ARNOBIUS OF SICCA

THE CASE
AGAINST THE PAGANS

ADVERSUS NATIONES

Ancient Christian Writers

THE WORKS OF THE FATHERS IN TRANSLATION

EDITED BY

JOHANNES QUASTEN, S. T. D.
*Professor of Ancient Church History
and Christian Archaeology*

JOSEPH C. PLUMPE, Ph. D.
*Associate Professor of New Testament
Greek and Ecclesiastical Latin*

The Catholic University of America
Washington, D. C.

No. 7

ARNOBIUS OF SICCA
THE CASE
AGAINST THE PAGANS

NEWLY TRANSLATED AND ANNOTATED

BY

GEORGE E. McCRACKEN, Ph. D., F. A. A. R.

Professor of Classics
Drake University, Des Moines, Iowa

VOLUME ONE
INTRODUCTION, BOOKS ONE – THREE

NEWMAN PRESS

New York, N.Y./Ramsey, N.J.

Nihil Obstat:

  Johannes Quasten, S.T.D.
   Censor Deputatus

Imprimatur:

  Patricius A. O'Boyle, D.D.
   Archiepiscopus Washingtonensis
   die 12 Februarii

Library of Congress
Catalog Card Number: 78-62458

ISBN: 0-8091-0248-X

PUBLISHED BY PAULIST PRESS
Editorial Office: 1865 Broadway, New York, N.Y. 10023
Business Office: 545 Island Road, Ramsey, N.J. 07446

PRINTED AND BOUND IN THE UNITED STATES OF AMERICA

CONTENTS

Volume One

ARNOBIUS OF SICCA

THE CASE
AGAINST THE PAGANS

SAINT JEROME'S TESTIMONIES ON ARNOBIUS

De viris illustribus 79: In the reign of Diocletian Arnobius taught rhetoric most successfully at Sicca in Africa and wrote the books *Adversus gentes* which are commonly available.

Chronicon (326-7 A. D.): Arnobius enjoys great repute as a rhetorician in Africa. While he was giving instruction in oratory to the youth of Sicca and was yet a pagan, he was drawn as the result of dreams to belief in Christianity. Failing, however, to obtain from the bishop acceptance into the faith which he had hitherto always attacked, he gave all his efforts to the composition of most splendid books against his former religion; and with these as so many pledges of his loyalty, he at last obtained the desired affiliation.

Epistula 70 (*ad Magnum*) 5: Arnobius published seven books *Adversus gentes* and his pupil Lactantius the same number.

De viris illustribus 80: ... Firmianus, who is also called Lactantius, Arnobius' pupil, in the reign of Diocletian . . . .

Epistula 58 (*ad Paulinum*) 10: Arnobius is uneven and prolix and without clear divisions in his work, resulting in confusion.

Epistula 62 (*ad Tranquillinum*) 2: I think Origen ought at times to be read for his learning, in the same manner that we treat Tertullian and Novatus, Arnobius and Apollinarius, and a number of ecclesiastical writers both Greek and Latin: we should choose out the good in them and shun what is contrary.

INTRODUCTION

In these two volumes we present in a new English dress what is in many ways the most remarkable patristic document now extant, the seven books of Arnobius *Adversus nationes*, the last surviving apology composed before the end of the persecutions.[1] Written from the point of view of a layman [2] not yet perfectly instructed concerning the nature of the Christian faith, this surprising work is now of primary interest because it affords us an opportunity to study the psychology of an eccentric personality who, though living at a critical moment in history, nevertheless seems to have been relatively unaffected by his times.

Despite the fact that the learning of Arnobius is impressive to many,[3] negative judgments are more frequently found. Indeed, one scholar of first rank speaks of him as " misinformed, virulent, and to us tolerant moderns, somewhat repulsive." [4] Another asserts that " the semi-philosophical, semi-religious discussions of the partially-instructed Christian . . . (are) . . . only the elegant refutation of an already dying system,[5] and a rhetorical statement of Christian truth, both incomplete [6] and imperfectly apprehended." [7] Still another [8] maintains that Arnobius is not a systematic but a " popular " philosopher, while a fourth [9] condemns him as neither a clear thinker nor a skillful writer who made no deep study. Finally, the book itself is, in the words of a great German scholar,[10] a " most infamous pamphlet " which compromised the Christian faith more than it helped.

While there is more than a grain of truth in all these severe

3

strictures, taken alone they are hardly fair to Arnobius who in modern times has suffered much from undeserved neglect.[11] Indeed, thus far the only first-rate study giving a favorable opinion on Arnobius' theological importance is a book by Rapisarda published as recently as 1945.[12] The *Adversus nationes* has hitherto been translated into our tongue but once and that as long ago as 1871.[13] Though our writer bristles with obscure allusions and unresolved problems which cry aloud for exegesis, we have hitherto had to depend for extended commentaries upon one German and a few Latin editions, the last of which appeared more than a century ago.[14]

Actually, the treatise has much of value for us today. Usually classified among the apologies [15] because it contains a vigorous defense of Christianity from slanderous charges brought by pagan opponents, it is, as a matter of fact, the most intense and the most sustained of all extant counterattacks upon the contemporary pagan cults.[16] When its testimony upon such matters is subjected to critical control, this fact makes it a mine of great richness for our knowledge of the religion which Christianity supplanted in the fourth century.[17] Indeed, the chief phase of that worship which Arnobius neglects to discuss is the cult of the emperors, an omission for which no convincing explanation has been offered.[18]

Modern neglect of our author, however, has merely paralleled the example of antiquity, for only one ancient writer, St. Jerome, who mentions him six times, tells us anything about Arnobius. Of these six testimonies, which are given in full on page 2, four are biographical; [19] the two which deal with his style and content will be examined later.

The data contained in the four biographical testimonies are not wholly consistent, nor are they in complete harmony with internal evidence to be found in the text of the *Adversus nationes* as it has come down to us, yet no scholar now seriously entertains doubt that Jerome is referring to the treatise with which we are dealing. There was, of course, another ancient writer of the same name, even more obscure, called " Arnobius the Younger " to distinguish him from our man, yet sometimes confused with him; [20] but since the younger Arnobius lived in the middle of the fifth century,[21] Jerome cannot have known of him and in any case the statements quoted do not fit his work at all.

Jerome is doubtless right in giving the name as ' Arnobius ' but the manuscript on which we uniquely rely for our knowledge of the text (*codex Parisinus* 1661) regularly spells it ' Arnovius.' [22] This, however, is only an apparent discrepancy, to be easily explained as the result of confusion, frequent in this manuscript, of the sounds of *b* and *v* in Late Latin. Etymologically, the name shows affinity with a number of Greek personal names,[23] but we cannot therefore conclude that Arnobius was himself of Greek origin, though he may have been. So far as we know, he had no other name,[24] a fact which may argue that he was indeed Greek in race.

Note that in both instances where Jerome mentions the title, he gives it as ' *Adversus gentes* ' while the evidence from the manuscript [25] shows it to be ' *Adversus nationes*.' While both may be translated identically as " Against the Pagans," the witness of the manuscript has been generally thought better by more-recent scholars, since it is easier to understand how Jerome, perhaps citing from memory, could employ *gentes*, a more or less precise synonym for *nationes*, than to explain how a copyist could make the reverse substitution.[26] We should not, however, support this choice by alluding to the *Ad nationes* of Tertullian for, if Arnobius was consciously influenced by Tertullian's title, he might have used either noun with equal propriety. These verbal discrepancies are seen, therefore, to be of no particular significance.

That Jerome is right in stating that Arnobius was a rhetorician, no one who has read the *Adversus nationes* would ever doubt, since the style, of which we shall presently speak at greater length, bears all the earmarks of the practitioner of that profession. Moreover, although there are occasional passages which appear to treat rhetoric with some disdain, there are also instances in which the author's interest in that subject is ill-concealed.[27] Finally, the *incipit* to Book Five [28] actually calls him "Arnobius Orator," which furnishes additional corroboration, if more were needed.[29]

But that it was at Sicca in Africa [30] that Arnobius taught rhetoric is open to some question on two grounds, a point to which attention has not been previously directed. Nowhere does Arnobius mention Sicca, or for that matter any other place, as his home,[31] a silence surprising in view of what shall shortly appear.

The name of Sicca at first sight suggests that the town was founded by the Sicels before the occupation of this territory by the Phoenicians, and the site has been identified with certainty as that of the modern Tunisian town of Schak Benâr el Kef,[32] some ninety miles southwest of Tunis, near the Algerian border. From a study of several of Kiepert's maps we may infer that Sicca was originally part of the kingdom of Numidia, then became part of the proconsular province bearing the same name, and at the reorganization of the empire under Diocletian, found itself in the Province of Numidia, a part of the Diocese of Africa.[33] Therefore, Jerome's allusion to Sicca in Africa, though not precise, is not incorrect.

Now we know rather little about Sicca. It is first mentioned by Polybius,[34] who reports a revolt of the Carthaginian mercenaries as having taken place there in the year 241 B. C. According to Valerius Maximus,[35] writing in the first century of our era, the town possessed a shrine of Venus in which the Punic women *used to* practice temple prostitution. Arnobius' complete silence on this social evil, which would have provided him with perhaps the most disgraceful single charge which he could have brought against the pagans, is therefore surprising. Other apologists do not hesitate to utilize a similar charge,[36] and it seems difficult to believe that even a professor of rhetoric could have been ignorant of the temple, had he really lived in Sicca. It will not help much to point out that in Halm's edition of Valerius Maximus, the passage in question reads *Cirtae* and not *Siccae*, for the best palaeographical evidence is definitely against this reading of Halm's.[37] Even if it is right, the reference could still be to Sicca and not Cirta, since the full Roman name of the town was *Colonia Iulia Veneria Cirta Nova Sicca*,[38] that is, Sicca was regarded as a sort of New Cirta. But note that Valerius Maximus uses the past tense, implying the discontinuance of the practice in his day,[39] and we are probably justified in assuming that the religions which Arnobius attacks were all current when he wrote. Sicca may therefore really have been his home, as Jerome says, but we do not know that he was also born there,[40] though he may have been.

We have now to consider the important and vexed question of Arnobius' date. In the two passages from the *De viris illustribus* Arnobius is placed in the reign of Diocletian which lasted from 284 to 304 A. D., but the passage in the *Chronicon* of Eusebius—it is the first item in the section which Jerome added to this work—is dated, according to the three chronological systems here employed,[41] in the 2343rd year from Abraham,[42] the twenty-first year of the reign of Constantine, and the third year of the 276th Olympiad, all of which equal the latter part of 326 or the early part of 327 A. D.[43] Now it has been pointed out that " the Saint inserted his notices with a lighthearted disregard for chronology," [44] but this date of 327 A. D. not only is inconsistent with the statements in the *De viris illustribus* but also runs counter to the testimony of chronological deductions which can be made from the text of the *Adversus nationes* itself.[45]

Persecutions are there mentioned many times [46] and while the words do permit us in some instances to assume that at the moment of writing a vigorous persecution was not actually in progress, there is not the slightest suggestion that the period of the persecutions had ended.[47] There is no allusion, not even a veiled one, to the Peace of the Church under Maxentius in 311 A. D.[48] The year 311 therefore becomes a *terminus ante quem* which is absolute: the entire work was completed before that time.[49] This shows at least that the date of the passage from the *Chronicon* must be an error [50] or, if it is correct, then it is not the date of the composition of the *Adversus nationes* but of something else unspecified. A group of scholars [51] assumes it to be the year of Arnobius' death, but Bardenhewer [52] questions this too-easy solution of the problem. On the other hand, his doubts are probably based on the prevailing belief, for which there seems to be no evidence, that Arnobius was an old man when he wrote.[53] Oehler takes the view, approved by Bryce-Campbell [54] as probable, that the error derives from a confusion of the *vicennalia* of Diocletian (304 A. D.) with those of Constantine (celebrated in the East in 325 and in the West in 326), that is, that Jerome intended to date the entry in the *Chronicon* in 304 but through error inserted it at the place of Constantine's *vicennalia*. On the contrary, it appears at the next year and only after Jerome has inserted between the entries for 326 and 327 a note to the effect that all entries thereafter were written by himself.[55] If, on the other hand, Oehler is right in thinking that Jerome was confused about which emperor's *vicennalia* coincided with Arnobius' date, then we could correct the error by transferring the item to the year 304, and as we shall shortly see, there is some other evidence tending to favor this period.

We should now examine additional chronological data to be found in the *Adversus nationes*. In 1.13 Arnobius says that " it is almost three hundred years, more or less, since we began to be Christians and to be known on the earth." [56] This calculation is doubtless computed from the Birth of Christ [57] rather than the beginning of the Ministry or the Crucifixion [58] or the adoption at Antioch [59] of the name ' Christians' to designate the followers of Christ, since the last three alternatives would each give a date later than 311 A. D. which, as we have seen, is impossible. Arnobius has, however, been studiously inexact and so we cannot use this passage for fixing the date of composition more precisely than in the reign of Diocletian, not much before or after 300.

A second chronological allusion is to be found in 2.71 where the age of the City of Rome is given as " a thousand and fifty years [60] . . . or not much less than that." Here again there is inexactness and an embarrassment of alternatives, since the founding of Rome was variously dated [61] by L. Cincius Alimentus [62] in 728 B. C., by Q. Fabius Pictor [63] in 747, by Polybius [64] in 750, by M. Porcius Cato [65] in 752, and by M. Terentius Varro [66] in 753 B. C. Depending upon which of these dates is accepted as correct, Rome reached the age of 1050 years in, respectively, 322, 303, 300, 298, or 297 A. D.

By which system of chronology would Arnobius be likely to compute his date? Here we can be almost certain, as Bryce-Campbell [67] maintain, since not only was the Varronian system by far the most popular in later times, being regularly used in computing all dates *ab urbe condita*, but Arnobius actually does use it in 5. 8 where he says that according to Varro there were, from the Deluge to the consulship of Hirtius and Pansa (43 B. C.), not quite two thousand years. Frequent allusions elsewhere to Varro [68] also support this contention.

On the other hand, there is in 4.36 a reference to burning of Christian books and destruction of Christian meeting-places which to many scholars [69] can only be an allusion to the persecution of Diocletian in 303 A. D. described by Eusebius.[70] Arnobius' words are as follows: " For why, indeed, have our writings deserved to be given to the flames? Why should our meeting-places be savagely torn down? " [71] Perhaps these scholars are right but the opinion is certainly not unanimous [72] and the passage itself seems rather general in its terms and application.

Let us here recapitulate the chronological evidence presented up to this point: so far as Book One is concerned we can reach no more precise year than about 300 A. D. For Book Two, the possibilities are many, depending on the system of chronology chosen, ranging from 297 to 303, with strong preference shown for the earlier date, but in any case, no one year can be taken as *exactly* right, since the statement is not precise. For Book Four, what evidence there is points to 303 or thereafter, assuming the allusion in 4.36 to be to the persecution of Diocletian. The other books contain no chronological data at all.[73] Such is the evidence upon which Monceaux,[74] and Moricca [75] following him, base their theory of a divided composition. In their view, Books One and Two are to be dated about 297 but the other books not until 303 or thereafter.

There is something to be said for this compromise, yet all conclusions based on the theory that the first two books were composed as one unit and the last five as a separate and later unit fall to the ground when the books themselves are examined.

At the beginning of Book Two (2.1) and again at the beginning of Book Three (3.2) there is unmistakable evidence that Arnobius regarded Book Two as a sort of digression from the theme begun in Book One and resumed in Book Three. Thus, the break between Book Two and Book Three cannot be taken as a resumption of composition after an interval—if it is significant, it tends to show that Book Two is an interpolation between One and Three, and any attempt to see breaks in composition elsewhere must be regarded as purely subjective. There are, to be sure, two passages which suggest that composition was not continuous in the order in which the books, or parts of books, now stand. There is an allusion in 4.3 to something said " previously " but the subject has not been touched upon previously and it is probable, as Bryce-Campbell think, that the author really refers to 4.8. In 4.37 and 7.9 there are locutions which seem to anticipate a story introduced later. While these passages tell us something of the method of composition, they have no bearing on the date of composition. The Monceaux theory therefore is unproven at best—it is really highly improbable.

In view of the many questions that arise from the consideration of the evidence just discussed, it is not surprising that the dates assigned to our author by various writers show a very wide divergence, covering the period from 296 to

313![76] One of these scholars[77] would go so far as to assert that Arnobius was martyred between 303 and 305.[78] Harnack even maintains that his birth was before 250 A. D.[79] on the basis of the psychology of the work which indicates, so he thinks, that Arnobius must have been sixty years of age when he wrote. This view appears to me wholly subjective. Others[80] put the birth as about 250 A. D. but we really do not know when or where Arnobius was born; when, where, or how he died. We do know that he wrote prior to 311 A. D. and probably in the reign of Diocletian, not much before or after the year 300, and with the present evidence we ought not to attempt any more precise dating.

Before passing to another topic we should note, however, that except for the date given for the entry in the *Chronicon*, which as we have seen must certainly be an error, all of the *chronological* details of Jerome may have been derived from internal evidence, but since Jerome's testimony also involves other items which could not have been deduced from a reading of the book itself, we need not assume that he was without independent sources of information as to the date. Inasmuch as he was writing not quite a century later, he may even have derived his knowledge of Arnobius from oral tradition.

At any rate, he tells us also that Lactantius was Arnobius' pupil. Though most scholars who have discussed this problem, in particular Micka,[81] the latest to deal with it at length, find this statement not easy to accept, it has apparently been rejected *in toto* only by Ffoulkes.[82] The stumbling-block consists of the fact that Lactantius never mentions Arnobius, a silence the more surprising since there is in the *Divinae institutiones* a passage[83] in which its author mentions three of his predecessors, Minucius Felix, Tertullian, and Cyprian, in that order, which is chronological. Had Lactantius merely heard of Arnobius, much less been his pupil, he might well have added his name to the list.

This raises the question at once as to which of the two works is earlier, a point on which we have no conclusive evidence. It will help us little to assume, however, that Lactantius is the earlier, for we shall then have to explain why Arnobius does not mention Lactantius. This might be somewhat easier to explain, since Arnobius mentions no Christian predecessors by name. We do not, however, know exactly when the *Divinae institutiones* were written and the date given by Micka,[84] 304-13, is doubtless based in part on the assumption that the work of a pupil would be later than that of his teacher. Such an assumption may be right but we have no way of proving it so, and it may actually be wrong. Moreover, Micka's date may be in conflict with the testimony of Jerome where the words " in the reign of Diocletian "[85] can apply either to Lactantius' school days, or to the date of composition of his great work, or merely to his *floruit*.

In the absence of definite statements to the contrary, we may with justification take it that Jerome means us to understand that Lactantius was Arnobius' pupil *when the latter was teaching rhetoric at Sicca*. Yet we do not know how much older the master was than the pupil, if at all. The period of Arnobius' life during which on *a priori* grounds it is possible that Lactantius studied under Arnobius may easily have extended for fifty years. It is generally further assumed that both master and pupil were still pagans at the time of their association. The pupil may be presumed to have finished his course of study and then to have left Sicca. Later the master became a Christian and wrote his remarkable book, but by this time it is possible, even probable, that the pupil was far away. Indeed, we know that Lactantius was at

Nicomedia in Bithynia as early as 290 A. D.[86] Therefore, he may never have heard of his former teacher's conversion or known that he had written a book. Much of this is mere assumption but we have no way of disproving it and it furnishes, at least, a possible explanation of Lactantius' failure to mention Arnobius in the passage cited.[87]

Though there are great differences between the two writers,[88] as we should expect, some scholars have been impressed by the resemblances. Both composed their works in seven books, a parallel noted even by Jerome, and this makes Brandt [89] think that Lactantius was writing his work as a sort of silent protest against Arnobius.[90] Moricca[91] and Molignoni [92] attribute to Arnobius the love of metaphysical discussion displayed by Lactantius,[93] while Brandt,[94] Pohlenz,[95] and Micka [96] profess to see passages where the similarities imply interdependence of some kind or other. The last named,[97] who is sure that Lactantius could not have read the *Adversus nationes*, attempts to explain the resemblances as follows:

> The similar passages of Lactantius can be sufficiently explained by the attestation that he knew of Arnobius' doctrine from the time he spent with him as his pupil.[98] . . . And during the time he (= Arnobius) was Lactantius' teacher, the pupil readily became acquainted with his teacher's views and what they involved.[99]

While a pupil may often recall much of his master's teaching, we are hardly justified in believing that Lactantius studied under Arnobius any other subject than rhetoric. Note also that Micka elsewhere [100] inconsistently suggests that the failure to mention Arnobius may be motivated on grounds of style, that is, that the fine taste of the " Christian Cicero " [101] was repelled by the barbarisms of Arnobius. This view exaggerates the defects of Arnobius' style, and if Lactantius' taste were so sensitive, it is strange that he would have gone to that very same man for instruction in the art of rhetoric. Moreover, he does mention and criticize Tertullian whose style is sometimes conceded to be inferior to that of Arnobius.

At a later point we shall discuss certain parallels between the *Adversus nationes* and the *Divinae institutiones* which may be thought to show interdependence. Here we may anticipate the results of that discussion by stating that the investigation hardly proves conclusive.

Let us now turn to the statement that dreams figured in Arnobius' conversion. In the two allusions which our author makes to his espousal of Christianity (1. 39, 3. 24), there is no mention of the motive which led him to his act, much less the suggestion that a dream figured in it—the point which he drives home is the recency of his conversion, which we should perhaps have expected him to conceal. Moreover, in 1. 46 he speaks of "empty, unsubstantial dreams," and in 7. 39 he tells a pagan story in which Jupiter appears to a man in a dream.[102] For these reasons Oehler [103] and Bryce-Campbell [104] deny the possibility that the conversion was caused by a dream or series of them. On the other hand, Coxe [105] and Rand [106] accept the story at its face value. Other writers explain the conversion differently: Freppel,[107] for example, says that it was not brought about by reading Scripture, a conclusion reached from the paucity of references to the Scriptures, a point we shall discuss later. According to Freppel and Moule,[108] it was the heroism of the martyrs that impressed the rhetorician. Gabarrou [109] thinks that Arnobius was also greatly impressed by the miracles of Christ and by the failure of philosophy, but that the dreams won him finally. Cruttwell,[110] approving Neander's skepticism on the story,[111] says that the conversion must have been the result of a long dissatisfaction with paganism, an element surely present in every genuine conversion. Cumont [112] thinks that the conversion was based on the fear of his soul's death.

Some scholars attempt to date the conversion: Gabarrou [113] at about Arnobius' fiftieth year (295-6); de Labriolle [114] at about his sixtieth year; Monceaux [115] and Moricca [116] in 295 or 296, while Bryce-Campbell [117] are sure that the conversion did not take place in a time of persecution. This last conclusion is probably correct. Nock, [118] however, warns that the statement of the details of the conversion as Arnobius gives them should not be taken too literally, since the story agrees with the style of other similar narratives elsewhere.

To sum up, the dream story is not really inconsistent with what Arnobius says about the conversion, for he there does not mention motives, and we now know that some dreams, at least, are the subconscious repetition of ideas impressed upon the mind during consciousness. There is no reason why Arnobius, already drawn to Christianity by what he had observed of its adherents or had been told of its nature during his waking hours, should not have dreamed of it also, and should thus have been led to take the final step leading to his becoming a Christian.

In the testimony found in the *Chronicon* Jerome tells us also that upon Arnobius' expressing his desire to be received as a Christian, his sincerity was doubted by the bishop because he had always been an opponent of the Faith. So far as I am aware, this is the only example of a Christian bishop in the early period exhibiting such skepticism about the profession of a convert, but that is no reason to reject the story. On the other hand, it must be admitted that the very act of wishing to become a Christian involved a prospective convert in such great danger as to discourage the insincere trifler. There is, moreover, no allusion in the entire work to the bishop nor to any other specific Christian, clerical or lay, and the introductory chapters of Book One are completely silent on any such stimulus to composition. Neander and Schaff,[119] indeed, maintain that Arnobius wrote more from an inward impulse than from outward occasion. The story is treated with skepticism by Bryce-Campbell [120] and Rapisarda,[121] and Sihler [122] regards it as very improbable. On the other hand, it is accepted at its face value by LeNourry,[123] Freppel,[124] Rand,[125] Geffcken,[126] Salvatorelli,[127] and Amatucci.[128] So also Moule [129] who says it was the church at Sicca that demanded the pledge.

If the story is to be accepted, we can be sure that it was really a bishop at Sicca and not the bishop of Carthage who was involved, for we know that the church at Sicca had a bishop of its own, suffragan to the See of Carthage, at least as early as 1 September 256 A. D., when Castus of Sicca is recorded as having attended the Seventh Council of Carthage.[130] That Bishop Castus had survived to the conversion is, of course, extremely unlikely in view of the length of time and the frequency of death in persecutions experienced by Christians in those days.

The biographical details of Jerome's testimony which we have thus far discussed may in general be accepted without *much* question except for those three items contained only in the entry in the *Chronicon*: (1) the date of 326-7; (2) the dream; and (3) the attitude of the bishop. Inherently these three items are such as to cause us the greatest difficulty and they are unsupported elsewhere. Of the three the date is the most easily explained and the least serious. Note however, that though in the whole entry there are facts supported by other testimony, it possesses a somewhat romantic

flavor. *Se non è vero, è ben trovato.* Yet the imperfection of
Arnobius' knowledge of Christianity fits in rather well with
the passage. In fact, it may be that the story is a slightly
fictionalized version of deductions made by Jerome or his
source from the book itself.[131] Curiously enough, much the
same objections have also been raised again and again against
a similar biographical passage in the very same *Chronicon*,
that dealing with Arnobius' master, the Roman poet Lucretius,[132] and perhaps there is an element of fiction in both.[133]

Before passing to the work itself, we should note certain
other biographical details. The Benedictine Ioannes Trithemius [134] tells us categorically that our writer became a *presbyter*
and also wrote a work called *De rhetorica*. The second part
of this statement is apparently a misunderstanding of what
Jerome says, but there is now, at least, no ancient evidence for
the first, and Trithemius in the fifteenth century is unlikely
to have possessed a source since lost. The idea that Arnobius
received ordination is completely at variance with everything
in the *Adversus nationes* and we know nothing whatever of
the author's history subsequent to the completion of the book.
At the time of writing Arnobius was too ill-informed to have
become a *presbyter;* [135] indeed, it has been maintained that
he was then only a *catechumen.*[136] If so, he was a remarkable
catechumen indeed. This view, moreover, has been carried
to a completely untenable extreme by Colombo [137] who suggests that Arnobius was never a Christian at all and that the
Adversus nationes is merely a mighty rhetorical *tour de force,*
a mere exercise in composition! No other scholar would
entertain such an idea for a moment.[138]

✦   ✦   ✦

To learn more of Arnobius we must turn to the " most
splendid " books themselves in which, as Gabarrou [139] acutely

remarks, his physiognomy is clearly revealed. For, while he is most reticent about himself, the frankness with which he handles his materials and the remarkable individuality of his views permit us to use his unconscious self-revelations to round out our picture of the man.

On the style Jerome tells us also that " Arnobius is uneven and prolix and without clear divisions in his work, resulting in confusion." [140] He is certainly uneven and prolix but the composition as a whole shows organic unity and each book discusses in thorough fashion the topic assigned to it.[141] Passing allusion, to be sure, is frequently made to topics treated in great detail at other points,[142] but this is no defect. The subjects discussed in the central part of the work (Books Three to Five) are really parts of a larger whole, but the author should hardly be criticized because the magnitude of a topic extends beyond the limits of a single book.

Book One is devoted in general to a refutation of certain charges brought against the Christians by pagans,[143] the chief of which is the slander that the cause of certain calamities which the opponents pretend to have noticed in recent years is the anger of pagan gods at not having received their proper worship from the Christians. Arnobius' refutation of this charge, which seems considerably stronger than the defense which St. Cyprian includes in his *Ad Demetrianum*, may be summarized briefly as follows:

As a matter of fact, no new types of calamities have been noticed and actually there have been fewer of the older types in the Christian era, as well as times of relative prosperity. The origin of the calamities may be possibly found in nature itself. Moreover, such anger tends to demean the gods. Since the Christians are really innocent of any wrongdoings, it is the pagan priestlings who have stirred up the accusation because their income has been reduced. Indeed, the pagan gods are ridiculous, a point which will form the general theme of Books Three to Five.

A second charge to which attention is here directed is that the Christians worship a human being and, at that, one who has been crucified. The refutation is a demonstration [144] that Christ was divine, attested by His own miracles and those of His disciples, as well as by the expansion of Christianity subsequent to the Crucifixion. The third and final charge discussed in this Book is that Christian literature lacks an exalted style, a stricture which we might think was chiefly a reflection of Arnobius' experience as a rhetorician, were not the same charge also quoted and refuted by Clement of Alexandria. [145] The Book ends with some sections on the Incarnation and the Crucifixion which have been thought to have a Docetic ring. [146]

Book Two, the longest and in many ways the most interesting of the seven, is, as we have seen, regarded by its author as a kind of digression from the main theme. [147] After a preliminary section which consists of praise of Christ, Arnobius compares Him with the pagan philosophers to their discredit, and he does this by a lengthy attack upon the Platonic doctrine of the immortality of the soul. [148] For Arnobius the soul can only be mortal and he appears to be of the opinion that this view is orthodox Christianity. Among the most interesting parts of the Book is a section devoted to description of a controlled experiment in which an attempt was to be made to demonstrate that the soul at birth is what philosophers since Locke call a *tabula rasa*. [149] This Book also contains a denial of the value of philosophic and scientific investigation which leads de Labriolle [150] to remark that Arnobius is the first of the apologists to found religious dogmatism upon philosophical Pyrrhonism. The Book ends with a demonstration that the charge against Christianity of being recent in origin may be refuted by showing the relative recency of the pagan religions themselves. Book Two shows Arnobius at the height of his powers; indeed, McGiffert,[151] who says that only Books One and Two are of interest for us, admits that they are very fresh and original and present an extreme skepticism for his own day.

Following the digression in Book Two, Arnobius resumes the argument by attacking the pagan conception of the gods as anthropomorphic and centers his polemic in particular on the fact that they were represented as having sex and sexual characteristics and also as having a 'division of labor' by which one god rules over a limited province and cannot trespass on the territories of another.[152] The Book ends with a description of various pagan gods whose very nature is ridiculous.

The same argument is continued in Book Four where the identical method is applied to the Roman deifications of abstract qualities, to the *indigetes*, to the sinister gods, to 'multiple' deities (a syncretism of a number of local divinities into an unharmonious whole), and, finally, to the disgraceful legends concerning the great god Jupiter himself.

In Book Five this method of attack is turned against two well-known myths, the story of Jupiter Elicius and Numa, and the legends of Attis and the Great Mother of the Gods, while the criticism of these myths is followed by a powerful and devastating polemic against certain of the pagan mysteries. These three Books, while not attaining the sublimity of the first two, received from Orelli[153] the high praise of being called worthy of Lucian himself.

Book Six is devoted to an attack upon the pagan consecration of temples to the gods and upon the images erected therein, while Book Seven involves a polemic against the pagan rituals, in particular the blood sacrifices, and the offerings of wine and incense.

We have already alluded to the question of the order of the composition of the respective Books.[154] Kettner[155] is probably right in claiming that the work was hastily put together and Bryce-Campbell[156] that it was never revised and finished. In 7. 44 appears a long passage which is a slightly-differing variant of the preceding section.[157] The best explanation of the repetition is that it is an alternative version actually prepared by Arnobius himself and that, being preserved with his notes, it was erroneously included when the individual pages were amalgamated into a finished manuscript. Another section which in most editions appears as 7.35-37 seemed to Orelli so admirable a conclusion to the whole work that, following the suggestion of an unknown French scholar, he actually transposed it to the end, renumbering these chapters as 7. 49-51. Indeed, the final chapter (7. 51 = 7. 48 Orelli) appears to break off somewhat abruptly.[158] Moreover, throughout the work the author so frequently employs two almost synonymous words or phrases for a single idea that many times I have wondered whether such doublets were not intended to be eliminated in a final revision by the ultimate selection of one of the alternatives.[159] While it is now my considered judgment that they are but an expression of a passion for redundancy apparent not only in the locutions but also in the ideas as well,[160] Arnobius' style betrays throughout a mind working at almost incredible speed, a quality which I hope has been carried over into the translation.

Earlier scholars[161] were apt to complain that Arnobius

writes " impure Latin " but this lament is doubtless based on the now-exploded theory that any deviation from the Ciceronian norm constitutes a blemish. The view of Jülicher [162] that the books show disorder and bad style has been recently challenged by Festugière.[163] A comment of Brandt [164] that the style is wild is less open to objection. Freppel [165] finds it impossible to approve Orelli's view that Arnobius is both " sapiens et sobrius." Yet few would go so far as to attribute to Arnobius, as does Foakes-Jackson,[166] the best Latinity of his age. In this connection we may do well to quote the words of Bryce-Campbell: [167]

> His style is, in point of fact, clear and lucid, rising at times into genuine eloquence; [168] and its obscurity and harshness are generally caused by an attempt to express a vague and indefinite idea. Indeed, very considerable power of expression is manifested in the philosophical reasonings of the second book, the keen satire of the fourth and fifth, and the vigorous argument of the sixth and seventh.

De Labriolle [169] also aptly refers to " son éloquence continue, son érudition compacte, son ironie massive," and says he may be compared with Voltaire but is less subtle.[170]

Yet, in spite of the undeniable excellence of many passages,[171] the defects of the style are precisely those which we should expect to find in a book written, not by a great master, but by a pedantic professor of rhetoric who uses all the tricks of his trade, and sows constantly with the sack, rarely with the hand. Arnobius is never content to make a point with lightning thrust and then pass on—he invariably continues to drive home each argument with seemingly endless repetition.[172] The book would have profited much by the judicious use of an editorial blue pencil.

As for language, Sihler [173] remarks that the style is consciously archaic and the reader of the Notes will be impressed by the number of parallels cited from Lucretius and other early writers. The parallels to Lucretius, which display apparent borrowings of both locutions and ideas, can hardly be explained as accidental—it is clear that Arnobius had read Lucretius long and well.[174] But the archaistic tendency as a whole, which was noticed by Freppel,[175] may be better explained by his wise suggestion that many such locutions had remained firmly fixed in the standard Latin of North Africa to the end of the third century, though they had long before become obsolete elsewhere.[176] That Arnobius writes in the same style as the other Africans is pointed out by Oehler,[177] yet in the words of the great expert on prose style, Eduard Norden,[178] he exhibits a tendency to preserve a more classical style than the others, Apuleius, for example. He employs all the figures of speech and no one is so addicted to rhetorical questions.[179]

Scholars interested in the study of prose rhythms, notably Stange,[180] Lorenz,[181] Löfstedt,[182] and Hagendahl,[183] have subjected the Latin text of Arnobius to the minutest examinations. They conclude that in ending his clauses Arnobius observes the laws of metrical *clausulae*, Lorenz defining four such patterns, Löfstedt only three.[184] Many text critics even use such principles in textual emendation, a practice recently criticized by Jones.[185]

Jerome's final dictum on the content of the work needs some comment: [186] " I think Origen ought at times to be read for his learning, in the same manner that we treat Tertullian and Novatus, Arnobius and Apollinarius, and a number of ecclesiastical writers both Greek and Latin: we should choose out the good in them and shun what is contrary." It is clear that Jerome was offended by what he read in Arnobius. So also have been many others, and one of the chief complaints is that Arnobius, to use a phrase of Micka's,[187] appears to have a poor grasp of Christianity. This probably is what Geffcken [188] means when he says that Arnobius begins a secularizing tendency in the apologies.

Indeed, Arnobius is the only apologist who does not show close familiarity with Scripture and does not appeal to the authority of the prophets.[189] Not only does he never quote from the Old Testament, there is good evidence to show that he must have been largely ignorant of it.[190] It is universally conceded that he does quote from the New Testament,[191] some scholars admitting one quotation, others two, but even this statement needs to be qualified. In 2. 6 appears the following: " Has that well-known saying never struck your ears that *the wisdom of man is foolishness with God* who is Chief? " The italicized words are a free translation of 1 Corinthians 3. 19 which reads, *The wisdom of this world is foolishness with God.* The divergence between Arnobius and the extant New Testament manuscripts, both Greek and Latin, forces us to choose between two alternatives: either Arnobius is quoting exactly but from a different text of the Epistle, or he is quoting from memory, inexactly. The first alternative is actually accepted by Newton [192] but is less probable than the second. Consider the phrase, " that well-known saying," [193] which suggests that Arnobius knew of the words only from hearsay: indeed, it is not even clear that he knew the saying had the support of Apostolic authority behind it. Moreover, the saying is exceedingly sententious, easily remembered, and apt to be frequently quoted by Christians. Certainly, there is no proof here that he had read the Epistle.[194]

The second supposed quotation is even less exact and consists of a sentence with which Reifferscheid [195] compares four New Testament passages. Speaking of Christ, Arnobius in 1. 6 says: " we . . . have learned from His teachings that *evil should not be repaid with evil.*" The passages referred to are Matthew 5. 44, where the correspondence is not very close, and Romans 12. 17, 1 Thessalonians 5. 15, and 1 Peter 3. 9. Yet here also the phrase which we find in Arnobius is so central a theme in Christian teaching that it is neither necessary nor possible to assume a knowledge of the New Testament to explain it.[196] Doubtless, this Christian truth was one of the first to be imparted to the new converts, if indeed they had not already deduced it from observance of Christian practice while yet pagans.[197]

A word of caution must be inserted at this point. We must not overdo the *argumentum ex silentio* since the fundamental purpose of Arnobius, to impress the pagans with their own guilt, rather than to win them to Christianity,[198] would not necessarily require him to make use of Scripture and other evidence drawn from Christian sources. The pagans would hardly admit such material as evidence—their position must be attacked on the basis of illogical elements inherent in it.

Yet this *caveat* will not fully explain the sparseness of Christian testimony in the *Adversus nationes*, for in addition there is positive evidence to show that its author was definitely ignorant of the New Testament[199] as well as of the Old.[200]

In 7. 7 it is objected against the pagan gods that they have never been seen:[201] could a Christian who knew that John 1. 18 states that *no man hath seen God at any time* have used such an argument? Again, in 7. 16, with heightened sarcasm Arnobius suggests to the pagans that they ought to offer their gods sacrifices of cumin, cress, turnips, and other such vegetables: could a Christian knowing Matthew 23. 23 have

employed such an argument? Possibly. The remarks in 7. 8
imply ignorance of the Redemption.[202] Finally, the long passage in 1. 38 in which praise of Christ appears to have been
drawn not from the Gospels but from Lucretius' eulogy of
Epicurus, certainly implies genuine ignorance of the Gospel
narrative concerning the teaching of Christ.[203]

The *Adversus nationes* is also singularly silent on the
stories of the Birth of Christ and of the Resurrection of which
nothing is said except that it was merely the human body that
died on the Cross.[204] Arnobius vacillates, according to Mc-
Giffert,[205] between modalism [206] and ditheism.[207] This would
be evidence, if McGiffert is right, of an Arianizing tendency
noted also by Cruttwell.[208] Micka [209] merely says that in
Arnobius Christ is in some way subordinate to the Father,
while Brunner,[210] who attempts without much success to
show that Arnobius is orthodox, maintains that he clearly
distinguishes between the pre-existence of Christ and the
Incarnation. In any case, we look in vain for any reference
to the Third Person of the Trinity.[211] While in general
Arnobius takes a pessimistic [212] view of the depravity and
worthlessness of man,[213] Marchesi [214] maintains that he knows
nothing of original sin. At least, he never alludes to the
story of the Garden of Eden or its theological implications,
but Rapisarda,[215] on the other hand, cannot believe Arnobius
ignorant of this dogma and cites the *ingenitae infirmitatis
vitium* mentioned in 1. 27.

At some points our writer appears to Cruttwell [216] to be
dangerously near agnosticism, but in this Cruttwell seems to
misunderstand his meaning: Arnobius denies that man can
know many things about God but he never doubts man's
ability to know that God exists. There is also evidence that
points suspiciously to Gnostic influences, but Marchesi [217]

3 *

absolves him from the charge of being a Gnostic and Mc-
Giffert [218] wisely says on this point: " The accusation betrays
the inveterate habit of mistaking superficial resemblances for
real relationships, a habit which has wrought untold confusion in history." Few writers, indeed, have suffered so
much at the hands of those who read isolated passages and
then derive general conclusions therefrom without benefit of
a thorough examination of teaching elsewhere.[219]

We find, moreover, nothing in this book on the Sacraments.[220] There is nothing whatever on ecclesiastical polity.
Arnobius says nothing about forms of Christian worship save
that in the Christian meeting places (conventicula) the
Christians pray to the Supreme God asking peace and pardon
on behalf of those in authority, for armies, kings, friends and
enemies, the living and the dead.[221]

There remain, however, two phases of Arnobius' thinking
which require more extended comment. The first is that
while Arnobius, unlike his pupil Lactantius, consecrated no
special book to the teaching of the Divine Anger,[222] he
repeatedly reiterates the belief that display of anger is wholly
inconsistent with divinity. This typically Arnobian doctrine
has been subjected to searching analysis in the masterly dissertation of Micka which we have previously had occasion
to cite many times. Micka has convincingly demonstrated [223]
that this view, which is a corollary of Arnobius' doctrine of
' aloofness ' of God,[224] is out of harmony with Scripture.[225]
Earlier Christian writers do not, it is shown by Micka, present
a united view on this doctrine. Indeed, there is a group
which includes [226] Aristides, Athenagoras, Justin Martyr,
Theophilus of Antioch, Cyprian, and Commodian, who exhibited no awareness that the problem of the Divine Anger
even existed. A second group of Fathers,[227] including Ire-

naeus, Tertullian, Novatian, the author of the Pseudo-Clementine *Recognitions*, and Origen, concern themselves with combatting the heretical view of Marcion [228] that there were two Gods, one free from anger and one displaying anger, and take the opposite view that the doctrine of the Divine Anger is orthodox. Now Arnobius' teaching on this important point ranges him neither with the first group, nor with the second, nor even with the Marcionites. It is with the pagan philosophers,[229] as distinct from the people,[230] that Arnobius' view places him, particularly with Epicureanism [231] but also to some extent with Stoicism.[232] There can be no doubt whatever that Arnobius is unorthodox on this point, a charge from which LeNourry [233] has vainly attempted to absolve him.[234]

Allusion has already been made to the frequent use which Arnobius has made of the Epicurean poet Lucretius.[235] This led Klussmann to suppose that Arnobius had actually been an Epicurean and had failed to make the transition from Epicureanism to Christianity complete.[236] There are, however, in 1. 31 some anti-Epicurean attacks,[237] which, to be sure, might not necessarily vitiate Klussmann's view, but the allusion to the conversion suggests that Arnobius had been a worshipper of fetishes and that hardly seems congruent with the belief that he was actually an adherent of Epicureanism itself.[238] Jessen [239] and Dal Pane,[240] however, take the strong position that he had not been an Epicurean but was merely an imitator of Epicurus and Lucretius, and in this view, they are joined by Röhricht [241] who thinks that Lucretius was probably the only source of Arnobius' Epicureanism. Rapisarda [242] maintains, on the contrary, that many other contemporary sources existed and that while Arnobius uses Epicurean arguments when they suit his purpose, he never

shares their position, and, indeed, Marchesi [243] maintains that
Arnobius was an "avversario sdegnoso" of Epicureanism,
while Atzberger [244] thinks that he stands midway between
Epicureanism and Neo-Platonism, an astute observation.
Whatever the explanation of the Epicureanism in Arnobius,
the fact that it exists is undeniable. Though there are traces
of Stoicism here and there, [245] our author appears not to have
been much influenced by that school and Freppel [246] maintains that in Book Five he actually attacks the Stoic view.
Arnobius was, according to Micka, [247] not an adherent of any
school but an eclectic philosopher. This is probably the truth
—he did not construct a system of his own. [248].

He lacks as a philosopher, so Cruttwell [249] says, the metaphysical depth of Origen, but when the same scholar also
maintains that he is without the uncompromising candor of
Tertullian, he certainly under-estimates Arnobius. He further complains that as a scientist Arnobius cannot distinguish
between the discoverable and the undiscoverable, but admits
that in some points " he is beyond his age, e. g. he sees the
possibility of contradictory propositions being put forward
with equal *à priori* plausibility on many important subjects,
e. g. the immortality of the soul, the corporeity of God,
&c." [250] Again, he points out [251] that Arnobius shows affinities
with non-Christian modes of thought and in that he is,
according to Cruttwell, a precursor of Calvinism. In any case,
Arnobius does not believe that the soul is by nature immortal [252] though it is capable of becoming so by grace, [253] and
on human nature he is sometimes pessimistic, sometimes
optimistic, [254] and a skeptic concerning the possibility of
knowledge. He is, according to Halliday, [255] in harmony with
the prevailing trend of his time against rationalism.

An impressive group of scholars [256] charge our author with the mistaken belief that the pagan gods exist as a sort of secondary divinity subordinate to the Christian God. This opinion is by no means unanimous,[257] but dissenters are not numerous. Cruttwell [258] and Leckelt [259] think that he identifies these gods with the *daemones*,[260] but in every instance in which this word appears [261] it is clear that he distinguishes between them and the gods of the pagan cults. Our present inquiry concerns, therefore, not the demons but the well-known gods of the Graeco-Roman pantheon, Jupiter, Juno, and the rest.

Examination of what Arnobius actually says about these gods shows that in 3. 28-35, 4. 9, 4. 11, 4. 27, 4. 28, 5. 44, 6. 2, and 6. 10 there is highly convincing evidence to support the view that he is sure such gods cannot exist. To these passages we should add two others (5. 2 and 5. 8) where the same opinion is expressed about specific gods. In 3. 44, 7. 2, and 7. 7 he expresses doubt as to their existence without reaching the negative conclusion expected from an orthodox and well-informed Christian, but there is nothing here that suggests that he really believed the divinities exist. He alludes to the fact that pagans " suppose " they exist in 6. 8 and 7. 35, while in 6. 2 he holds back from even imputing virtues to the gods. The reference in 2. 3 to the " lesser gods " occurs in a quotation from a supposed pagan opponent and since he is regularly careful to compose these " quotations " in complete harmony with the pagan view, if, indeed, as some have thought, they are not actually borrowed from an actual pagan attack upon Christianity, no evidence of Arnobius' own opinions may properly be deduced from a phrase put into the mouth of a pagan. In 4. 13 there is an allusion to one supreme god and the many who pretend to be gods; in 3. 6 he expresses a willingness to worship the pagan gods but demands to know about them first, i. e. that they exist. An allusion to the " gods who dwell in heaven " (5. 15) is probably only rhetorical. If these passages were all we had, no one would have raised any question as to Arnobius' orthodoxy on this point.

There are, on the other hand, several passages which, taken at first glance, seem to favor the opposite view. In 7. 18 there is the concession: " So far as we are concerned, let them (the pagan gods) be whatsoever they are believed to be." In 3. 3 he maintains that though the Christians do not worship the pagan gods, in their rendering homage to the One God, the other gods are included—" if they are royal in descent and are sprung from the primal Head." (Does not the fact that admittedly the Christians do not worship the pagan gods imply, at the very least, belief in their falsity?) Again, he states: " If we all grant there is but one Father of things, immortal, and alone unbegotten, and that nothing is found prior to Him . . . , it follows that all those whom human fancy has believed to be gods of mortal men, have been either begotten by Him or brought forth by His command." And again,[262] " since all the gods, be they true gods or only said to be such by hearsay and conjecture, are immortal and eternal by reason of His will," and " what greater honor or distinction can we bestow upon them than to put them in the same place as the Head and Lord of the universe and the Supreme King himself, to whom the gods, in common with us, owe their consciousness of their own existence and that they are possessed of living substance? " [263]

These are the passages which, read out of their context and without due consideration of the impressive evidence to the contrary, have led some scholars to assert that Arnobius believed that these pagan gods existed as a sort of lesser divinity subordinate to the God of the Christians.[264] Such a view is erroneous and unfair to Arnobius: in arguing with the pagans he constantly does so on the basis of their own premises—he will concede for the sake of argument what he would never positively maintain: on this point consider the following judgment of Marchesi with which I am generally in agreement: [265]

> Arnobius tends to believe, he even does believe, in the existence of heavenly powers, subordinate to God and created by God and by God made sharers in divine attributes; but in no passage does he affirm that the pagan divinities are among these heavenly powers. It is true that in no passage does he exclude them; [266] but the constantly-dubitative tone which he uses in considering among the 'dii minores' the deities of paganism reveals to us a polemic concession rather than a personal conviction.[267]

Thus, the assertion that the pagan gods are included in the worship of the True God is merely a concession of this kind. Where our author is possibly at fault is in hastily stating that the gods of human fancy " are begotten by Him or brought forth by His command " and " are immortal and eternal by reason of His will."

While enough has been said to show that Arnobius is hardly orthodox [268] at every point, it would be quite another thing to accuse him of being heretical. No evidence exists to show that he was *strongly* influenced by any heretical sect, and his divergence from accepted Christian belief is the result, not of a willful choosing of views known to be dissident, but of an imperfect acquaintance with Christian teaching and a tendency to carry over into the new faith certain pagan ideas which he did not realize were incompatible with Christianity.

Yet it is not surprising to find that in the sixth-century *Decretum de libris recipiendis et non recipiendis* [269] once

ascribed to Pope Gelasius I (492-96) the "opuscula Arnobii" are included among the apocrypha "a catholicis vi-
tanda."[270] In this respect, Arnobius enjoys the company of
both Tertullian and Origen. Bardenhewer[271] thinks that the
inclusion of Arnobius in this list is a reflection merely of the
criticism of St. Jerome already noted, but if so, it is surprising
to observe that neither Novatus nor Apollinarius, both also
mentioned by Jerome in that passage in an unfavorable light,
is condemned in the *decretum*.

                    ⸗   ⸗   ⸗

We must now turn our attention to the much-vexed question of the sources used in the compilation of the *Adversus
nationes*, a problem which has a double aspect since, while
Arnobius mentions many a pagan source, he never refers by
name to any of his Christian predecessors. Indeed, all Christian literature is lumped together in the extremely indefinite
phrase "res vestrae."[272]

To begin with the Greek sources, the names of fifty-one
philosophers and writers are mentioned at least once each,
while Plato or one of his works is mentioned fourteen times,[273]
and Aristotle, Sophocles, and the very obscure writers
Mnaseas of Patara, Myrtilus, and Posidippus, are each mentioned twice. Names which appear only once are the following: Aethlius of Samos, Antiochus, Apollodorus, Arcesilas,
Archytas, Arrian, Butas, Carneades, Sextus Clodius,[274] Chrysippus, Crates of Mallos, Cronius the Neo-Platonist, Ctesias,
Democritus, Diagoras of Melos, Ephorus, Epicharmus, Epictetus, Euhemerus, Heraclitus, Hermippus, Hesiod, Hieronymus, Hippo of Melos, Homer,[275] Leandrius of Miletus, Leon
of Pella, Metrodorus, Nicagoras of Cyprus, Numenius the
Neo-Platonist, Panaetius, Panyassis of Halicarnassus, Patro-
cles of Thurium, Philostephanus, Pindar, Plutarch, Polemon,

Ptolemaeus of Megalopolis, Pythagoras, Sosibius, Thales, Theodorus of Cyrene, Timotheus, Zeno the Stoic, and Zeno of Myndus. There is also an allusion to an unnamed Tarentine poet who has been thought by some to be Rhinthon, and to such philosophers as the Epicureans and the proponents of the Middle and New Academy. Moreover, the *Orphica* are quoted and there is an allusion to Hermes Trismegistus. It will be readily apparent from this list that some of the names are household words among classicists but that others are very obscure indeed.[276].

Of Latin writers, M. Terentius Varro heads the list with fifteen citations, and P. Nigidius Figulus and Granius Flaccus follow with four each,[277] while M. Tullius Cicero, L. Cincius Alimentus, Cornificius Longus, and T. Manilius appear as authority three times each, and Ennius is once named and once cited anonymously. Latin writers mentioned once only are: Aelius Stilo, L. Caesellius Vindex, Caesius, Cornelius Epicadus, Q. Fabius Pictor, a Flaccus who may be Granius Flaccus or Verrius Flaccus (certainly not the poet Horace), Lucretius, Nisus a grammarian, L. Calpurnius Piso Censorius Frugi, Pomponius the writer of farces, Q. Serenus Sammonicus, Q. Terentius Scaurus, Trebatius, Valerianus,[278] Valerius Antias, and Verrius Flaccus. There are also occasional references to anonymous writings such as the *annales*,[279] the *memorialia scripta*,[280] the theologians,[281] and unspecified histories,[282] as well as to pseudonymous writings like the *libri Acherontici*[283] ascribed to Tages the Etruscan and the *Indigitamenta*[284] which bore the name of Numa Pompilius. As in the Greek list, we have here a combination of well-known writers with most obscure.[285]

Considered alone, these two lists with fifty-one Greek names and from twenty-two to twenty-four Latin names, depending upon how one counts ' Flaccus ' and ' Valerianus,' give the impression that the learning of Arnobius was both broad and profound. Sihler,[286] for example, concludes that Arnobius was in touch with the entire range of philosophy and ancient literature. Probably he is right but the evidence tends to suggest the wisdom of caution in deducing from a casual reference to an ancient writer proof that Arnobius himself had read the author's works, much less used them as a source. (We have, of course, included in both lists allusions to a philosopher or writer even when the context suggests that he is mentioned merely by way of illustration.)

To give an example, in 4. 24 there is the familiar charge against Aesculapius that he was slain because he became greedy and tried to exact pay for his cures, Pindar the Boeotian being cited as the source. We might conclude that Arnobius was himself familiar with Pindar, were it not for the fact that the same story is also told twice by Tertullian and once by Clement of Alexandria, both of whom also cite Pindar as their source. Either of these two apologists might theoretically have been an intermediate source, though a study of the parallels shows that it is unlikely that Tertullian was here used.[287]

A somewhat different type of aetiological problem is posed by a phrase in 3. 31 concerning Aristotle. Here Arnobius' choice of words suggests that he is unacquainted with Aristotle's works but has learned about him through the intermediary source, Granius, whom he names. A pair of passages in Cicero,[288] are so strikingly like the phrases of Arnobius, except, of course, that Granius is not mentioned, that we can be certain that ultimately the passage is to be derived from Cicero.

Furthermore, when we compare Arnobius with such encyclopaedic writers as Clement of Alexandria and Lactantius, we see clearly that he exhibits both a more superficial and a narrower acquaintance with pagan literature than they. He is more sparing in direct quotation, and there are relatively fewer allusions which embroider the plain argument, less that is incidental or digressive, by way of citation.

A glance at the lists will show some surprising omissions, though we must not expect Arnobius to mention every ancient writer known to us but only those who might presumably furnish good material for his purpose. Vergil is never mentioned, for example, but three scholars [289] have collected examples of Vergilian imitations and on *a priori* grounds we should expect Arnobius to be well acquainted with the poet. Herodotus, and, above all, Lucian, would have furnished good ore for Arnobius' furnaces but they are never mentioned and the same is true also of the *Fasti* of Ovid.

Arnobius' references to Plato and his works have been subjected to close scrutiny by both Röhricht [290] and Gabarrou [291] who are united in concluding that the evidence shows direct acquaintance with the Greek originals, rather than, for example, with such a possible Latin intermediary as the version of the *Timaeus* by Cicero. Neither of these two scholars considers the possibility that Arnobius was following closely, not Plato himself, but some book about Plato, perhaps a Neo-Platonist work, which accurately represented Plato. The number and character of the borrowings from Plato render this possibility, however, rather unlikely. [292]

Lucretius is cited but once but this is no indication of the extent of the borrowings from the author of the *De rerum natura*, [293] a debt so great, indeed, that, as we have seen, it has given rise to the speculation that Arnobius had been prior to his conversion a member of the cult of the Garden. Lucretius is also a source, hardly, I think, the only one, of Arnobius' idea that the gods cannot be angry and still exist.

The abundant proof that Arnobius utilized Varro presents no special problem although it is possible that at least some of the citations may have been derived indirectly. Indeed, Arnobius has at times been given the soubriquet of the " Christian Varro " [294] but the term might better have applied to the learned Lactantius, also called the " Christian Cicero " because of the excellence of his style.

As for Cicero,[295] it seems highly probable that his *De natura deorum* and *De divinatione* have been exploited, and, less certainly, the *Tusculanae disputationes*.[296] To the first of these works Arnobius refers once in a vague way but that does not mean that he did not use it extensively, as will be shown in the Notes. The failure to mention the *De divinatione* may, I think, possibly be attributed to the fact that it contains a trenchant criticism by a pagan of one of the more preposterous aspects of the pagan cult.[297] Yet Arnobius was quite willing to allude to the similar criticism coming from Euhemerus [298] and from Varro,[299] so this argument may be somewhat weaker. It seems scarcely probable, however, that, even giving due force both to the known decline in classical culture growing ever progressively greater in the first three centuries of our era and to the fact that Arnobius was a provincial, a professor of rhetoric could have been ignorant of the works of Cicero.[300]

But the most complex of these aetiological problems is that involved in the theory, until recently quite popular, that among the more important sources was Cornelius Labeo, known to us only from a few fragments [301] and never mentioned by Arnobius himself.[302]. The very date of this shadowy figure is a matter of controversy, Bousset,[303] who thinks that

Labeo utilized not the Neo-Platonist Porphyry but hermetism and the *Oracula Chaldaica*, dating him in the second half of the first century A. D. Boehm,[304] who devotes an entire dissertation to the question, concludes that the *terminus ante quem* is 125 A. D. Niggetiet[305] and Kroll,[306] on the other hand, favor a much later date and make Labeo a contemporary of Arnobius.

The partisans of the Labeo myth,[307] for such it has now been recognized to be, have the following factual basis for their position. In 3. 26 Arnobius distinguishes between *dii laevi* and *dii boni* but ascribes this information to no source. Now since St. Augustine[308] attributes a similar distinction between *numina bona* and *numina mala* to Labeo (he does not use the *gentilicium*[309]), the Labeonians immediately conclude that Arnobius *must* have derived his knowledge of these divinities from Labeo. At this point we should admit that Labeo is certainly a possible source but he is by no means the only one.

Having concluded to their own satisfaction, however, that Labeo is the source in 3. 26, these scholars proceed to see him lurking behind many another passage in Arnobius for which they are unable to suggest some other derivation! Fortunately for them, so little is known of Labeo that they are never embarrassed by facts difficult to fit into their theory. Passages in which one or another scholar have professed to see the hand of Labeo include the following: 2. 13-62, 2. 35, 2. 36-43, 3. 23 f., 3. 26, 3. 29-42, 3. 37, 3. 40, 3. 41, 4. 5, 4. 12, 4. 16, 5. 18, 7. 23 f., and the whole of Book Seven. I do not propose to repeat here what I have said about these passages in the Notes: it should be sufficient to state that the Labeo myth has, in my opinion, been thoroughly exploded in the fundamental dissertation of Friedrich Tullius[310] and the ex-

cellent article on the special sources of Book Two by the
Dominican Festugière.[311] Let us hope that the ghost of Labeo
has now been laid.

Tullius' dissertation consists of a detailed study of passage
after passage in Books Four to Six (as well as of some in Book
Three) in an attempt to identify the source of each. We shall
have occasion shortly to consider his conclusions in regard
to a possible use of the *Protrepticus* of Clement of Alexandria
—here we need only state that he thinks the real source in
Books Three and Four is a theological manual in existence
at least as early as 100 A. D. and not by either Varro or
Labeo; [312] that in his estimation Arnobius used also a *Liber
de mysteriis* and a book on the allegorical interpretation of
the pagan myths; [313] and that he believes the source in 4. 25
is a mythographic handbook.[314] All of these sources are now
lost and were by unknown hands. Indeed, Tullius seems to
be constitutionally unable to admit that Arnobius could
possibly have used any source still preserved, Cicero, for
example.

While the care with which Tullius examines the text is
great, and his conclusions frequently seem valid, it should
be pointed out that his method does not, in my opinion,
allow sufficiently for any knowledge derived from personal
observation or previous reading, and Tullius' enthusiasm for
the theory of the lost source sometimes leads him to press a
point far too strongly. Moreover, his handling of this problem
in aetiology suggests that he cannot divest himself of the
" single-source " theory which in the nineteenth century produced such disastrous results in the criticism of Livy. I cannot eliminate from my thinking the possibility that some of
the divergences which he thinks significant are merely the
reflection of personal differences which we should expect.

From Tullius' point of view, nothing can have been added by Arnobius himself—every detail must have been found in the source being followed. This seems to misunderstand the method of literary composition and grossly to underestimate our author.

To turn now to Festugière, however, we find a very different story. Here the investigation is limited to Book Two, which did not fall within the compass of Tullius' study, and the writer proves, to my mind quite conclusively, that in that Book Arnobius displays a considerable acquaintance with hermetism,[315] Neo-Platonism, the *Oracula Chaldaica*, Gnosticism (as reported in Plotinus), Zoroaster, Osthanes, and magical papyri containing Mithraic liturgies.[316] Whether this knowledge was the result of independent study or not, is hard to say, but it seems clear that whatever the source, Arnobius possessed it when he wrote the *Adversus nationes*. This does not mean, nor does Festugière maintain that it does, that Arnobius was himself influenced by these intellectual forces. In fact, he attacks the views which he cites.

We have already stated that Arnobius nowhere names a single Christian predecessor,[317] from which silence we might conclude at once that he knew none, or at least used none, in the composition of the *Adversus nationes* but for the fact that there are a great many passages which show resemblance to one or another of the earlier apologists. These have led many a scholar to conclude that he was acquainted with these predecessors. Thus, Cruttwell[318] thinks that Arnobius had read Justin Martyr; Colombo,[319] that he had surely read Cyprian's *Ad Demetrianum* 2, Tertullian's *Ad nationes* 1. 9 and *Apologeticus* 40; Coxe,[320] and Gabarrou,[321] that he had learned of Tertullian and Cyprian; the latter,[322] that he had read the *De anima* of Tertullian; de Labriolle,[323] that he borrows from Tertullian; Amatucci,[324] that he knew Minucius, Tertullian, Cyprian, and Clement; while Freppel [325] compares some of his ideas with the *Contra Celsum* of Origen. Geffcken [326] says that he is a follower of Tertullian in his attack on the gods and a precursor of Lactantius in his use of Roman authors to refute the Roman cults. From many passages in the Notes it will be seen that I am well aware of many of these resemblances, some even in such writers as Tatian, Athenagoras, and Theophilus of Antioch, who are not mentioned by my predecessors.

Yet we cannot demonstrate from passing resemblances that Arnobius was really indebted to a given precursor. That a great many other writers of the early Church also attacked the ridiculousness and scandal which they saw in the pagan cults makes it almost inevitable that just by chance more than one would independently touch upon the same allusions, utilize the same myth, make the same charge. Unless, therefore, there is in each instance some better reason to accept interdependence as a fact, we can hardly afford to be dogmatic.

In the case of the *Protrepticus* of Clement of Alexandria, however, the resemblances are so numerous and so strikingly parallel that many scholars have concluded the dependence of Arnobius upon Clement is clearly proven. Thus, Le-Nourry,[327] says that Arnobius borrows from Clement; Bryce-Campbell,[328] that from Clement whole sentences have been taken unchanged; Kettner,[329] that Books Four to Six show the influence of the *Protrepticus*; Coxe,[330] that Arnobius " economizes " (= condenses?) Clement; Brakman,[331] that the five Minervas in 4.14 are derived from Clement; and others [332] either list Clement among the sources or allude to Arnobius' indebtedness to him. The great exponent of this view, however, is Röhricht [333] who devotes his dissertation to the problem of the relationship of Arnobius to Clement, reaching the conclusion that Arnobius must have had Clement before him as he wrote.

The evidence which he adduces is extremely impressive. The parallels between the two authors are so exact that we must accept one of two possibilities: either (1) Arnobius was using Clement as a source, or (2) both were following a common source. There can be no possibility of accidental similarity such as might be suggested if we were dealing with a few isolated passages. Except possibly for an incidental remark of Bouchier,[334] no voice has been raised in opposition to Röhricht's conclusion save that of Tullius in the dissertation to which we have already alluded. After minute examination of the parallel passages Tullius convinces himself that Arnobius exhibits sufficient divergence from Clement as to make it impossible for him to be following Clement. He therefore is forced to believe that both authors had a common source.[335]

Following the appearance of Tullius' dissertation in 1934, Hagendahl [336] briefly expressed his disagreement with Tullius' method, but it was left to Rapisarda to publish a thorough-going criticism of Tullius' conclusions in his book *Clemente fonte di Arnobio*, which though published in 1939, was not available to me until my own work was completed.[337]

While Tullius is clearly right in seeing elements in Arnobius which cannot have been taken from Clement since they are not there, he is wrong in concluding that Arnobius could not know Clement or borrow from him. Tullius does not allow sufficiently for two factors: the fund of knowledge which Arnobius possessed and the possibility that he would, even in copying, vary the phraseology to a considerable degree

in the interests of rhetoric and his own independence. That
Arnobius might easily have found a copy of Clement's
Protrepticus in one or another of the Christian libraries in
North Africa seems to me highly probable. I am therefore
inclined to think that the present state of our knowledge
points to a position more nearly that of Röhricht than Tullius.

Two apologists whom we might expect most to find among
Arnobius' sources are Minucius Felix and Tertullian. A careful search of the *Octavius* has revealed a fair number of
parallel passages in which there is sufficient resemblance to
justify closer scrutiny. In a majority of these instances it is
possible to conclude either that evidence of dependence is
entirely lacking or that some concomitant feature suggests
another source at the point in question.[338] In four other
instances, however, we cannot eliminate the possibility of
dependence, though proof is lacking,[339] but three present
evidence adequate to prove that Arnobius had read the
Octavius.

When in 3. 29 Arnobius refers to the tradition that Janus
founded the Janiculum, he calls it a town (*oppidum*). The
error is interesting and I think came about through a mis-
reading of Minucius (*Octavius* 21. 6): *itaque latebram
suam, quod tuto latuisset* (sc. *Saturnus*), *vocari maluit
Latium, et urbem Saturniam idem de suo nomine et Ianiculum Ianus ad memoriam uterque posteritatis reliquerunt.*[340]
In this passage Saturn and Janus are coupled together as
having given each his name to something in Italy, Saturn to
the city of Saturnia, Janus to the Janiculum, the latter not
being specified as a hill. If Arnobius read the passage hur-
riedly, however, it is conceivable, that he might, having implanted in his mind the fact that Saturn named a city, carry
over this thought to the Janus clause and, not knowing or

forgetting that the Janiculum was a hill, set down a word that does not fit.

The second parallel which I think significant is found in the opening sentence of 4. 32, a quotation from the presumed pagan opponent: *Sed poetarum, inquiunt, figmenta sunt haec omnia et ad voluptatem compositae lusiones.* With this compare the *Octavius* 23. 1: *Has fabulas et errores, ita ab imperitis parentibus discimus, et quod est gravius, ipsi studiis et disciplinis elaboramus, carminibus praecipue poetarum, qui plurimum quantum veritati ipsi auctoritate nocuerunt.*

Finally, in 6. 16, which refers to the presence of vermin in and around the pagan cult statues, there is a passage so strikingly like the *Octavius* 24. 1 (which I have quoted at length in the Notes *ad loc.*) that the resemblance appears causal, as was rightly maintained by Orelli in his commentary, by Heinze [341] and by Kroll, [342] though as usual denied by Tullius. [343]

The number of parallels between Arnobius and Tertullian is much greater. This might be expected from the relatively larger bulk of Tertullian's writing, but, as we shall see, the parallels are rather generally confined to the two shorter works, the *Apologeticus* and *Ad nationes*, so the greater percentage of resemblances carries weight.

Arnobius may have been influenced in his choice of title by the *Ad nationes.* [344] Both authors make abundant use of ' retorsion,' the twisting back of an opponent's argument upon himself. [345] Both also employ the device of an *adversarius* or assumed opponent who is a sort of straw man set up to be knocked down. [346]

Moreover, a number of passages show extremely close parallelism. Among these are the emphasis laid on the point that Christ performed the Miracles by a single word; [347] a very significant passage concerning the use by pagans of expressions implying monotheism;[348] the allusion, in a single sentence of Arnobius, to the relationships of slave-master, wife-husband, and child-parent, with another sentence in Tertullian in which the same relationships appear, though in a different order (wife, child, slave);[349] an extremely striking parallelism between Arnobius 2. 67 and the *Apologeticus* 6 in which a number of the illustrations are identical: the conservative Roman respect for ancestral institutions, sumptuary laws, the Roman view that a woman should abstain from wine, and the fact that though the Christians are criticized for bringing in something new, the pagans themselves introduce novelties. Another passage in the same Book contains ideas found in various places in Tertullian: Faunus is the son of Picus,[350] Saturn is the earliest god,[351] the pagan gods are relatively recent in origin,[352] and in the consulship of Piso and Gabinius the Egyptian divinities were expelled from Rome.[353] Finally, both authors elsewhere[354] maintain that the pagan gods have more reason to complain against the pagans than against Christians.

To these parallels, which are so close that I regard it as almost beyond doubt that Arnobius borrowed from Tertullian in each instance, we may add another group where the similarity is striking but dependence not so clearly proven. A statement of Arnobius concerning the swallowing-up of cities may be a condensation of several passages of Tertullian.[355] There is a very close similarity between parallel statements that the Christians were attacked for worshipping a human being, but this idea is so commonplace that we must not conclude dependence from it alone.[356] The idea for the ' controlled experiment ' may have been suggested to Arnobius by the account of a somewhat similar experiment con-

ducted by Psammetichus of Egypt, which Tertullian relates,[357] and Tertullian is a possible source in the case of the
allusion to the ass's head.[358] While the examples cited in this
paragraph are by no means absolutely certain, they lend
cumulative support to the group described in the preceding
paragraph.

So also another group of parallels which are close but still
less certain: an allusion to the etymology of Cronus from
chronos,[359] which is commonplace; a reference to Jove's love
for his sister;[360] references to the wounding of Venus and
the chaining of Mars,[361] and to the services of gods rendered
to human masters;[362] a criticism of horse-racing;[363] and, less
clearly, an allusion to gods dwelling in the air.[364] Among the
rare words which Arnobius uses are two which Tertullian
employs in a single chapter,[365] and Tertullian's statement
that Christians should be punished if they fail to worship
real gods should be compared with several of Arnobius'
somewhat similar statements expressing beliefs in the existence of the gods.[366]

We should note, however, certain evidences of sharp difference between Arnobius and Tertullian. Arnobius' doctrine of the impassibility of God is in direct conflict with the
orthodox position which appears in the *De anima* 16 where
both God and Christ are represented as capable of anger.
This difficulty should not trouble us—it is merely evidence
that Arnobius had not read the *De anima*.[367] Moreover,
despite Tertullian's willingness to have the pagan gods worshipped, *if they are real gods*, Tertullian leaves no doubt that
he was sure they did not exist.[368] But this presents a difficulty
only if we take the view that Arnobius thought they did
exist. Finally, as we have noted, though Tertullian twice
presents a charge of greed against Aesculapius, it is more

probable that it was from the *Protrepticus* that Arnobius borrowed the story.[369]

In the light of the generally inadequate and inaccurate information concerning Christianity which our author displays, this evidence that he almost certainly had read and borrowed from the *Protrepticus*, and knew and utilized the *Octavius* and *Apologeticus* and *Ad nationes*, or at least one of these last, is somewhat surprising. Yet it seems quite reasonable to suppose that when, soon after his conversion, our author determined to write, knowing as yet rather little about the faith which he had espoused, he took himself to the libraries which were accessible. That he there found copies of all these works I am convinced. Surely the Church in North Africa would have possessed copies of the *Protrepticus* and the *Octavius*, and even the fact that Tertullian had in his later years fallen away from orthodoxy would not have meant, in fact, did not mean, that books written in his orthodox period were destroyed. But if Arnobius used the work of these predecessors, why was he silent about their names? The answer is that there was no point in naming them. That Clement or Minucius or Tertullian had previously used a given argument has no real effect upon the validity of the argument, and the modern conception of plagiarism never bothered any ancient—to the ancient, imitation was the greatest compliment of all. Yet he does cite pagan authors in profusion. Quite so. That Euhemerus, a pagan philosopher, had attacked the pagan cults heightens the argument. Remember constantly that the *Adversus nationes* is addressed to the pagans; indeed, the preposition *adversus* itself means not only 'against' but also 'toward.'[370]

In discussing the question of the date of Arnobius[371] we have had occasion to mention the view of certain scholars that there is interdependence between Arnobius and the *Divinae institutiones* of his pupil Lactantius which were being composed at about the same time as the *Adversus nationes*. Let us now examine the evidence on this point which is to be found in nine pairs of parallel passages which show some resemblance.[372] Two of the pairs have to do with the Miracles of Christ. Consider the following from Lactantius:[373] " For as He Himself, when He was living among men, put to flight all the demons by a word, and restored to their former senses the minds of men which had been excited and maddened by their evil attacks, so now His followers, in the name of their Master and by the sign of His passion, banish the same polluted spirits from men." Here, in briefer form, is the content of *Adversus nationes* 1. 50, in which our author also emphasizes the fact that the miracles of the followers of Christ were performed by verbal means, not by magic.[374] The second passage referred to is too long for quotation but is itself a shorter version of the same argument which Arnobius uses in describing Christ's own Miracles.[375] Lactantius' account is in harmony with the Gospels, whereas Arnobius attributes to Christ a miracle not there recorded.[376] While there is in general a fairly close harmony between the two passages, the material which they here utilize must have been of common knowledge in the Church, and so the resemblances, striking as they are, do not prove interdependence.

A comparison of passages[377] in which both writers cite Sextus Clodius for a story about Fenta Fatua, and another pair[378] in which they both tell the story of the sacrilegious temple-robbing of Dionysius the Younger, tyrant of Syracuse, will reveal in each instance that Arnobius' account is considerably the shorter and that there is nothing in his version not found in that of Lactantius which might not be attributed to rhetorical differences. To judge from these passages alone, Arnobius may well have been condensing Lactantius but it is more probable that they are following a common source. Here also the evidence is far from being conclusive.

In another pair of correspondences the same circumstances do not obtain. In 2. 35 Arnobius unfolds his doctrine that the souls are of a medium quality, that is, neither mortal nor immortal, an idea also found in Lactantius.[379] The second parallel is between a statement of Arnobius in 2. 51 that surmise, rather than certainty, is all that philosophers can reach by their investigations, and a similar statement in Lactantius.[380] In these instances it is tempting to think that one author had read the other but there is no way to determine which may claim priority, and in fact these parallels also may be purely accidental.

Adversus nationes 2. 39-42 is a long and florid passage in which the author asks whether the Creator sent the souls into the world for the purpose of having them commit a large variety of evil acts—the implication, of course, is that God is not the Creator of the souls. This list of impious deeds includes (in 2. 42) several that are parallel to items in a similar list of vicious acts attributed by Lactantius [381] to the worshipers of the pagan divinities. Crimes which appear in both lists are: brigandage, forging of wills, poisoning, acts of lust and of perversion, but the remainder of both lists differs so much that we can hardly hold the resemblances as more than accidental. Indeed, if two persons were asked to write down a list of crimes, it is probable that independently they would prepare lists more closely parallel than these.

Finally, we should note the striking use by both authors [382] of the word *caducus* in the sense of mortal, and two exceedingly close clauses:

Adversus nationes 1. 62: homo quem induerat et secum portabat
Divinae institutiones 4. 10: homini . . . quem induerat gerebat.

But these phrases are, I believe, commonplaces.

To summarize this evidence, probable common sources
may easily account for four of the nine passages, and two of
the others are either of no great significance or are commonplaces. In only two out of nine are the parallels not easily
explainable, but note that both of these come from Book Two,
the sources of which, despite the able article by Festugière,
are neither well-known nor sure. It is possible that even here
a common source is followed.

Particularly attractive is this view of the independence of
the two authors when we consider the implications of the
alternative. To believe in interdependence, as do Buonaiuti
and Rapisarda,[383] we must be able to show how either writer
might have seen the book of the other. Such a problem is
of no great difficulty in the case of Arnobius' knowledge of
Clement, Minucius, or Tertullian, but with Lactantius in
Nicomedia and Arnobius in Sicca, writing about the same
time, the difficulty of transporting a copy of the product
of either to the other sufficiently soon seems well-nigh
insurmountable.

*   *   *

And what of Arnobius' *Nachleben?* That a copy was available to St. Jerome, of course, is obvious and from his statements concerning the *volumina quae vulgo exstant* we must
assume that the book had at least a moderate distribution by
his time. Yet, except for Jerome and the compilers of the
Decretum Gelasianum in the sixth century, no writer mentions Arnobius until the first edition of Trithemius' *De
scriptoribus ecclesiasticis*, published at Basel in 1494.[384]

Two scholars have noted parallels, chiefly linguistic in character, between the *Adversus nationes* and the *De errore profanarum religionum* of the Christian writer Firmicus Maternus, and I myself have found parallels of subject matter as well. Ziegler [385] does not go so far as to maintain that Firmicus Maternus had really read Arnobius—he merely cites the resemblances in the notes to his edition of Firmicus. [386] But Brakman [387] seems quite convinced that Firmicus copied from the pages of Arnobius. I can hardly take so extreme a position since too many of the parallels are of dictions which might have been and probably were commonly current in the period, and the similarities of content may be presumed to come from frequent identity of topics. [388] It is possible that the author of the *De errore profanarum religionum* had read Arnobius but it is not proven. Rapisarda credits Arnobius with having given great impetus to a new literary genre, the *Quaestiones* of later Christian writers, [389] and we should also cast a glance at a curious fragment preserved in one of the manuscripts of Tertullian [390] but long recognized as certainly not by his hand. This is the *De execrandis gentium diis* which has been convincingly dated by Bickel, [391] after a masterly study of the text, in the sixth century. The reason for mentioning this fragment here is that it shows more remarkable parallels with Arnobius than does even Clement of Alexandria. One wonders at once whether the anonymous author had derived his information from the *Adversus nationes*. Possibly so, but at least he had before him some other source, since he refers in the fifth chapter to four laws (the *Lex Falcidia et Sempronia, Lex Papinia, Lex Iulia,* and *Lex Cornelia*) which are not mentioned by Arnobius.

The failure of Vincent of Beauvais († 1264) to mention

Arnobius in the third part (*Historiale*) of his *Speculum maius* is puzzling to Colombo [392] but a silence much more surprising is that of the celebrated Bishop of Hippo. The many places in which Arnobius uses material also exploited by St. Augustine in the *De civitate Dei* will be evident from the frequent citations to that work in the Notes. Moreover, we can hardly suppose that a work known to Jerome in many copies was likely to have escaped the notice of his great contemporary, particularly one who lived in the vicinity of Arnobius' home Sicca. St. Augustine may have been offended by Arnobius for various reasons. [393]

✶   ✶   ✶

Translators of previous volumes in this series have had the good fortune to deal with relatively-sound texts and have thus not been forced to pay much attention to matters of textual criticism. Yet, despite the accumulated labors of a host of scholars in the last four centuries, the text of Arnobius is still in a lamentable state. This is largely the result of the fact that since our knowledge of it is dependent upon a single manuscript, the *codex Parisinus* 1661, now preserved in the *Bibliothèque Nationale* in Paris, [394] and usually referred to as ' P,' the numerous errors in that *codex* can be eliminated only by the ingenuity of emendations.

What appears in P as the ' liber octavus ' or eighth book of Arnobius is in reality the *Octavius* of Minucius Felix, first correctly distinguished from the *Adversus nationes* by Franciscus Balduinus who published the earliest separate edition of the *Octavius* at Heidelberg in 1560. [395]

Besides *codex P*, there is preserved in the *Bibliothèque Royale de Belgique* in Brussels another *codex* of these same two works bearing the collocation 10846-10847 (formerly

Burgundiacus D 685) which has been dated variously: in the eleventh century,[396] in the eleventh or twelfth,[397] in the twelfth,[398] and as late as the sixteenth.[399] Despite this disagreement as to date, all scholars who profess to have seen the manuscript are agreed that it is a copy of P. If such be the case, the Brussels *codex* has no value as an independent witness for the text. In any case, its testimony was made available from a collation by F. Modius used by Godescalcus Stewechius in the edition which he published at Antwerp in 1604 and another collation, transcribed in the nineteenth century by L. Lersch, convinced Reifferscheid that this manuscript may be safely ignored.[400]

The *editio princeps* of the *Adversus nationes* was published at Rome in the year 1542, according to the colophon, or in 1543, the date of the preface, by Franciscus Sabaeus who used as the basis of his text our *codex* P, then his private property. Though Sabaeus was at the time in charge of the Vatican Library, he had brought the *codex*, as it would appear from statements in the preface which are not quite clear, from somewhere in the north. In any case, soon after the publication of the printed edition bearing a dedicatory epistle to Francis I of France, the editor presented both a copy of his edition and the *codex* itself to that monarch from whom it ultimately passed to its present owner.

Since that day a total of at least twenty-eight editions of the complete Latin text have been printed.[401] In addition, there are separate editions of Book One, twice thereafter reissued, and of Book Two.[402]

All earlier editions of the *Adversus nationes* were, however, superseded by the excellent edition of August Reifferscheid published as the fourth volume of the then newly-established *Corpus scriptorum ecclesiasticorum latinorum* (Vienna 1875, reprinted 1890). For the first time the text of Arnobius was firmly established on the basis of rigid principles of textual criticism, being prepared from a fresh examination [403] of the *codex* P in the light of the principal editions published hitherto.[404] Reifferscheid did not however, hesitate to mark many a lacuna with the asterisk (*) and many a *locus desperatus* with the obelus (†): the text was hardly yet in a satisfactory condition.

In the years following the appearance of this text much good work was done on the improvement of the more difficult passages without, however, reaching general agreement.[405] This was the situation when Concetto Marchesi issued a new text as volume 62 of the *Corpus scriptorum latinorum Paravianum* (Turin 1934).[406] Marchesi's text, which at first received acclaim,[407] was marked by greater conservatism in adhering to the reading of the manuscript and it had the advantage of being able to include references to the work of scholars who had written in the six decades since the Vienna edition. In recent years, however, Marchesi's caution has been under attack, chiefly from the brilliant Swedish school of Wiman, Hagendahl, and Axelson,[408] from whom it is to be hoped we may soon expect a new and better text. Their chief complaint against Marchesi has been his failure to mark palpable lacunae and to accept what they regard as certain emendations. While I am inclined to think that they have carried this criticism of Marchesi to extremes, in the main I believe it to be sound.

In preparing the present translation the text of Marchesi has been used as a base, but Reifferscheid's readings have frequently been preferred, as have many appearing in critical work published since 1875, which has been thoroughly examined. In addition, some emendations of my own, published in the *Vigiliae Christianae* 3 (1949) 39-49, have been adopted, but in every case where a reading different from Marchesi's has been followed, that fact has been noted in the commentary. Citations to critical work earlier than 1875 have been made on the basis of the apparatus provided by the two editors usually without independent examination. The eclectic Latin text thus created will be published, it is hoped, together with the results of further critical study, in a European series.

Notwithstanding the fact that the commentary has been prepared entirely from original research, much help was derived from the notes in the variorum Latin commentary in Orelli's edition and reprinted in *ML* 5. This contains not only the fruit of Orelli's own studies but also a vast amount which he copied, with due credit, from his predecessors.[409] There is, in addition, a brief commentary in Oehler's edition and longer ones will be found in Hildebrand's and in the German translation of von Besnard mentioned below, but these three commentaries have been consulted only when occasion demanded.

The sole previous English translation, by Archdeacon Hamilton Bryce and Hugh Campbell, *The Seven Books of Arnobius Adversus Gentes*, which first appeared as volume 19 of the *Ante-Nicene Christian Library* edited by Alexander Roberts and James Donaldson (Edinburgh 1871) and was reprinted, with some additional notes and elucidations by the Episcopal Bishop A. Cleveland Coxe, in volume 6 of *The Ante-Nicene Fathers* (Buffalo 1886), though frequently faulty and now completely outmoded, has proved invaluable. On occasion reference has also been made to two German translations, the first by Franz Anton von Besnard, *Des Afrikaner's Arnobius sieben Bücher wider die Heiden, aus dem Lateinischen übersetzt und erläutert* (Landshut 1842),[410] and the second by J. Alleker, *Arnobius sieben Bücher gegen die Heiden, ins Deutsche übersetzt* (Trier 1858). No copy of the only other translation known to me, that in Dutch by Joachim Oudaan, *Arnobius d'Afrikaner tegen de Heydenen vervat in zeven bocken* (Harlingen 1677) has been available.[411]

My sincerest thanks remain to be expressed to the many who have contributed to the preparation of this book by furnishing me bibliographical information at their disposal or by making available for my use copies of their own publications or rare books owned by them. Professor Kevin Guinagh of Antioch College very kindly lent me for an unlimited period several volumes from his extensive collection of Arnobiana. Through the courtesy of Professor Axel Boëthius of Göteborg I have received copies of articles from the editors of *Eranos* and from Professors Bertil Axelson and Gerhard Wiman; while at the moment of going to press Professor Emanuele Rapisarda provided me with a copy of a work of his for which I had long searched in vain.[412] Without the assistance of these friends, the present translation and commentary could not have been made.

BOOK ONE

PAGAN SLANDERS OF THE CHRISTIANS REFUTED

*The charge: the Christians have brought calamities
upon mankind.*

1. The claim has been made, as I have learned, by some
who believe profoundly in their own wisdom and speak in an
oracular fashion as if they were the mouthpiece of some god,[1]
that after the Christian race began to exist on earth, the world
went to ruin, mankind was afflicted with many and varied
ills, and even the denizens of heaven themselves, as the
result of the abandonment of the ceremonial sacrifices by
which they were formerly induced to look after our affairs,
were exiled from the regions of the earth. For this reason I
have decided to oppose this prejudiced view, insofar as my
competence and my modest command of language permit,[2]
and to refute these slanderous charges. These people must
not harbor the delusion that they have said something significant when they have merely spread abroad common rumors,
or think that, if we on our side refrain from engaging in controversy, they have won because our view is inherently defective, when it really is only because of the silence of the
defenders.[3]

I would never deny that the charge is most serious and
that we wholly deserve the odium of being public enemies,[4]
if it were proved that we are the reason why the world has
wandered from the path of natural law, the gods have been

exiled far from us, or so great a swarm of mortal woes have been brought upon mankind.

The refutation: no new calamities have occurred.

2. Let us therefore examine the precise significance of the belief they hold, having laid aside entirely the spirit of contention [5] which usually confuses or glosses over the consideration of the facts, and let us weigh the merits of each side and determine whether this statement be true or not.

It will surely be brought out by the juxtaposition of arguments in logical sequence that not we but they, rather, are shown to be godless and that they who profess to be worshippers of the gods [6] and to be devoted to the ancient religious practices are themselves found guilty of that charge they advance.

And first, in friendly and unimpassioned manner, we ask of them answers to these questions:

After the name of the Christian religion began to be used on earth, what phenomenon never before observed, or never before recognized, or what sensation or experience contrary to the laws laid down at the beginning of time, has ever come to the so-called 'Nature of Things'? [7] Have any of those primordial elements of which it is agreed all things are composed ever gone through a transmutation of their basic qualities? [8]

Has the construction of this massive mechanism [9] which covers us all and in which we are held inclosed [10] in any way been shaken or destroyed? Has the revolution of the earth, varying from the speed of its primal motion, begun to be slower or to be accelerated in precipitate rotation?

Have the stars begun to rise where they formerly set and have the constellations begun to set in the place they used to rise? Has the sun itself, the sovereign of the stars, with whose light all things are clothed [11] and by whose warmth all things are brought to life, blazed forth in greater heat, grown less warm, and thus deteriorated by changing to opposite conditions the well-regulated temperature it used to have? Has the moon ceased to refashion herself and to recreate her older contours by constant re-establishment of new ones?

Has winter, has summer, have the intervening seasons, been destroyed by the mingling of seasons of unequal character? [12] Has winter begun to have long days and has the summer's night begun to invite back the dawn at its tardiest pace? [13]

Have the winds ceased to blow? And have their blasts died down so that the sky is not gathered together into clouds and the fields do not submit [14] to be moistened by the storms? Does the earth refuse to receive the seeds entrusted to it or are the trees unwilling to leaf out? Has the flavor in edible fruits or the vine with its juices been changed? Is foul gore squeezed out from the olive berries and has the lamp, gone out, lost its source of supply?

Do the animals accustomed to the land and those that pass their life in the seas have no mating season? Do they fail to protect, each according to its own habits and its own law of instinct, the young which they have generated in their wombs?

Finally, do men themselves, whom the first creation [15] scattered over the habitable [16] shores, not contract marriages with the proper nuptial rites? Do they not beget children they love most dearly? Do they not carry on public and private and family business? Do they not, as each pleases, direct their talents to varied arts and different kinds of learning, and reap the profits of their cleverness and zeal?

Do those to whom fate [17] has given such privileges fail to exercise rule, do they fail to issue commands? Do they fail to experience daily advancement in honorable offices and powers? Do they not preside over discussions in the courts of law? Do they not give interpretations of laws and rights? [18] All other things by which human life is encompassed and in which it is contained—men practice these, do they not, in their own tribes after the established customs of their ancestors? [19]

Such calamities as have occurred are of a type long familiar.

3. Since these are the facts and no unusual factor has appeared to break [20] into the eternal succession of events by disturbing their courses, why is it that it is said that a plague was brought upon the earth after the Christian religion appeared in the world and revealed the mysteries [21] of hidden truth?

" But pestilence," they say, " and droughts, wars, famines, locusts, mice, and hailstorms, and other harmful things with which human affairs are visited, are brought upon us by the gods in their anger at your wrongs and evil-doings." [22]

Now if in matters that are perfectly clear and need no defense it were not stupid to delay longer, I would certainly show by unfolding the story of former ages that those evils you speak of were not unknown, and that these plagues did not suddenly burst in upon us, and mortal affairs did not begin to be infested by a variety of dangers after our race merited the happiness of being called by this name. [23] If we are to blame and it is for our punishment that these calamities have been devised, from what source did men of old derive the names of these misfortunes? Whence did they obtain a word for wars? How could they have given meaning to "pestilences" and "hailstorms" or introduced them among the words that form lucid speech? If these ills are entirely new and derive their existence from recent sins, how could it happen that past generations created words for these things which they neither knew themselves nor had learned that they had been experienced in the times of any of their ancestors?

"Poverty of agricultural produce," they say, "and scarcity of grain have a more relentless grip on us."

Were earlier centuries, even the most ancient, ever free at any time from such periods of great need? Do not the very names that label these evils bear witness and loudly testify that no human being was ever immune to them? And if the matter were really hard to believe, we could specify by the testimony of authors how great the nations were that experienced dire famine and perished in devastation piled on devastation, and to what nations and how often it happened.

"Hail storms occur very frequently and ruin everything." Well, do we not find it expressly stated in ancient literature that even showers of stones [24] demolished whole areas? [25]

"Hard [26] rains cause the crops to die and bring on barrenness to the lands." Was antiquity ever free from these evils when we have known of mighty rivers drying up and the mud parched? [27]

"Contagious diseases consume the human race." Run through the annals [28] in various languages: you will learn that whole nations have often been laid desolate and bereft of their inhabitants. [29]

"Every kind of crop is ruined and eaten by locusts, [30] by mice." [31] Go through your own historical records and you will be taught how often a former age was affected by these pests and brought to the wretchedness of poverty.

" Shaken by violent earthquakes, cities totter to their destruction." What? did not times gone by see cities with their populations swallowed up by huge rifts? [32] Or were they fortunate enough not to experience such disasters?

4. When was the human race ever destroyed by a flood? [33] Was it not before our time? When was the world set on fire [34] and reduced to coals and ashes? Was it not before our time? When were magnificent cities engulfed by tidal waves? [35] Was it not before our time? When were wars carried on with wild beasts and struggles with lions? [36] Was it not before our time? When was ruin brought on entire populations by venomous serpents? [37] Was it not before our time? Yes, as for this habit of yours to impute to us the causes of frequent wars, the devastation of cities, the invasions of Germans and Scythians—you must pardon me for saying it—in your passion for calumnies you obviously fail to see the actual facts behind your statements.

5. When ten thousand [38] years ago, as Plato tells us, [39] a great force of men who utterly destroyed and blotted out countless nations broke forth from the island which is called Neptune's [40] Atlantis, were we the cause? When between the Assyrians [41] and the Bactrians under Ninus and Zoroaster [42] of old not only was there a conflict with the sword and with brawn but even with the esoteric arts of the Magi and Chaldaeans, [43] was this cause for hostility to us? When Helen was carried off under the leadership and instigation of the gods [44] and became a dreadful bane to her own and later times, was this charged against our religion? When that monstrous Xerxes [45] let in the sea upon the land and walked across the

seas, was this brought about by any wrong on the part of our people? When from the borders of Macedonia one young man [46] arose and conquered the kingdoms of the East, reducing their populations to the state of prisoners and slaves, was this our doing and did we provoke the causes? When the Romans more recently, like some mighty flood, submerged and overran all nations, did we, indeed, urge the gods to this madness? But if there is no man who would dare impute to our times those things which took place long ago, in what way can we be the causes of the present misfortunes, when nothing new is taking place, but all these things are old and were not unheard of by the ancients?

There have actually been fewer calamities since Christians appeared.

6.   Actually, regarding the wars which you say were begun on account of hatred for our religion, it would not be difficult to prove that after Christ [47] was heard on earth, not only did they not increase but in great measure were reduced as a result of the repression of fierce passions.[48] For when we, so large a number as we are, have learned from His teachings and His laws [49] that *evil should not be repaid with evil*; [50] that it is better to suffer wrong than be its cause, to pour forth one's own blood rather than to stain our hands and conscience with the blood of another: the world, ungrateful as it is, has long had this benefit from Christ by whom the rage of madness has been softened and has begun to withhold hostile hands from the blood of fellow beings.

And if all without exception who understand that ⟨they⟩ are men, not through the form of their bodies but through the power of reason, would for a little while be willing to lend an ear to His wholesome and peaceful commandments, and would believe not in their own arrogance and swollen conceit but rather in His admonitions, the whole world, long since having diverted the use of iron [51] to more gentle pursuits, would be passing its days in the most placid tranquillity and would come together in wholesome harmony, having kept the terms of treaties unbroken.

What is the origin of these calamities?

7. "But if," they say, "no inconvenience has come to human affairs by your agency, what is the source of these evils which have for a long time oppressed and afflicted pitiful humanity?"

You ask me an opinion that has no pertinence to the matter at issue. For I have not undertaken the present discussion regarding it, to show or prove by what causes or for what reasons each of these things took place but that I might show that the reproaches for so great a crime lie far from our door. And if I succeed—if by reason of the fact [52] itself, or by most formidable arguments, the truth of the matter is made manifest—I care not whence these evils come or from what sources or first causes they flow.

Perhaps the cause is in nature itself.

8. Still, lest when I am asked what I think about matters of this kind I may seem to have no opinion at all, I can say: [53]

What if that primal matter, which is diffused through the four elements [54] of things, contains the causes of all these misfortunes wrapped up in its very nature? What if the motions of the heavenly bodies create these evils in certain signs, [55] regions, seasons, and limits, and impose upon the things beneath them the necessity of undergoing various hazards? What if at stated times changes take place and, as in the fluctuations of the tides, at one moment favorable circumstances make you ride high and at another unfavorable ones bring you low again, good times alternating with evil? What if the dirt we tread upon in walking has this property given to it, of breathing forth the most harmful exhalations by which the air is befouled and brings disease to the body and cripples man's activities? What if—and this is nearest the truth [56]—what seems adverse to us is not really evil to the world itself, and that judging all things in terms of our own advantage, we blame the results of nature because of unproved opinions?

Plato, that sublime head and pillar [57] of philosophers, has stated in his writings [58] that those dread floods and world-wide conflagrations are a purification of the earth, and that wise man was not afraid to call the overthrow of the human race— its destruction, ruin, death, and burial—a renewal of things, for [59] by this reintegration of powers a certain youthfulness was brought about.

9. " There is no rain from heaven," my opponent says, " and we suffer from an extraordinary lack of food."

Well, do you insist that the elements serve your needs, and to permit you to live more comfortably and extravagantly, the obedient seasons are under obligation to give themselves over to your conveniences? What if in this way a man who wants very much to go sailing should complain that for a long time now there have been no winds and that the breezes of heaven have been stilled? Is it therefore to be said that the tranquil sky is wicked because it hinders travelling merchants [60] from realizing their aspirations? What if someone, accustomed to sun himself and to dry out his body in this manner,[61] in like manner should complain that by the prevalence of cloud the pleasure of a clear sky is taken away? Would you have us say, then, that the clouds hang over the sky with an injurious covering because one cannot at his ease tan his skin to his taste and provide an excuse for drinking bouts? All these events which take place and happen under this mass of the universe are not for our creature comforts but should be regarded as in the arrangements and plans of nature itself.

10. If anything occurs which fosters us and our affairs with but little happy success, it is not therefore an evil and to be regarded as pernicious. The world either rains or does not rain; it is for itself that it rains or does not rain, and though perhaps you do not know it, it either evaporates excessive moisture with drying heat or it moderates a long spell of dryness by showers of rain. It produces pestilences, diseases, famines, and other deadly forms of evil. How can you tell whether it does not remove what exists in excess, to this end that by forcing things to take losses, it may set moderation upon their tendency to develop riotously?

11. Would you venture to say that this and that thing in the world, the origin and final cause of which you cannot explain or analyze, is bad, and because winter possibly hinders you from enjoying delights and pleasures, would you say that it is a pernicious, austere thing? Does it follow that because cold weather does not happen to agree with your body and chills it and benumbs the warmth of your blood, there must be no winter? And because you cannot bear or put up with the hottest rays of the sun, ought summer to be eliminated from the year and another plan of nature be set

up with other laws opposite in character? Hellebore is a poison to men: [62] ought it for this reason not grow? The wolf [63] lies in wait at sheepfolds: is nature at all to blame because it has created a beast most dangerous to the wool-bearer? By its bite the serpent takes away life: would you really condemn the foundation of things because it added to living creatures monsters so fierce?

12. You are conceited in the extreme, considering that you are not your own master and are even the property of another, to want to dictate terms to the more powerful, so that what you wish may take place, not what you have found in the state of things made immutable by their ancient constitution.

Therefore, if you wish your complaints to have a place for consideration, you must, my good men, first tell us whence and who you are; whether the world was produced and fash-ioned for you, or whether you have come into it, as tenants hailing from other regions. And seeing that it is not in your power to say, and you cannot explain for what cause you live beneath this vault of heaven, stop thinking anything belongs to you, since those things which take place take place not for the benefit of one individual but arise for the good of the whole. [64]

Not only calamities but seasons of prosperity have occurred.

13. "Because of the Christians," [65] they say, "the gods contrive [66] all these evils and destruction of crops is produced by the heavenly deities."

I ask, do you fail to see that when you say this you are slandering us wickedly with open-faced and demonstrable lies? It is almost three hundred years,[67] more or less, since we [68] began to be Christians and to be known on the earth: in all these years have wars been without interruption? Have bad crops been continuous? Has there been no peace on earth? Has there been no time at all when things have been cheap and abundant? For this must first be made out by our accuser, that these calamities have been continual and consecutive, that never at all have mortal beings had a chance to get their breath, and that without any days off,[69] as the expression has it, they have passed through manifold critical situations.

14. And do we not see that in these intervening years and intervening seasons many victories over conquered enemies have been won, that the boundaries of the empire have been extended and nations with names hitherto unheard-of, have been brought under our sway;[70] that very often there have been years with the most abundant produce; that there have been so many periods of low prices and abundance of commodities [71] as to cause an amazing paralysis of all business undertakings by the low price level?[72] For how could business be carried on and how could the race of mortals endure to this day, had not the fruitfulness of nature supplied all things requisite for life?

15. Of course, there were at times a few seasons of scarcity, but these were again relieved by abundance. Certain wars were carried on contrary to what we should wish [73] but afterwards this situation was rectified by victories and successes. Well, now, what are we to say—that the gods were at times mindful of our wrongdoings and at others unmindful? If when there is a famine they are said to be angered at us, it follows that when there is abundance, they are not

angry and harsh. And so it boils down to this that capriciously they lay aside and take up their anger and are constantly returning to their former attitude when the remembrance of our sins has been laid aside.

16. Yet the true meaning of these statements cannot be established by any logical reasoning. If they willed that the Alamanni,[74] the Persians, and the Scythians be subdued because Christians lived and dwelt among those peoples, how did it happen that they granted victory to the Romans [75] when Christians lived and dwelt among those peoples also? If they decreed mice and locusts to swarm forth in huge numbers in Asia [76] and Syria because here, too, Christians dwelt among those peoples, why was it that at the same time nothing similar took place in Spain or Gaul, since innumerable Christians lived in these same provinces also? If among the Gaetuli and the Zeugitani,[77] they for this reason sent exceeding drought, why did they in that year grant to the Mauri and the Nomads the fullest harvests, when again this religion existed in these regions as well? If in any state you wish to cite they have made many die of hunger because of their hatred for our name, why have they in the same state made richer, not only people who do not belong to our body, but also Christians, some even very wealthy? [78] The conclusion is: either all together should have gone without prosperity, if we are the cause of evils, for we are in all nations; or when you see favorable circumstances mixed with undesirable, cease to attribute to us what is harmful to your fortunes, since we in no way affect your blessings and prosperity. If by my [79] agency your affairs turn out badly, why do I not prevent them from ever turning out well? If what I am is the cause of great dearth, why do I not prevent the greatest of harvests from taking place? If when in wars a wound is

received, I am said to bring the misfortune, why, when enemy warriors [80] perish, am I not a bad omen [81] and why do I not bring evil to prosperity through my being an evil portent?

The gods demean themselves by anger against Christians.

17. And yet, you great devotees and priests of the deities, do you assert that those most august gods are angered with Christian peoples? Do you really not notice, do you not see how shameful, how disgraceful are the mad feelings [82] which you thus impute to the deities? What else is anger than madness, than rage, than to be carried on to a lust for vengeance and having become savage with the torments [83] of the grief of another, to revel in the senselessness [84] of heart? The great gods, then, know, suffer, and feel what wild beasts, what monsters, what deadly snakes contain in their poisoned fangs. It is claimed by you that that superior nature, which is solidly based on eternal righteousness, knows the fickleness of man and what is blameworthy in earthly life. And what necessarily follows from your statement but that from their eyes fiery flashes shine out,[85] their breast gives forth a pant, foam rushes from their mouth, and from their burning words their lips become dry and pale? [86]

18. But if this is true and it has been examined and proven certain that the gods boil with anger and are shaken by emotion and disturbance of this sort, they are not immortal and eternal nor should they be thought to possess any of the quality of divinity. For where there is any disturbance, there, of necessity, as the philosophers think, must be passion; and where passion exists,[87] there emotional excitement is a

logical consequence. Where emotional excitement is, there grief and sorrow are; where grief and sorrow are, there is room for lessening of powers and for decay,[88] and if these two cause trouble, dissolution is near at hand—death which ends all and takes away life from every sentient being.

19. "Why?" Because in this way you represent them as not only capricious and excitable but also—something agreed by all to be farthest from the gods—that they are unjust and evil and that they possess nothing at all of even moderate fairness.[89] What is so unjust as to be angry at some and to harm others; to complain about men and to ruin the harmless crops of grain; to hate Christianity and to ruin its worshippers with every loss to them?

20. But do they therefore rage also against you in order that aroused by the wounds you yourselves [90] receive, you may rise up for their avenging? If so, the gods are seeking defense from human beings and, were they not protected by your advocacy, they are themselves not competent, they are not strong enough to repel the insults shown them, to defend themselves.[91] Indeed, if it be true that they burn with anger, let them have the power of defending themselves and let them put forth and make trial of their own powers for the avenging of their insulted majesty. They can slay us, if they wish, with heat; they can slay us with most fell cold; they can slay us with pestilential winds; they can slay us with the most unheard-of diseases; they can consume us, and can exile us completely from all human association; or if it is a bad plan to attack us with violence, let them send forth some sign of judgment from which it may be clear to all that we are living under heaven most contrary to their pleasure.

The gods appear to treat pagan and Christian alike.

21. Let them give to you good health and to us bad, even the worst. Let them water your farms with showers at the proper time and from our tiny little fields let them drive away all the rains even in the form of dew. Let them see that your flocks of sheep are multiplied with many lambs: let them bring to our folds luckless barrenness. From your olive trees and vineyards let them make the autumn's harvest full, but from ours let them forbid one little drop to be pressed out from the vines. And as the very worst they can do, let them decree that in your mouth fruits should keep their natural taste but in ours, on the contrary, let honey be made bitter, let the flowing oil of olives grow rancid, and let the deceitful wine, passing from the cups to the lips, be suddenly turned sour.[92]

22. Well, since the facts themselves bear witness that nothing like this ever takes place, and it is agreed that the blessings of life reappear no less to us and no greater to you,[93] why is there such great desire to maintain that the gods are hostile and unfriendly to the Christians who, as you see, in the most unpleasant circumstances, as well as in joyful, differ from you in no way? If you permit the truth to be told and to be expressed without flattery, these are words, words only; indeed, matters believed by accepting slanderous accusations, not clearly proven by examining any witness.

True gods would react differently.

23. But the true gods and those who fully deserve to hold, to bear the authority of this name, neither grow wrathful, nor indulge a grudge, nor do they devise cunning stratagems to harm any one. For it is truly profane and surpasses all

sacrilege to believe that that wise and most blessed nature considers it a great thing for any one to bow down before it in humble worship, and that if this be not done, it believes that it is despised and has fallen from the topmost pinnacle. It is childish, weak, and pitiful, and scarcely becoming to those whom for a long time now the experience of the learned has called *daemones* [94] and " wanderers," [95] not to be acquainted with heavenly matters [96] and to concern themselves with the coarser things of earth in place of their own natural condition.

The criticism really originates from neglected priestlings.

24. These are your thoughts, they are your ideas, conceived with impiety and believed still more impiously. No, rather, if I am to state this more truthfully, the diviners,[97] the interpreters of dreams, the soothsayers, the seers, and the custodians of shrines, always vain, have contrived these stories. In order that their own arts may not perish and that they may not exact only paltry fees from those who now very infrequently come to them for advice, whenever they find you inclined to let their occupation come into disrepute, they keep on screaming:

" The gods are neglected and in the temples attendance [98] is woefully slight! The ancient ceremonials are now laughed at and the august old rituals formerly held sacred have fallen under the superstitions of new religions! Rightly is the human race oppressed by so much misery and distress, tormented by so many hardships and tribulations! And men, stupid people and people unable because of their innate blindness to see things in plain daylight, dare in their frenzy to assert as true what you in your right senses do not blush to believe! " [99]

Christians are guilty only of worshipping the true God.

25. And lest any one should think that we, through a lack of confidence in our reply, grant the gods the gift of tranquillity, and that we attribute to them minds that harbor no harm and are far removed from every excitement, [100] let us allow them, as you wish, to direct their anger against us, to thirst after our blood, and let us admit that for a long time they have wanted to remove us from the generations of mortals. But if it is not troublesome, not too hard; if it is a matter of duty, common to both, to discuss the points of this discussion not according to one's pleasure but in accordance with the truth, we demand to hear from you what is the cause, what is the reason on account of which against us alone the gods above rage, and men in their anger grow hot.

" You practice your wicked religions," they say, " and rites unheard-of in the world."

What statement is this that you, men who have a share of reason, dare to make? What do you dare to blab out? What are you trying to bring out through the recklessness of rash speech? To worship God as the Ruler, [101] the Master of all the things that are, occupying the topmost peak of all the heights; to call upon Him with obedient reverence; to cling to Him, as it were, in all moments of weariness; [102] to love Him, to look up to Him—is this an accursed and unholy religion, full of sacrilege and impiety, polluting by the superstition of its newness the ceremonies established in olden times? [103]

6 [7]

For this Christians are persecuted.

26. Is this, I ask, that bold and heinous crime on account of which the supreme gods in heaven aim the sharp sting of their wrath and indignation against us; on account of which you yourselves, whenever the fierce passion enters you, despoil [104] us of our goods; drive us from our ancestral homes; inflict capital punishment upon us; torture, mangle, burn [105] us, and at last cast us to the wild animals and to the clawings of monsters? Should whoever condemns that in us, or considers that it ought to be held in some way against us, be called by the name of man, even though he appears such to himself? Or should he be believed a god, even though he claims to be such through the mouths of a thousand prophets? Does the Trophonian [106] or the Dodonian Jupiter [107] call us wicked, and will he himself be named a god and be thought to belong to the number of deities, who places a charge of impiety against the servants of the Most High King or is tormented himself because His majesty and His worship are preferred? Is Apollo, whether he be called Delian, [108] or Clarian, Didymaean, Philesian, Pythian, Sminthian, to be held a diviner, when he either does not know the Most High Ruler [109] or is unaware that He is prayed to each day by us? If he knew not the secrets of our hearts and was unacquainted with the innermost feelings we possess, he could know by using his ears, or could recognize by the tone of our voices which we use in prayers, that we are invoking the Most High God and that it is from Him we ask what we need.

27. This is not yet the place to show who or whence come all those who condemn us; what their authority or their knowledge may be; why they quaver at mention of Christ; [110] why they regard His disciples as hostile and hateful; but to

those who give promise of human intelligence let us set it down in terms applicable to all of us: we Christians are nothing more than worshippers of the Most High King and Ruler [111] under Christ as Master.[112] If you think about it, you will find nothing else is involved in that hated religion. This is the sum total of every action; this is the ordained limit of all religious duties, this is the end. Before Him we all according to our custom fall down and worship; to Him we pray in common supplications. From Him we ask just and honorable things, worthy for Him to hear, not because He Himself has need of us as suppliants or loves to see the veneration of so many thousands laid before Him. Our benefit is involved and our need. For we are prone to faults and to varied passions and lusts because of the defect of our innate weakness. He suffers Himself always to be comprehended in our thoughts so that when we pray to Him and struggle to merit His bounties, we may receive a will to purity and may cleanse ourselves from every spot by the cutting-off of all sins.

The pagan gods are ridiculous and even wicked.

28. What do you say, you interpreters of sacred, of divine law? Are they who worship the *Lares Grundulii* [113] the *Aii Locutii*,[114] and *Limentini*,[115] possessed of a better case than all of us who worship God, the Father of all things, and from Him ask protection when we are tired and weary? Even they seem to you shrewd, wise, and most sagacious, worthy of no criticism, who worship *Fauni*,[116] *Fatuae*, and the *genii* of cities; who worship *Pavores* and *Bellonae*. On the other hand, we are pronounced dull, stupid, silly, obtuse, and dumb, having surrendered ourselves to a God by whose nod

and judgment everything in existence has been formed and is immovable in the eternity of His nature? Do you hand down this opinion, do you establish this law, do you proclaim this decree that anyone who shall worship your slaves shall be decorated with the fullest honors and that whoever makes a petition to you, the masters themselves, shall be worthy of the extreme penalty, crucifixion?

In the greatest states and in the more powerful peoples public sacrifices are made to harlots who formerly sold themselves and prostituted themselves to the passion of the mob,[117] yet in the gods this causes no swelling of indignation.[118] Temples with the loftiest roofs have been dedicated to cats,[119] beetles, and heifers.[120] The powers of the deities thus mocked are silent and experience no envy when they see sacredness attributed to base animals on a par with their own selves. To us alone are they hostile? To us are they the bitterest enemies because we worship their Father by whom, if they really exist,[121] they began to be and have the substance of their power and majesty; and having been allotted by Him, so to speak, their very deity, they feel that they exist and realize that they are numbered among the things that exist, and by His will and decision they can both perish and be dissolved and not perish and be not dissolved? For if we all agree that there is only one Beginning before whom in the antiquity of time nothing else comes, it follows of necessity that after Him are all things born and put forth and have burst forth into their own individual nature. And if this is established and agreed upon, we will admit as a consequence that the gods are creatures of birth and that they derive their beginnings from the primal fount of all creation. If they are born and begotten, they in any case are exposed to destruction and dangers.[122] Yet they are believed to be eternal, immortal, and subject to no end. Hence, this is also the gift and bounty of God the Father, that through unending ages they have deserved to be the same, since they are by nature subject to perishing and dissolution.

Praise of the true and eternal God and Creator.

29. Would [123] that it might be granted to me here to address the whole world gathered together as in one assembly and that I might be placed within hearing of the whole human race. Are we therefore in your judgment guilty of an impious religion, and because we worship the Head and Pillar of things with reverent obedience are we to be pronounced undesirables and godless, to use the terms of your abuse? And who would more rightly bear the odium of such words than the one who either acknowledges or asks about or believes another god before this God of ours?

Do we not all owe to Him this as the very first obligation, the fact that we are; that we are called men; that as ⟨souls⟩ either sent forth by Him or fallen [124] from Him, we are kept in the blindness of this body? Does it not come from Him that we walk, that we breathe and live, and by the very force of living does He not cause us to be and to be moved by animation? Do the causes not flow out from Him by which our health is supported with the abundance of varied pleasures? To whom does that world in which you live belong and who granted you the right to keep its produce and its possession? Who gave that common possession, light, by which you may see, touch, and examine all things beneath it? Who has established the fires of the sun to warm [125] the vital elements and make things grow lest the elements of life become listless through being held in a stupor of inactivity? Since you believe the sun is a god, are you not interested in his founder and maker? Since with you the moon is a goddess, do you not care to know who begot and fashioned her?

30. Has the idea not entered into your mind of reflecting, of considering, in whose possessions you live; in whose property you are; whose land that is which you wear out; whose is that air which you breath in and out; whose springs you consume, whose water; who has arranged for the blasts of winds; who has devised the wavy clouds; who has granted to the fruitful powers of seeds their special characteristics? Does Apollo rain for you, does Mercury [126] rain for you; have Aesculapius,[127] Hercules, or Diana arranged the plan of showers and storms? And how can this be when you claim that they were born on earth and that at a certain time they acquired living senses? For in the ancient days the world preceded them and before they were born nature was acquainted with showers and storms. Those born afterwards possess no right to send rain nor can they foist themselves upon programs which they found here already in progress, and derived from a greater Author.

31. O Greatest,[128] O Highest Procreator of ⟨visible and⟩[129] invisible things! O Thou who art Thyself invisible and never understood by the things of nature! Worthy, worthy art Thou truly—if only mortal lips may call Thee worthy— to whom all breathing and understanding nature should never cease to be grateful and to give thanks; to whom throughout the whole of life it should fall on bended knees to pray to Thee with unending petitions. For Thou art the first cause, the place and space [130] of things created, the basis of all things whatsoever they be. Infinite, unbegotten, ever-

lasting, eternal alone art Thou, whom no shape may represent, no outline of body define; [131] unlimited in nature and in
magnitude unlimited; without seat, motion, and condition,
concerning whom nothing can be said or expressed in the
words of mortals. To understand Thee, we must be silent;
and for fallible conjecture to trace Thee even vaguely, nothing must even be whispered. Grant pardon, O King Most
High, to those who persecute Thy servants and by reason of
the kindliness which is part of Thy nature, forgive those who
flee from the worship of Thy name and religion.

It is not to be wondered at if Thou art unknown—it would
be a matter for greater marvel if Thou wert understood. Perhaps some one dares—for this remains for raging madness to
do—to be in doubt, to be uncertain whether that God exists
or not; whether He is to be believed in by the proved truth of
faith or by the imaginings of vain rumors. For we hear that
some who give themselves to the study of philosophy deny [132]
that there is any divine force, and that others daily inquire
whether it exists; [133] that others [134] construct the whole sum
of things by chance accidents and random collisions and
fashion it by the propulsion of different-shaped things. [135]
With these we shall at this time engage in no controversy at
all regarding such obstinate theories. For those who have
good sense say that to oppose stupid views is greater stupidity.

32. Our discussion is with those who, agreeing that there
is a divine race, are in doubt about the greater ones, while
they confess that there are inferior and lower deities. Is the
conclusion, then, that we struggle and strive to arrive at
results of such great moment by arguments? Let such a
foolish idea depart from us and let this madness be far, far
hence, I say—in the words of the old saying, [136] let it be averted
from us. For it is as dangerous to attempt to demonstrate

that God is Supreme as by reasoning of this kind to want to know that He exists. It matters very little and makes no difference whether you deny that He exists or assert and admit that He does, since both an assertion of such a thing and the denial of an unbelieving opponent are equally blameworthy.

33. Is there any human being who has not entered the day of his nativity with a knowledge of that Beginning? [137] To whom is it not an innate idea; in whom has it not been impressed, indeed, almost stamped into him in his mother's womb; in whom is it not deeply implanted that there is a King and Lord and Regulator of all things which are? In fact, if the dumb beasts themselves had the power to utter thoughts, if they could enjoy the use of our tongues; yes, if trees, clods, stones, animated by living perception, could produce the sound of a voice and utter comprehensible speech, would they not, following nature as their leader and teacher with faith of a simple purity, understand that God exists and cry out that He alone is Lord of all?

Jupiter is not the true and eternal God.

34. " But in vain," says some one, " do you assail and attack us with misrepresentation and a slanderous charge, as if we were going to deny that there is a greater god, since Jupiter is by us called and held to be both the Best and Greatest,[138] and since to him we have dedicated the most sacred seats and the huge Capitol."

You are trying to join unlike things together and to force them into one group with resultant confusion. For it has been unanimously agreed by the common consent of all mortals that the Omnipresent God is known not to have been begotten nor to have been brought forth to new light at any ⟨instance⟩of time nor in any age to have begun to be. For He himself is the Source of things, the Sower of the ages and seasons. They do not exist of themselves but from His eternal perpetuity they move forever in unbroken line. Yet Jupiter,[139] as you say, has both father and mother, grandfathers, grandmothers, and brothers; now recently, ⟨it is asserted,⟩ [140] being conceived in the womb of his mother, and being perfectly developed in ten months, he burst, feeling life in him, into the light hitherto unknown to him. Therefore, if this is a fact, how can Jupiter be God when it is agreed that that God is everlasting,[141] while the other is represented by you to have had a birthday, and frightened by the new experience, to have squalled like an infant? [142]

35. But let them be one and the same, as you wish, and not different in any power of divinity or majesty. For what possible reason, then, do you persecute us with unjust hatred? Why do you shudder at any mention of our name as a very bad omen, if we also worship the god whom you worship? Or why do you in the same argument maintain that the gods are your friends, but hostile and most antagonistic to us? For if we and you have one religion in common, the anger of the heaven dwellers is stopped. If they are hostile to us alone, then it is clear that both you and they do not know God; that God is not Jupiter is clear from the very wrath of the deities.

But the Christians worship a human being and one
crucified.

36. " But," they say, " the gods are not hostile to you because you worship the Omnipotent God but because you

maintain that a man,[143] born a human being, and one who suffered the penalty of crucifixion,[144] which even to the lowest of men is a disgraceful [145] punishment, was God, and you believe that He still exists and you worship Him in daily prayers."

If it is not asking too much, my friends, set forth which are these gods which believe that Christ worshipped by us tends to harm them. Is it Janus,[146] the founder of the Janiculum,[147] and Saturn [148] who established the Saturnian state? Is it Fauna Fatua,[149] the wife of Faunus,[150] who is called the Good Goddess [151] but is better and more praiseworthy when wine is drunk? Is it those *Indigetes* [152] who crawl to the river and pass their days in the shallows of the Numicius [153] with the frogs and little fishes? Is it Aesculapius [154] or Father Liber,[155] the former the son of Coronis [156] and the latter struck out of his mother's womb by lightning? Is it Mercury,[157] the outpouring of the womb of Maia [158] and, what is more divine, Maia the bright? Is it the archers Diana [159] and Apollo, carried about in the exile of their mother and in floating islands scarce safe? Is it Venus [160] of the race of Dione, mother of the children of a Trojan man, and the advertiser of her personal beauty? Is it Ceres [161] born in the land of Trinacria, and Proserpina,[162] seized while gathering flowers? Is it the Theban or the Tyrian Hercules,[163] the latter buried within the borders of Spain, the former burned up in the flames of Mount Oeta? Is it the sons of Tyndareus, the Castors,[164] the one accustomed to taming horses, the other a good pugilist and invincible with the rough boxing-gloves? Is it the Titans [165] and the Moorish Bocchores and the Syrian gods [166] that were hatched from eggs? Is it Apis,[167] betrayed in the Peloponnesus and in Egypt called Serapis? [168] Is it Isis [169] burnt black by the Ethiopian suns, mourning her lost son and

her husband torn limb from limb? We pass by and step over
the royal offspring of Ops [170] which your writers have written
about in their books to explain to you who and what they
were.

Do these then hear with wounded [171] ears that Christ is
worshipped and accepted by us and regarded as a divine
being? And having forgotten what lot they had a little before
and what condition they then had, they want no one else to
share in what was granted to them? Is this the justice of
heaven's inhabitants, this the holy judgment of the gods?
Is it not a kind of envy and greed, a mean sort of disparage-
ment, to want only their own fortunes to prosper and those
of others to grow less and to be trodden upon in lowly
contempt?

The pagans have deified many human beings.

37. We worship one born a man.[172] What of that? Do
you worship no one born a man? Do you not worship one or
another, yes, countless others? Indeed, have you not elevated
from the level of mortals all those you now have in your
temples and made a gift of them to heaven and the stars? [173]
For if by chance it escapes you that they once were partakers
of human lot and condition, open up your most ancient
literature [174] and run through the writings of those who, being
near to antiquity, set forth everything without any flattery in
clear truth. Surely you will then learn from what fathers,
by what mothers each was procreated, where they were born,
of what family; what they did, accomplished, suffered, were
employed in; what favorable or unfavorable fortunes they experienced in performing their exploits. If you, however,
knowing that they are the fruit of wombs and that they pre-

served their life by eating the products of the earth, nevertheless complain that we worship a human being, you are acting
very unjustly in condemning in us what you yourselves do
constantly, or what you allow to be right for you to do but
are unwilling for it to be right for others.

The teachings of Christ are divine.

38. But let us grant, yielding [175] to you for the moment,
that Christ was one of us [176] in mind, spirit, body, weakness,
and condition in life: is He not deserving of being called
God and being felt God [177] by us on account of the favor of
so many blessings?

For if you enrolled Liber [178] among the list of gods because
he found a use for wine; Ceres, because she discovered bread;
Aesculapius,[179] the use of herbs; Minerva, the use of the
olive; [180] Triptolemus, the invention of the plough; [181] Hercules because he subdued and restrained wild beasts, thieves,
and many-headed serpents: [182] with how many distinctions
should He be honored by us who has withdrawn us from
great errors by introducing truth to us; [183] who when we were
walking like blind men everywhere without a guide, drew
us back from the precipices, from the pathless tracks, to
smoother places; who has pointed out to us what is especially
fruitful and wholesome for the human race, what God is,
who He is, how great, and of what character; who has permitted us and taught us to receive and understand, so far as
our moderate ability was able, His depths and indescribable
profundity; who, with the greatest of kindness has made it
known by what Founder, by what Father this world has been
established and made; who has explained [184] the nature of its
birth and essential substance never before comprehended by

anyone; whence the life-giving warmth is added to the rays of the sun; why the moon is forever in motion, and whether from the same or other causes [185] she is believed to alternate her periods of light and darkness; what is the origin of animals; the law of seeds; who designed man himself; who fashioned him or from what kind of material did He mold together the very constructions of bodies; what the senses are, what the soul, and whether it flew to us of its own will or was planted and created within our very organs; whether it lives with us a sharer in death, or has been endowed with everlasting perpetuity; what state remains for us when we have departed from our bodies relaxed in death; whether we shall see or have no memory of our perceptions and recollection; [186] who restrains our arrogance and has made our necks, uplifted with pride, to confess that they have a measure of weakness; who has shown that we are living beings without form, trusting in vain imaginings, without understanding of anything, knowing nothing, not seeing what is placed before our eyes; who has led us from false religions to the true one, a blessing which surpasses and exceeds all others; who has uplifted us from the worship of statues inanimate and formed from the vilest clay to the stars and heaven and has made us to mingle the words of our prayers and the conversations of our supplications with God, the Lord of the universe!

Arnobius only recently became a Christian.

39. Recently,[187] O blindness, I worshipped images drawn from furnaces, gods fashioned on anvils and with hammers, elephant's bones,[188] paintings, ribbons on trees [189] hoary with age. Whenever my gaze fell upon an anointed stone daubed

with olive oil,[190] I would, as if there were some power in it, show great respect to it; I would speak to it, and ask blessings of it though it was a block without feeling. And those very gods of whose existence I had convinced myself, I treated with the greatest slanders since I believed that they were sticks of wood, stones, and bones, or that they dwelt in matter of this ⟨kind⟩. But now, having been led into the paths of truth by so great a Teacher, I know all those things for what they really are. I have worthy feelings about things that are worthy.[191] I offer no insult to any divine name; and what is owed to each person or head, with clearly understood differences and distinctions, that I grant. Is Christ therefore not to be deemed God by us and should ⟨He⟩ in no other way be honored with divine worship, from whom for a long time we have received so many gifts while we live and hope for more when " the Day " comes? [192]

Christ's crucifixion in no way lessens His divinity.

40. " But He died nailed to the cross." [193]

How does that affect the argument? For the sort and disgrace of His death do not change His words or deeds, nor will the authority of His teachings seem less, because He departed from the bonds of the body not by a natural death but went away because of the violence borne against Him.

Pythagoras [194] of Samos was burned to death in a temple as the result of an unjust suspicion that he aimed at assuming power. Did what he taught lose its peculiar effectiveness because he breathed forth his spirit not willingly but as the result of a cruel assault? Likewise, Socrates [195] paid the supreme penalty of death when he was condemned by the courts of his city. Are his discussions about character, virtues,

and duties, made of no value because he was wrongly banished from life? Many another, prominent in fame or valor
or reputation, experienced the most bitter forms of death like
Aquilius,[196] Trebonius, Regulus. Were they therefore after
life judged shameful because they perished not by the common law of fate but torn and tortured by the most painful
kind of death? No guiltless person, foully slain, is ever dis-
graced thereby, nor is he stained by the mark of any shame-
fulness who suffered severe punishment without desert but
because of the savagery of his tormentor.

41. And yet, you who laugh at us for worshipping a man
who died ignominiously, do you not also honor Father
Liber,[197] whom the Titans tore limb from limb, by the dedication of shrines to him? Have you not proclaimed the
discoverer of medicines, Aesculapius,[198] the guardian and
protector of health, well-being, and safety, after he suffered
the penalty and punishment of being struck by lightning? [199]
Do you not call upon the great Hercules himself with sacrifices, offerings, and incense, Hercules whom you yourselves
say was burned alive [after punishment] [200] and consumed on
funeral pyres? [201] Do you not bear witness, with the approval
of the Galli,[202] to the fact that that Phrygian Attis, mutilated
and deprived of his manhood, is a gracious god, a holy god,
in the shrines of the Great Mother? Do you not say that
Father Romulus [203] himself, who was torn to pieces by the
hands of a hundred senators,[204] is Quirinus Martius,[205] and
do you not honor him with priests and couches, and worship
him in great temples [206] and after all these things swear that
he went up into heaven? Therefore, either you are to be
laughed at also who think that men slain by the heaviest of
tortures are gods and worship them, or if there is a sure

basis for your thinking you should act as you do, then allow
us to know for what reasons and grounds you [207] do this.

Christ's teachings and miracles are proof of divinity.

42. " You worship one born a human being."
Even if that were true, nevertheless, as has been said in
former passages, on account of the many gifts which have
come from Him to us, He ought to be called and addressed as
God. Since He really is God, and without the shadow of any
considerable doubt, do you think we shall deny that He is
worshipped by us as much as possible and that we call Him
the Protector [208] of our body?

" So, then," some raving, angry, and excited man will say,
" is that Christ a god? " We shall answer: God and God of
the inner powers,[209] and—what may torment unbelievers the
more with the bitterest pains—it was for the greatest of
purposes that He was sent to us by the Most High King.
Perhaps he will ask, having become madder and more frenzied, whether what we have just said can be proved. No
greater proof exists than the credibility of His acts, than the
unusual quality of His miracles; [210] than all those ordinances
of fate broken and dissolved, which the peoples and tribes
saw brought to pass in broad daylight with not a single
disagreeing voice; nor will those whose ancient and ancestral
laws He showed to be full of vanity and the most empty
superstition dare to charge Him with falsity.

Christ's miracles were not performed with the aid
of magic.

43. Perhaps my opponent will return to the attack with
those many other childish slanders: " He was a Magian; by

secret arts He performed all these things; from the temples of the Egyptians He stole the names [211] of powerful angels and esoteric learning."

Why do you talk, you scholar-dunces, about things not examined by you and prattle with a loose and rash tongue about things you do not know? Were therefore those things which were done the tricks of demons [212] and the stunts of magic arts? Can you point out to us, show us from all those Magi [213] who ever existed through the ages, any one that ever did anything resembling what Christ did, even to the thousandth part; who accomplished this without the assistance of incantations, without the juice of herbs and grasses, without any anxious observance of sacrifices, drink offerings, seasons? We do not press the point and ask what they promise to do or in what kind of acts all their teaching and experience are usually comprised. Who is not aware that these men are eager to know in advance what is about to happen, things which will come to pass in any case, whether they wish it or not, as a natural result of their inherent character; or to inflict a deadly disease upon anyone at all, or to break up the affections of families, or to open locked rooms without keys, or to bind the mouth in silence, or to weaken, increase the speed of horses in chariot races [214] or slow them, or to inspire in the wives and children of others, both males and females, the flames and frenzied passions of illicit love; or if they seem to attempt anything useful, to be able to do it not by their own force but by the power of those they pray to?

44. But it is agreed that Christ did all He did without any paraphernalia, without the observance of any ritual or formula but only through the power of His name, and as was proper, becoming, and worthy of a true god, He granted with the generosity of His benevolent power nothing harmful or hurt-

7 ⁷

ful but only what was helpful, wholesome, and full of aids
for us.

A summation of Christ's miracles.

45. What do you say again, o you . . .? [215] Was He then
a mortal or one of us whose authority, whose voice, expressing
ordinary and daily speech, put to flight sicknesses, diseases,
fevers, and other torments of the body? [216] Was He one of us
whose presence, whose sight, that tribe of demons sunk into
the vitals of men could not bear, and terrified by the strange
power gave up possession of the body? [217] Was He one of us
to whose command ugly skin diseases [218] were obedient and
left a healthy color to flesh [219] formerly spotted? Was He one
of us at whose bare touch hemorrhages [220] stopped and stayed
their excessive flows? Was he one of us whose hands caused
the jaundiced fluids in the skin [221] to flee, hands which that
penetrating fluid avoided and because of which the swellings
of the abdomens went down with the relieving dryness? Was
He one of us who urged on the lame to run [222] and was it a
⟨small⟩ accomplishment [223] that the withered stretched forth
their hands [224] and unbent the movements of joints stiff
from birth; that paralytics rose, and those who a little while
before were borne on the shoulders of others now carried back
their beds; [225] that those deprived of sight saw, and those born
without eyes now looked upon the sky and light of day? [226]

46. Was He one of us, I say, who by a single intervention
once restored to health a hundred or more afflicted with
various weaknesses and diseases; [227] at whose mere voice the
raging and maddened seas stilled themselves, the whirlwinds
and storms subsided; [228] whose foot crossed over the deepest
whirlpools, not touched by water; [229] who trod the ridges of
the sea and the very waves themselves were amazed that

nature entered into bondage to Him; who fed to satiety five thousand of His followers with <five> loaves,[230] and lest this seem a trick to the unbelieving and hard of heart, piled up the fragments in twice-six baskets? Was He one of us who commanded the breath long since breathed out to return to bodies,[231] and those who had been buried in tombs to come forth, and the third day after burial to be unwrapped from the shrouds of the undertakers? [232] Was He one of us who clearly saw in the hearts of the silent what each one was pondering, what they tried to conceal in their innermost thought? [233] Was He one of us who when He uttered a single word was thought by different peoples who speak in languages of different sound to be uttering words familiar to each and to be using the tongue that each spoke? [234] Was He one of us who when He taught His followers the duties of the religion established as true, then and there filled out the entire world and by revealing the immensity of His authority, showed His real greatness and His real identity? [235] Was He one of us who when His body had been laid away revealed Himself to countless people in open day, who both spoke and obviously listened to others speaking, who taught, rebuked, admonished; who, lest they think they were led astray by empty imaginings, showed Himself once, twice and oftener, in conversation with His friends; [236] who appears even now to very righteous men of incorruptible character who love Him, not in empty unsubstantial dreams but in an appearance of pure simplicity; whose name when heard puts to flight harmful spirits,[237] imposes silence upon the soothsayers, causes fortune-tellers to lack consultants,[238] nullifies the deeds of boastful magicians, not by the dread power of His name, as you say, but by the freedom of a higher power?

Christ performed these miracles to reveal the nature
of God.

47. And this summary account has not been given in the belief that the greatness of the One who did these things was to be seen clearly in these miracles alone. For however great these things, how light and trifling will they be found to be, if it should be known, from what realms, as the minister of what power, He has come! [239] Those things which were done by Him were constantly performed, not that He might vaunt Himself with idle display of power but that men hard of heart and unbelieving might know that what was promised was not false, and that from the kindliness of His deeds they might be taught to imagine what a true God is. Likewise we wish it to be known, that when, as was said, a list of His deeds was given in summary form, not only could Christ do what He did but He even overcame the laws of the fates. For, if as is clear and agreed, ailments, and bodily sufferings, [the deaf, the deformed, and the dumb],[240] and if shrivelling of the sinews and loss of sight happen and are brought on by the decrees of fate; [241] if Christ alone has corrected, restored, and healed these ailments, it is clearer than the sun itself that He was more powerful than the fates when He unloosened and overpowered those things which were bound by everlasting knots and immovable necessity.[242]

Similar claims for pagan gods are clearly false.

48. "But," says some one, "in vain do you claim so much for Christ, since we know and have heard of other gods, who gave medicines to many sufferers and healed the diseases and sicknesses of many men." [243]

I do not inquire, I do not demand to know, what god or

when, to whom such assistance was given or what broken man he restored to health—this only do I desire to know: whether it was without adding any substance, that is, any medication, by mere touch, he bade the diseases to fly away from men; commanded or brought it about that the cause of the ailment ceased to exist and the bodies of the sick returned to their natural state. For we know that Christ, by applying His hand to the ailing part or by a single command, opened the ears of the deaf, removed blindness from eyes, gave speech to the dumb, loosened the stiffness of joints, gave power to walk to the paralytic, regularly healed with a word and cured by a command skin diseases, agues, dropsical diseases, and all other kinds of ailments which some evil, cruel power willed the bodies of men to endure.

What similar act have all these gods done by whom you say aid was borne to the sick and the critically ill? For if they ever, as the story goes, ordered some to be given medicine, or certain food to be taken, or a potion of any particular kind to be drunk, or a poultice of juices of plants and grasses to be laid on the places causing distress; or that persons should walk, rest up, or refrain from anything harmful: then it is clear this is no remarkable thing and deserves no respect at all. If you care to give it attentive examination, you will discover that physicians heal in this same way, a creature born of earth, not trusting to the truth of science, but employing the art of guessing and wavering in conjecturing possibilities.

And no miracle is involved in removing conditions by medical means. The beneficial qualities are inherent in the things, they are not the powers of the healers, and though it is praiseworthy to know by what drug or method it is suitable for persons to be healed, the occasion for this praise is with man, not with the god. It is no disgrace that a person should have improved the health of a man by things taken from without—it is a disgrace to the god that he is unable to do these things of himself but that he grants health and safety through the aid of external things.

49. And since you compare the other deities and Christ with respect to the benefits of health given by them, how many thousands of sick people do you want us to show you; how many suffering from wasting diseases whom the applications of no medicine restored, although as suppliants they went through all the temples; although they prostrated themselves before the faces of the gods and swept up the thresholds themselves with kisses; [244] when, as long as life remained, they wore out with their most piteous prayers and vows Aesculapius himself, the giver as they call him of health? Do we not know that some died of their ailments; others grew old under the torments of their diseases; still others began to conduct themselves wickedly, after they had worn out their days and nights in continual prayer and hope for clemency? What good is it, then, to show that one or another was possibly cured when to so many thousands no helper has come and all the shrines are full of the wretched and unfortunate?

But, perhaps, you say that aid is brought by the gods to the good and that the misfortunes of evil men are ignored. Yet Christ gave assistance in equal measure to the good and the evil and no one who in adversity asked aid against the attack and wrongs of fortune was rejected by Him.[245] For it is the property of a true God and of royal power, to deny this kindness to none and not to give thought as to who is deserving or not, since it is natural weakness [246] that makes a man a sinner, not will and [247] deliberate choice. To say, moreover, that aid is borne by the gods to those who are meritorious in their distresses, is to keep the question raised by your assertion unanswered and doubtful, so that he who has been cured seems to have been preserved by accident, and he who has not may be believed to have been unable to banish sickness through a heaven-sent ⟨lack of⟩ strength, not because of his own deserts.

Christ also delegated His miraculous power to His disciples.

50. Moreover, those miraculous deeds, which we have listed above in summary form and not in accordance with the importance of the matter, He not only performed by His own power but, and this was more sublime, He has allowed many others to attempt them and to do them in His name.[248] For when He saw that you would be detractors of His deeds and divine work, in order that there might survive no lurking suspicion that He had bestowed these gifts and blessings by using magical arts, He chose from the huge multitude of people who with wonder pursued His favor, fishermen, workmen, farmers, and that kind of uneducated people, those who being sent through various nations, were to perform all those miraculous deeds without any dissimulation and without any material aids.

By a word [249] He soothed the torments of aching bodies, and by a word they soothed the aches of maddening sufferings. By one command He cast out demons from bodies and to the lifeless He restored their senses; they also by no different command returned to health and soundness those laboring under the torments of these demons. He by applying only His hand wiped off the marks of the whitening skin

infections; they also by a touch no different restored the body
lines. He bade the watery swollen organs to recover their
natural dryness, and His servants in this way stayed the
wandering waters and ordered them to glide through their
proper courses without danger to the body. He within the
time of a single word curbed from incessant feeding sores of
large extent that refused to heal, and they no differently com-
pelled the stubbornness of the fierce cancer to confine itself
to a scar by limiting its ravages. He gave the power of walking to the lame, sight to blinded eyes, He called back the
dead to life: no less did they also loosen the tightness of
sinews, fill the eyes with light now lost and ordered the dead
to walk out of the tombs, in a reversal of the funeral services.
And nothing was ever done by Him to cause wonder [250] by
all who were amazed at it, which He has not granted to be
done completely by those humble and rustic men, and did
not put in their power.

The pagan gods never delegated similar authority
and power.

51. What do you say, o minds unbelieving, stubborn,
hardened? Did that Jupiter Capitolinus [251] ever grant power
of this kind to any mortal? Did he ever grant this power to
any *curio*,[252] or to the *pontifex maximus*,[253] or even to the
flamen Dialis,[254] because he is his creature? [255] I shall not
say power to arouse the dead, to restore light to the blind, to
restore the natural state of the body to the bent and the
paralyzed, but to check either by a command of his voice or
a stroke of his hand a blister, a hangnail, a pimple? Was
this therefore a human power or could such a right be granted
by word of mouth? Could such a privilege come to one

nourished on the produce of fertile earth? Was it not rather divine and sacred, or, if the hyperbole is in place, more than divine and sacred? If you yourself do what you can and what is consonant with your strength and power, there is no excuse for an exclamation of astonishment: you will have done what you could and what your own power ought to have accomplished, so that there should be a correspondence between the deed and its doer. To be able to transfer to a man your own power and to grant and to share what you alone can do with the weakest thing, this is the characteristic of power established over all things, which holds subordinate to itself the causes of all things, and the natures of methods and means.

The magicians have been unable to perform such miracles.

52. Well now,[256] if you will, let through the zone of fire [257] come some magian Zoroaster,[258] from a far part of the world, if we accept the authority of Hermippus.[259] And with him let the Bactrian come whose deeds Ctesias relates in the first book of his histories; [260] Armenius,[261] too, the grandson of Zostrianus, and Pamphylus the friend of Cyrus; let Apollonius,[262] Damigeron,[263] and Dardanus; [264] Belus,[265] Julianus,[266] and Baebulus,[267] and if there is any other who is said to have primacy and repute in such magic. Let them allow one of the people to have the power of causing the mouths of the dumb to become articulate, to unstop the ears of the deaf, to create for those born without sight the powers of the eye, and to restore feeling and animation to bodies long cold. Or if that is too difficult and they cannot permit others to possess the powers of such acts, let them themselves do them, and let them do them with their own rites. Whatever

poisonous grasses the bosom of the earth nourishes; whatever
powers the muttering of words and the accompanying indispensable incantations, let them add—we do not envy them
this; let them marshal them—we have no objections. Finally,
let them try and determine whether they can bring to pass
with the help of their gods what has been done time and time
again by uneducated Christians with bare commands.

Not magic but God in Christ performed the miracles.

53. Cease, you men of no knowledge, to meet such great
deeds with curses which will in no way harm Him who did
them, but will bring danger to you; no small danger, I say,
but one based on great, on important considerations, if indeed
the soul is a valuable thing and no man can find anything
dearer than himself. There was nothing magical,[268] as you
think, nothing human, deceitful or crafty; no deception
lurked in Christ, though you may jeer, as usual, and split
your sides with hilarious laughter. He was God sublime,
God from His innermost roots, God from realms unknown,
and was sent by God the Ruler [269] of all as a Savior, whom
neither the sun itself nor any stars, if they have feeling, nor
the rulers and princes of the world, nor the great gods, or
those who, making themselves out as such, try to frighten the
whole race of mortals, were able to know or even to guess
whence or who He was. And rightly so. But, freed from
the body which He carried about as a small part of Himself,
He afterwards suffered Himself to be seen and allowed it to
be known who and how great He was. All the elements of
the world were confused [270] with terror at the strange phenomenon; the earth trembled,[271] the sea was stirred up to its

depths; the air was veiled with clouds of darkness; the fiery orb of the sun was stopped and its heat became less. For what remained to take place, after He who for a long time had been reckoned to be one of us was recognized as God?

The miracles are well attested by testimony of the witnesses.

54. Of course you do not believe these things. But those who viewed them taking place and saw them happening under their very eyes, the best witnesses and the surest authorities, both believed them themselves and handed them down to us their descendants with confirmation of no small weight. You are interested to know who these are? Tribes, peoples, nations—indeed that skeptical human race which, if the fact itself were not plain and, as the saying is, clearer than day itself, would never give its corroborating assent to events of this kind. But shall we say that the men of that time were such deceivers and liars,[272] were so stupid and brutish, that they imagined that they had seen what they had never seen, and that they published by false testimony and corroborated with childish assertions things that had never taken place at all, and that when they were able to live in harmony with you and to establish pleasant relations, they went out of their way to incur hatred and to be held in contempt?

The expansion of Christianity corroborates the testimony.

55. But if our writers are liars in relating this, as you allege, how did it happen that in so short a time the whole world was filled with that religion? How could nations settled far from each other, separated by the winds and convexities

of heaven,[273] have come to unite on one conclusion? They have been attracted by bare statements, led on to empty hopes, and have been willing of their own accord to let themselves in for the risks of capital punishment [274] by reason of their rash desperation, although they had seen no such thing which could have aroused them to adopt this worship as a result of something strange and wonderful? No, but because they saw all these things were done both by Himself and by His heralds,[275] who, having been sent through the whole world continually bore the blessings of the Father and God's gifts to souls and bodies.[276] Conquered by the force of truth itself, they surrendered to God and considered it a matter of no weight that they cast their bodies before you and offered their flesh to be torn.

56. But you say that our authors have put forth these statements mendaciously; they have made too much of unimportant deeds, and have greatly exaggerated minor matters with boastful pretense. But would that all things could have been reduced to writing, both what had been done by Himself and what had been completed by His heralds with like right and power! So great an array of miracles would make you more skeptical, and perhaps you would be able to point to a place to which it would seem highly probable that additions were made to facts and that false statements were interpolated in writings and commentaries. But in unknown nations and those which did not possess the art of writing,[277] all the deeds could not have been written down or have reached the ears of all men; or if any were entrusted to written and connected forms, by the malevolence of demons—and it is their painstaking concern to kidnap this truth—and of men like them, certain insertions and additions, in some places changes and omissions of words, syllables and letters, would

have been made, so that they might forestall acceptance of them by the judicious and impair the authority of the deeds. At any rate,[278] they will never be happy that the question who Christ was, can be decided on the basis of written testimony; and the only reason that His cause has been set down in writing is that if what we say be accepted as true, it be shown by the admission of all that He was God.

Truth of the Christian religion and falsity of the pagan.

57. You do not believe our writings and we do not believe yours. We, you say, fabricate falsehoods about Christ, and you bandy about empty and false statements about your gods. For no god has come down from heaven or with his own hands has delineated your system [279] or in like manner has discredited our religious system. Ours was written by men—yours also was written by men, expressed in human phrases, and whatever you have in mind concerning our authors, consider and remember that about yours the same has been said with equal force. You want what is contained in your writings to be true, and those things which are certified to in our writings, you must admit of necessity that they are true. You charge our system with falsity and we charge yours with falsity.

" But," you say, " ours is more ancient, and for this reason fullest of trustworthiness and truth ": as if, indeed, antiquity were not the most prolific mother of errors and did not herself bear those things which have in disgraceful stories placed upon the gods the most shameful stigmas. Could not false things be both heard and believed ten thousand years ago? Or is it not most likely the truth that confidence may be placed more upon those things which are near us in time than those which are remote because of the long space of time that intervenes? For our position is based on witnesses, yours upon opinions, and it is much more probable that there will be less fiction in recent accounts than in those far removed in the gloom of antiquity.

Pagan criticism of the style of Christian literature.

58. " But they were written by uneducated and ordinary men and therefore they should not be believed without question as soon as heard."

Be careful, or this may prove all the more reason why they have not been befouled with any lies, set forth as they are by men of pure hearts who knew not how to embellish them with meretricious ornaments.

" The language is commonplace and of low quality." [280]

Never has truth given herself to rouge and lipstick nor does she suffer what has been carefully examined and is sure, to be led on into indirection and verbosity. Syllogisms,[281] enthymemes, definitions, and all those figures of speech by which respect for a statement is sought, give assistance to those trying to make statements, but they do not clearly reveal the features of truth. On the other hand, one who knows what he is talking about, neither defines, nor syllogizes, nor goes after any other tricks of language, by which audiences ordinarily are captivated, and are induced by figures of speech to agree.[282]

59. " Your narratives," says some one, " are overrun with barbarisms and solecisms and vitiated by ugly faults."

A criticism that is childish and reveals a narrow mind, for if we grant that it is valid, let us refrain from using certain kinds of fruits because they grow with prickles on them and other parts that must be cut out, which cannot contribute to our nourishment, and yet on the other hand do not prevent us from enjoying what is particularly excellent and what nature has meant to be most wholesome for us. How, I ask you, does it impede or how does it retard comprehension whether something is expressed with clean-shaven smoothness or with shaggy roughness; whether that is accented with the acute which ought to be accented with the grave; [283] or how is any statement less true if there is a mistake in number or case, in preposition, participle, or conjunction? Let that ostentation of diction and oratory according to rhetorical rules be reserved for assemblies, for lawsuits, for the forum, and for courts of justice, and let it be given to those who, seeking for soothing pleasures, put their whole zeal into the brilliance of words.

When the question at issue is far removed from mere display, what is said should be considered, not with how much charm it is said, nor how it soothes the ears, but what profit it brings to those who listen, especially since we know that some who devote themselves to philosophy [284] not only threw away refinements of style but even, when they could have spoken with greater elegance and richness, zealously strove after a commonplace and humble style, lest perchance they might spoil the stern gravity and revel rather in sophistic display. Indeed it is characteristic of a depraved heart to seek for pleasure in matters of grave importance, and, when you have to deal with persons in poor health and sick, to pour forth upon upon their ears honeyed sounds, instead of applying medicine to their wounds.

Although, if you look at the truth, no kind of speech is naturally perfect; likewise none is defective. For [285] what natural reason is there or what law written in the constitution of the world, that *hic* [286] should be used with *paries* and *haec* with *sella*, since neither noun has a sex which is indicated by the male and female gender; nor can any good scholar inform me what *hic* and *haec* are, or why one of them designates the male sex and what follows is used with feminines. These things are human conventions and are certainly not indispensable to all persons for use in creating language. For *paries* could perhaps have been used with *haec* and *sella* with *hic* without any complaint, if it had been agreed from the beginning that this would be said, and if by following ages this practice had been preserved in common speech.

And yet, you who charge our writings with the disgrace of defective diction, do you not also have these your solecisms in those very great and most wonderful books of yours? Do you not say in one place [287] *haec utria* [288] and in another *hos utres; caelus* [289] and *caelum*; likewise *pileus* [290] and *pileum, crocus* [291] and *crocum; fretus* [292] and *fretum?* Have you not also used *hoc pane* [293] and *hic panis, hic sanguis* [294] and *hoc sanguen?* Are not *candelabrum* [295] and *iugulum* in like manner also written *iugulus* and *candelaber?* For if each noun cannot have more than one gender and if nouns cannot be of this gender and of that, for one gender cannot pass into another, he sins as much who pronounces masculine genders under the laws of feminines as the one who prefixes feminine genders with masculine pronouns. Notwithstanding we see you making masculine objects ⟨into feminines⟩ and feminine objects into masculines, and what you call neuter you use in this way and that with no distinction. Therefore, it is no fault for us to use these words indifferently; and in vain you say that our works are disfigured by the impropriety of solecisms, or if the manner in which each ought to be used is determined and fixed, you yourselves are involved in the same faults, even though you have on your side all such people as Epicadus,[296] Caesellius, Verrius, Scaurus, and Nisus.[297]

The Incarnation.

60. "But if Christ was God," they say, "why did He appear in human form? And why was He slain in the manner of men?"

Could that invisible power which has no corporeal substance have in any other way brought itself to earth, adapted itself to the world, and participated in the councils of men, than by taking upon itself some covering of more substantial material, which might receive the gaze of eyes and upon which the eye of even the most unintelligent contemplation could fasten itself? For who is there among mortals who could have seen Him, who recognize Him, if He had decided to come to earth such as He is in His primal nature and such as He Himself has willed [298] to be in His own character and divinity? Therefore He took upon Himself [299] the form of man and under the likeness of our race he enclosed His power, so that He could be seen and gazed upon, utter words and teach, and might carry out all those things, for whose accomplishment He had come into the world, having preserved without impairment the sovereign power and direction of the Most High King.

61. "Well, now," says our opponent, "was the Most High King unable to accomplish all those things which He had decreed should be done in the world, without pretending [300] to be a man?"

If it were necessary for these things to be done in the way you say, perhaps He would have done so—because it was unnecessary, He did otherwise. Why He willed it to be done in this way and not in that is unknown, shrouded in mystery and scarcely to be comprehended by any. You might perhaps have been able to understand these causes, had you not long been prepared not to understand them and were not boldly preparing yourself for unbelief before what you sought to know and hear was explained to you.

Only Christ's human body was crucified.

62. " But He was slain after the manner of men."

Not He Himself, for it is impossible that death fall upon what is divine nor that that which is one and uncompounded [301] and not created by the uniting of any parts, should disappear in the breaking-up of death.

" Who then was seen hanging on the cross? Who, dead? "

The human form which He had put on and which He carried about with Him.[302]

" This saying is unbelievable and shrouded in blind obscurity."

If you please, it is not blind and it is established by a very close analogy. If the Sibyl [303] when she was uttering and pouring forth those prophesies and oracular responses, being filled, as you say, with the power of Apollo, had been slain by wicked men and by robbers was bereft of life, would Apollo be said to have been killed within her? If Bacis,[304] if Helenus, if Marcius, and other soothsayers, had been deprived of life and light while in the midst of their prophesying, would anyone say that those who, speaking through their mouths, had unfolded the ways of things to inquirers had ceased to exist according to the laws of humanity? That death of which you speak was of the human form assumed, not His own; of the thing borne, not of the bearer; and this a power so great would not have stooped to suffer if so great [305] a thing did not have to take place and the inscrutable plan of fate [306] did not have to be revealed in hidden mysteries.

Christ chose voluntarily to suffer death on the cross.

63. "What," you will say, "are these hidden and shadowy mysteries which neither men nor even those who are called gods of the world can at all fathom by imagination or thought, except those upon whom He had thought it fitting to bestow the blessings of such great understanding and to lead into the hidden recesses of the inner treasury?"

You do see, then, that if He had been unwilling that any-one should lay hands upon Him, He ought to have struggled to the utmost to repel His enemies from Him with all His power? Could He who had restored sight to the blind not make enemies blind if that were necessary? Was it hard or troublesome for one who had given strength to the weak to render enemies weak? Did He who used to bid the lame to walk not know how to tie up the movements of the limbs and sinews of His enemies by making them stiff? Would it have been difficult for Him who drew the dead out of their tombs to decree death on whom He willed? But because reason demanded that those things which had been foreordained should take place both here in the world itself and in no other way than it was done, that inconceivable and unbelieveable gentleness, considering the wrongs of men suffered by Him to be but childish trifles, permitted the most violent and hardened soldiers [307] to lay their hands on Him. And He did not think it worth while to consider what their temerity had planned for Him, if only He might show His own people what they ought to expect from Him.

For when, thinking much about the dangers of souls, and also on the other hand, about their evil tendency to vice,[308] the Introducer, Master, and Founder directed His laws and ordinances to the end of fitting duties, did He not destroy the haughtiness of pride? Did He not quench the flames of passion? Did He not suppress the craving of greed? Did He not twist the weapons from their hands and cut them off from the hotbeds of every vice? Finally, was He not Himself gentle, agreeable, easy to approach, friendly to address? Was He not sympathetic to every human misery and to all in any way afflicted with troubles and physical ailments and diseases? Did He, pitying them with His unparalleled kindness, not return and restore them to health?

Why do the pagans persecute Christ and His followers alone?

64. What therefore forces you, what urges you on to curse, to rail at Him, to show implacable hatred toward Him whom no man can accuse, can indict, as guilty of any crime? Your tyrants and kings, who, having laid aside the fear of the gods, plunder and pillage the votive treasuries of temples;[309] who, by proscriptions,[310] exiles, murders, denude a state of its aristocracy; who, with licentious force ruin and rob the chastity of married women and maidens—[311] these you call *indigetes* and *divi*,[312] and to those whom you ought to have attacked with most bitter hatred, you sacrifice with couches, altars, temples, and other worship, and by observing their birthdays with games.

And all [313] who by writing books attack in many forms public morals with biting criticism; who slash, scorch, and scourge your luxurious lives; [314] who hand down to posterity through the permanence of writings the stigmas of their own times; men who seek to persuade us that marriages should be held in common; [315] who cohabit with boys, beautiful, lustful, naked; [316] who proclaim [317] that you are brutes, runaways, exiles, slaves of the lowest type, mad and crazy—all these with wonder and approval you raise to the stars of heaven, place them in secret places in libraries, [318] endow them with chariots and statues, and as far as in you lies, grant them a certain kind of immortality, by the witness of immortal titles.

Christ alone you wish to reproach, to tear in pieces, if you can do so to a god. Indeed, if you could, you would gnaw Him alone with bloody jaws after the manner of wild beasts, and gulp down His shattered bones. On account of what desert, I ask you, do you say this, because of what fault? What was done by Him to bend the course of justice and to arouse you to hatred made fierce by the Furies' lashings? Because He told you that He was sent by Him who alone is King as a guardian for your souls? Because He brought to you immortality which you are certain you already have, persuaded by the statements of a few?

But even if you had the certainty that He spoke falsehoods, that He even promised the most unfounded hopes, even so I see no reason why you would have to hate Him, to condemn Him with bitter reviling. Indeed, if your spirit had been kind and gentle, you ought to embrace Him for this alone, that He promised to you things which you might wish for and which would be favorable to you; that He was the messenger of good tidings; that He preached those things which would harm no mind but rather fill all with less-anxious hope.

65. O thankless and wicked age, prepared [319] for its own destruction by the unbelievable stubbornness of its heart! If any physician had come to you from far-away countries and from regions never known to you, promising medicine which would ward off from your bodies absolutely all kinds of diseases and complaints, would you not all have run to him vying with one another to reach him first? Would you not have received him within your family walls with every kind of attention and showered him with honors? Would you not want that kind of medicine to be very reliable, genuine, which guaranteed that you would be free from innumerable bodily ills even to the end of your lives? Even if the matter were doubtful you would yet put yourselves in his care and you would not hesitate to drink down the unknown dose, induced to do so by the prospect set before you of gaining health and by a love of security.

Like a bright light Christ appeared to us as the herald of very great news, bringing also an omen of prosperity and a message of good health [320] to those who believe. What is this cruelty, what this great barbarity? Indeed, to speak truly, what is this pride, arrogance, this tearing to pieces of the herald and bearer of so great a gift not only with verbal revilings but even with dread warfare, [321] and this pursuit of Him with all the weapons that can be showered on Him and with destruction? His words do not please you and it hurts you to hear them—so you put them down as a soothsayer's [322] equivocations. You have Him speaking pure nonsense and promising air castles—so you laugh, you as men of wisdom, and leave His stupidity to welter among the errors it makes.

What is the meaning of this brutality, to repeat what I have said so often? What is this passion, so bloodthirsty, to declare implacable war on one who did not deserve it from you; to want to tear Him limb from limb if you could, who not only brought evil to no man, but spoke with equal kindness to enemies concerning the salvation that was being brought to them from God the Ruler; concerning what had to be done so that they might escape death and receive an immortality unknown to them? And when the strangeness of these things and the unheard promises troubled the minds of those who heard them and caused them to hesitate to believe, the Lord of every power [323] and the Destroyer of death itself,[324] allowed His human form to be killed, so that from the results they might know that the hopes which they had long entertained about the salvation of the soul were safe and that in no other way could they avoid the danger of death.

BOOK TWO

Attack on Philosophy: The Mortality of the Soul

What is the reason for the persecution of the blameless Christ?

1. At this point, if it were at all possible, I should like to have a little talk with all those who hate the name of Christ, digressing for a moment from that defense originally set up. If you think it no disgrace to answer when asked a question, tell us, and speak out: For what reason or for what cause do you pursue Christ with such determined hostility? Or what wrongs of His do you recall that at the mention of His name you boil over with the heat of maddened hearts?

Did He ever, as He claimed royal power for Himself, infest the whole world with fiercest legions, and of nations at peace from the beginning did He destroy and exterminate some and force others with necks bent under the yoke to be obedient to Him? Did He ever, inflamed with greedy avarice, claim by right of His own possession all the abundance with which the human race strives eagerly to enrich itself? Did He ever, impassioned by lust, forcefully break down the bars of chastity or stealthily lay an ambush for the wife of another? [1] Did He ever, swollen with arrogant conceit, perpetrate wrongs and slanders right and left with no distinction of persons?

2. Did He not rather extend [2] to all men the light of life and remove the peril of ignorance? [3] If He did not deserve

114

your attention and belief, you should not have despised Him precisely because He showed you things bound up with salvation,[4] and because He chose [5] for you highways to heaven and hopes for immortality.

Christ drove the pagan religions from the earth.

" But, certainly, He deserves to be hated because He has driven religions from the earth, because He has prevented access to the worship of the gods."

Is He then charged with being a destroyer of religion and a promoter of impiety, who brought true religion into the world, who opened the doors of piety to men blind and truly living in impiety, and pointed out to whom they should be submissive? Or is there any religion more true, more eager to serve,[6] more powerful, more just, than to be acquainted with the God the Beginning; to know how to pray to God the Beginning who is the only Head and Fount of all good things, the Father and Founder and Creator of lasting things, through whom all that is on earth and everything in heaven breathes and is given vitality [7] and whose non-existence would surely imply that nothing would bear a name or have substance?

3. Perhaps you doubt the existence of that Ruler [8] of whom we speak, and rather believe that Apollo, Diana, Mercury, Mars,[9] do exist. Put the decision up to a child [10] and looking around at all these things we see, it will doubt more whether the other gods exist than have any hesitation in the case of the God whom we all know from nature, whether when we cry out " O God! " [11] or when we make God the witness of the wicked and raise our face to heaven as if He saw us.

" But He forbade men to pray to the lesser gods." [12]

True—but do you know who or where the lesser gods are? Has mistrust or mention of them at any time seized you so that you justly are annoyed that worship has been taken from them and they have been bereft of the granting of honor? If in this matter conceit and what is called *typhus* [13] by the Greeks did not stand in your way and impede you, long ago could you have known what He forbade to be done or why; within what limits He wanted true religion to stay; how much danger arose for you from what you consider obedience or out of what evils you would rise up if you were to renounce your deadly delusion.

The truth of Christ's religion is clearly demonstrated.

4. But all these things will be demonstrated more plainly and more clearly when we shall proceed further. For we shall show that Christ did not teach nations impiety but that He delivered woefully ignorant and wretched men from the worst bandits. [14]

" We do not believe," you say, " that what He says is true."

Well, now, are you clear about the things you say are not true, when lying in the future and having not yet taken place, they can in no way be subjected to disproof?

" But He Himself does not prove what He promises." [15]

That is so, for, as I said, there can be no demonstration of matters still to take place. Since, then, it is the nature of things which are still in the future that they cannot be grasped and understood by the touch of anticipation, is it not better reasoning that, of two alternatives which are both un-certain and hang in doubtful suspense, we should believe the one which affords some hopes rather than the one which

offers none at all? [16] In the former case there is no danger
⟨if⟩ what is said to be in the future proves vain and idle;
and in the latter there is the greatest loss, specifically the loss
of salvation, if when the time has come, it be made patent
that there was no deceit.

The extension of Christianity throughout the world.

5. What can you say in your ignorance, you for whom we
might well shed tears of pity? Are you not very much afraid
that after all these things may be true which you despise and
which provide you with a reason to laugh? And do you not
at least in your own private ponderings give thought to the
possibility that because today in your stubborn perversity
you refuse to believe, time may later convict [17] you and unquenchable remorse punish you? [18] Do not even these considerations give you faith to believe: the fact that through
all lands in such a short period of time the sacred doctrines [19]
of this great name have been spread abroad; that there is now
no nation of so wild a character and so impervious to gentle
sentiments which has not under the influence of His love
softened its harshness, and, adopting tranquillity, passed over
into peaceful dispositions? that men endowed with great
ability—orators,[20] grammarians, rhetoricians, lawyers, and physicians, even those who explore the profundities of philosophy
—eagerly seek instruction in these things, having abandoned
those to which a little while before they were devoted? that
slaves choose to be tortured by their masters rather than to
follow their orders,[21] couples to be divorced, children to be
disinherited by their parents, rather than to break the Chris-
tion faith and desert their colors in the struggle for salva-

tion?[22] that although you have established such a great variety
of punishments for those who follow the mandates of this
religion, the thing grows the more, and against every threat
and fearful prohibition the people struggle with even stouter
heart, and are spurred to greater zeal for belief, as if whipped
by the sting of this restriction?

Do you believe that these things take place at random and
by chance,[23] that these attitudes are the result of accidental
encounters?[24] Is this not, then, a case of something sacred
and divine? Or is God not present when minds are so
changed that, although the executioners' hooks and countless
other torments threaten, as we have said, those who believe,
with full comprehension they accept the conditions as if swept
away by a certain sweetness and a love of all virtues, and
prefer the friendship of Christ to all the things of the world?

The pagans arrogantly claim wisdom as their possession.

6. But perhaps those who now throughout the world are
acting in concert and uniting in agreement of " credulity "[25]
seem to you stupid and silly. But tell me: do you, alone
seasoned[26] with the pure potency of wisdom and understanding, see something different and profound? You alone comprehend that all these things are trifles; you alone, that what
we declare will come from the King Supreme, are words and
childish stupidities. From what source,[27] I ask, has so much
wisdom been given you? Whence, so much penetration and
wit? Or from what teachings of science were you able to
acquire so much heart, to drink in so much power of pro-
phecy? Because you know how to inflect[28] verbs and nouns
through the cases and tenses; because you know how to avoid
barbarisms and solecisms; because you have learned how to

express yourselves in rhythmic, balanced, and properly-arranged language or to know when it is unpolished; because you keep sealed in your memory [29] the *Fornix* of Lucilius [30] and the *Marsyas* of Pomponius [31]; because you know what the points in dispute in law cases are, how many kinds of cases there are, how many of speaking in court; what the genus is, what the species; how an opposite differs from a contrary—do you therefore think you know what is false, what is true; what can take place or what cannot; what is the nature of the lowest and the highest? Has that well-known saying never struck your ears that *the wisdom of man is foolishness with God* [32] who is Chief?

7. You yourselves, moreover, clearly see that whenever you discuss subjects that are obscure and are eager to uncover the mysteries of nature, you are ignorant of the very things you talk about, affirm, and frequently maintain with deadly earnestness; and that each one defends with obstinate opposition his own notions ⟨as⟩ proved and apprehended. For, if I am to perceive the truth, how, though all the ages be made available for searching out the facts, can we, left to ourselves, have knowledge, we whom some unfortunate something with ill will [33] brought forth into existence in such a condition of blindness and pride that although we know absolutely nothing, we nevertheless deceive ourselves and are raised to the point of believing we do know by the swelling of our conceited heart?

For example—to pass over divine matters and those enveloped in obscurity by their nature—is there anyone who can explain what the famous Socrates could not understand in the *Phaedrus*: [34] what man is and whence he is, wavering, changeable, fickle, deceitful, manifold, and complex; for what purposes he was brought forth; by whose genius he was planned; what he is to do in the world; why he suffers so many swarms of evils; whether the earth transformed by some putrid slime brought him to life like worms, like mice; [35] or whether he received the outlines of his body and his face's shape at the hands of some fashioner and maker?

Can he, I say, know these obvious things which have their place in the experience of all: by what causes we sink into sleep, by what we awaken; by what means dreams take place, by what they are seen; indeed, a point about which Plato in the *Theaetetus* [36] is in doubt, whether we ever are awake or whether what is called being awake is a part of everlasting slumber, and what we seem to be doing a dream; whether when we say we see, we see by the extension of rays and light [37] or images of objects fly to and light on our eyes; whether flavor resides in the objects or takes place in contact with the palate; by what causes the hairs lay aside their natural blackness [38] and grow white, not all simultaneously but one by one; why it is that all liquids when mixed make one body and oil alone refuses to permit others to be dissolved into itself but remains always clearly suspended in its own nature; finally, why the soul [39] itself which is said by you to be immortal and divine,[40] is sick in sick people, dull in little children, and having been worn out in old age, prattles [41] about things to come and things silly? [42] The weakness and ignorance of these statements is the more pitiful because,[43] since it is possible for us by accident sometimes to say something true, we are yet uncertain even of this very point, whether what we have said is true at all.

The pagans also are guilty of "credulity."

8. And [44] since you are accustomed to laugh at our faith, and with witty jests to gibe at this our "credulity," tell us,

jolly wits soaked and saturated with the unmixed [45] draught of wisdom, is there in life any sort of undertaking requiring one to be right busy and active which the doers do not accept, undertake, and begin, without an initial act of *faith* in it? Do you go on trips, take voyages, not *believing* that you will return home when the business has been successfully completed? Do you cut the earth with hoe and fill it with different kinds of seeds, not *believing* that you will receive a harvest at the turn of the seasons? Do you unite in marriage, not *believing* that it will be chaste and that the alliance will confer benefit to the married parties? Do you undertake to rear [46] children, not *believing* that they will come through unharmed, and, passing through life's stations, will come to the goal of old age? Do you entrust your bodies' ailments to the hands of the physicians, not *believing* that the diseases can be relieved by the lessening of their severity? Do you carry on wars with enemies, not *believing* that you will come back victorious from the battles? Do you worship and show devotion to the gods, not *believing* that they exist and will lend sympathetic ears to your prayers? [47]

9. And again, have you seen with your own eyes and have you held those things in your own hands regarding which you yourselves write, which are your daily reading, matters that escape human understanding? Does each one of you not *believe* this authority or that? What anyone has persuaded himself another has truly said, does he not defend as if by an agreement of *faith*? Does [48] one who says that the origin of all ⟨things⟩ is ⟨fire,⟩ or water, not show *belief* in Thales or Heraclitus? [49] One who ascribes causes to numbers, in Pythagoras of Samos, in Archytas? [50] One who thinks of the soul as distinct from the body, in the Socratic Plato? [51] One who adds a fifth element [52] to the primary causes, in Aristotle,

father of the Peripatetics? [53] One who threatens the world
with fire and says that when the time comes, it will burn,[54]
in Panaetius, Chrysippus, Zeno? [55] One who is always manu-
facturing worlds from atoms, and destroying them, in Epicurus, Democritus, Metrodorus? [56] One who ⟨says⟩ that
nothing is understood by man and also that all things are
shrouded in blind obscurity, in Arcesilas,[57] Carneades—in
somebody, in fine, who is a devotee of the old or later
Academy? [58]

10.   Finally, do not the chief exponents and fathers of the
above-mentioned views say what they say on the basis of a
trust in their own guesswork? [59] Did Heraclitus see things
come into being through changes brought about by fires,
Thales by the condensing of water? Did Pythagoras see
numbers combining; Plato the bodiless forms; Democritus the
collisions of the atoms? Or do those who assert that nothing
at all can be understood, know whether what they say is true,
so that they may understand that the very thing which they
posit is a truthful declaration?

Since, therefore, you have learned and understand nothing, and are led by " credulity " to assert all that you write
and " comprehend "[60] in thousands of books: what is this
judgment, I ask you, which is so unjust as to let you make
fun of our faith [61] which you see you share in common with
our " credulity "? [62]

But, of course, you " believe wise men and men well educated in all branches of learning." Yes, men who accept
nothing and make no unified and harmonious declaration,
who wage wars on behalf of their opinions with their opponents and constantly fight like swordsmen with stubborn
hostility; who overthrow, destroy, uproot the one the other's

conclusions, render everything doubtful and from their very disagreement have shown that nothing can be known.[63]

Christ possessed powers not held by the pagan philosophers.

11. But [64] let us grant that these things must ⟨not⟩ hinder and in no way prevent you from believing and following them in great measure: and what reason is there that in this respect you should have more and we less? You believe Plato,[65] Cronius,[66] Numenius, or any one you please: we believe in and assent to Christ. How unfair it is, that when both of us take our stand on authorities and both of us have in common one and the same thing, namely, belief, you should wish to be given the right to receive what is thus said by them but are unwilling that we should hear and see what is brought forth by Christ!

And yet if we should want to balance causes, sides with sides, we are in a stronger position when we show what we have followed in Christ, than you are in showing what you have followed in the philosophers. And here is what we have followed in Him: His glorious works and mighty powers which He brought out publicly in various miracles, so much so that anyone could be brought to the necessity of belief and could confidently [67] decide that they were not human but performed by some divine and unknown power.

What powers did you follow in the philosophers that you ought to believe them more than we Christ? Could any one [68] of them by a single word or by the bidding of a single command—I shall not say forbid, restrain the madness of the sea and the ragings of the storms; restore light to the blind or give it to those born without sight; call back the dead to life; end the sufferings of years, but what is the easiest by far to do—heal by one rebuke a boil, an itch,[69] or sliver stuck in hard skin? Not that we deny that they are praiseworthy for the purity of their characters or that they are equipped with every kind of research and learning: we know right well that they speak in the most splendid [70] language and that they are fluent in smooth [71] composition; that they draw up their syllogisms most acutely; that they arrange their conclusions in proper sequence; that they express, divide, and distinguish their basic principles in definitions; that they have much to say about the phases of mathematics, many things about music, and that they also demonstrate the science of geometry with its axioms and postulates.

But what does this have to do with the case? Do enthymemes, syllogisms, and other such things vouch that these men know the truth, or are they therefore so worthy that one must of necessity believe them on very obscure matters? A comparison of persons must be weighed, not by the vigor of eloquence, but by the miraculous power of the deeds they have done. He is ⟨not⟩ to be called a good authority who has expressed his meaning lucidly but the one who follows up what he promises by the guarantee of divine works.

The pagans foolishly reject the testimony of Christianity.

12. Propose your arguments [72] to us and your subtle surmisings: if Christ Himself were to use these in the meetings of the peoples—let me beg His pardon for saying this—who would agree? Who would listen? Who would conclude that He makes any clear promises, or who, when He bandied about such gross and bare statements, would follow Him, however naïve and good-naturedly stupid he might be? His miraculous powers have been set before your eyes and that

unheard-of power over nature, both those done in public by Himself or practiced through the whole world by His heralds. It [73] quenched the fires of passions and made races and peoples and the most disparate nations hasten with one mind to consent to one and the same faith.

For the deeds can be counted and numbered [74] which were done in India,[75] among the Seres,[76] Persians and Medes, in Arabia,[77] Egypt, in Asia, Syria, among the Galatians, Parthians, Phrygians; in Achaea, Macedonia, Epirus; [78] in all the islands [79] and provinces on which the rising and setting sun shines, and, finally, in Rome, too, the mistress, where, though there are men who give themselves to King Numa's arts [80] and superstitions, there was yet no tarrying in abandoning the ancestral traditions [81] and identifying oneself with the truth of Christianity.[82]

For they [83] had seen the chariot of Simon Magus [84] and the fiery four-horse team blown to pieces by the mouth of Peter [85] and vanish at the mention of Christ's name. They had seen him, I say, trusting in false gods and abandoned by these same in their fear, hurled headlong by his own weight, lying there with his legs broken; then afterwards carried to Brunda,[86] exhausted by his sufferings and his disgrace,[87] again casting himself down from the roof of a very high house.

All these happenings you neither know nor wanted to know nor have you ever deemed them essential for you, and while you trust your own hearts and call what is conceit wisdom, you have given to impostors, to those criminals, I say, who make it their business to discard the name of Christ, an opportunity to cloud over and bury in darkness matters of such capital importance; to rob you of faith and to replace it with scorn, in order that, seeing as they do, that an end in accord with their deserts threatens them, they might also give you cause to approach danger and be bereft of God's mercy.

The pagans unfairly mock at Christianity.

13. Meanwhile, you who show surprise, who marvel at the pronouncements of the learned and of philosophy, do you not consider it most unfair to ride, to mock us, as if we were saying stupidities and ineptitudes when you are found saying the same or similar things at which you laugh when said or stated by us? And here my concern is not with those who, scattered through the various bypaths of the schools,[88] have created this and that party by divergence of views. It is you I address, you who follow after Mercury,[89] Plato, and Pythagoras,[90] and you others who are of the same view and march with unity of sentiments through those same ways. You dare to laugh at us because we worship and cherish the Father of Creation and the Lord, and because we give and entrust our hopes to Him?

What does your Plato say in the *Theaetetus*, to mention him in particular? Does he not advise the soul to flee from the earth and to busy itself as far as possible [91] in thought and contemplation concerning Him? [92] Dare you laugh at us because we say that there will be a resurrection of the dead,[93] a fact which we admit we say but maintain that you hear it in a sense different from ours? What does that same Plato say in the *Politicus*? [94] Does he not write that when the world has begun to rise from the west and to incline towards the turning point of the rising sun, men will again burst forth from the earth's bosom—old men, white-haired, worn out, and when the remoter years begin to approach, they will sink back through those same steps by which today they advance in growth, to the cradles of their infancy? [95]

Dare you laugh at us because we look out for the health of our souls, that is, ourselves for ourselves? For what are we human beings except souls shut up in bodies? Is it not true that you, all of you,[96] go to every limit in preserving them unharmed? As for the fact that [97] you refrain from every fault and passion, is not this the fear which possesses you, that you may cling to your bodies as if nailed to them with spikes? What is the meaning of those esoteric ceremonials [98] in which you address powers I know not which to get them to be propitious to you and not put any hindrances in your way as you journey back to your ancestral homes?

Plato and Christ on the immortality of the soul.

14. Dare [99] you laugh at us, when we speak of Gehennas and certain unquenchable fires into which we have learned that souls are cast by their enemies and foes? [100] Does that same Plato of yours in that book he wrote on the immortality of the soul [101] not name the rivers Acheron, and Styx, and Cocytus, and Pyriphlegethon,[102] in which he declares that souls are rolled, sunk, consumed by fire? And a man of wisdom not perverse [103] and of careful and balanced judgment, he undertakes an insoluble question, with the result that while saying that souls are immortal, everlasting, and possessing no bodily substance, he yet says that they are punished and are subject to a sense of pain. But what man fails to see that what is immortal, what is uncompounded,[104] cannot be subject to any pain; that, however, what feels pain, cannot have immortality? Nevertheless, his view does not stray far from the truth.[105] For, although that gentle and benevolent man believed it to be inhumane to sentence souls to death, he yet not inconsistently entertained the view that they are cast into rivers raging with balls of fire and loathsome in their muddy abysses. They are hurled in, and being an-

nihilated, they vanish in the frustration of everlasting destruction. They are of intermediate character,[106] as is known from Christ's teaching; and they are such as to perish if they fail to know God, but can also be delivered from death to life, if they have given heed to His warnings [107] and graces, and ignorance is cleared up. This is the true death of a human being,[108] this leaves nothing remaining behind—for that which is seen before one's eyes is merely an uncoupling of the souls from the bodies, not the final end of destruction— this, I say, is the true death of a human being when the souls which know not God shall be consumed in long-enduring torments by fierce fire into which they shall be cast by certain fiercely-savage beings [109] who were unknown before Christ and unveiled only by the one who knows.[110]

Criticism of the view that the souls are immortal.

15. Wherefore [111] there is no reason that we should be deceived by what promises us vain hopes, something said by certain upstarts [112] carried away by an extravagant opinion of themselves, namely that souls are immortal, very near in degree of rank to the Lord and Ruler of Creation, brought forth by that Begetter and Father; divine, wise, learned, and not touchable by any contact with the body. Because this is true and certain and we have been brought forth by the Perfect One in a perfection that is capable of no correction, we are living blameless and therefore incapable of criticism; good, just, and upright, possessing no faults. No passion subdues us, no lust dishonors us. We preserve and renew the practice of every virtue, and because the souls of all of us have flowed out from a single source, therefore we feel alike and are in agreement. We differ neither in morality

nor beliefs. We all know God [113] and there are not as many opinions in the world as there are men,[114] nor are these divided by infinite variety.

16. And while we are sliding and hastening to our human bodies, from the world's circles causes [115] pursue us by which we are evil and most wicked; burn with passions and wrathfulness, pass our lives in shameful deeds and are condemned [116] to public lust by prostitution of our bodies for hire. But how can bodies unite with that which is bodiless, or things created by God the Supreme be transformed by weaker causes into degrading vices? Are you willing, gentlemen, to lay aside that deep-seated arrogance [117] and conceit, you men who claim God as your Father and maintain that you have the same immortality as He? Are you willing to inquire, to search out, to investigate [118] what you yourselves are, whose you are, of what father you are thought to be, what you are doing in the world, how you are born, in which manner you leap into life? Are you willing, having laid aside partiality,[119] to reach the conclusion in your silent thought that we are animate beings either in all respects like the rest or separated from them by no great difference? [120] After all, what is there to show that we differ from them? Or what extraordinary quality is there in us so that we should refuse to be enrolled in the number of animals? [121]

Their bodies are founded upon bones [122] and are bound together by a network of sinews: and in like manner our bodies are founded upon bones and are bound together by sinews. They breathe in the air through nostrils and give it out again in exhalations: and we in the same way draw in our breath and breathe it out again in a continuous to-and-fro. They are separated in female and male kinds: and we too have been fashioned by our Creator into as many sexes. They produce their young from wombs and beget them through bodily union: [123] we, too, are born from bodily embraces and are brought forth and sent out from the wombs of mothers. By food they are sustained and by drink, and the impure excess they cast out from the lower parts: we, too, are sustained by food and by drink, and what nature is ready to reject, we pour out by the same channels.

All of them take care to repel death-bringing hunger and of necessity to watch for food. What else do we do in life's great preoccupations except to seek for those things by which the danger of hunger is avoided and unhappy anxiety is laid aside? They feel diseases and starvation and in the end are weakened by old age. Are we by any chance immune to these evils and not broken in the same manner by the inconvenience of diseases and destroyed by the decline of old age?

But if this also is true, as is said in the more hidden mysteries, that the souls of the wicked go [124] into cattle and other beasts after they have been removed [125] from human bodies, it is more clearly demonstrated that we are near them and not removed from them by any appreciable difference; for there is a factor in both us and them by reason of which animate beings are said to exist and to have the power of living motion.

Is man really superior to the animals because he has reason?

17. "But *we* possess reason and surpass in understanding every species of dumb animals." [126]

I would believe this to be most truly spoken, if all men lived rationally and wisely, held to the course of duty, refrained from the forbidden, had nothing to do with base activities, and no one through his depraved intellect and blindness of ignorance asked for what is alien and even hostile to himself. I should, however, like to know what this reason is by which we are to be preferred to all species of animals. Because we have made dwellings for ourselves in which we can avoid the cold of winter and heat of summer? Do you mean to say that other animate beings have no foresight of this kind? Do we not see some building dwellings of nests for themselves in places most suitable; others covering and fortifying themselves in rocks and hanging crags; still others burrowing into the soil of the earth and preparing in dug-out pits places of protection and lairs for themselves? And if Mother Nature had been willing to give them hands to help them, there would be no doubt that they themselves would also have built towering fortifications and would have struck out new works of art. Yet even in those things which they make with their beaks and claws, we see that there are many images of reason and wisdom which we human beings are unable to copy with any amount of thought, although we have hands that work for us and are masters of every sort of perfection.

18. "They have not learned to fashion clothing, chairs, ships, and ploughs, nor the other equipment which daily life demands."

These are not the blessings of knowledge but the inventions of paupers—necessity.[127] Nor did the arts drop down with the souls from the innermost heart of heaven, but they have all been carefully sought for and come to birth here on earth and through painstaking thought have been devised gradually in the progress of time. And if in this regard the souls possessed the knowledge which a race that is divine and immortal ought by all rights fittingly to have, all men would have known all things from the beginning and there would have been no age unacquainted with any art or not possessed of the advantage of experience with things. But now a life that is destitute and lacking many things, observing that certain things happen to its advantage by chance, while it imitates, experiments, and tries, while it makes errors, revises, makes changes, by a constant process of rejection has assembled little smatterings in the arts and has brought them to one issue, the joint improvements of many ages.

Skills in arts and crafts no proof of a divine soul.

19. Now if men either knew themselves through and through or had received an understanding of God to the extent of even the slightest conjecture,[128] never would they claim for themselves a divine and immortal nature nor would they think themselves something great because they have made for themselves gridirons, basins, and bowls; because they have made undershirts, linen jackets,[129] mantles, cloaks, ceremonial robes, knives, breastplates, and swords; because they have made rakes, hatchets, the ploughshare. Never, I say, would they believe, exalted by their arrogance and conceit, that they are deities of the first class and equals of the Highest in His sublimity, just because they had begotten grammar, music, oratory, and geometrical forms.[130] We do not see what is so surprising in these arts that from their discovery it should be believed that the souls are superior to the sun and all the stars, surpassing in glory and substance this whole world of which these things are only parts.[131]

And what else can these promise to be able to assimilate or to impart to others than that we may learn the rules and differences of nouns, the tonal intervals of sounds; that we may speak convincingly in lawsuits; that we may measure the extent [132] of the lands? If the souls had brought these with them from the heavenly regions, it would of necessity follow that all should know them; long since they would be dealing with them over the whole earth, nor would any race of men be found which would not be uniformly and equally instructed in all these matters.

But now how few in the world are musicians, logicians, and geometers, how few orators, poets, grammarians.[133] From which it seems clear, as has been stated repeatedly, that these things were discovered through pressure of times and places and that the souls did not fly here divine and instructed, because neither are they all learned nor can all learn, but among them are many relatively dull-witted and stupid, and are forced to apply themselves to a zeal for learning by the coercion of stripes.

But if it were really true that what we learn are recollections,[134] as has been accepted in ancient beliefs, it would have been necessary for us all, coming as we do from a single truth, to learn alike and to recall alike, not to have differing beliefs nor to have a great number of inconsistent beliefs. But as it is, seeing that we assert some one thing and some another, it is at once manifest that we brought nothing from heaven but learned what here came into being and make claims for what has established itself in our thought.

A controlled experiment.

20. And that we may show you more clearly and more patently of what worth is man whom you believe to be very like the Higher Power, conceive this idea in your minds and, because it can be done if we put ourselves to it, let us assume

we have and let us hold it by positing an analogy.[135] Let us therefore take a place dug out in the ground, fit for habitation; having the shape of a bedroom, enclosed by a roof and walls; not cold in winter, not too warm in the hot season, but with the temperature so regulated that we feel neither cold nor the summer's strong heat. Here let no sound, no cry penetrate at all, of bird, of beast, of storm, of man—in fine, of any noise or of heavy crashes of thunder. Let us then devise some way to provide light, not from fire brought in or from exposure to sunlight but something artificial,[136] to counterfeit daylight in the darkness that has been introduced. Let there be only [137] a single door, and there must not be a direct entrance; let the approach be made through twists and windings; and let it never be opened except when necessity demands.

21. Now that we have prepared a place for our idea, let us next take some one just [138] born into this lodging which is to contain no article of any kind and should be empty and bare. Let it be some one of the race of Plato [139] or Pythagoras, or of some one of those who, they say, were of the divine wit or were named most wise by the oracles of the gods.[140] This done, it follows that he be given his necessary nourishment and be brought up on suitable sustenance. Let us therefore also provide a wet nurse who shall always come to him naked, always silent, speaking not a word nor opening her mouth and lips to say [141] anything, but when she has nursed him and attended to the following duties, let her leave him given over to sleep, close the door, and remain outside day and night, for usually a nurse's care is required to be at hand and to watch his movements from time to time.

But when the child begins to require the support of solid foods, they should be carried in by the same nurse, laying aside her clothes, as we said, and preserving the practice of silence. Moreover, let the food itself which is brought in be always one and the same, not different in substance nor varied by different flavors, but let it be gruel of millet or bread of spelt, or, to copy the ancient centuries, acorns [142] taken from the coals or berries from wild branches.

Let wine be absolutely unknown to him for drink and let him be given nothing else for settling his thirst except pure water untouched by the heat of fire, and, if it can be done, this served to him by the hollow of the hands. For custom, made familiar from habit, will become second nature and his desire will interest itself no further, unaware that there is anything further to be sought after.

The testing of the subject.

22. " Well, what is the purpose of all this? "

Our purpose is that, since it has been believed that the souls are divine and therefore [143] immortal, and that they fly to the bodies of men with every kind of learning, we may make a test from this person whom we have proposed to bring up in this way, whether the thing can be believed or whether it has been lightly accepted and taken for granted in consequence of vain preoccupations. Let him grow up, then, nourished by us in secluded isolation, to an age of your choice: do you say twenty? thirty? Yes, let him reach forty years, and then bring him to the assemblies of men and if it is true that he is part and particle [144] of the original being, lives here sprung from fountains of such auspicious [145] life, before he acquires knowledge of anything or is initiated to human speech, let him give answer to the questions: who he is and from what father, in what locality he was born, in what way or by what method was he given sustenance, practicing what work or business previously, he has come through the period of his existence in the past.

Will he not stand there more stupid and duller than any cattle, log, stone? When introduced to new experiences and things never known to him before, will he not before all else be ignorant of himself? Will he be able, if you ask, to show what the sun is; the earth, seas, stars, clouds, mist, rains, thunder, snow, hail? Will he be able to know what trees are, plants or grasses, a bull, horse, or ram, a camel, elephant, or kite? [146]

23. If when he is hungry you give him a grape, a must-cake,[147] an onion, an artichoke, a cucumber, a fig, will he know that his hunger can be satisfied by all of these or of what kind each ought to be for eating? If you made a bonfire or surrounded him with poisonous creatures, would he not go through the midst of flames, vipers, spiders, ignorant that they are harmful and unaware of what fear itself is? And, indeed, if you place in front of him clothing, utensils, both for city and for country use, will he be able to distinguish, to tell them apart, for what work each is fitted, for the discharge of what service each is adapted?

Will he point out for what clothing purpose a coverlet [148] was made, a turban, a chaplet,[149] a fillet,[150] a pillow, a handkerchief, a cloak, a veil,[151] napkin, sheepskin,[152] slippers, sandals, shoes? What if you go on to ask what a wheel is or a flail, winnowing fan, jar, cask, oil mill, ploughshare, or sieve, a millstone, plough-beam, or hoe; an armchair, a needle, a strigil, a washbasin, an easy chair,[153] a ladle, a platter, a candlestick, a goblet, a broom, a cup, a bag?

What if you ask about a lute, a pipe, silver, bronze, gold, a codex,[154] a rod, a roll? What if you ask about the other articles which surround and sustain human life? Will he not, as we have said, like an ox or an ass, a pig, or if there is any animal more slow-witted, look indeed at these things, examining their different shapes,[155] but be ignorant of what they individually are and unaware of for what purpose they are possessed? Should he by any necessity perforce utter a sound, would he not, as is usual with mutes,[156] merely cry out something inarticulate with gaping mouth?

Criticism of Plato's doctrine of recollection.

24. Why, Plato, do you in the *Meno* [157] seek to learn certain things from a young slave, using the rational function,[158] and strive by his answers to prove that what we learn we do not learn but return to a recollection of the things which we knew in a time long past? If he [159] answers you truly—it would be unbecoming if we denied credence to what you say—he is led on not by a knowledge of the facts but by his intelligence, and from the fact that he has some acquaintance with numbers from his daily experience, it happens that he understands the questions and the process of multiplication itself constantly leads him on.

But if you are really certain that the souls when they fly hither are immortal and full of knowledge, cease to question that young fellow whom you see to be acquainted with the facts and possessed of human faculties. Call to you that forty-year-old and ask him not anything abstruse or complicated, not about triangles or squares or what a cube is or a power, the ratio of nine to eight or even of four to three,[160] but what is evident of itself: ask what sum twice two make, what, twice three.

We are anxious to see, we are anxious to know, what he would answer when asked, whether he finds a solution to the posited problem. In such a state will he perceive, though his ears be open, whether you say anything or ask anything, or require that he answer you something? And will he not stand there like a log or, as it is said, like Marpesian granite,[161] tongue-less and dumb, not understanding or knowing even this—whether it is with him or with another that you are speaking, whether your conversation is with another or with him,[162] whether that is speech which you utter or the sound of a voice meaning nothing but drawn out to a vain purpose?

25. What do you say, gentlemen, who overreach your-selves in claiming excellence which belongs to others? Is this that learned soul you speak about—immortal, perfect, divine, holding fourth place after God the Master of things and after the twin intellects[163] and flowing from living mixing bowls?[164] This is that precious human being endowed with the loftiest powers of reason, who is said to be a microcosm,[165] and formed and fashioned into the appearance and likeness of the macrocosm[166]—no better, as became apparent, than cattle, more stupid than wood, stone? One who would be unacquainted[167] with human beings and constantly live and linger in silent isolation, he in his inert existence would never be equal to the task of ⟨identifying⟩ anything at all,[168] though he were to live to numberless years and never be released from the bonds of his body. But when he reaches the schools and becomes educated through the instructions of teachers, he is made wise, learned, and rids himself of the ignorance which he recently had. Both an ass and an ox, as well, learn, when forced by constant practice, to plough and to turn the mill; a horse to bear the yoke and to recognize changes in direction; a camel to kneel down when he takes on or lays off loads; a dove[169] when set free to fly back to its master's house; a dog, when it has found the quarry, to

repress and hold back the bark; a parrot to articulate speech and a crow to utter names.

If the soul once had knowledge, why did it forget it?

26. But when I hear the soul called something out of the ordinary, near and next to God, that it hurries here knowing everything about former centuries,[170] I do not want it to learn but to teach, and not to step down, so to speak, from the scholar's chair to the primary classes [171] but retaining what it had, to bind itself to earthly bodies. For unless such is done, how can it be discerned whether it recollects or learns what it hears, since it is much easier to believe that it learns what it does not know than that it has forgotten what it knew a little while before?

"From the interposition of the body it loses remembrance [172] of former things."

And what has happened to that statement that bodiless [173] souls have no substance? [174] Evidently, that which is incorporeal is not hindered by the interposition of any second thing nor can anything of itself [175] destroy that which is not susceptible to the touch of anything set against it. Just as, for example, a number which has existence apart from bodies,[176] even though it be buried in a thousand bodies,[177] remains untouched and secure, so it is necessary that souls, if they are bodiless, as it is claimed, suffer [178] no forgetting of former things, however thoroughly they may be encompassed by material ties.

What of the fact that this same reasoning not only shows they are not bodiless but also deprives them all of immortality and subjects them to the normal limits of all life? Whatever by the intervention of some cause is so changed and affected that it cannot maintain its natural state, must of necessity be

10 *

adjudged as passive by nature. But that which is liable to and is exposed to suffering [179] declares itself subject to corruption by the very presence of its capacity for suffering.

27. If, therefore, souls lose everything they knew when held by the fetters of the body, they of necessity suffer something which forces them to don the blindness of forgetfulness. For, if they experience no change whatsoever, it is impossible for them to part with factual knowledge and at the same time preserve their previous identity, or to pass over to other states of existence without incurring the risk of change in themselves.

Be that as it may, we for ourselves think that what is one, immortal, simple, always of necessity retains its own individual nature, and is neither obligated or capable of suffering anything, as long as it thinks it is everlasting and remains steadfast within the bounds of the immortality that is its own.

For all suffering is the door [180] to ruin and destruction, a path leading to death and bringing to things inescapable dissolution. If souls feel it and yield to its touch and attacks, they have life on a basis of tenancy,[181] not handed over to them by legal purchase,[182] however differently some conclude and place confidence in their own arguments in regard to so weighty a matter.

28. However, not to depart [183] from you without having learned something—what do you mean when you say that souls, when enveloped in earthly bodies, have no recollection of the past, while when they are actually placed in bodies and are rendered almost incapable of feeling through their close union with them, they retain with unfailing tenacity in their memory things which a good many years before—if you wish, say eighty or more—they either did, or suffered, or spoke, or heard?

If it is brought about by the hindrance of the body that they do not remember the things which they used to know a long time ago before they were attached to a human body,[184] so much the more [185] ought they to forget what, shut up within bodies, they continue from time to time to do, than those they did when existing apart, not yet yoked to human forms. What withdraws recollection of former things from what has entered it, ought likewise to obliterate by complete forgetfulness the things done within it. One cause cannot bring out two mutually exclusive effects, so as to deaden the memories of some things and to permit others to be recollected by the doer.

But if souls, as you call them, are prevented by the hindrance of their body's members from remembering their activities, especially those of old, how is it that they remember[186] when established in those very bodies, and know that they are souls and that they, exalted by their quality of immortality, have no bodily substance; what rank they hold in the world of things, in what order they have been set apart by God the Father; by what means they have reached these nethermost parts of the universe; what properties they have acquired and from what circles while they were gliding [187] towards these places?

How, I say, do they know that they were very learned and have lost what they knew through the hindrance of bodies? For if it were true that union with the body brought some deterioration, then, too, this is precisely the thing they were bound not to know. To know what you were and what today you are not, is no sign of a lost memory but a demonstrative proof of one preserved.

Belief in the soul's immortality is destructive of
morality.

29. Since these are the facts, stop, I beg you, stop ap-
praising at enormous values things that are little and of
trifling importance.[188] Cease to assign man, seeing that he
is only of the proletariat,[189] to the highest classes; [190] and, to
the first ranks, seeing that he is merely counted by the head [191]
because he is destitute, has only a poor *lar*,[192] and a poor
shelter, and is never entitled to be declared of patrician [193]
lustre. For while you as true [194] supporters of right and
integrity ought to subdue arrogance and conceit on the wings
of which we are all borne aloft and are puffed up with inane
vanity, you not only hesitate to strike at [195] these evils but—
what is much more serious—you have encouraged the increase
of vices and given permanence to the incorrigibility of
wickedness.

What man is there, although he be of a character that ever
flees from the realm of infamy and shame, who, when he
hears expressly stated by the wisest of men that souls are
immortal and not subject to the laws of the fates, would
not rush headlong into every kind of shameful deed [196]—
would not, free from fear and without qualms, engage in and
trespass into unlawful things—would not, finally, gratify his
desires in everything commanded by incontinent [197] passion,
emboldened even still more by freedom from punishment?

What will prevent him from doing so? The fear of a power
above and divine judgment? And how will he be deterred by
the dread of any fear who has been convinced that he is
immortal just as is the Supreme God Himself and that by
Him no judgment against Himself can be passed, since there
is one and the same immortality in each and the one cannot

be troubled by the other in view of the identical nature of the other? [198]

30. "But the well-known penalties in the lower world and the many different kinds of punishment, what about them?" [199]

But who will be so lacking in sense and so unaware of the consequences of events as to believe that when the souls are incorruptible the shades of Tartarus can do any harm, or rivers of fire, or swamps with muddy whirlpools, or the twirlings of flying wheels? That which is not near and is actually far removed from the laws of dissolution, may be surrounded by all the flames of raging [200] rivers, rolled in mud,[201] buried by falls of overhanging rocks and by the destruction of huge mountains, yet it must of necessity remain uninjured and untouched and take to itself no sensation of deadly suffering.[202]

And, what is more, the conviction mentioned not only is a stimulus for vices giving as it does free rein to sin, but it also removes the *raison d'être* of philosophy itself and shows the futility of taking it up because of the difficulty that it leads to nothing. For, if it is true that souls know no end and march along with every century in the unbroken line of the ages, what danger is there when the virtues, by which life becomes somewhat limited and unattractive, are despised and neglected and one surrenders himself to pleasures and permits the untempered heat of wild desire to rampage through lust of every kind? The danger of falling away under indulgence and of being ruined by the enervation of vices? But how can that be ruined which is immortal, which exists forever and is not subject to any suffering? The danger of growing filthy and defiled by the hideousness of shameful acts? But how can that be befouled which has no corporeal substance? Or where can corruption place itself when there is no place in which the mark of this corruption can attach itself?

And again, if the souls approach the gates of death, as is laid down in the doctrine of Epicurus,[203] even so there is no cogent reason why philosophy should be sought out, even if it is true that by it the souls are cleansed and become pure from every uncleanness.[204] For if they pass away in common [205] and in the bodies themselves the sense of life dies and is blown out,[206] not only is it a colossal mistake but stupid blindness to curb innate passions, to restrict life within narrow limits, not to indulge nature, not to follow the behests and urgings of desire: no rewards will await you for such great toil when the day of death comes and you are freed from the body's chains.[207]

Souls possess a neutral or intermediate character.

31. A certain neutral character, therefore, and an undefined and doubtful nature of the souls, has begotten a place for philosophy and has invented a reason why it should be sought after, while, you might say, that fellow [208] is fearful of danger arising from evil deeds confessed by him and another man entertains good hopes if he does no evil and passes his life dutifully and righteously. Hence it is that among scholars [209] and men endowed with superior ability there is a controversy about the nature of the souls and some say that they are mortal and cannot partake of divine substance, but others that they are everlasting and cannot degenerate into mortal nature. This is the result of the law according to which they [210] have a neutral character: some have arguments ready at hand by which it is found they are subject to suffering and perishable, and others on the con-

trary have arguments by which it is shown that they are divine and immortal.

32. Since this is the case and since by the highest authority [211] we have received the view that the souls are established not far from the gaping jaws of death; that, nevertheless, they can be made long-lived by the gift and favor of the Supreme Ruler, if only they try and study to understand Him—for knowledge of Him [212] is a sort of leaven of life and a glue to bind together in one elements otherwise not cohesive—let them, then, having laid aside their wild and barbarous ways, take up more gentle natures, so that they can be prepared for what will be given. [213] What reason is there that we should be judged by you as stupid and brutish, if on account of these fears we have surrendered and delivered ourselves to God as liberator? Against harmful blows and the poisoned bites of serpents we often look for remedies and protect ourselves by lamina [214] brought from Psylli [215] or Marsi or other peddlers and quacks, and to prevent periods of cold and consuming heat from causing discomforts, we provide with anxious care and foresight the protection of houses and clothing.

Christian and pagan views of the soul compared.

33. Since the fear of death, that is, the destruction of our souls, threatens us, is it not true that we act from an instinct of what is good for us, an instinct by which we all love ourselves, in holding fast to Him and embracing Him who promises that He will free us from such danger, and preferring Him to our very souls, provided such transfer—right in itself—is possible? You rest the safety of your souls on your own selves and are confident that by your personal

effort you become divine; but we on the other hand promise
nothing to ourselves from our weakness, realizing that our
nature is powerless and by its own proclivities is defeated in
every struggle for anything. You, the moment you are freed
from the bonds of your bodies and depart, think wings will
be ready for you [216] to enable you to hasten to heaven and soar
to the stars; we shrink from such presumptions and do not
think it has been placed in our power to reach the world
above, holding as we do that even this is a doubtful matter,
whether we deserve to receive life and to be excepted from
the law of mortality.[217] You take it for granted that you will
return to the Lord's palace as to your own home, of your
own choice and with no one to stop you; but as for us, we
neither have hopes that this can be done without the Lord of
things nor believe that so much power and privilege is
granted any man.

34. Wherefore, since such is the case, why this unfair-
ness that we should seem to you stupid in that "credulity"
you criticize, when we see that you *believe* like things and
entertain the same hope? If we are thought deserving of
ridicule because we promise ourselves hope of this kind, the
same ridicule also awaits you who adopt for yourselves the
hope of immortality. If, moreover, you have and follow any
rational thinking, grant us also some portion of that rationality.

If Plato ⟨in⟩ the *Phaedrus*, or another of this tribe,[218] had
promised these joys to us, that is, a way to flee death, and
could provide it and redeem [219] his promises, it would have
been appropriate for us to undertake the worship of him
from whom we might expect so great a gift and favor. Now
since Christ has not only promised it but also has demonstrated by His extraordinary powers [220] that it can be fulfilled, what outlandishness do we practice or on what grounds

are we guilty of the charge of folly, if we prostrate ourselves before His name and majesty, to whom we look for both, power to flee a death of torture and to be granted life eternal?

Not only the souls but the pagan gods are of neutral character.

35. "But," they say, "if the souls are mortal and of neutral character, how can they become immortal from their neutral character?"

If we should say that we do not know this and only believe what we have heard from a more powerful authority, how will our "credulity" seem to have slipped if we believe that to the Omnipotent King nothing is hard, nothing difficult; [221] if what is impossible for us to accomplish is possible for Him and ready, as it were, to obey?

Is there anything which can oppose His desires, or does it not necessarily follow that what He wills be done? Or shall we possibly gather from our distinctions what can be done or cannot? And shall we not believe that our powers of reason are as mortal as we are ourselves and of no weight with the Supreme?

And yet, listen, you who do not believe that the souls are of neutral character and have their existence on the borderline midway between life and death: are not absolutely all whom fancy supposes to exist, gods, angels, demons [222]—or whatever other name they have—are not they also of a neutral character, tottering in the condition of their doubtful lot?

If we all grant [223] there is but one Father of things, immortal and alone [224] unbegotten, and that nothing is found prior to Him possessed of any name, it follows that all those whom fancy has believed to be gods of mortal men [225] have been either begotten by Him or brought forth by His command.[226] If they are brought forth and begotten, they are of a later order and time; if of a later order and time, they must necessarily have origin and beginnings of birth and life; and as for what makes its entrance and has a beginning of incipient life, it must necessarily have an end also.[227]

36. " But the gods are said to be immortal."

Not by nature, as became clear, but by the will and favor of God the Father. In that way, then, in which He granted the gift of immortality to the gods who were on a certain ⟨day⟩ brought forth, in the same manner will He deign to grant immortality to the souls, although savage death seems capable of blotting them out and of annihilating them in immutable destruction.

That divine Plato,[228] who expresses many worthy opinions about God which are not shared by the multitude, in that dialogue which bears the title *Timaeus*,[229] says that the gods and the world are by nature corruptible and in no way free from disintegration, but that by the will of God, the King and Chief, they are preserved by an everlasting bond.[230] For, as he states, what has been properly bound and tied together with the most perfect knots, is preserved by the goodness of God; and by no other than by Him who bound them can they, according as the case requires, be destroyed, or given the order of salvation.[231]

Consequently, if these are the facts in the matter, and no other opinion or belief is consonant with the facts, why do you show astonishment that we speak of the souls as having a neutral character, when Plato says that the deities themselves have neutral natures but that their life is made continuous and undying by the kindness of the Supreme Being?

But if by chance you do not know it and hitherto it was not understood by you owing to its novelty, then at this late date hear and learn it from Him who knows and has published it abroad—from Christ—namely that the souls are not the children [232] of the Supreme King, nor did they, begotten by Him, as is stated, begin to identify themselves and speak of themselves in terms of their essential origin [233] but that they have some other creator,[234] removed from the Supreme Being by a very great inferiority in rank and power, yet of His court and ennobled by the sublimity of their highborn stations.[235]

" Immortal souls " need never have left Heaven.

37. But if, as the story goes, the souls were the Lord's offspring and the descendants of the Supreme Power,[236] nothing would have been lacking for their perfection, since they were begotten, in that case, by most perfect virtue; [237] all would have been of one mind and one accord; they would always dwell in the royal court, and they would not, leaving behind the seats of blessedness in which they came to know and remembered the most sublime teachings, unwisely seek these earthly parts, only to pass their lives enveloped by gloomy bodies amid phlegm [238] and blood—these dung-sacks and filthy urinals! [239]

" But it was necessary that these parts, too, should be populated and therefore Almighty God sent forth the souls into so many colonies, as it were."

And of what use are men in the world, and for what reason are they essential, if we are not to believe that it was to no purpose that they had to live in this region and tenant an earthly body? [240]

" They make a certain contribution to the completing of

the integration of this mass, and unless they are added to it, this totality of the universe is imperfect and defective." [241]

Does it follow, then, that in the absence of men the world ceases to function? Will the stars not pass through their changes? Will there be no summers and winters? Will the blasts of winds grow silent and will the clouds not gather and hang low and showers not fall upon the earth to bring relief in droughty seasons? No, on the contrary, all things must of necessity travel through their courses and not depart from the continuity of the established order, even though no name of man be heard in the world and the earth remain still with the silence of unpeopled solitude. How, therefore, can it be boasted that an inhabitant had to be added to these areas, when clearly man has no contribution to make to the world's perfection, all his pursuits always look to his personal comfort, and he never deviates from his own advantage?

The earth receives no advantage from being populated.

38. For, to begin with important matters, what advantage is there to the world from the fact that mighty kings are here? What advantage that there are tyrants, lords, and all the countless other magnificent potentates; that there are generals, masters of military science, experts in the taking of cities; soldiers unyielding and utterly invincible in cavalry battles or in infantry combat? What, that there are orators, grammarians, poets; writers, dialecticians, musicians; pantomimes, mimics, actors, singers, trumpeters, flutists, and pipers? That there are runners, boxers, charioteers, bareback riders, stilt-walkers, rope dancers, jugglers? That there are pitch vendors,[242] salt dealers, fishmongers, perfumers, gold-

smiths, fowlers, weavers of winnows and baskets? That there are fullers,[248] wool combers, embroiderers, cooks, confectioners, muleteers, pimps, butchers, harlots? What do the other kinds of dealers, of professors and of arts,[244] for listing which the whole of life would be too short, contribute to the organization and constitution of the world, that it should be believed that without mankind it could not have been founded and that it would not have reached its completeness, unless the struggle of a poor and useless animal had been added to it?

Did God send the souls so that they might be evil?

39. But [245] perhaps the King of the Universe [246]—and for human lips to say this is consummate rashness—for this reason sent hither the souls begotten from Himself, that they who had been divine [247] with Him, not having any share in contact of body or the bounds of time,[248] should be sunk into human seeds, spring forth from the wombs of women, give forth and keep up the most stupid wailings, suck and drain breasts, smear and spot themselves with their own filth, then in their fright be hushed by the rocking of the nurse and by the sound of rattles.[249]

Did He send the souls [250] so that they who had recently been possessed of purity and of innocent goodness, should learn in human bodies [251] to pretend, to dissemble,[252] to lie, to cheat, to deceive, to cajole by the false humility of the flatterer; to have in mind one thing, to promise another to a man's face; [253] to lay snares, to deceive the unwary with tricky traps; by countless arts to seek out the venoms of malice and to meet the occasion, to put on the guise of fickle flattery?

Did He send the souls so that passing their days in calm and serene tranquillity, they might take on from bodies the causes by which they might become fierce and savage, might carry on hatred and enmities; sow wars among themselves; attack and overthrow states; burden themselves with and surrender themselves to the yoke of slavery; and at last become subject the one to the other's power, having changed the status into which they were born?

Did He send the souls so that being made unmindful of the truth and having forgotten what God was, they should pray to images that move not; address pieces of wood, of bronze, and stones as divinities; beg from the gore of slaughtered animals; make no mention of Himself; indeed, that some of them should even doubt that they themselves exist, or deny that anything whatever exists?

Did He send the souls so that they who in their proper habitation had been of one mind, being equals in understanding and knowledge, should, after they had put on mortal forms, be separated by differences of opinions; that what is just, useful, and right should seem to some to be one thing, to others another; that they should fight about what should be sought after and what shunned; that some should establish the limits of goods and evils [254] in one way, others differently; that desiring to know the truth of things they should be opposed by obscurity, and as if bereft of the sight of their eyes they should see nothing with certainty and be led through doubtful paths by the error of their ideas?

40. Did He send the souls that while other living beings were nourished on what sprang spontaneously into being and was produced without seeding, and looked for no shelter or covering of houses [255] or clothing, they should be burdened with the wretched necessity of building houses for themselves with the greatest expense and no end of sweat and toil;

fabricate coverings for their limbs; produce a variety of utensils for their daily need; borrow aids for their weakness from dumb animals; do violence to the earth and make it produce not its own grasses but yield up the fruits commanded; and when they had used up all their energies in subduing the earth, they might be forced to lose the hopes they placed in labor through rust, hail, drought,[256] and in the end, forced by hunger, to take to human corpses; and by gradual deterioration of the body to be alienated and separated from their human forms?

Did He send the souls so that they who, as long as they tarried with Him, never had had any longing for possessions, should here become most greedy and with insatiable desire be consumed by covetousness; that they should excavate lofty mountains and turn the hidden bowels of the earth into materials of a different designation and purpose; that at the risk of their heads they should force their way through strange nations, and in the exchange of goods should always be on the lookout for high and cheap prices; that they should exact a greedy and most unfair rate of interest, and aggravate their insomnia [257] by counting up the thousands coming from the blood of the poor; that they should be forever extending the bounds of their properties,[258] and although they were to reduce whole provinces to a single country estate, should wear away the forum by litigation for one tree, for one furrow, and bring upon themselves feuds with their friends and brothers that can never be settled?

41. Did He send the souls so that they who formerly had been gentle and strangers to rousing savage passions, should establish for themselves butcher shops and amphitheaters, places of blood and public wickedness, in the one of which they should see human beings devoured and torn to

pieces by wild beasts—see themselves slay others for no reason of guilt but for the favor and delight of the spectators and should pass those very days on which so heinous a deed was committed in general enjoyment and consecrate the holidays with gaiety; but in the other place they should tear up the flesh of poor animals, some snatching one part, some another, as is the practice of dogs and vultures; chew them up with their teeth and give them over to their most cruel belly, and that in the midst of such savage and horrid practices those whom the stringencies of poverty forbade to enjoy such tables, should bewail their lot; that they should be regarded as living blissfully happy lives whose mouths and countenance such barbarous spreads defiled?

Did He send the souls so that foregoing their divine great-ness and dignity, they should get for themselves gems, pre-cious stones, pearls, at the expense of their purity, should wind these around their necks, pierce the lobes of their ears, compress their foreheads with fillets, procure rouges to call attention [259] to their bodies, darken their eyes with mascara, [260] and though bearing the features of males, should not blush to curl [261] their hair with curlers, remove the wrinkles from the body; [262] to walk with bare knees and with every other modish fad to cast away the strength of manhood and to be enervated by the manner and dalliance of women?

42. Did He send the souls so that some should infest the highways and byways, others should lie in wait for the unwary, forge false wills, [263] brew poisoned cups; that they should break into homes at night, seduce, alienate, [264] lie and betray; that they should strike out tasty dainties for the palate; that in cooking fowls they should know how to catch the dripping fat; that they should make twisted cakes and

sausages,[265] mince meat, tit-bits,[266] Lucanian sausages, with these a sow's udder, and iced sausage?

Did He send the souls so that beings of a holy and most noble race should here practice music and the arts of the piper; that in blowing the flute, they should puff out their cheeks; that they sing smutty songs; that they raise a din by the rhythmic shakings of the castanets by which numbers of other souls should want only to give themselves up to bizarre motions of their bodies, dance, sing, jump around in circles [267] and, finally, raising their haunches and hips, should sway with the rippling motion of their loins?

Did He send the souls so that among males they become pederasts and in women harlots, sambucists,[268] harpists; that they let their bodies for hire; that they make their vileness public property—ready in the brothels, to be met with in the archways, willing to submit to anything, even ready for the defilement of their sacred mouth? [269]

If not, how did they then become evil?

43. What do you say, offspring and progeny of the Supreme Deity? Did then the souls, wise and sprung from their first causes, learn to know these kinds of profligacies, crimes, and iniquities and in order to practice, carry on, and constantly repeat these evils, did they receive orders to depart from thence [270] and dwell in these regions and be clothed with the cloak of the human body?

And is there any mortal possessed of any sense of reason, who thinks the world was established through them, and not rather that it was made by them into a seat and home in which daily every wrong might be perpetrated, all crimes take place together—conspiracies, impostures, deceits, greed, robberies, assault, wickedness, audacity, obscenity, ignominy,

infamy, all the other evils which men the world over spawn
with wicked purpose and plot for each other's ruin? [271]

Why did God not prevent the soul's degradation?

44. "But," you say, "they came by their own desire, not
sent by the King."

And where was the Almighty Father, where the authority
of His royal sublimity, that He did not prevent their departure and not allow them to fall into ruinous pleasures?
For if He knew that by changing places they would degenerate—as the Founder of all causes He should have known
—or that something from without would influence them and
would cause them to forget their dignity and honor, then—I
would ask Him a thousand pardons—there is no other cause
of all these ⟨errors⟩ [272] than Himself; yes, indeed, He suffered
them freely to stray who, He foresaw, would not preserve
the state of innocence. And so the result is that it makes no
difference whether they came of their own free will or
whether they obeyed His command, since by not forbidding
what should have been forbidden, by His carelessness He
made the fault His own and by neglecting to hold them, He
first [273] allowed it.

45. But let the heinousness of this wicked idea depart far
away, that Almighty God, the Sower and the Founder of
great and invisible things, the Creator, should be thought to
have begotten souls so fickle; [274] souls possessing no serious-
ness, character, or steadfastness; prone to slip into vices; with
a proclivity for all kinds of sins; and, when He knew that
they were such and of this kind, to have ordered them to go
into bodies, having put on which, they should in prisons [275]
daily carry on under the blasts and storms of fortune, and now

do shameful things, now suffer shameful treatment; perish in shipwrecks, catastrophes, the fires of holocausts; that poverty should press hard on some, on others beggary; that some should suffer to be torn to pieces by wild beasts; others perish by the venom of tiny flies; that some should walk with a limp, others lose their sight, others stay glued to their chairs on account of stiff joints; and, in fine, should be subjected to all the diseases which poor and pitiful mortality experiences from the agony of different punishments. Then, at last, forgetful that they are of a single source, of a single Father and Head, they should uproot and shatter the rights of kinship, overthrow their cities, lay waste their lands as enemies, enslave the free, do violence to virgins and the wives of others, hate each other, covet the joys and good fortunes of others, then, finally, all curse, revile, and mangle each other with the teeth of savagery.[276]

God did not do this because the souls are not sprung from Him.

46. But, to say the same things over and over again, let this idea, so monstrous and wicked, be far from us, that He who is the Salvation of things, the Head of all virtues, and the Acme [277] of benevolence, and—to exalt Him with human praise—the Most Wise, the Just, who makes all things perfect and retentive of the fullness of their perfection, either made anything defective or not wholly appropriate, or was to anything a cause for misfortunes or dangers or ordained, commanded, and enjoined the very acts by which human life is spent and employed, to deflect from His dispositions.

These things are beneath Him and are destructive of the power of His greatness and so far removed is He from the thought that He should be the Author of such things that the charge of blasphemous impiety [278] is incurred by anyone who imagines that from Him is sprung man, a thing unhappy and wretched,[279] who is sorry that he exists, who despises his own condition and mourns, who understands that he was begotten for no other purpose [280] than to prevent evils from being without material for their diffusion and that always there might be wretches on whose torments some lurking power and cruelty adverse to man should feed.[281]

Investigation of the true origin of the souls is pointless.

47. " But if God," you say, " is not the Parent and Father of the souls, by what source were they begotten and in what manner have they been brought forth? "

If you wish to hear the unvarnished truth, not spun out in wordy display, we likewise admit that we do not know this,[282] are ignorant of it, and the knowledge of so great a matter, we believe, transcends not only our weakness and frailty but also that of all the powers that are in the world and which in the minds of mortals have assumed the place of deities.

But because we deny that they are of God, are we obligated to show whose they are? That does not necessarily follow at all. If we were to deny that flies, beetles, and bugs, doormice, weevils, and moths, are the work of the Almighty King, it would not of consequence be demanded of us that we should say who made them and gave them a place. For without incurrring criticism we can be ignorant as to who gave them their beginning and at the same time maintain that not by the Higher God were they brought forth such useless, pointless, purposeless creatures—indeed, in some instances even bringing harm and inescapable injuries.

48. So here also, in much the same manner, when we deny that the souls are the offspring of God Supreme, it does not forthwith follow that we must explain from what parent they have been brought forth and by what causes they have come into existence. After all, who is there to forbid us either to be ignorant of whence they have taken birth and being or to know that they are not the descendants of God?

" For what reason," you say, " in what way? "

Because it is absolute truth and positive certainty that nothing, as has often been said, is done, made, or determined by the Supreme Being except what is right and becoming, except what is whole and entire and finished in the perfection of its integrity.[283]

Further, we see that men, that is, the souls themselves—for what are men but souls bound to bodies?—themselves show by the perverseness of countless vices that they are not of the noble lineage but are scions of ordinary families.[284] We see some harsh, criminal, bold, rash, reckless, blind, false, deceitful, liars, haughty, overbearing, greedy, covetous, lustful, fickle, weak, and unable to observe their own rules; which they would certainly not be if nobility derived from the Supreme Being [285] had begotten them and if they traced their high descent from the Head of the universe.[286]

Though a few men are good, the average of all men is bad.

49. " But," you will say, " there are also good men [287] in human-kind—wise, just, of blameless and wholly irreproachable character."

We are not raising the question at all as to whether at any time there were such in whom that same integrity which is referred to was lacking in no respect. Granted that they were exceptionally noble and praiseworthy, that they reached the topmost peak of perfection and in their life they at no time stumbled and fell into any fault: we would yet beg to hear how many they are or were, that from the size of their number we may gauge whether comparison has been made that is fair or evenly balanced. One, two, three, four, ten, twenty, a hundred: certainly they are limited in number and perhaps capable of being accounted for by name.

But the proper thing is to appraise and weigh humanity not by the standard of a very few good men, but by all the rest. For the part is in the whole, not the whole in the part, and the totality ought to account for the individual parts, and the parts not serve as a standard for the totality. What if you were to say, for example, that a man maimed in all his limbs and shrieking from his agony was entirely well merely because no pain was suffered in one little fingernail? Or that the earth is made of gold because in a little eminence of a single hill there are tiny grains which, when smelted, yield gold and wonder is excited when it is laboriously collected? [288]

It is the totality of the element that shows the material it is made of, not tiny particles, fine enough to be blown about, nor is the sea straightway sweet if you add or cast into it a few drops of more palatable water. The minute quantity is swallowed in its measureless mass; and that must be regarded ⟨not⟩ only as [not] [289] of little significance, but of none whatever, which, being diffused through all, loses its identity and is cut off in the great vastness of the body.

*Even the few " good " men are proof of the soul's
mortality.*

50. You may say that in the human race there are good
men, who are perhaps believed to be such as the result of
comparing them with the worst. Who are those men? Tell
us.

The philosophers, I suspect, who assert that they are alone
most wise and on the strength of this name [290] have raised
their eyebrows—yes, those who fight daily with their passions
and struggle to drive out from their souls deep-seated desires
by the persistent opposition of their virtues; who, lest they
may be allured into vices by the stimulus of some opportunity,
flee from inheritance and wealth and remove from themselves
causes for stumbling. But when they do this and take pains
about it, most clearly do they show that the souls are subject
to falling and ready from weakness to plunge into vice.

In our view, however, what is good by nature requires no
correction or chastening; nay, it should not even know what
evil is, if the individual of each class is bent on the preserva-
tion of its own integrity; for a contrary cannot be implanted
in a contrary or equality ⟨in⟩ an unequal, or sweetness be
contained in bitterness. Hence the man who struggles to
correct the innate perverseness of souls,[291] most clearly proves
himself imperfect,[292] incapable of correction, although he may
strive with every effort and firmness on the other side.

*The philosophers deal with surmises, not with
knowledge.*

51. But [293] you laugh at our reply, because when we deny
that the souls are royal progeny, we for our part do not
account for the causes and sources from which they have been

produced. But what kind of crime is it either to be ignorant of anything or to admit that you do not know what you do not know, without any pretense? And who seems to you to be the more deserving of derision, the one who claims for himself no knowledge of some shadowy thing, or the one who thinks that he himself, of himself, knows most clearly what transcends human knowledge and what is wrapped up in blind obscurities? [294]

If the nature of everything were submitted to a searching examination, your own case is similar to the one you criticize in us. Because you say that the souls come down from the King Himself and enter into human forms,[295] you are not therefore stating anything as examined and placed in the light of the clearest truth. You are merely guessing, not knowing. You merely suspect, you do not understand. For if to know is to retain in your mind what you yourself have seen or learned, none of those things which you assert can you say you ever saw, namely, that the souls come down from a home and region above.

You therefore make use of surmise, not the trustworthiness of knowledge achieved. And what is surmise except a doubtful imagining of things and a casting of the mind upon nothing that is available for examination? [296] He therefore who surmises does not possess knowledge nor does he walk in the light of it. But if this is true and certain, in the view of judges who are really such and possessed of great wisdom, that surmise of yours, in which you have confidence, must be adjudged ignorance.

Further criticism of the pagan position.

52. Now, lest you think that you alone can make use of suppositions and surmises, we also can employ them since what you ask concerns us both.

"From where," you say, "do men come, and what and whence are the souls of these same men?"

Whence are elephants, oxen, stags, mules, asses? Whence are lions, horses, dogs, wolves, panthers, and what and whence are the souls of these living beings? Certainly it is not plausible that from that Platonic bowl [297] which Timaeus prepares and mixes, their souls came or that the locust, mouse, shrew, cockroach, frog, centipede should be believed to have received the spark of life. For, what if [298] they actually have the cause and origin of their coming into being from the elements themselves, if there are present in these hidden and wholly unrecognizable means for generating animals which subsist in each of these? And here we see that some philosophers say that the earth is the mother of men; that others add water, that still others join the breath of air to those; and that some claim the sun to be their artisan and that being quickened by its heat, they are stirred by the activity of life.[299] What if it is not these either and it is something else—some other cause, some other system—some other power, finally, bearing a name unheard of by us and unknown to us, which may have fashioned humankind and fitted it into the universe's planned arrangement? Is it not possible that men could have originated in such a manner and that the authorship of their birth does not go back to the Supreme God?

What reason do we think motivated that great Plato, a philosopher of goodness above reproach, when he took away from the Supreme God the fashioning of man and gave it to some sort of lesser gods, and when he would not have the souls of the human race to be composed of that same pure mixture [300] of which he had made the soul of that universe, except that he thought the making of man unworthy of God and the fashioning of something feeble as incompatible with His exalted greatness?

53. Since, then, such is the case, it is not absurd and foolish for us to believe that the souls of men are of neutral character,[301] that is to say, they are not of the first rank,[302] subject to the law of death, of powers small and fallible; that they are endowed with the gift of immortality <if> they base their hope of so great a gift upon the Supreme God who alone has the power to bestow such immunity from corruption.

But, of course, we are stupid for believing this. What is that to you, you consummate fool, you simpleton? [303] Where do we harm you or what wrong do we do or inflict on you, if we are confident that Almighty God will have a regard for us when we begin to depart from our bodies and will, as is said, deliver us from the jaws of Hell? [304]

The problem of evil.

54. "Well, then," someone will say, "can anything happen without the will of God?" [305] We must carefully consider and examine with not a few pains, lest, while we think that we do honor to God by such a question, we fall into the opposite sin by tearing down the primacy of His majesty.

"In what way? For what cause?"

Because, if all things take place in accordance with His will, and without His assent nothing in the universe can either succeed or fail, it follows of necessity that all evils also are understood to arise by His will. But if, on the other hand, we should wish to say, not referring to Him the causes of evils, that He is aware of evil but the author of none, the worst things will begin to make their appearance either against His will or—a thing monstrous to say—while He is ignorant, unconscious,[306] and unaware of them.

And again, if we should choose to say that there are no evils, as we have found has been thought and believed by some, all races and all nations will protest loudly, showing us their tribulations and the manifold types of dangers with which at each moment the human race is harassed and tormented.

Then they will ask of us: "Why, if there are no evils, do you hold back from certain deeds and actions? Why do you not do everything which impetuous passion bids and commands? Why, finally, have you with most dreadful legislation fixed punishments for the wicked?" After all, can a more prodigious stupidity be found than to maintain that there are no evils and to condemn sinners to destruction as if they were evil?

55. When,[307] defeated, we agree that these exist and not without reason [308] admit that all human affairs abound in them, it will follow that they will ask:

"Why, then, does Almighty God not take away these evils but suffers them to exist and to march on through all the ages in steady continuance?"

If understanding comes to our aid from God the Supreme Ruler and it is not our determination to wander through unholy vagaries of conjecture, we must answer that we do not know those things and what could not be grasped by any powers we possess, we have not sought after or endeavored to know. And your reasoning [309] will be better and preferable, indeed even safer,[310] if you choose to plead ignorance and inexperience, rather than to state that except for the will of God nothing is made, which at once results in taking Him both as the instigator of evils and the author.

"Whence, then," you will say, "are all these evils?"

From the elements, say the philosophers, and from their instability. But how it is possible that things which have no sense or judgment are said to be malicious and pernicious, or that not rather He is malicious and pernicious who in order to bring about some result took on things which were bound to be extremely bad and harmful—this is a matter for the scrutiny of such as make the statement.

What, then, are we? Whence are we? [311] There is no need to answer. For whether we are able to give the answer, or are unequal to the task and cannot, in either case it is a small matter with us. Nor do we regard it as of any real significance either to be ignorant of it or to know it. We are satisfied to have established one thing only: that nothing comes from God Supreme which is harmful and destructive.[312] This we grasp, this we know, on this one truth of understanding and knowledge we stand, that nothing is done by Him except what is wholesome to all, what is pleasant, what is overflowing with joy and gladness, what has boundless and undying pleasures, what each asks in all his prayers to happen to himself, and regarding which he thinks that everything else is destructive and death-bringing.

Other philosophical questions need not be examined.

56. And all other matters, whatever they be, which usually turn up when controversial problems are threshed out—what parents they have, or who gives them their being—we neither make any effort to know nor do we give any care to inquiry and investigation of the subject; we leave all things to their causes and we do not regard them as connected with or involved in what we ask for ourselves.[313]

What is there that human ingenuity with its penchant for controversy dares not undermine, destroy, however clear and evident and secured by the seal of truth that may be which they endeavor to weaken? Or, again, what are they not able to maintain with plausible arguments, even though it is most clearly false, even though it is an evident and manifest lie? When a person has convinced himself that something exists or does not exist, he loves to assert his opinion and to outdo others in subtlety, especially if the matter under discussion is out of the ordinary and abstruse and of its nature obscure.

Certain philosophers think that the world has neither been created nor will at any time perish; [314] some,[315] that it is immortal, although they are authority for the statement that it was born and begotten; while a third group [316] are satisfied that it was born and begotten, and that as the result of the necessity common to all, it will perish. And although of these three views only one can be true, nevertheless, all have arguments by which to support their own opinions and destroy [317] and undermine the tenets of others. Regarding this same world some teach and declare that it consists of four elements; [318] others that it is formed from twin elements; [319] a third party that it is from one; [320] there are those who say that it is from none of these but that atoms [321] are its substance and primary origin. And although of these only one opinion is true, but none of them certain, here again in like manner all have arguments to hand by which to establish the truth of what they say and show up the falsehoods present in the opinions of others. So, too, some deny categorically that gods exist; [322] others say they doubt whether they exist anywhere; [323] others, to be sure, that they exist but care nothing for human affairs;[324] and others, of course, maintain that they do take part in affairs of mortals and control events on earth.[325]

57. While this is so and it cannot be otherwise than that only one of all these opinions is true, still they all battle with arguments and none of them lack something plausible to say,

whether they state their own position or dispute the views of others. It is not different and quite the same story when these people discuss the character of souls. This one, for example, thinks [326] they are both immortal and survive the death of mortals; that one does not believe they survive but perish with the bodies themselves.[327] The opinion of another is that they suffer nothing immediately, but after the human body has been put away, they are given a little longer to live,[328] then come under the laws of mortality.

And while all these opinions cannot be identified with truth, nevertheless all support them by so strong and so valid demonstrations that you can find nothing which appears false to you, although from all sides you see expressed a diversity of views and the discord of controversies. This would assuredly not take place if human desire for knowledge could achieve any certainty, or if what seems to have been discovered by anyone might be demonstrated by the approval of all others. Therefore it is a most inane thing and a purposeless task to bring something forward as if you knew it, or to wish to maintain that you know something which, even if it be true, you see can be refuted, or to accept as true what perhaps is not, and is brought forth after the manner of men deceived by their own delusions.

And this is so for a good reason. For we do not weigh and guess at divine matters by divine but by human reasoning, and just as we think something ought to have taken place, so we maintain that it must have taken place.

Pagan philosophers are ignorant about many questions.

58. Well, does it follow that we alone are ignorant, without knowledge of who is the Creator of the souls, who their

Establisher, what cause fashioned man, whence evils have burst forth, or why the Supreme King suffers them to exist and to be perpetrated and does not oust them, ward them off from human affairs? Do you know any of these things as the result of investigation and knowledge? If you care to expose your reckless guesswork—can you explain and disclose whether the world which holds us is ⟨un⟩begotten or was at some period of time established? If it was established and made, by what kind of act or because of what thing? [329] Can you bring forward and explain the reason why it does not remain fixed and immobile but is constantly being rotated in a circular path? Does it revolve of itself and by its own choice, or is it turned by the propulsion of some power? [330] What is the place itself and space [331] in which it is located and continually revolves? Is it unlimited, limited, void or solid? Does an axis, resting on pivots at its extremities, support it, or does it rather keep itself aloft by air which is carries within itself?

Can you, when you are asked, make clear [332] and demonstrate from the fullness of your knowledge, what opens out the snow into feathery flakes? For what reason and cause the dawning day [333] should not rise from the regions where the sun now sets and put out its light in the place where it now rises? How the selfsame sun by one and the same touch produces results so differing—even opposites? What the moon is? What the stars? Why the former does not always remain in the same shape, or why it was desirable and necessary that in the case of the latter those little bits of fire [334] should stud the entire body of the universe? Why some of these are smaller, others fuller and larger; why some have dim light, others a clear and shining brightness?

59. If what we wish to know is at our beck and if science

is an open matter, explain and tell us how and by what system showers come about, so that in the upper regions and in the midst of the air water is held in suspense, a thing naturally subject to falling and so ready always to flow and run downwards?

Explain, I say, and tell us what it is that hurls down hail, what makes the rain fall in drops, what causes showers to fall, spreads out the snowflakes into leafy foliage; [335] whence the wind rises and what it is; why the changes of the seasons were established, when one alone could have been instituted [336] and with it a single kind of climate, so that nothing should be wanting to the undivided state [337] of the universe.

What is the cause, what the reason, that the seas are salty or that of the waters of the land some are sweet ⟨or warm⟩, [338] others are bitter or cold? From what kind of material has the flesh [339] of human bodies grown compact and strong? Whence have the bones become solid? What has given the intestines, the veins their tubular shape and made them capable of being passed through?

Why, when it would be more practical to furnish sight to us by several eyes against the danger of blindness, are we limited to only two? For what purpose have such limitless and countless kinds of monsters and snakes been fashioned or brought forth? What business do owls, falcons, hawks have in the world? What place, the other winged creatures and flying fowls? [340] What place, the different ants and worms that grow into varied pests and dangers? What, fleas; what, pesky flies, spiders, shrews, mice, bloodsuckers, water spinners? What, thorns; what, brambles; what, wild oats; [341] what, tares? What, the seeds of grasses or shrubs either sweet to the nostrils or disagreeable in smell? Yes, if you think that anything is knowable or understandable, do tell us what wheat is, what spelt, barley, millet, chickpea, beans, lentils, honey, oil, wine,[342] the scallion, leek, onion. For though they are useful to you and are established among the ordinary kinds of foods, it is not a quick and easy matter to know just what each kind is; why they have been shaped into the forms they have; whether there was any need that they should not have other tastes, other smells, other colors, than the ones they severally have, or whether they could have taken on others also. Finally, what are these very things, taste, I mean [that is, taste],[343] and the others; from what reasons do they derive distinctions of qualities?

" From the elements," you say, " and from the first beginnings of things."

Well, are the elements bitter or sweet? Are they possessed of a certain odor, <of a certain> [344] color, that we should think that from their union qualities were imparted to what grew out of them, by which sweetness comes into being or something offensive to the senses is produced?

Christ taught us to disregard such futile questions.

60. While, therefore, the origins, the causes, the reasons, of so great and so many things escape you yourselves also, and you can neither say nor explain what has been made or wherefore, or why it ought not to have been, you would pull and tear apart our reserve, who confess that we do not know what cannot be known, and have no desire to seek out or investigate [345] what, it is most clear, cannot be understood, though human conjecture should stretch and extend itself through a thousand hearts.

And therefore Christ,[346] who, though that does not meet with your approval, is God, *Christ God*—yes, this must be

stated often for the bursting and splitting of infidel ears—
spoke by command of the Supreme God, in human form:
knowing the nature of mortals to be blind and that it cannot
understand a single truth even of things placed squarely before the eyes, that it regards as ascertained and understood
whatever it persuades itself is so, and that on behalf of its
conjectures it does not hesitate to instigate and prolong quar-
relsome discussions, He taught us to leave behind and disregard all those things, and not to spend our time on fruitless
consideration of those things which are far from our understanding. On the contrary, to the extent that is possible, we
are to approach the Lord of the universe with whole mind
and spirit, to be lifted up from these places and to commit to
Him the doubtful waverings of the heart, to be ever mindful
of Him; and although His true being escapes all imagination,
yet we should form some sort of image [347] of Him. For He
said [348] that of all things which are subsumed in the un-
fathomable mystery of exalted divinity, He alone is beyond
doubt; He alone is true, and about Him no one, except a
madman and one possessed of reckless desperation, can be in
doubt. To know Him is enough, though you have learned
nothing else; and if you have been intent upon the comprehension of God, the Head of the universe,[349] you have
achieved the true and greatest knowledge.

61. " What is it to you," He says,[350] " to examine, to investigate who made man, what origin the souls have, who
conceived the causes of evils; whether the sun is larger than
the earth, or measures only a foot across; [251] whether the moon
shines by the light of another or by its own beams? [352]

" There is no gain in knowing these things nor any loss in
not knowing them. Leave these things to God and allow Him
to know what, wherefore, and whence something is, whether

or not it had to be; whether something transcends birth[353] or has first beginnings; whether it should be annihilated or preserved, whether consumed, dissolved, or be repeatedly renewed. Your intellects are not free to involve you in such things and to trouble themselves uselessly[354] about matters so removed from you. Your own good is at stake, and I mean the salvation of your souls; and unless you busy yourselves in acquiring a knowledge of the Supreme God, grim death awaits you when you are freed from the body's bonds, not bringing sudden extinction but over a period of time consuming you by the bitterness of torturing punishment."

Magic powers and prayers cannot make the soul immortal.

62. And let not that which is said by some who have a smattering of knowledge and take a great deal upon themselves, intrigue you or flatter you with vain hope, that they are born of God and not subject to the laws of fate; that if they lead a life of fair restraint,[355] His palace lies open to them and that after the death of the body, they are brought back without any hindrance at all to their ancestral seat, as it were; nor what the magicians promise,[356] that they have intercessory prayers,[357] moved by which certain powers provide easy routes for such as are anxious to fly to heaven; nor those things which in Etruria[358] are promised in the Acherontic[359] books, that when the blood of certain animals is given to certain divinities,[360] the souls become divine and are made immune to the laws of mortality.[361] These are empty delusions and the nutriment of empty desires.

No one except Almighty God can preserve souls nor is there anyone else at all[362] who can make them long-lived and grant to them the breath of eternity, except alone Him who is immortal and eternal and limited by the restriction of no time. Since all the gods, be they true gods [363] or only said to be such by hearsay and conjecture, are immortal and eternal by reason of His will and the favor of His kindness, how is it possible that they can impart to another [364] what they themselves are, when actually they have this not as their own but as something bestowed by the might of a greater? [365]

Let them sacrifice as many victims as they wish in Etruria; let the philosophers deny themselves all that is human; let the magicians appease and cajole all powers: unless souls have received from the Lord of the universe what reason [366] demands, and that by His command, there will some day, when the feeling of death approaches, be great regret for having been an object of derision.

The fate of the centuries before Christ came.

63. " But if," they say, " Christ was sent by God for this purpose that He might free the unhappy souls from the destruction of extinction, what were the former centuries guilty of which before His coming were annihilated by the lot of mortality? "

Well, now, are you in a position to know what has happened to the souls of mortals who belong to the most ancient past, whether they too have not received help, care, and foresight of some sort? [367] Can you, I say, know what could have been learned had Christ taught it: whether the ages which have passed since the human race began to be on earth are unlimited or limited; when the souls were first united with the bodies; who was the author of that union, yes, indeed, who was the maker of man; whither the souls of former men have departed; in which regions and sections of the universe they were; whether they were corruptible or not; whether they could have approached the danger of death, had not Christ the Preserver appeared at the proper time?

Put aside these cares and leave off inquiries into things you do not understand. The King's mercy has been granted also to them, and the divine benefits have gone out to all men alike. Their souls have been preserved, their souls have been freed, and have laid aside the lot and condition of mortality.

" How is that? What? When? "

If arrogance, if pride, if conceit, were strangers to you, long since would you have been able to know these things from ⟨Christ⟩ as your authority.

Christ is no respecter of persons.

64. " But if Christ came as the Preserver of the human race, as [368] you say, why does He not free all without exception with equal kindness? "

Does He not free all alike who summons all alike? Or does He thrust away or repel anyone from the Supreme Benevolence who grants to one and all the privilege of coming to Him—to the mighty, the humble, slaves, women, children? " The fountain of life," He says, " is open to all [369] and no one is denied the right to drink or turned away." [370] If this has so little attraction for you that you refuse the kindness of the proffered favor; yes, indeed, if you are so superior in wisdom that you term what Christ offers farce and folly, what can He expect to gain by continuously inviting you,[371] when His only function is to set before you the fruit of His kindness? God, says Plato,[372] does not cause any man to choose his lot in life,[373] nor can the will of another be rightly imputed to anyone, since freedom of the will was placed in the power of the same who willed it.[374] Or must you be begged to deign to accept from God the bounty of salvation, and must the grace of divine kindness be poured into your lap while you reject it and flee far from it? Are you willing to take what is offered and to turn it to your own purposes? Then you will act to your own advantage. Do you disdain, despise, and look down on it? Then you deprive yourself of the advantage of the gift. God forces no one. He intimidates none with fear that forces obedience. And, of course, our salvation is not necessary to Him so that he would gain anything or suffer loss, were He to make us gods [375] or allow us to be annihilated in the destruction of corruption.

God grants free will to every soul and forces none.

65. "But I beg your pardon," he says, "if God is powerful, merciful, a preserver, let Him change our minds and make us to trust in His promises despite our unwillingness to do so."

Such a thing is force, not kindliness or the generosity of the Supreme God but a childish eagerness for mastery and the straining of an empty spirit.[376] For what is so unfair as to twist forcefully the desires of persons who are reluctant, who are unwilling, to the opposite; to ram down into their souls what they do not want and what they shrink from; to do them harm rather than good, and having taken away a former view to deliver them over to a view and opinion not their own? You who wish yourself to be changed and to suffer violence so that you may do and experience compulsion to do what you do not want, why do you refuse to take on voluntarily what you desire to do on being changed and transformed?

" I do not want to," he says, " and I have no desire."

Well, then, why do you accuse God as if He were remiss in bringing aid to you when you long for it, He whose gifts and favors you not only scornfully reject and flee but also term them empty talk and make them the subject of witty jokes?

Christ is the only hope of salvation.

" Then, unless I become a Christian, I cannot have the hope of salvation? "

Yes, just as you state. For the office [377] of granting salvation and of giving to the souls what was proper to be bestowed and necessary to be added, He alone holds it, as a trust and commission from God the Father—an arrangement based on reasons that escape us in their profundity.

For as with you certain gods have certain spheres of influence, prerogatives, powers, and you do not demand of any one of them what is not within his power and privilege, so it is the power and right [378] of Christ alone to give salvation to the souls and to assign them the breath of eternity.

To illustrate: if you believe that Father Liber [379] can give a vintage, cannot give a cure; if you believe that Ceres can give crops, Aesculapius [380] health, Neptune one thing, Juno [381] another; that Fortuna,[382] Mercury, Vulcan,[383] are each givers of certain and particular things: then you must also accept this necessarily from us, that from no one can the souls receive the power of life and of safety from harm except from Him whom the Most High King has placed over this duty and office. The Almighty Ruler has willed this to be the way of salvation, this, as it were,[384] to be the door [385] of life, through which [386] alone is entrance to the light; and there is no other possibility, either of creeping in or walking in: everything else has been closed off and secured by an impregnable bulwark.[387]

The charge that Christianity is new is wholly unfair.

66. Therefore, though you are pure and have been cleansed from every stain of vices, have won over those powers and prevailed upon them ⟨not to⟩ close the roads and erect barriers to your passage on your return to heaven, you will not be able to arrive at the reward of immortality by any struggles unless you understand through Christ's gift what constitutes immortality and have received admission to the true life.

For in regard to the charge you are wont to throw up against us, that our religion is a new one,[388] and arose only a few days ago, as it were, and that we should not have abandoned the religion of our fathers to be led over into barbarous and foreign rites,[389] this is urged entirely without reason. For what would you say if in this manner we should wish to throw blame on those ages of long ago because when crops [390] were discovered, they despised acorns and rejected wild berries; [391] because they stopped covering themselves with barks of trees [392] and wrapping themselves in skins, once woven clothing was devised, more useful and convenient to wear; or because when houses were built and more elegant dwellings were introduced, they lost their affection for their little old huts and preferred not to lie under rocks and in caves like the beasts?

It is a trait shared by all men and handed down almost from the cradle itself to prefer good things to bad, to place the useful before the useless, and to strive after and to seek for that which proves itself more valuable and pleasing, and to base on it the hope of well-being and the things that promote welfare.

The pagans have also been guilty of adopting novelties.

67. And so, when you urge against us abandonment and deviation [393] from former centuries, you should look at the reason, not the fact, and not set forth against us what we have abandoned but examine what in particular we have followed. If it is any fault or crime at all to change an opinion, and to leave behind ancient institutions for other things and bents that are new, such an indictment also involves you who many times have changed your manner of living and practice, who have transferred to other habits and other ceremonies with the condemnation of the past. [394]

Do you, for instance, have the people divided into five classes, as your ancestors formerly had them? [395] Do you choose officials by popular vote? Do you know what military, city, and popular assemblies [396] are? Do you observe the sky and do you cause a cessation of public functions when adverse omens are reported? [397] When you are preparing for war, do you put out a standard on the citadel? [398] Or do you observe the fetial laws? [399] Do you by an official threat of war demand the return of plunder? Or when in a crisis you turn to Mars, do you take hope from the spearhead auspices? [400]

When entering upon offices, do you observe the laws relating to the appointed year? [401] In the matter of gifts,

presents, do you obey the Cincian laws? [402] In restricting
expenses, do you obey the laws of the censors? [403] Do you
maintain, as formerly, ever-burning fires on the innermost
hearths? [404] Do you consecrate tables by the placing of salt-
cellars [405] and with images of the gods? When you enter
wedlock, do you spread the couches with a toga and do you
invoke the genii of married couples? [406] Do you stroke the
hair of brides with the bachelor's lance? [407] Do you carry the
togas of the girls to the temple of Fortuna Virginalis? [408] Do
your matrons work in the atria of their homes displaying their
industry? [409] Do their relations by marriage and their kins-
men have a right to kiss them,[410] to prove that they are sober
and abstemious? [411]

68. On the Alban Mountain [412] in ancient times it was not
permitted to sacrifice other than snow-white bulls: [413] have
you not changed that custom and observance and has it not
been enacted with the approval of the senate that reddish
ones may be offered? While during the reigns of Romulus
and Pompilius [414] the inner organs, thoroughly cooked and
made soft,[415] were burnt up to the gods, did you not begin
under King Tullus,[416] with disregard of the ancient custom,
to offer these to them half-raw and slightly warmed? [417]

While prior to the coming of Hercules to Italy, at the
instance of Apollo sacrifice was made to Father Dis [418] and to
Saturn with human heads, have you not again with a bit of
clever deceit and some playing on words [419] changed this
custom? Since you yourselves have followed at one time
those customs, at another other usages, and when mistakes
were recognized and better things were observed as such,
you rejected, repudiated many things, what have we done
contrary to common sense and judgment,[420] if we have given
preference to the great and the certain, and have not suffered

ourselves to be held back by any religious scruples regarding frauds?

Did not all things once have a beginning?

69. But our name is new and the religion which we follow was born but a few days ago. To grant for the moment that the objection made to us is not a false premise, what is there in human affairs that is either done by the work of the body and with the hands, or is mastered by the training and perception of the mind alone, which did not at some time have a beginning and enter into the practice, the experience of mortals?

Medicine, philosophy, music, and all the other arts upon which life is built and refined—did these originate at the same time as human beings? Rather, was it not in modern times— indeed, practically just a short time ago—that these began to be practiced, understood, and to receive universal recognition? Before Tages [421] the Etruscan touched the shores of light,[422] was any man aware or did he trouble himself about knowing and learning whether there was any significance in the fall of thunderbolts or in the veins of the entrails? When did the movements of the stars or the practice of horoscopy begin to be known? Was it not after Theutis the Egyptian [423] or after Atlas [424]—as some say—the bearer, carrier, pillar, and mainstay of heaven?

Even the pagan gods had a beginning.

70. But why do I speak about such trifles? The immortal gods themselves, whose shrines you now approach and whose divine powers you pray to as suppliants, did not they, as is stated in your records and in your beliefs, begin to exist,[425]

to be known at definite times, and to be designated by the nomenclature given them?

If, for example, it is true that from Saturn and his wife Jupiter was begotten with his brothers, before Ops was married and bore issue, Jupiter never existed, both the supreme Jupiter and the Stygian; [426] nowhere was the lord [427] of the sea, nowhere was Juno; nay, more, no one lived in the seats of heaven save only the two parents, but from their embrace they were conceived and born and drew the breath of life. At a definite time, therefore, Jupiter began to exist as a god; at a definite time to receive worship and sacrifices as his due; at a definite time to be preferred before his brothers in powers.

And again, if Liber, Venus, Diana, Mercury, Apollo, Hercules, the Muses,[428] the Castors, sons of Tyndareus,[429] and Vulcan, the lord of fire, were begotten by Father Jupiter and fathered by a parent of Saturn's line, before Memoria,[430] before Alcmene,[431] Maia,[432] Juno,[433] Latona,[434] Leda,[435] Dione,[436] and then also Semele,[437] became pregnant from cohabitation with Diespiter,[438] then these, too, had no previous existence anywhere [439] or in any part of the universe, but they were begotten and born from intercourse with Jupiter and began to have some consciousness of themselves. These, too, therefore, began to exist at a definite time and receive ritual invocation as belonging to the holy divinities, which same thing we may say in like manner with regard to Minerva. If, as you state, she sprang from the brain of Jupiter, unbegotten, before Diespiter was generated and received the forms and shape of his body in the womb of his mother, it is of course certain that Minerva did not exist and was not counted among things or as having any substance at all; but from the moment she was born from Jupiter's head, she, too, began to be something established in reality. She, therefore, has a primal origin and at a definite time began to be called a goddess, set up in holy temples, and to be consecrated by inviolable religion.

Since these are the facts, when you speak of the novelty of our religious observances, do your own not come to mind, and do you not trouble yourselves to see when your gods originated, what sort of origins they had, what caused them to be, or from what roots they have burst forth into the light of day? Moreover, how shameful, yes, how shameless to criticize another for what you see yourself doing, to seek an occasion for depreciation and incrimination which can in turn be used as counter-charge against you!

The pagan religion is not more than two thousand
years old.

71. But what we are doing is new: and what you are doing is outdated and too encumbered by antiquity. And how does that either help you or detract from our cause and argument? The thing which we cherish is new, and some day it, too, will become old: what you are doing is old but in the times when it began, it was new and suddenly there. The authority of a religion, however, is not to be appraised in terms of time but by the divinity it worships and it is proper for you to examine not on what day you begin to worship but what.

" Four [440] hundred years ago your religion," he says, " did not exist."

And your gods did not exist two thousand years ago.

" By what computations or what calculations can that be deduced? "

Not by difficult ones, not by abstruse ones, but by those

which anyone may see and feel, as the saying goes, in his hands.[441]

Who begot Jupiter with his brothers? [442]

" Saturn," as you say, " sprung from Caelus [443] and Hecate,[444] on the marriage couch with Ops."

Who begot Picus,[445] father of Faunus and grandfather of Latinus?

" Saturn," as you likewise hand down in your writings and authors. Therefore, if this is so, it follows that Picus and Jupiter are united to each other by the ties of kinship, since they were begotten from one blood and one seed.

" Obviously it is as said."

How many generations are there from Jupiter and Picus down to Latinus?

" Three, as the line of descent shows."

Are you willing to agree that Faunus, Latinus, and Picus, lived a hundred and twenty years each? As you know, beyond this it is denied that the life of man can be prolonged.[446]

" The reckoning is correct and clear."

There have been then full three hundred and sixty years since their time?

" The fact is as the calculation shows."

Whose father-in-law was Latinus?

" Aeneas'."

Aeneas [447] was the father of whom?

" Of ⟨Ascanius,⟩ the founder of the town of Alba."

How long was there a kingdom at Alba?

" Almost four hundred and twenty years."

What age do the annals indicate for the City of Rome?

" It is a thousand and fifty [448] years old, or not much less than that."

Therefore, from Jupiter, who is the brother of Picus and

also the father of the lesser and the remaining gods, to the present time, there are nearly two thousand years,[449] or if we give good measure, fully that.

Since this cannot be refuted, not only is the religion which you follow shown to be recently arisen, but the gods themselves, to whom you pile up bulls and other victims with the risk of corruption,[450] hitherto are infants and small fry who ought still to be fed from breasts and on drops of milk.[451]

Christianity is not really new but only recently revealed.

72. But your religious observances precede the one we espouse by many years, and for that reason they are truer because fortified by the authority of age. And of what use is it that they are senior by ever so many years, since they began at a specific time, or of what length are two thousand years compared with so many millennia?

And lest, however, we seem to betray our cause by such long hedging, tell us, if it is not asking too much: does the Almighty and First God seem to you to be something new, and those who reverently worship Him to be devising and introducing religious observances that are unheard of, unknown, suddenly on the scene? Is there anything older than He? Or can anything be found that precedes Him in being, time, name? Is He not the only one uncreated, immortal, and alone eternal? Who is the Head and Fountain of things? Is not He Himself? To whom does eternity not owe the very fact that it is called eternity? Is it not to Him?

Is not the fact that the ages proceed in infinite succession effected from His eternity? This is beyond question and true. Therefore, not what we follow is new, but late in time we have learned what we should follow ⟨and⟩ cherish, or where it is proper to place our hope of safety and to apply the aids leading to salvation. Not yet had He shone forth who was to point out the way to the straying [452] and to let in the light of understanding to those standing in deepest darkness,[453] and to strike away the blindness of their ignorance.

Foreign deities have been introduced into the pagan pantheon.

73. But is a charge of this sort turned alone against ⟨us⟩? Tell me, did you after the consulship of Piso and Gabinius [454] not bring into the number of your gods the Egyptian divinities named Serapis [455] and Isis? [456] Yes, did you not begin to know and be acquainted with and to hallow with inviolable [457] sanctity the Phrygian mother,[458] said to have been founded by Midas [459] or Dardanus, when the Punic Hannibal [460] was plundering the wealth of Italy and claiming world dominion?

Is it not an established fact that the rites of Mother Ceres [461] are called " Greek," because they were unknown to you, taken over a little while ago, their name witnessing to their very newness? Do not the writings of the learned [462] contain the fact that the rituals of Pompilius [463] are unacquainted with the name of Apollo? From which fact it appears and is clear that he was also unknown to you, but afterwards at some later time began to be known.

Should anyone, therefore, ask you why you have so lately undertaken the worship of those divinities to whom we have made allusion, it is certain that you will answer—either: " because we were recently unaware that they belonged to the gods," or " because now we have been put in mind of them by the seers," or " because in most adverse circumstances we have been preserved by their kindness and assistance."

But if you consider this to be a proper answer, then consider that from our side, too, a reply was made after the same fashion. Our religion has just now come into existence, for just now has He arrived who was sent to reveal it to us, to lead us into its truth, to show us what God is, to call us away from things that are merely imaginary to His worship.

The reason for the late revelation is unknown to man.

74. " And why," he says, " did God the King and Prince decide that barely a few hours ago, as it is said, Christ should be sent from the heights of heaven as Savior? " [464]

On the other hand, we ask you also: what cause, what reason is there, that sometimes the seasons do not return in their months, but winters occur later, summer and autumn later also? [465] Why does it occasionally happen that after the crops have been parched and the harvests destroyed, rains fall, which should have come down while things were still unharmed, serving the needs of the times? Rather, let us ask this: if Hercules had to be born, if Aesculapius, [466] Mercury, Liber, and some others, so that they could be added to the councils of the gods and bring something useful to mortals, why were they given forth by Jupiter so late, that only the period of those who came after would know them while the past age of their predecessors remained unacquainted with them? You will say that there was some reason. Here also there was a reason, therefore, why the Savior of our race should come not recently but today.

" What, then, is the reason? "

We are not denying that we do not know. It is impossible for anyone to see the mind of God, or how He has arranged His affairs. Man, a blind animal and one who does not know himself, has no means whatever by which to arrive at what ought to be done, when, or in what manner; the Father of all things Himself knows, the Ruler [467] and Lord alone knows. Nor, if I shall be unable to explain to you the causes why something takes place in this way or that, does it straightway follow that what was done becomes undone and that a thing loses its plausibility which was shown to be beyond doubt by so many kinds of miracles [468] [and by the powers] of powers.

Christ came in the fullness of time.

75. You may object and rejoin: "Why was the Savior sent so late?"

In limitless, everlasting ages nothing at all must be called late. Where there is no end and beginning, nothing is too early, nothing late. For time is recognized as such from beginnings and endings which a succession and unmeasured duration of ages cannot have.

Moreover, what if the very situation, [469] to which it was necessary to bring help, demanded precisely that as the opportune time? What if ancient times had one kind of circumstances, following ages another? What if it was necessary to give aid to the ancients in one way, to care for later men in another? Do you not hear, remembering your own writings, that there once were men who were demigods, heroes, with enormously huge bodies? Do you not read of infants a hundred feet long [470] giving forth a wail on the breasts of their mothers, whose bones dug up [471] in different parts of the world made their discoverers hardly credit them as the remains of human limbs?

It can be, therefore, that Almighty God, who alone is God, sent Christ forth only when the race of men began to be more frail and our nature weaker. If what has been done today, could have been done thousands of years ago, the Supreme King [472] would have done it: or if these same thousands of years hence it were necessary for what has been done today to be fulfilled, nothing forced God to refrain from waiting the necessary measures of time. His affairs are administered in fixed ways and what once has been determined to be done cannot be superseded in any way.

Why does God permit the persecution of the Christians?

76. " Why,[473] therefore," he says, " if you serve the Almighty God and trust that he has care for your health and safety, why does He suffer you to suffer through so many persecutions and to undergo every kind of penalty and punishment? "

And now let us ask in turn why, in the face of the fact that you worship so many gods and establish for them holy temples, fashion images of gold, slaughter herds of animals, pile up all the boxes of incense upon full altars, why you do not spend your days immune to so many dangers and storms, by which fatal fortunes of so many kinds press you each day. Why, I say, do your gods fail to avert from you so many kinds of diseases and ailments, shipwrecks, catastrophes, fires, epidemics, barrenness, loss of what you have pledged,[474] and confiscation of property; dissensions, wars, feuds; captures of cities and enslavements, with loss of freeborn rights?

But to us also God grants no help at all in such misfortunes. The reason is plain and clear. Nothing has been promised us by God in respect to this life,[475] nor has any aid been pledged to us or help decreed to those established in the husk of this petty flesh.[476] Indeed, we have been taught to consider

and value as of small import all the threats of fortune, whatever they are, and if ever any particularly serious blow assails
us—and this must come to an end—to acquiesce willingly [477]
in misfortune and not to fear or flee so that the more easily
we may put off our bondage of body and escape the shadows
of blindness.

Persecution is really a deliverance from the body.

77. And so that bitterness of persecution of which you
speak is our deliverance, not persecution, nor will our being
harassed bring punishment to us but will bring us out to the
light of freedom. It is the same as if some stupid dullard
should think that a man put into a prison ⟨without⟩ an
exit [478] was not receiving, when subjected to questioning by
torture, penalties sufficiently severe and frightful, unless he
rage against the prison itself, demolish it and burn the roof,
wall, doors, and strip off, throw down, dash down the other
parts of the building, ignorant of the fact that thus light was
being given to the one he thought he was injuring, and that
the accursed darkness was being removed. In the same way
you do not snatch life from us by flames, banishments, tortures, beasts, with which you tear in pieces and rend our
bodies, but you take hides and skins,[479] unaware that to the
extent you attack and continue to rage against these our
shadows and forms, to that extent you free us from tight and
heavy bonds and, cutting through the knots, make us fly
upward to the light.

*Amid persecutions let us entrust ourselves to God
alone.*

78. Wherefore, men, cease by senseless investigations to
obstruct your hopes, nor if anything is otherwise than you

think, ought you to trust your own beliefs rather than an august thing. The times, full of dangers, press us, and deadly penalties threaten.[480] Let us flee to the God of salvation [481] and not insist on the reason for the gift offered. When it is the salvation of our souls and ourselves that is involved, something must be done even without a reason, as Arrian [482] assents to what Epictetus said. Though we were to hesitate, though we were to doubt and were to suspect that what is said is not fully worthy of belief: let us entrust ourselves to God, and let not our unbelief prevail more with us than the greatness of His name and power. Otherwise, while we of ourselves are seeking for ourselves arguments to make that seem false which we want [483] to be and strive to make true, the last day may steal upon us and we may be found in the jaws of the enemy—death.[484]

BOOK THREE

Pagan Gods are Really Anthropomorphic

The Christian religion needs no defense from pagan witnesses.

1. All these charges, or to label them for what they actually are, these diatribes, have long ago been answered with all the detail and accuracy required, by men who are masters in this field and who are entitled to know the truth in the matter; [1] and no single point of any question has been passed over without being subjected to rebuttal in a thousand ways and on the strongest grounds. Therefore, there is no need to linger longer on this part of the case. For neither is truth unable to stand without supporters, nor will the fact that the Christian religion has found many to agree with it and has gained weight from human approval prove it true. It is satisfied to rest its case upon its own strength and upon the basis of its own truth. It is not despoiled of its force though it have no defender, no, not even if every tongue oppose it and struggle against it and, united in hatred, conspire to destroy faith in it.

Resumption of the argument after the digression on the soul.

2. Now let us go back to the point which we had to abandon a little while ago,[2] to prevent our defense, if interrupted any longer, from being said to have conceded to our

detractors the prize of a proven charge. They have this to put forward:

"If religion means anything to you, why do you neither worship the other gods with us nor reverence them nor join our [3] nations in common sacrifices and a united religious ceremonial?"

Tentatively we can say this: in attending to the worship of the Godhead, the First God—the First God, I repeat—the Father of things and the Lord, the Establisher and Governor of all things, is enough for us. In Him we worship everything that must be worshipped. We pray to what we ought to pray to. We serve with the acts of reverence what demands the homage of reverence. For when we hold to the Head of divinity itself from which the divinity of everything divine is derived, we think it superfluous to ⟨go⟩ through them all one by one individually: we simply do not know who they really are and what they are called and, furthermore, we cannot clearly understand or establish how many they are.

If the gods really exist, Christians worship them in rendering homage to the Supreme God.

3. And as in earthly kingdoms we are forced by no necessity to show reverence by name to those who, along with the sovereigns, compose the royal families, but whatever respect is attached to them is tacitly understood to be implied in homage to the kings themselves, so in precisely the same manner, these gods, whoever they are whom you suggest for our worship, if they are royal in descent and are sprung from the primal Head, though they receive no worship from us by name, nevertheless understand that they receive homage in common with their king and are included in acts of reverence accorded Him.

And this, let me state, has been put thus only if it is clear and agreed that in addition to the King and Prince Himself there are other divine individuals [4] who when sorted out and counted, form, as it were, a sort of plebeian mass.

And please do not show us, instead of gods themselves, likenesses of gods in the holy temples and, at that, images which you also understand—but [5] refuse and are unwilling to admit—are shaped from the commonest clay and the childish fabrications of craftsmen. And when we speak of what concerns divinity, we demand you show us this, that there *are* other gods,[6] in nature, power, name—not such as are merely represented in visible images which we see, but in that substance in which it is fitting that the power that goes with so great a name ought to be believed to exist.

Where and how did the pagan gods receive their names?

4. But in this part of the discussion I do not purpose to tarry lest we seem to be wishing to stir up conflicts of the most serious proportions and to sow the seeds of riotous contests.

Let the mob [7] of divinities exist, as you state; let there be countless families of gods—we agree, assent, shut our eyes, nor do we by any form of questioning puncture the doubtful and equivocal position which you hold. Nevertheless, we demand to know from you—and we ask you the source of your information and how you came to grasp it—whether *these* gods in whose existence you believe and whom you worship, are actually in heaven; or whether it is some others, whose existence and identity still remain to be heard of. For it is indeed possible that those you do not think of as existing do exist and that those you are sure of are nowhere to be found. You know, you have never flown up to the stars of heaven, looked at the face and features of each, and, remembering the gods you saw there, began to worship them as known and seen.

But again we here ask also whether they got from you these names by which you call them, or assumed them themselves on the days of purification.[8] If these names *are* divine and celestial, who told them to you? But if they got these names of theirs from you, how could you give appellations to those you never saw,[9] and of whom you did not have the slightest knowledge as to what they were or who they were?

How many pagan gods are there?

5. But—as you wish and believe and have persuaded yourselves—let these be gods; let them also be called by those names by which the common herd [10] considers them [11] to be listed. But how can you decide [12] if the ones known by names complete the census of this class or whether there are any unknown to you and who were never introduced to your worship [13] and acquaintance? Evidently, it is not readily known whether their multitude is fixed and certain as to number [14] or whether it is without any maximum number and not limited at all. Let us, for example, imagine that you worship a thousand gods—no, let it be five thousand: but in the universe [15] there are possibly a hundred thousand gods! There can be more. Yes, as we said a moment ago, it is possible that the sum total of the gods is unnumbered, unlimited.[16]

Therefore, either you also are lacking in piety who omit your duties toward all but a few gods, or, if you ask pardon for your ignorance of the others, you will win the same pardon for us also, when in precisely the same way we refrain from worshipping those we do not know in the least.

Criticism of anthropomorphic gods.

6. And yet let no one think that we are perversely unwilling to take upon ourselves allegiance to the other divinities, whoever they are. For we raise up devout spirits and our hands in supplication, and we do not refuse to go wherever you invite us, provided only we learn who those " divine beings " are whom you urge upon us and who may rightly be associated with the Supreme King and Prince in worship.

" Saturn," he says, " and Janus are such; Minerva, Juno, Apollo, Venus, Triptolemus, Hercules, and the rest [17] to whom antiquity in reverence dedicated magnificent temples in almost all the cities."

Perhaps you could have summoned us to the worship of those " divinities," had you not yourselves been the first to fabricate such stories about them with the foulness of shameful fancies, as not only to smear their reputation but to demonstrate by the characters you assigned them the fact that they do not exist at all. [18]

For in the first place we cannot be induced to believe this, that that [19] immortal and most extraordinary nature goes by a division of sexes, one part males, the other part females. [20] This point, indeed, has long ago been fully expounded by men of genius [21] both in the Roman and in the Greek languages, and Tullius, [22] before all others the most eloquent of the Roman race, having feared no hostility from a charge of impiety, has nobly, firmly, and freely shown with greater piety what he felt about such fancy. Now, if you proceed to accept from him judgments corresponding to fact rather than his brilliant language, this case would have reached its concluding phase, nor would it demand of us, who compared with him are mere youngsters, any ' second pleadings,' [23] as they are called.

Some would burn not only Christian books but also Cicero's.

7. But why should I say that men seek him out for word-catching [24] and brilliance of diction, when I know that there are not a few who loathe and shun his books on this topic [25] and are unwilling to lend their ears to some reading which would refute their prejudiced opinions; when I hear others angrily muttering and saying that " the Senate ought to decree the destruction [26] of those writings " by which the truth of the Christian religion is demonstrated and the influence of antiquity is counteracted?

Yes, if you are certain that you are saying something about your gods which has been shown by examination to be true, then by all means convict Cicero of error; refute, rebut, and prove that he is forever given to rash and impious talk. For assuredly to do away with written works and to want to suppress a text is not to defend the gods but to fear the evidence of the truth.

Christians do not believe that God has sex.

8. Now, lest some heedless person should in turn falsely accuse us, as though we believe God whom we worship to be male [27]—the reason being, of course, that when we speak of Him we employ the masculine gender—let him not understand sex but that His name and designation is so expressed according to the usage of everyday speech. For God is not male [28] but His name is masculine in gender, something you

in your religion cannot say. You are accustomed in your prayers to say "whether thou art god or goddess," [29] a doubtful expression which makes clear from the very distinction that you attribute sex to the gods.

We therefore cannot be induced to believe that the gods have bodies; [30] for, if they are males and females, bodies must be distinguished by separation of genders.[31] But who with ever so small a trace of sense does not know that that Founder of all earthly creatures has established and fashioned the sexes of different genders for no other reason than that through marital intercourse of bodies, a thing that is prone to fall and lapse may be perpetuated and renewed through an eternal succession? [32]

9. Now, then, shall we say that gods beget, that gods are born, and that they have been given reproductive organs to make them equal to the task of bearing offspring,[33] and that with the arrival of each new spawning, a recurring substitution might supply what the former age took away? Well, if such is the case, that is, if the gods above procreate and under [34] these laws of sex live together and are immortal, not growing impotent with the frigidity of old age, the whole universe then ought to be full of gods and countless heavens incapable of accommodating their multitude, for, on the one hand, they themselves are constantly begetting, and, on the other hand, increased through offspring of offspring, their numberlessness is ever multiplied. Or if, as is proper, the obscenity of intercourse is far from the gods, what cause or reason will be pointed out why they are distinguished from each other in those places by which the sexes customarily recognize each other, prompted by their own desires? It is improbable that these anatomical organs exist without a purpose [35] or that nature wanted to play a wicked trick [36] on

them by affixing to them these parts for which there would be no use. As hands, feet, eyes, and other members have been established for certain purposes, each for its own duty, so it is logical to believe that *these* parts have been provided for the performance of their proper function; or one must confess that in the bodies of the gods there is something purposeless, fashioned vainly and uselessly.

10. What have you to say, you holy and undefiled priests of the religions? Do the gods, then, have sexes, and do they carry about them the hideousness of the genital organs, to mention which by their names is disgraceful for modest mouths? What, then, remains for us except to believe that after the manner of filthy quadrupeds they are transported into madnesses of passions, enter with raging desires into mutual embraces and in the end, their bodies broken and dissipated, become feeble through the disintegration of lust?

And since there are functions peculiar to the female sex, we must then believe that goddesses, too, fulfill the conditions that bind them when the months roll round, conceive and remain pregnant with nausea, suffer miscarriages,[37] and in premature delivery sometimes give birth to seven-month infants.

O pure, o holy divinity, and separated and detached from every blot of shame! Lust is eager and burns to see in those great halls [38] and in the palaces of heaven, gods and goddesses with bodies uncovered and naked—Ceres, " full-breasted," as the muse of Lucretius [39] says, " from Iacchus "; the Hellespontian Priapus [40] among the virgin and mother goddesses, carrying about the things that are ever ready for the encounter of battles. It is eager, I say, to see pregnant goddesses, goddesses with child, with their bellies daily swelling in size; some faltering with the irksomeness of their inner burden;

others giving birth after long delay and seeking the midwife's hands; still others shrieking, writhing as agonizing pangs and acute pains stab them, and through it all imploring the aid of Juno Lucina.[41]

Is it not far better to abuse, to revile the gods and to heap other indignities upon them than under pretense of piety to stoop to imagining such monstrous ideas about them?

Not Christians but pagans thus insult the gods.

11. And you dare to charge us with offending the gods, although, if the matter come to trial, it will be found that such offense most certainly is on your side and that it involves a disgrace ⟨other⟩ than you think![42] For if the gods, as you say, are moved with anger and mentally grow hot with indignation,[43] why should we not think they take it badly, very badly indeed, that you ascribe to them sexes with which dogs and pigs are formed, and that, since you believe this, this is precisely the way you represent them and that you make a disgraceful spectacle of them?

Such, then, being the case, it is you who are the cause of all woes, you urge on the gods, you arouse them to inflict the lands with every evil and daily to raise up new misfortunes by which they can take vengeance in irritation at suffering so many wrongs and slanders from you. By slanders, I say, and wrongs, which, partly in your shameful tales, partly in the disgraceful beliefs, your theologians,[44] your poets, you yourselves, too, celebrate in shameful ceremonies, you will find that human affairs are ruined and that the gods have thrown away the helm, if indeed the guidance and disposition of men's fortunes is their concern. For with us they certainly have no reason to be angry whom they see and perceive neither worshipping nor mocking them, as it is said, and thinking, believing much more worthily than you concerning the dignity of their name.

The shapes of the gods are anthropomorphic.

12. Enough about sex.[45] Now let us come to the appearance[46] and shapes by which you believe that the gods above are defined, yes, in which you fashion them and place them in the most splendid quarters of the temples.

And here let no one bring up against us Jewish fables[47] and those of the sect of the Sadducees,[48] as though we also attribute forms[49] to God, for this is thought to be said in their writings and corroborated as if certain[50] and authoritative. These stories have nothing to do with us, absolutely nothing in common with us, or if, ⟨as⟩ is thought, they do share something with us, you must seek out teachers of higher wisdom and learn from them how you may best remove the clouds that obscure those writings.

Our opinion on this matter is as follows: all divine essence, which neither at any time began to be nor at any time will come to an end of life, is without features of body and possesses nothing like the forms by which the external delimitation of members usually defines and bounds the body's frame. For whatever is like this, we think is mortal and subject to perishing, and we do not believe anything can attain to life eternal which an unavoidable end hems in, however remote the terms of its existence.

13. But as for you, you are not satisfied to enfold the gods in the measured limits of forms—you even confine them to human shape,[51] and what is far more degrading, you restrain them to the configuration[52] of earthly bodies.

What are we to say then? That the gods bear a head com-

pressed [53] into a smooth roundness, bound to the back and to
the chest by a network of muscles, and that for the necessary
bending of the neck it is supported by combinations of verte-
brae and by a bony foundation? Now, if we assent to this
as true, it follows that they have ears pierced by curved
windings, rolling eyeballs, shaded by fringes of eyebrows; a
raised conduit,[54] nostrils, through which the snivelling and
air may pass; teeth for the mastication of foods, of three
kinds [55] and adapted to a threefold function; hands to serve
for tasks, made facile of motion by jointed fingers and flexible
elbows; feet for supporting their bodies, regulating their
steps, and prompting the initial motions of walking.

But if there are these obvious things, logically there must
also be those which are hidden away under the framework of
the ribs by the skin and by the fatty membranes—the wind-
pipes, stomachs, spleens, lungs, bladders, livers, tracts of
winding intestines and the veins of scarlet blood coursing
through all the flesh and joined with the arteries which bear
the air.[56]

14.   Do the bodies of the denizens of heaven possibly lack
these ugly things? And because they abstain from mortal
foods,[57] are we to believe that like little ones they are tooth-
less, and are without all inner organs, inflated like bladders,
hanging there, because of the emptiness of their swollen
bodies? If this is so, you must ponder carefully whether the
gods are all alike or have different shapes and contours.[58]
For if each and every one has an identical shape, it is not
unreasonable to suppose that they make mistakes and err in
recognizing each other. If, however, they differ in features,
one must then understand these dissimilarities to have been
given them for no other reason than that they might be able
to recognize each other by the peculiarities of distinguishing

marks. So it must be said that some among them are big-heads,[59] beetle-brows, broad-heads, blubber-lips; [60] other are long-chinned, have moles and big noses; some have broad nostrils, others are snub-nosed; some with bulging jaws or chubby-faced [61] by reason of their puffed cheeks; dwarfed, tall, middling, lean, plump, fat; here some curly-locks with crinkled hair; others with shining bald pates. Your workshops also indicate and declare that our opinion is not false, since in fashioning, forming the gods, you represent some with long hair, others as smooth-shaven, [calm] [62]—old men, youths, boys, swarthy, fair-skinned, tawny, half-naked, uncovered, or, lest cold cause discomfort, covered with flowing garments thrown over them.

15. Does any man, affected even by a tinge of reason, believe that hair and down grow on the bodies of the gods; that among them there is the distinction of age; that they go clad with various types of coverings and clothes and shield themselves from heat and cold?

But whoever believes this true, necessarily also accepts this as true, that the gods are fullers,[63] barbers, who wash their sacred garments or trim the locks when matted with the fleece of growing hairs. Is it not shameful, full of disrespect and impiety, to assign to the gods characteristics of mortal and fallible creatures; to distinguish them with those parts which no decent man would dare to mention, to dwell on, or to picture in his imagination, without a shudder at such height of indecency?

Is this that contempt you show, that proud wisdom, with which you despise us as ignorant [64] and think all knowledge of things lies exposed to you? You laugh at the mysteries [65] of the Egyptians because upon the divine causes [66] they ingrafted the forms of dumb creatures, and because they wor-

14 [7]

ship [67] these same images with much incense and with the rest of the paraphernalia of rituals: you yourselves worship images of men as if they were powers vested with divinity; and you are not ashamed to give them the features of an earthly creature,[68] to blame others for their stupid error, and to be caught erring on the same point.

If the gods are not anthropomorphic, to represent them as such is insulting.

16. But,[69] perchance, you will say that the gods of course have other shapes and that you have attached to them the appearance of mortals for the sake of honor and form. But this is much more insulting than from ignorance to have made some mistake. For, were you to say that you had given the divine the shapes which your conjecture believed they possessed, it would have been less wrong to have made that mistake upon a belief by presumption. But now, when you believe one thing and fashion another, you both insult those to whom you attribute what you admit does not exist in them, and you reveal yourself as lacking in piety when you worship what you fashion, not what you think exists and in very truth really does exist.

If asses, dogs, pigs possessed something of human wisdom and the skill of fashioning things, and at the same time wished to do us reverence by some worship and to honor us by the dedication of statues, how great flames of passion, what storms of indignation would they arouse in us if they wanted our images to bear the shape of their bodies? [70]

How great flames of passion, I say, would they provoke, would they fan, if the founder of the City, Romulus, were to stand there with an ass's head; [71] if the holy Pompilius [72] had a dog's head; if under the likeness of a pig the name of Cato [73] or Marcus Cicero were inscribed?

So, then, you think that your stupidity is not laughed at by your divinities—if they do laugh—or, since you think that they are capable of anger, that they do not rage, do not grow furious, and that for so great wrongs and insults they do not wish to be avenged and to hurl upon you what wrath is wont to hurl and the bitterness of hatred to threaten! How much better to have given them the forms of elephants, panthers, or tigers, bulls, and horses! For what is there beautiful in man —what, I ask, admirable or becoming, except that some writer wanted him to possess in common with the ape? [74]

The Christians really do not know many things about God's shape, but are confident He is not anthropomorphic.

17. " But if," [75] they say, " you do not like our view, you point out, you tell us, with what form a god is endowed."

If you wish to hear an opinion which is the true one—God either has no form, or if He is to be identified with some form, we certainly do not know what it is. And assuredly we consider it no disgrace not to know what we never saw, [76] nor are we therefore debarred from refuting the opinion of others merely because on this point we ourselves have no belief to offer. For just as, if the world should be said to be made of glass, of silver, iron, or to be rolled together and molded out of brittle clay, we would not hesitate to maintain that this is false, although we do not know of what material it is: so when the discussion involves the appearance of God, we prove that it is not what you maintain, even though we are unable to say what it is.

18. " But tell me, then," some one will say, " does a god not hear? Does he not speak? Does he not see? Does he not observe what is placed before him? "

In His [77] own way, possibly, not in ours. For in a matter so important we cannot know the truth at all or ferret it out by guesswork, which, in our case, it is clear, is unfounded, hazardous, and like empty dreams.

If, for example, we said that He sees in the same ways by which we also see, one must then understand Him to have lids above His eyeballs; that He winks, blinks, sees by rays or images; or what is common to all eyes, sees nothing at all without the presence of light from another source.

This same thing must be said in like fashion about hearing and the form of speech and the utterance of words. If He hears by ears, these He also has penetrated by winding channels through which the sound can creep to report the meaning of speech; or if His words pour forth from a mouth, He has lips with teeth, by the manifold contact and motions of which the tongue articulates sounds and fashions the voice into words.

One must not even dare to impute virtues to God because He is ineffable.

19. And if you do not refuse to listen to the conclusions of our thought, far from attributing to God bodily character-istics, we are even afraid to ascribe to so great a thing the distinctions of soul and the very virtues in which it is scarcely granted a few to excel.

Who will say, for instance, that God is brave, steadfast, upright, wise? Who, that He has integrity; who, that He is temperate; who, indeed, that He knows anything, under-stands anything, takes care of anything? Who, that He guides to definite moral ends of their duties the decisions by which He acts? All these good qualities are human, and because they are the opposites of the vices, have acquired the praiseworthy reputation they have.

And who is so dullhearted, stupid, as to say that God is great in terms of human good or that the reason why He surpasses all others in the majesty of His name is that He lacks the ugliness of vices? Whatever you say about God, whatever you conceive in the silence of your mind, passes over and is corrupted into human applications nor can it have the mark of a meaning of its own because it is expressed in our own words and words designed for human affairs. There is only one thing most certainly understood by man concerning the nature of God: your realization and conviction that mortal man's speech is powerless to set forth anything about Him.

The second insult to the gods: that they are skilled in arts and crafts.

20. And this insult about the shapes and sexes is the first which you—noble defenders, indeed, and guardians of religion—offer your divinities. But what implication is there in what comes next,[78] your contention that some of the gods are mechanics,[79] others physicians,[80] others wool-workers,[81] sailors,[82] guitar-players,[83] flute-players,[84] hunters,[85] shepherds,[86] and—all that was wanting—farmers! [87]

"That god," he says, "is a musician, and this other one is a soothsayer." [88] Yes, indeed—the other gods are not ⟨musicians⟩ [89] and from their lack of skill and their ignorance of the future they do not know how to foretell what will come to pass! [90] One is instructed in the arts of midwifery, another has been taught the learning of the physicians. Are they, therefore, each competent in his own province and when called to aid, can they give no assistance in other fields? This one is eloquent of speech and quite adept in the construction of periods,[91] but the others are stupid and cannot say anything elegantly, if a speech is to be made?

21. And, I ask, what reason is there, what necessity so relentless, what cause, that the gods above should know and have these handicrafts like common mechanics? In heaven,[92] for instance, there is singing and playing of music, so that the nine [93] graceful [94] sisters may harmonize pauses and rhythms of tones. In the motions of the stars [95] there are forests, there are thickets, there are groves, ⟨that⟩ Diana may be regarded the mighty mistress of hunting expeditions. The gods are ignorant of the future and they live and pass their time according to the fates allotted to them, that the Latonian [96] seer may unfold and reveal to them what tomorrow or the hour may bring to them. He himself is inspired by another god and is urged on and shaken by the power of a greater divinity, so that he may rightly be said and held to be a diviner.[97] The gods are seized by diseases and can be wounded,[98] harassed by anything, so that in a given case the Epidaurian helper [99] may give them aid. They labor, they bear, so that Juno Lucina may soothe and take away the trying pangs of childbirth. They occupy themselves with farming or devote themselves to the military profession so that Vulcan, the master of fire, may forge them swords [100] or hammer out the implements of the countryside. They need the covering of garments so that the Tritonian maiden [101] may diligently weave cloth and give them to wear, as the season demands, either triple-twilled tunics or silken ones. They make accusations and refute charges so that Atlas' descendant [102] may bear off the prize of eloquence, acquired by assiduous practice.

22. "But you are mistaken," he says, "and are in error, for the gods are not themselves artisans but suggest these arts to the talents of men and, so that life may be better provided for, equipped, they hand on to mortals the knowledge required."

But he who gives any training to the unknowing and ignorant, and strives to make him efficient in the knowledge of some work, must first himself know what he has decided the other should cultivate. For no one is capable of imparting any science without having mastered the fundamentals of what he teaches and without grasping its method through incessant practice.[103]

The gods are therefore the first artisans, whether because they themselves, as you say, endow with knowledge, or because, being immortal and never begotten,[104] they surpass everything on earth in the duration of time.[105]

This, then, is the question: since there is no place or need for these arts among the gods, and their nature requires no ingenuity or knowledge of any craft, why should you say that they are skilled, are experts, some in one capacity, ⟨some⟩ in another, so that, owing to a distinction according to what is known of the sciences, one is superior to the other?

Inconsistencies in the theory that the gods merely preside over the arts and crafts but do not practice them.

23. Well,[106] perhaps you say the gods are not artisans; but they preside over these arts, care for them; yes, everything we perform, carry on, has been placed under their protection and by their foresight they make sure that it has a good and happy outcome.

This statement would, indeed, seem to have merit and

plausibility, if everything we undertake, carry on, or all we risk in human business, always progressed according to wish and purpose. But since every day things turn out to the contrary, and the results of actions do not correspond to the desired aim, it is a delusion to say that over us as guardians are gods who are but fictions of our imagination, whose recognition is not that of certified truth.

⟨Matuta⟩ [107] provides [108] safe voyages to those traversing the seas; but [109] why has the raging sea so often cast up the flotsam of dire shipwrecks? Consus [110] supplies our thoughts with helpful and trustworthy advice; and yet, why does an unexpected change constantly effect outcomes contrary to the desired ones? Pales and Inuus [111] preside as guardians over flocks of cattle and sheep; and yet, why do they, with harm-bringing inactivity, fail to see to it that fierce epidemics and pestilent diseases are turned away from the summer pastures?

And that mother [112] Flora, venerated in lewd games, looks after the blossoming of the fields; but why does the baneful frost [113] daily sear buds and luscious vegetation and destroy them? Juno has been made the patroness of childbirths and gives aid to pregnant mothers; but why do thousands of them perish each day, snatched away in murderous travails? To Vulcan belongs the guardianship of fire and the stuff which feeds it has been placed under his direction; but why are holy edifices and sections of cities permitted to fall to ashes devoured by flames?

The Pythian [114] grants the knowledge of divination to the soothsayers; but why does he often give and pass off answers that are equivocal, doubtful, and involved in misty obscurities? Aesculapius [115] is in charge of the profession and art of healing; but why cannot more kinds of ailments and diseases be brought through to recovery, whereas, instead, at the hands of those who care for them, they even become worse? Mercury takes care of the arenas,[116] presides over boxing bouts and wrestling matches; but why does he not make invincible all over whom he has charge? [117] Why, when he is placed over the duty of a single task, does he suffer some to share in victory, others to be laughed at for the ignominy of their weakness?

Criticism of the theory that the gods benefit only worshippers.

24. " To the tutelar divinities," he says, " no one makes supplication and for this reason one after the other fails us in the services and helps associated with them."

We may say, then, that unless they receive incense and salted barley meal, the gods cannot do good, and unless they see their little altars besmeared with the blood of cattle, they abandon and abdicate their guardianships? [118] And yet, up to very recently [119] I used to think that the benevolent acts of the divinities were spontaneous and that from them flowed the gifts of kindness, voluntary and unexpected. Yes—and the King of the Heavens,[120] is He perhaps solicited by any libation or sacrifice to bestow upon the tribes of mortals all those conveniences which go with life? Does God not grant the life-giving heat of the sun and the nighttime, the winds, rains, harvests to all alike, to the good, the wicked, ⟨the just⟩,[121] the unjust, to slaves, the poor, the rich? This is the property of a god powerful and true, to offer the benefactions unasked to beings weary [122] and weak and ever hemmed in by hardship of many kinds. Verily, to grant what you are asked on the basis of sacrifices performed is not to help those who ask but to sell the largess of your own kindness. We men play and trifle about so great a matter, and having forgotten who

God is, and what the magnificence of His name, associate with the tutelar divinities whatever base or sordid thing we can invent in our morbid credulity.

The pagans worship gods disgraceful and ridiculous.

25. "Anointings," he says, "are presided over by Unxia,[123] the loosening of bridal knots by Cinxia; the most holy Victua [124] and Potua [125] take care of eating and drinking." [126]

O extraordinary and unique interpretation of the powers of divinities! If brides did not smear the doorposts of their husbands with greasy ointment, if bridegrooms, aglow with passion, did not eagerly unloosen the maiden's bonds, if human beings did not drink and eat, then the gods would be without names? In addition, not satisfied to have subjected and involved the gods in concerns so disgusting, you even attribute [127] to them natures fierce, cruel, monstrous, ever rejoicing in evils and in the destruction of humankind!

Evil deeds of the god Mars.

26. We shall not mention at this point Laverna,[128] goddess of thieves, the Bellonae,[129] the Discordiae,[130] the Furies,[131] and those unpropitious [132] deities which you set up we pass [133] by in utter silence. Mars alone we shall bring up and that good-looking mother of the Desires,[134] one of whom you place in command of battles, the other of loves and the passion of desire.[135]

"Mars," he says, "has power over wars."

To cause those in progress to cease, or to stir them up when things are quiet and peaceful? If he is a calmer of martial insanity, why is it that every day wars continue? If, on the other hand, he is their instigator,[136] we should say that at the inclination of his own pleasure the god sets the whole world at variance; sows the seeds of discords and strife among far-separated nations of the earth; brings together from different places so many thousands of mortals and, before you can say a single word, piles the fields with corpses; causes bloody torrents to flow; destroys the most firmly established empires; levels cities to the ground; takes away freedom from the free-born and places on them the condition of slavery; rejoices in civil strife, in the fratricidal slaughter of brothers [137] dying together, and, finally, in the horror of murderous conflict between sons and fathers.

Evil deeds of the goddess Venus.

27. This same argument we may apply to Venus in exactly the same way. For if, as you assert and believe, she enkindles the flames of love in human minds, one must then understand that to the wounds of Venus must be attributed whatever disgrace or misdeed arises from such madness. Is it, therefore, under compulsion from the goddess that even the noble frequently surrender their honor to harlots of the worst repute; that the firm ties of marriages gradually loosen; [138] that relationship by blood is inflamed ⟨toward⟩ incestuous passions; [139] that mothers nurture a mad love for their children; that fathers turn to themselves the longings of their daughters; that flouting the dignity that goes with their age, old men are filled with youthful passions for filthy gratifications; that wise and brave men, [140] living in dissipation of the sinews of their manhood, exchange the demands of constancy for effeminacy; that people hang themselves; [141] and, commonly enough, [142] cast themselves—leaping deliberately—from the heights of jagged cliffs. [143]

No such god deserves the respect of worship.

28. Can any man exist possessed of even traces of incipient reason, who could befoul or deface the essence [144] of
divinity with a morality so filthy? Who would credit the
gods with dispositions such as human gentleness often won
over and tamed down in the beasts of the field? Where, I ask
you, is that theory that the gods are far removed from disturbing emotion,[145] that they are gentle, peaceful, mild; that
in the completeness of their virtue they preserve the peak of
perfection and the topmost summit of wisdom itself?

And why do we pray to them to avert from us things unfavorable and hostile, if we find that they are the authors of
all the evils by which daily we are harassed? Call us wicked,
impious, or atheists, as much as you please—never will you
make us believe in gods of loves, gods of wars; that there are
gods who sow strife, who stir up minds with the stings of
the furies' whips. Either in very truth they are gods and do
not do the things you tell about them ⟨or, if they do⟩ what
you say, without any doubt they are not gods.

Pagan testimony results in eliminating many of the
gods: Janus and Saturn.

29. And yet,[146] even so we might take from you these
ideas rife with wicked fabrications, were it not for the fact
that you yourself, by bringing forth about the gods many
statements inconsistent and mutually contradictory, force us
to refrain from agreement. For in your rivalry, one en-
deavoring to outshine the other in profundity [147] of knowledge, you both remove those very gods whom you imagine
and supplant them with others who clearly do not exist; each
one says something different about identical things; and you

put down those whom the consensus of men has always accepted as individuals, as being infinite in number.

Accordingly, let us too, as is customary, begin with Father Janus.[148] Some of you represent him to be the world,[149] some the year,[150] some the sun.[151] Now if we are going to accept this as true, the necessary conclusion follows that no Janus ever existed, who, they say, sprang from Caelus [152] and Hecate, was the first to rule in Italy, founded the town [153] of Janiculum, was father of Fontus,[154] son-in-law of Vulturnus,[155] husband of Juturna; [156] and so you rub out the name of the god whom you place first in all your prayers,[157] and whom you believe obtains for you a hearing before the gods.

And again, if Janus is the year, it is once more impossible for him to be a god. For who does not know that the year is a fixed period of time and that that which is delineated by the lapse and computation of months [158] does not have the essence of divinity?

This very same point can be made similarly in the case of Saturn. For if by this name time is meant, as the Greek philologists declare, making *Kronos* identical with *chronos*,[159] then Saturn is no divinity at all. Who is so crazy as to say that time is a god when it is merely the measuring of a certain period included in a continuous perpetual succession? [160] And so that fellow too, will be removed from the list of denizens of heaven, one whom hoary antiquity declared and handed down to the later ages as having Caelus for his father, to be the progenitor of the "great gods," planter of the vine,[161] bearer of the pruning hook.[162]

Jupiter and Juno are eliminated.

30. But what shall we say about Jupiter [163] himself, whom wise men have frequently said is the sun,[164] driving winged

chariots, followed by a crowd of deities; [165] some, that he is ether burning with powerful flame [166] and with a tremendous unquenchable fire? If this is an established fact, then according to you there is no Jupiter at all, who, having Saturn for his father and Ops [167] for his mother, is reported to have been concealed in the territories of the Cretans [168] in order to avoid the mad fury of his sire.

And now does not a similar line of reasoning remove Juno from the list of the gods? If she is the air, a pun which by an inversion of the Greek name you make a practice of stating over and over again,[169] she is found to be no sister and consort of all-powerful Jupiter,[170] no Fluvionia, no Pomana, no Ossipagina, no Februtis, Populonia, Cinxia, Caprotina, and so the fiction of that name of hers, spread abroad by the popularity of a groundless belief, will be found to amount to absolutely nothing.

Minerva, Neptune, and other gods are eliminated.

31. Aristotle,[171] an unusually powerful intellect and an extraordinary scholar, as Granius [172] tells us, shows by plausible arguments that Minerva is the Moon [173] and demonstrates it by written authorities. Others have said that she is the crest of ether and its utmost height; [174] some that she is memory, whence the very name Minerva as if derived from *meminerva*.[175] But if this view is accepted, then there is no daughter of Metis,[176] no Victory,[177] ⟨no one⟩ born [178] of the brain of Jupiter, no discoverer of the olive, no accomplished mistress of the arts and the various sciences.

"Neptune," they say, "is addressed as such and has received his name from the fact that he covers the earth with water." [179]

Therefore, if the covering of water is the meaning of this

name, there is no god at all named Neptune, and so is ousted
and eliminated from the scene the full brother of the Stygian [180] and of the Olympian Jupiter, armed with the iron
trident, lord of sea monsters and little fishes, king of the salty
depths and shaker of the trembling earth.[181]

Mercury, Tellus, Ceres, and Vesta.

32. Mercury's name, too, means something like a kind of
go-between; [182] and because conversation runs between two
speakers [183] and speech is reciprocal, hence the agreement of
the character suggested by this name. Accordingly, if this is
the case, Mercury is not the name of a god but of speech and
the exchange of sound, and thus is blotted out and annihilated
that Cyllenian [184] bearer of the caduceus,[185] born on a cold
mountain, the deviser of words and names, the barterer of
market wares and merchandise.

The Earth, because it furnishes food to all living creatures,
some of you have said to be the Great Mother.[186] Others
declare that this same thing is Ceres [187] because it brings
forth crops of wholesome seeds; and some, that it is Vesta
because in the universe it alone stands still,[188] the other parts
being fixed in constant motion.[189]

But if this is advanced and maintained on sure grounds,
again by your interpretation three divinities do not exist. No
Ceres, no Vesta will be reckoned in the roster of gods, nor,
finally, can the Mother of the gods herself, whom Nigidius [190]
declares to have been married to Saturn, rightly be named a
goddess, if, indeed, these are all but names of the one earth
and in these designations it alone is meant.

Vulcan, Venus, Proserpina, Liber, and Apollo.

33. To escape prolixity we pass at this point over Vulcan whom you unanimously all declare to be fire; [191] Venus because she comes [192] to all, and Proserpina,[193] so named because plants steal forth, when planted, to the light—where once more you erase the heads of three divinities from the list, if, indeed, the first is the name of an element, a word signifying no sentient power; the second, a passion pervading all living creatures; while the third means seeds raising themselves, and upward movement of growing crops.

Moreover, when you maintain that Liber, Apollo, the sun [194] are but one divinity multiplied by three names, is the list of gods not shortened by your notions and does not the stated belief collapse? For if it is true that the sun is the same as Liber and the same as Apollo, it follows that in " the nature of things " [195] there is no one such as Apollo or Liber, and so by you yourselves is blotted out, obliterated, the son of Semele,[196] the Pythian,[197]—the one the giver of filthy merriment, the other the bane of Sminthian mice.[198]

Diana, Ceres, Luna.

34. Among you there are men who, neither uninformed nor given to small talk, declare that Diana, Ceres, the moon, are but one godhead in three-way union,[199] and that these are not three distinct persons as there are three separate names; that in them all it is the moon that is invoked and that to her name the list of the other surnames has been added on. But if this has been ascertained, if this is established and the truth of the matter shows it so, once again the name of Ceres is meaningless and that of Diana means nothing, and so the matter is brought to the point that by

your own initiative and authority, that discoverer of grain, as you call her, is nothing, and Apollo is robbed of his sister, upon whom once, as she washed away the grime from her body in the crystal clear fountain, that antlered hunter [200] gazed and paid the penalty for his curiosity.

Criticism of the deification of parts of the universe.

35. Men noteworthy in the study of philosophy and men whom your encomiums have placed on the pinnacle in that discipline [201] declare with commendable earnestness that in their deliberate opinion the whole mass of the world, by whose expanses we are encompassed, are covered, and are supported, is but a single living being [202] possessed of wisdom and reason.[203] Now, if the opinion of these men is true and established as certain, those whom a little while ago [204] you set up in its parts, with names unchanged,[205] straightway also cease to be gods. As a single human being cannot, so long as his body remains entire, be split into many human beings, and again, many men, as long as the difference of their individuality is preserved, cannot be fused into the unity of a single sentient being,[206] so, if the world is a single animate being and is moved by the impulse of a single mind, it cannot be dispersed into several divinities nor can particles of it, if they are gods, be united and turned into the consciousness of a single living being.

The moon, sun, earth, ether, stars, are members and parts of the world. Now, if they are parts and members, they are certainly not independent living creatures, for the parts of a given thing cannot be the same as the whole, or think for themselves or feel for themselves. This cannot be accomplished by any activity of their own without the cooperation of the whole living organism; and this established and settled,

15 *

the whole matter boils down to this, that the sun is no god,[207] nor the moon, nor the ether, earth, and the rest. They merely are parts of the world, not the proper names of divinities, and so it is brought about by your muddling and meddling in all things divine that the world is established as the one and only god in the universe; [208] all others are driven out—yes, and that too, set up to no purpose, as vacuities and things without reality.

It is the pagans who are responsible for the gods' anger against men.

36. If in so many ways and by so many arguments we were to undermine belief in your gods, there would be no doubt that aroused to raging anger you would demand for us fire, wild beasts, and swords, and the other death-dealing torments with which you are wont to slake your thirst in its passion for our blood.

But while you yourselves with your ostentation of brilliance and scholarship do away with practically the entire race of gods, you have the audacity to insist that it is because of us that human affairs are oppressed by the gods, when as a fact, if it is true that they exist at all and grow hot with the flames of wrath, they would have no juster reason for raging against you [209] than that you deny their existence and their presence in nature.

Conflicting opinions concerning the Muses.

37. That [210] the Muses are the daughters of Tellus [211] and Caelus is the view advanced by Mnaseas; [212] others declare that they are Jupiter's by his wife Memory [213] or Mind.[214] Some write that they were virgins, others that they were

matrons. You see, we wish briefly to touch also upon those points in which you show yourselves as holding different opinions on one and the same matter, the one saying this, the other that. Ephorus,[215] then, says that they are three in number; Mnaseas, whom we mentioned, four; Myrtilus [216] brings in seven; eight are asserted by Crates; [217] finally, Hesiod puts forth nine with names, enriching heaven and the stars with gods.[218]

Unless we are mistaken, this difference of opinion is a sign of persons who know nothing about the truth,[219] and does not derive from the truth of the case. If the fact at issue were clearly known, the voice of all would be one and the agreement of all would tend towards and reach the conclusion of the same belief.

38. How, then, can you give [220] to religion the full force of the power when you are in error concerning the gods themselves? Or invite us to their reverential worship [221] when you have nothing certain to teach us on the concept of the divinities themselves? To say nothing about the authorities intervening—either the first one mentioned [222] strikes out and slays six divine Muses, if it is agreed there are nine, or that last one mentioned at the end [223] adds six who do not exist at all to the three who in reality alone exist, with the result that it cannot be known or understood which ones ought to be added, which taken away; and the performance of religious observance itself is forced to run the danger either of worshipping what does not exist or perhaps of overlooking what does exist.

The Novensiles.

Piso [224] believes that the Novensiles are nine gods set up among the Sabines at Trebia.[225] Granius [226] thinks that these are the Muses, which is in agreement with the view of Aelius.[227] Varro[228] hands down to us that they are nine in number because in undertaking anything that number is always held to be the most powerful and greatest.[229] Cornificius,[230] that they preside over renewals because by their care things are renewed and endure. Manilius,[231] that they are the nine gods whom alone Jupiter allowed to have the power of hurling his thunderbolt.[232] Cincius[233] pronounces them to be foreign divinities so called from their very newness; the Romans, in fact, were accustomed in some instances to spread the religions of conquered cities privately through the families and in other cases they consecrated them publicly; and lest through the great number of the gods and on account of the fact that they were unknown, some of them might be passed over, for the sake of brevity and economy all were invoked alike under one name—*Novensiles*.[234]

39. There are, in addition, some[235] who say that those who from being men were made gods are marked by this name, as is Hercules, Romulus, Aesculapius, Liber, Aeneas. These are all, it is clear, different opinions, and by the nature of things it cannot be that people who differ in their beliefs should all be regarded as authorities of one and the same truth. If the opinion of Piso is true, Aelius and Granius are mistaken; if what they say is certain, Varro, most learned as he is, is mistaken, because in place of what is established reality he substitutes the most inane and foolish. If the number nine produces the name of *Novensiles*, Cornificius is convicted of talking nonsense, in giving to the gods presiding over renewal the force of another's power. But if the opinion of Cornificius is true, Cincius is found to be ignorant for associating the gods of conquered cities with the power of the divinities called *Novensiles*. And if they are such as

Cincius says they are, Manilius will be found to be mistaken, for he comprehends under that name such as hurl another's thunderbolt. And if what Manilius asserts is verified as true, they who think that mortals raised and consecrated to divine honors are named thus [236] because of the newness of their honor, are particularly mistaken. But if the *Novensiles* are those who have merited to be exalted to the stars, after having done with the mortality of life, then there are really no *Di Novensiles* at all. As slaves, soldiers, teachers are not the names of individuals underlying the words, but of duties, ranks, and offices, so when we speak of *Novensiles*, if that is the name of those who from being in the human state deserved to be gods, it is at once obvious that no individuals are specifically identified but that newness itself is named by the designation of *Novensiles*.

The Penates.

40. Nigidius [237] taught that the *di Penates* are Neptune and Apollo who once on fixed terms surrounded Ilium with immortal [238] walls. The same man again in his sixteenth book explains, following Etruscan [239] teaching, that there are four kinds of Penates, and that some of these belong to Jupiter, others to Neptune, a third group to the gods of the lower world, a fourth class to mortal men—a sort of statement that is unintelligible. And Caesius,[240] of the same school, thinks that they are Fortuna and Ceres, the Genius Jovialis and Pales, but not that woman commonly understood but some male attendant and bailiff of Jupiter.[241]

Varro thinks they are the gods of whom we speak who are within and in the innermost recesses of heaven, and that their number and names are unknown. The Etruscans [242] say that they are the *Consentes* [243] and the *Complices* [244] and name

them because they rise together and sit together,[245] six males
and as many females, with unknown names and most sparing
of pity; [246] and that they are thought to be the counsellors and
princes [247] of highest Jupiter. And some wrote [248] that Jupiter,
Juno, and Minerva, were the *di Penates*, without whom we
cannot live and have intelligence and who guide our inner
selves with reason, warmth, and breath.

As you see, here, too, there is no agreement, nothing is
settled by a unanimous verdict, nor is there anything trustworthy on which the mind can stand, through conjecture
approaching near to the truth.[249] For the opinions are so
fallible and one idea is discredited by another, that there is
either no truth in them all or, if any one does utter it, it is
not so recognized amid the great diversity of statements.

The Lares.

41. We can,[250] if it is agreeable, briefly say something
also concerning the Lares,[251] whom the masses think are the
gods of streets [252] and roads [253] from the fact that Greece calls
streets *laurai*.[254] In his various writings Nigidius ⟨says⟩ in
one place that they are the guardians of buildings and houses,
in another that they are the Curetes [255] who are asserted to
have concealed once upon a time by clanging their weapons
the baby cries of Jupiter; [256] in another the Samothracian
Digiti, which five, the Greeks say, are named the Idaean
Dactyli.[257]

Varro with like hesitation states at one time that they are
the Manes and that therefore the mother of the Lares was
named Mania; [258] again, at another, that they are the gods
of the air [259] and are called heroes; at another, following the
opinion of the ancients, he says that the Lares are Larvae,[260]
certain genii, as it were, and the souls of the departed dead.

*The argument is finished: multiplicity of testimony
is useless.*

42. It would be a tremendous and endless task to go through each kind individually and to make it evident from the books alone that there is no god conceived or believed in by you concerning whom you have <not> given expression to uncertain and conflicting notions reflecting a thousand different points of view. But for brevity's sake and not to become boresome, what has been said must suffice; and it would prove too laborious to collect and mass a multitude of things, seeing as we do that one or the other case makes it manifestly clear that you are confused, hesitate, and that you have nothing certain to say concerning these things which you maintain.

But perhaps you will say: "Even if we do not personally know who the Lares are, who the *Novensiles* are, who the Penates, nevertheless the very agreement of the authorities proves that they do exist and that among the number of the heaven dwellers they are represented."

And how is it possible to know whether a given god exists, if there is utter ignorance as to what he is? Or how can a petition for benefits avail anything in the first place, if it is not ascertained and established who should be invoked for each appeal? [261] Every one who seeks to obtain an answer from some divinity, ought of necessity to know to whom he is making supplication, on whom he is calling, from whom he requests aid for human needs—particularly as you yourselves tell [262] us that not all the gods can grant all things and that the wrath and anger of each are appeased by very unlike ceremonials.

Ritualistic perfection demands information not pos-
sessed by the pagans.

43. If, for example, this one requires a black,[263] that one
a white hide; [264] to this one a person must sacrifice with head
veiled, to that with head bare; [265] that one is consulted about
marriages,[266] this grants remedies in cases of distress—can it
be immaterial whether this one or that one is a *Novensilis*,
since ignorance of the facts and confusion of persons is
offensive to the gods and of necessity ⟨forces⟩ [267] the contrac-
tion of guilt?

Imagine that I myself because of some distress or the avoid-
ance of danger, were to make supplication to any of these
divinities, saying: "Help me, do help me, divine Penates—
thou Apollo, and thou Neptune—and remove [268] by the
clemency of your divine power all these evils with which I
am consumed, am terrified,[269] am harassed." Will there be
any hope of getting aid from them if Ceres, Pales, Fortuna,
or Genius Jovialis [270]—not Neptune and Apollo—turn out to
be the *di Penates?*

Or if I call upon the Curetes in place of the Lares, whom
a group of your authorities say are the Samothracian *Digiti*,
how shall I be able to have them for helpers and patrons
when I have not given the latter their own names and have
given to the former names which do not belong to them?

Such is the urgency of the matter that we know the gods
individually and not be in uncertainty and doubt about the
power, the name of each one, ⟨lest⟩ if they should be invoked
by rites and designations not their own, they keep their ears
stopped and hold us bound in guilt that cannot be expiated.

44. Wherefore, if it is manifest to you that in the sublime palaces of heaven there dwells, exists that multitude of

gods you recount, it is for you to stand by the terms of one declaration of opinion,[271] and not destroy by divers divergent and self-contradictory notions confidence in these very things which you are building up as a system. If Janus exists, let Janus exist; if Liber exists, let Liber exist; if Summanus [272] exists, let Summanus exist: for this is to trust in, this to hold, to be settled in the comprehension of something proven, not to say after the manner of the blind and erring: "the *Novensiles* are the Muses—no, they are the gods of Trebia— no, their number is nine—rather, they are the protectors of cities overthrown"; and reduce things so important to this danger, that while some you remove and you replace others, it can rightly be doubted about all whether they exist anywhere.

NOTES

INTRODUCTION

The following list of abbreviations and bibliography are designed to eliminate unnecessary repetition in the references. An asterisk (*) indicates that, in spite of diligent search, no copy of the work has been found.

List of Abbreviations:

ACW	Ancient Christian Writers
ANCL	The Ante-Nicene Christian Library
ANF	The Ante-Nicene Fathers
CAH	Cambridge Ancient History
CIL	Corpus inscriptionum latinarum
CSEL	Corpus scriptorum ecclesiasticorum latinorum
Cumont	F. Cumont, *Les religions orientales dans le paganisme romain* (4th ed., Paris 1929)
DA	Dictionnaire des antiquités grecques et romaines
DACL	Dictionnaire d'archéologie chrétienne et de liturgie
DBM	Dictionary of Greek and Roman Biography and Mythology
DG	Dictionary of Greek and Roman Geography
DTC	Dictionnaire de théologie catholique
Fowler	W. Warde Fowler, *The Roman Festivals of the Period of the Republic* (London 1899)
LM	Ausführliches Lexikon der griechischen und römischen Mythologie
LTK	Lexikon für Theologie und Kirche
MG	J. P. Migne, *Patrologia graeca*
ML	J. P. Migne, *Patrologia latina*
P	Codex Parisinus 1661, containing the text of the *Adversus nationes* of Arnobius and the *Octavius* of Minucius Felix
Platner-Ashby	S. B. Platner-T. Ashby, *A Topographical Dictionary of Ancient Rome* (London 1929)
RE	Real-Enzyklopädie der classischen Altertumswissenschaft
TLL	Thesaurus linguae latinae
Wissowa	G. Wissowa, *Religion und Kultus der Römer* (2nd ed., Munich 1912)

Bibliographies of Arnobiana:

Schoenemann, K. T. G. *Bibliotheca historico-literaria Patrum latinorum* 1 (Leipzig 1792) 147-76 = Orelli 1. xix-xlv = ML 5. 354-66 = Hildebrand xix-xxxii. [Very useful for earlier editions.]

Richardson, E. C. *Bibliographical Synopsis* [of Arnobius], in *ANF* 10 (Buffalo 1887, repr. New York 1926) 76 f. [Useful but inaccurate.]

Ehrhard, A. *Die altchristliche Litteratur und ihre Erforschung von 1884-1900*, in *Strassb. theol. Stud.* Suppl. 1 (Freiburg i. Br. 1900) 481-4.

Guinagh, K. "Arnobiana," *Class. Weekly* 29 (1936) 69 f., 152.

Editions of the Latin Text:

Sabaeus, Faustus (Rome 1542 colophon; 1543 preface). [The *editio princeps*, containing, as Book Eight, the *Octavius* of Minucius Felix. All scholars agree that this was prepared from *codex Parisinus* 1661.]

Gelenius, Sigismundus (Basel 1546). [Contains Minucius. Cf. B. Ryba, "Sigismundus Gelenius a jeho vydání Arnobia a Minucia," *Listy Filologické* 52 (1925) 13-23, 91-108, 222-36, 337-41.]

Gelenius, Sigismundus (Basel 1560). [Reprint of the 1546 edition together with the edition of the *Commentary on the Psalms* by Arnobius the Younger, edited by Erasmus, both works being ascribed to the same author.]

La Barre, Renatus Laurentius de (Paris 1580). [Contained in his edition of Tertullian, 133-234. Includes Minucius. Apparently never examined by any subsequent editor of Arnobius.]

Canterus, Theodorus (Antwerp 1582). [Contains a commentary.]

[Ursinus, Fulvius] (Rome 1583). [So-called "second Roman" edition, without commentary, but contains Minucius.]

Elmenhorst, Geverhardus (Hannover 1603). [Text is combination of Gelenius and Ursinus. Also contains Minucius.]

Stewechius, Godescalcus (Antwerp 1604). [Contains commentary. Text generally that of Ursinus and with Stewechius' notes and a collation of the Brussels MS by F. Modius.]

Heraldus, Desiderius (Paris 1605). [Text largely based on Ursinus. Contains 378 pages of text, 428 pages of commentary, with voluminous indices to both. Also includes Minucius.]

Elmenhorst, Geverhardus (Hamburg 1610). [Text based on his 1603 edition with additions from Ursinus and Stewechius, not well chosen. Contains Minucius.]

Canterus, Theodorus (Cologne 1618). In Margarinus de la Bigne (and others), *Magna bibliotheca veterum Patrum*, etc., 3. 151 ff. [Not first edition of this collection but earliest to contain Arnobius.]

* Stewechius, Godescalcus (Douai 1634). [Contains summaries by Leander de San Martino (pseud.) = John Jones.]

[Salmasius, Claudius] and Thysius, A. (Leyden 1651). [Salmasius' name omitted from title where he is mentioned only as a 'vir celeberrimus.' Also contains annotations by Canterus, Stewechius, Elmenhorst, and Heraldus. Long the standard edition.]

Canterus, Theodorus (Paris 1654). In Margarinus de la Bigne, *Magna bibliotheca veterum Patrum*, etc., 15. 1-63.

* Priorius, Philippus (Paris 1666). [Text based on Salmasius and typographical errors are copied from that edition. This is in Priorius' edition of Cyprian.]

Priorius, Philippus (Lyons-Genoa 1677). In Margarinus de la Bigne, *Maxima bibliotheca veterum Patrum*, etc., 3. 430-514.

* Canterus, Theodorus (Leyden 1680). In *Sanct. bibliotheca Patrum*, etc.

* Gallandius, A. (Venice 1768). In his *Bibliotheca veterum Patrum*, etc. 4. 133-224. [Text based on Salmasius' Leyden edition with errors preserved and with addition of Priorius' notes. First edition to separate text into chapters.]

Oberthür, C. (Würzburg 1783). In his *Opera omnia sanctorum Patrum latinorum* 5. [Text is that of Canterus corrected from Salmasius. First edition to contain the chapter divisions subsequently adopted by all editors.]

Orelli, Joseph Conrad (Leipzig 1816-7, 3 vols.). [Voluminous variorum commentary—third volume contains addenda only.]

Caillau, A. B. (Paris 1829). In his *Collectio selecta SS. Ecclesiae Patrum* 15. 237-490.

* Anonymous (Paris 1836).

* Anonymous (Besançon 1838).

Hildebrand, G. F. (Halle 1844). [Contains commentary.]

Migne, J. P. (Paris 1844). In ML 5. 349-1372. [Contains complete verbatim reprint of Orelli, plus Schoenemann, plus LeNourry's *Dissertatio praevia*.]

* Anonymous (Lyons-Paris 1845).

Oehler, Franciscus (Leipzig 1846). In E. G. Gersdorf, *Bibliotheca Patrum ecclesiasticorum selecta* 12. [Commentary very limited.]

Reifferscheid, Augustus (Vienna 1875). In CSEL 4 (Vienna 1875, repr. 1890). [First critical edition, in many ways still standard.]

Marchesi, Concetto (Turin 1934). In *Corpus scriptorum latinorum Paravianum* 62. [To some extent supersedes Reifferscheid.]

PARTIAL EDITIONS OF LATIN TEXT:

Routh, Martin Joseph. *Scriptorum ecclesiasticorum opuscula praecipua quaedam* (Oxford, 1st ed. 1832, 2nd ed. 1840, 3rd ed. 1858). [The two later editions contain Book One only—no copy of 1st ed. has been found.]

Anonymous (Padua 1929). [Book Two only. Text consists of reprint of Reifferscheid, disregarding apparatus and failing to correct in accordance with his preface.]

TRANSLATIONS:

* Oudaan, Joachim. *Arnobius d'Afrikaner tegen de Heydenen vervat in zeven bocken* (Harlingen 1677).

Besnard, Franz A. v. *Des Afrikaner's Arnobius sieben Bücher wider die Heiden, aus dem Lateinischen übersetzt und erläutert* (Landshut 1842).

Alleker, J. *Arnobius sieben Bücher gegen die Heiden, in Deutsch übersetzt* (Trier 1858).

Bryce, Hamilton, and Campbell, Hugh. *The Seven Books of Arnobius Adversus Gentes*, in ANCL 19 (Edinburgh 1871), repr. in ANF 6 (Buffalo 1886) 401-572, with slight additions by the editor, A. C. Coxe.

CRITICAL ARTICLES SINCE 1875:

Armini, H. " Textkritiska bidrag," *Eranos* 28 (1930) 34-39.

Axelson, B. " Zur Emendation älterer Kirchenschriftsteller," *Eranos* 39 (1941) 74-81.

——. " Randbemerkungen zu Arnobius," *Eranos* 40 (1942) 182 f.

——. " Textkritisches zu Florus, Minucius Felix und Arnobius," K. *Humanistiska Vetenskapssamfundets i Lund* Årsb. 1944-5 No. 1.

Baehrens, W. A. [Rev. of Löfstedt's Arnobiana], *Berl. phil. Woch.* 37 (1917) 1291-8.

——. *Berl. phil. Woch.* 42 (1923) 352-4.

Bastgen, M. *Quaestiones de locis ex Arnobii Adversus Nationes opere selectis* (diss. Münster i. W. 1887).

Birt, T. " Marginalien zu lateinischen Prosaikern," *Philologus* 83 (1928) 164-82.

Brakman, C. *Arnobiana* (Leyden 1917).

——. *Miscella* (Leyden 1912).

——. *Miscella altera* (Leyden 1913).

——. *Miscella tertia* (Leyden 1917).

Corssen, P. " Zu Arnobius V 12 und 6," *Berl. phil. Woch.* 30 (1910) 382 f.

Damsté, P. H. " Emendatur Arnobius Adv. Nat. I 62," *Mnemosyne* 45 (1917) 165.

Ehwald, R. " Zu Arnobius und Cicero," *Philologus* 51 (1892) 747.

Eitrem, S. " Varia," *Nordisk Tidsskr. for Filol.* 10 (1922) 61.

Georges, K. E. " Kritische Bemerkungen," *Philologus* 33 (1874) 334.

Gomperz, H. " Zu Arnobius," *Rhein. Mus.* 64 (1909) 153-5.

Hagendahl, H. *La prose métrique d'Arnobe—contributions à la connaissance de la prose littéraire de l'empire*, in *Göteborgs Högskolas Årsskr.* 42 (1936) No. 1 (Göteborg 1937).

——. " En Ovidiusreminiscens hos Arnobius," *Eranos* 35 (1937) 36-40.

Havet, L. " Notes sur divers auteurs," *Rev. de Philol.* n. s. 1 (1877) 281.

Hidén, K. J. " Randbemerkungen zu Arnobius Adversus Nationes," in his *De Arnobii Adversus Nationes libris VII commentationes* 2 (Helsingfors 1921) extract from *Ann. Acad. Scient. Fenn.* ser. B, 15. 8.

Johnson, H. " Notes," *Class. Rev.* 23 (1909) 91 f.

Kirschwing, O. *Qua ratione in Arnobii libris ars critica exercenda sit* (diss. Leipzig 1911).

Kistner, K. " Arnobiana " (Progr. St. Ingebert 1912).

Koch, H. "Zu Arnobius und Lactantius," *Philologus* 80 (1925) 467-72.

Kroll, W. "Arnobiusstudien," *Rhein. Mus.* n. F. 72 (1917) 62-112.

——. [Rev. of Wiman's *Textkritiska Studier*], *Phil. Woch.* 52 (1932) 630 f.

——. [Rev. of Marchesi's edition], *ibid.* 55 (1935) 1082-4.

Löfstedt, E. "Beiträge zur Kenntnisse der späteren Latinität," in *Uppsala Univ. Årsskr.* (Uppsala diss. Stockholm 1907).

——. "Patristische Beiträge," *Eranos* 10 (1910) 7-29.

——. "Arnobiana: Textkritische und sprachliche Studien zu Arnobius" (Lund-Leipzig 1917).

Marchesi, C. "Per una nuova edizione di Arnobio," *Riv. Fil. Istr. Cl.* 60 (1932) 485-96.

McCracken, G. E. "Critical Notes to Arnobius' Adversus Nationes," *Vigiliae Christianae* 3 (1949) 39-49.

Meiser, K. "Studien zu Arnobius," *Sitzungsb. d. k. bay. Akad. d. Wiss., philosoph.-philolog. und hist. Kl.* 5 (1908) 19-40.

Pascal, C. "Emendationes Arnobianae," *Riv. Fil. Istr. Cl.* 32 (1904) 1-9.

* Pauly, F. *Zeitschr. oestr. Gymn.* 27 (1876) 900.

Phillimore, J. S. "Arnobiana," *Mnemosyne* n. s. 48 (1920) 388-91.

Polle, F. "Zu Arnobius," *Jahrb. f. class. Phil.* 135 (1887) 87.

Reifferscheid, A. "Analecta critica et grammatica," *Index lect. hib.* 1877-8 (Breslau 1877).

Souter, A. [Review of Marchesi's edition], *Class. Rev.* 49 (1935) 209.

Stangl, T. "Arnobiana," *Berl. phil. Woch.* 30 (1910) 126 f., 158 f.

——. "Bobiensia," *Rhein. Mus.* 65 (1910) 93.

Thörnell, A. "Patristica," *Uppsala Univ. Årsskr.* 1923 (Uppsala 1923) 1-21.

Thomas, P. "Observationes ad scriptores latinos: ad Arnobium," *Mnemosyne* n. s. 49 (1921) 63 f.

Wassenberg, F. *Quaestiones Arnobianae criticae* (diss. Münster i. W. 1877).

Wensky, H. "Zu Arnobius," *Fleckeisen's Jahrb. f. class. Phil.* 28 (1882) 495 f.

Weyman, C. "Textkritische Bemerkungen zu Arnobius adversus nationes," *Festschr. Sebastian Merkle zu seinem 60. Geburtstage gewidmet von Schülern und Freunden* (Düsseldorf 1922) 386-95.

Wiman, G. "Några Arnobius-ställen," *Eranos* 25 (1927) 278-80.

——. *Textkritiska studier till Arnobius*, in *Svenskt Arkiv för hum. Avhandl.* 4 (Göteborg 1931).

——. "Ad Arnobium," *Eranos* 45 (1947) 129-52.

Wölfflin, E. *Archiv. f. lat. Lex.* 2 (1885) 136.

ON ARNOBIUS AND HIS WORK:

Altaner, B. *Patrologie* (Freiburg i. Br. 1938) 109 f.

——. *Patrologia* (Rome 1944) 118 f.

Amatucci, A. G. *Storia della letteratura latina cristiana* (Bari 1929) 111-4.

16 ⁷

Atzberger, L. *Geschichte der christlichen Eschatologie innerhalb der vornicänischen Zeit* (Freiburg i. Br. 1896) 573-82.

Bardenhewer, O. *Geschichte der altkirchlichen Literatur* 2 (2nd ed., Freiburg i. Br. 1914) 517-26.

Baynes, N. H. *CAH* 12 (1939) 652 f.

Colombo, S. " Arnobio Afro e i suoi libri Adversus Nationes," *Didaskaleion* 9 (1930) 1-124.

Cruttwell, C. T. *A Literary History of Early Christianity* 2 (London 1893) 630-42.

Ebert, A. *Allgemeine Geschichte der Litteratur des Mittelalters im Abendlande* 1 (Leipzig 1889) 64-72 = French trans. by J. Aymeric and J. Condamin 1 (Paris 1883) 74-83.

Francke, K. B. *Die Psychologie und Erkenntnisslehre des Arnobius* (diss. Leipzig 1883) 74-83.

Freppel, C. E. *Commodien, Arnobe, Lactance, et autres fragments inédits* (Paris 1893) 28-93. [The lecture on Arnobius was delivered in 1869.]

Gabarrou, F. *Arnobe son oeuvre* (diss. Toulouse: Paris 1921).

——. *Le latin d'Arnobe* (Paris 1921).

Geffcken, J. *Zwei griechische Apologeten* (Leipzig-Berlin 1907) 287-90.

Godet, P. " Arnobe," *DTC* 1 (1930) 1895 f.

Goodspeed, E. J. *A History of Early Christian Literature* (Chicago 1942) 282-4.

Jirani, O. " Mythologické prameny Arnobiova spisu Adversus Nationes," *Listy Filologické* 35 (1908) 1-11, 83-97, 163-88, 323-39, 403-23.

Jordan, H. *Geschichte der altchristlichen Literatur* (Leipzig 1911) 229 f.

Jülicher, A. " Arnobius," No. 1, *RE* 1 (1894) 1206 f.

Krüger, G. " Arnobius," *New Schaff-Herzog Encycl. of Rel. Knowl.* 1 (1908) 300 f.

——. " Arnobius," *Realencycl. f. prot. Theol.* 2 (1897) 116 f.

* Labriolle, P. de. " Le cas d'Arnobe," *Revue de Fribourg* 40 (1909). [Probably identical with a section in the next item bearing same title.]

——. *Histoire de la littérature latine chrétienne* (2nd ed., Paris 1924) 252-67 = *History and Literature of Christianity from Tertullian to Boethius* (tr. by H. Wilson, New York 1925) 188-99. All citations, however, are to the 3rd French edition revised by G. Bardy, 1 (Paris 1947) 274-90.

——. " Arnobe," *Dict. d'hist. et de géogr. ecclés.* 4 (1930) 544.

Lardner, N. *Works* 2 (London 1815) 244-57; 3 (London 1831) 456-88.

Leckelt. *Über das Arnobius Schrift: Adversus Nationes* (Progr. Neisse 1884) 3-19.

LeNourry, N. " Dissertatio secunda in septem Arnobii disputationum Adversus Gentes libros," in his *Apparatus ad bibliothecam maximam veterum patrum* etc., 2 (Paris 1715), cols. 257-570 = " Dissertatio praevia " in ML 5. 365-714.

Lorenz, T. *De clausulis Arnobianis* (diss. Breslau 1910).

Marchesi, C. "Questioni arnobiane," *Atti del R. Ist. Veneto di Scienze, Lettere ed Arti* 88 (1929) 1009-1032.

———. "Il pessimismo di un apologeta cristiano," *Pègaso* 2 (1930) 536-50.

McCracken, G. E. "Arnobius Adversus Genera," *Class. Jour.* 42 (1947) 474 f.

McGiffert, A. C. *A History of Christian Thought* 2 (New York 1933) 39-45.

Micka, E. F. *The Problem of Divine Anger in Arnobius and Lactantius,* (Cath. Univ. Stud. in Christ. Ant. 4, Washington 1943).

Migne, J. P. "De Arnobio afro notitia historica," *ML* 5. 349-66.

Monceaux, P. *Histoire littéraire de l'Afrique chrétienne* 3 (Paris 1905) 241-85.

Moricca, U. *Storia della letteratura latina cristiana* 1 (Turin [1923]) 604-17.

M[oule], H. C. G. "Arnobius," in Wace and Piercy, *A Dictionary of Christian Biography and Literature* (Boston 1911) 49-51.

Neander, A. *General History of the Christian Religion and Church* 1 (7th Amer. ed., tr. by Joseph Torrey, Boston 1854) 887-9; 2 (Bohn ed., London 1853) 449-452.

Niccoli, M. "Arnobio," *Encicl. Ital.* 4 (1929) 551.

* Orsavai, F. *Mysterium ok Arnobiusnal* (diss. Budapest 1914).

Rand, E. K. *CAH* 12 (1939) 607-9.

Rapisarda, E. *Clemente fonte di Arnobio* (Turin 1939).

———. *Arnobio* (Catania 1945). (See the review by G. Quispel, *Vigiliae Christianae* 2 [1948] 123 f.)

Röhricht, A. *De Clemente Alexandrino Arnobii in irridendo gentilium cultu auctore* (diss. Kiel: Hamburg 1892).

———. *Die Seelenlehre des Arnobius nach ihren Quellen und ihrer Entstehung untersucht* (Hamburg 1893).

Salvatorelli, L. *Storia della letteratura latina cristiana dalle origini alla metà del VI secolo* (Milan 1946) 105-7.

Schaff, P. *History of the Christian Church* 2 (6th ed., New York 1892) 856-61.

Schanz, M., Hosius, C., and Krüger, G. *Geschichte der römischen Litteratur* 3 (3rd ed., Munich 1922) 407-13.

Scharnagl, J. *De Arnobii Maioris latinitate: Pars* 1 (Progr. Görz, publ. 1895).

Schram, D. *Analysis operum SS. Patrum et scriptorum ecclesiasticorum* 7 (Augsburg 1784) 91-250.

Schulze, E. F. *Das Übel in der Welt nach der Lehre des Arnobius, ein Beitrag zur Geschichte der patristischen Philosophie* (diss. Jena 1896).

Shahan, T. J. "Arnobius," *Cath. Encycl.* 1 (1907) 746 f.

Sihler, E. G. *From Augustus to Augustine: Essays & Studies dealing with the contact and conflict of classic paganism and Christianity* (Cambridge 1923) 167-73 = *Bibl. Rev.* 5 (1920) 259-65.

Spindler, P. *De Arnobii genere dicendi* (diss. Strassburg 1901).

Stange, C. *De Arnobii oratione*: 1. *De verbis ex vetusto et vulgari sermone depromptis*; 2. *De clausulis Arnobianis* (Progr. Saargemünd 1893).

Tixeront, J. "Arnobe," *Dict. prat. des conn. rel.* 1 (1925) 397 f.

Tschiersch, W. *De Arnobii studiis latinis* (Jena 1905).

Tullius, F. *Die Quellen des Arnobius im 4., 5. und 6. Buch seiner Schrift Adversus Nationes* (diss. Berlin: Bottrop 1934).

Weyman, C. "Arnobius der ältere," *LTK* 1 (1930) 689.

Wright, F. A. *Fathers of the Church* (London 1928) 139-56.

NOTES

[1] F. J. Foakes-Jackson, *Studies in the Life of the Early Church* (New York 1924) 203, calls Arnobius the last ante-Nicene writer, confusing him with Lactantius. He also says that Arnobius wrote the best Latin of the age, another point in evidence of the confusion.

[2] Cf. L. Salvatorelli, *Storia della letteratura latina cristiana* (Milan 1946) 107. F. Gabarrou, *Le latin d'Arnobe* (Paris 1921) 1, says that it is in Arnobius' spirit, nature, temperament that we are primarily interested.

[3] Orelli (1. iv) calls him "Varronem istum Ecclesiae Latinae," a dictum he credits to no one but which may have been derived from Voss to whom it is attributed by C. E. Freppel, *Commodien, Arnobe, Lactance, et autres fragments inédits* (Paris 1893) 87. Cf. E. Rapisarda, *Arnobio* (Catania 1945) 136. This highly important contribution to the literature on Arnobius became available to me only when my own work was ready for the press but I have attempted to take his conclusions into consideration wherever possible. While I disagree with Rapisarda on many minor points, I find him thoroughly sound in his effort to rehabilitate the reputation of Arnobius from the skeptical assault made on it by scholars of the nineteenth and early twentieth centuries. Conditions existing at the time he was writing naturally explain and excuse his failure to mention important work by others (e. g. Festugière) but the book has two serious defects: (1) the author often allows his enthusiasm for polemic to lead him to extremes, a fact which he himself recognizes (130); and (2) the passages he adduces in support of his contention that Arnobius was influenced by an earlier writer or himself influenced a later do not, in my estimation, always provide the necessary confirmation. Nevertheless, there are many unforgettable passages of which I quote the following (7): "[in Arnobio] si accendono luci e si stendono ombre, si illuminano speranze e si affaciano dubbi, che ripercuotono il tormento di un' anima che va in cerca di Dio."

[4] E. K. Rand, *The Founders of the Middle Ages* (Cambridge 1941) 41, but see his earlier view in *CAH* 12 (1939) 607. Cf. also J. W. Mackail, *Latin Literature* (London 1930) 255.

[5] Wisdom after the fact. Arnobius could hardly have realized that he was living on the eve of a new era.

[6] This criticism assumes that every work on Christianity must be a full exposition of its teaching.

[7] C. T. Cruttwell, *A Literary History of Early Christianity* 2 (London 1893) 641.

[8] E. F. Schulze, *Das Übel in der Welt nach der Lehre des Arnobius, ein Beitrag zur Geschichte der patristischen Philosophie* (diss. Jena 1896) 42.

[9] G. Krüger, *New Schaff-Herzog Encycl.* 1 (1908) 301.

[10] E. Norden, *Die antike Kunstprosa* 2 (Leipzig-Berlin 1909) 605 n. 1. Cf. also his *Die griechische und lateinische Literatur und Sprache* 2. 2 (2nd ed., D. *Kultur d. Gegenwart* 1. 8, Berlin-Leipzig 1907) 417 f. O. Bardenhewer, *Geschichte der altkirchlichen Literatur* 2 (2nd ed., Freiburg i. Br. 1914) 517, also compares him unfavorably with Cyprian. While this judgment is probably correct on the whole, there are phases in which he is superior to Cyprian. For still other unfavorable judgments, of which the most striking is the dictum of Cecchelli, "formicolante di errori" (errors like ants), in *Africa romana* (Milan 1935) 143, see Rapisarda, *Arnob.* 3-5. It is, however, refreshing to compare this negative verdict of the "moderns" with the perspicacity of Arnobius' first editor, Sabaeus, who in 1543 called him "pietatis christianae maximus dux et propagator."

[11] Freppel 39; Bryce-Campbell, *ANCL* 19 (1871) ix = *ANF* 6. 406. Cruttwell (2. 541) does not agree that Arnobius' neglect is wholly undeserved. H. B. Swete, *Patristic Study* (London 1909) 68, gives him only a short paragraph and omits him entirely from the suggested course of study (144-7) and from his article on "Fathers of the Church" in *Encycl. Brit.* 10 (11th ed., 1911) 200 f.

[12] Rapisarda, *Arnobio* (Catania 1945).

[13] For editions and translations consult the Bibliography (232-4) and the end of the Introduction (56 f.). No translation has as yet appeared or even been announced in the Loeb Classical Library.

[14] J. C. Orelli's variorum commentary appeared at Leipzig in 1816-7 and was reprinted in *ML* 5 (Paris 1844). In the latter year also G. F. Hildebrand published his edition at Halle. F. Oehler's commentary in E. G. Gersdorf's *Bibl. Patrum eccles. sel.* 12 (Leipzig 1846) is more restricted in scope. Only one commentary has been

published in any modern language, that accompanying the German translation of F. A. v. Besnard (Landshut 1842).

[15] For an excellent discussion of Arnobius' place among the apologists, see J. Geffcken, *Zwei griechische Apologeten* (*Samml. wiss. Komment. zu griech. u. röm. Schriftstellern*, Leipzig-Berlin 1907) 287-9.

[16] Rapisarda (*Arnob.* 54) terms it the most violent Christian attack on contemporary neo-Platonism.

[17] Since Arnobius is by no means an unprejudiced witness, his testimony must, of course, be handled with care. On the caution which must be observed in dealing with the works of the apologists as evidence for the pagan cults, see Cumont 12 f., 187 f., and cf. also P. de Labriolle, *Histoire de la littérature latine chrétienne* (3rd ed. rev. by G. Bardy, Paris 1947) 1. 179 f.

[18] Yet other apologists boldly attacked the cult. Cf. Theophilus, *Ad Autol.* 1. 11; Tertullian, *Apol.* 28-36. J. B. Lightfoot, *The Apostolic Fathers*, Part 2 (2nd ed., London 1889) 3. 376, wrongly cites Arnobius 7. 36 as testimony for the offering of incense to the emperors.

[19] St. Jerome, *De vir. ill.* 79; Arnobius sub Diocletiano principe Siccae apud Africam florentissime rhetoricam docuit scripsitque adversus gentes quae vulgo exstant volumina; *Chron., GCS Eusebius* 7. 231. 14 Helm = 2. 191 Schoene = 313 Fotheringham: Arnobius rhetor in Africa clarus habetur. Qui cum Siccae ad declamandum iuvenes erudiret et adhuc ethnicus ad credulitatem somniis compelleretur, neque ab episcopo impetraret fidem quam semper impugnaverat, elucubravit adversum pristinam religionem luculentissimos libros, et tandem veluti quibusdam obsidibus pietatis, foedus impetravit; *Epist.* (*ad Magnum*) 70. 5: septem libros adversus gentes Arnobius edidit totidemque discipulus eius Lactantius; *De vir. ill.* 80: Firmianus, qui et Lactantius, Arnobii discipulus, sub Diocletiano principe . . . .

[20] Chiefly by Trithemius (John of Trittenheim, 1462-1516) in his *De scriptoribus ecclesiasticis* (1st ed. Basel 1494) 53, and by the printer Froben of Basel who in 1560 reprinted in one volume as by the same author, both Erasmus' edition of the *Commentary on the Psalms* by the Younger Arnobius (preface dated 1 August 1522) and Gelenius' edition of the *Adversus nationes* (preface dated 1 January 1546).

[21] On Arnobius the Younger, see M. Schanz—C. Hosius—G. Krü-

ger, *Geschichte der römischen Litteratur* 4. 2 (Munich 1920) 533-6; O. Bardenhewer 4. 605 f.

[22] ARNOUII (gen.)—see the *explicits* of each Book, folii 27, 64, 80, 97b, 120, 134b, 162. The name does not appear at the beginning of Book One. Reifferscheid points out that this confusion is also found elsewhere in the manuscript.

[23] Cf. Ἄρνεος, Ἀρνίας, Ἀρνιάδας, Ἄρνιππος, etc.; Μηλόβιος, Ζηνόβιος, etc. See A. Reifferscheid, *Analecta critica (ad Arnobium), Index Lect. Hib.* (Breslau 1877) 9 f.; Bardenhewer 2. 518.

[24] Modern writers frequently refer to him as ' Arnobius Afer,' or as ' Arnobius Orator ' (in the title to Oehler's edition) or as ' Arnobius Maior ' (in the title to Scharnagl's article), but of these surnames only ' Arnobius Orator,' which is found in the *incipit* to Book Five, has ancient authority.

[25] Folio 64, *explicit* of Book Two, the only place in the manuscript where the title appears.

[26] *Adversus gentes* appears as the title of all editions down to that of Salmasius (Leyden 1651). L. Duchesne, *Histoire ancienne de l'Eglise* 2 (5th ed., Paris 1911) 52 n. 1, mistakenly says that the title is *De errore profanarum religionum* which he borrows from the work of Firmicus Maternus. It must be admitted that this title would have well fitted Arnobius' work.

[27] In 1. 58 f. Christian literature is defended from the charge of a lack of style and in 2. 6 the pagans are berated for their literary presumptions; but cf. 2. 5 and 4. 13.

[28] Folio 97b.

[29] I do not know any evidence for saying that Arnobius was " official professor " of rhetoric at Sicca, as does Duchesne 2. 42.

[30] Gabarrou (*Oeuvre* 7-10) makes a great deal of Arnobius' African patriotism, citing 1. 5, 5. 1, 5. 18, 6. 4, 7. 50, and 7. 51, as well as supporting statements from other African writers, but he admits (9) that Arnobius does not parade it much. None of the Arnobian passages cited furnishes good evidence for his point—they all merely criticize the Romans. In view of the general antagonism to Rome, I am surprised to find that Geffcken (290) maintains that the hatred of the warlike development of Rome found in earlier Christian writers is absent in Arnobius.

[31] Here and there we may note allusions to African places but too few to be impressive and if we did not know of Jerome's testimony, we might not see any significance in these scattered references.

[32] S. Pétridès, " Sicca Veneria," *Cath. Encycl.* 13 (1912) 771, gives

242   NOTES

other Arabic forms of the name: Shikka Benar or Shak Banaria.
Obviously, Schak, Shak, Shikka = Sicca; Benâr, Benar, and Banaria =
Veneria. El Kef means 'the Rock' which shows something of the
nature of the site. F. A. Wright, *Fathers of the Church* (London
1928) 139, renders Sicca as "Drytown."

[33] H. Kiepert, *Atlas antiquus* (10th ed., Boston and New York, no
date; 12th ed., Berlin, no date), tabulae 7, 10, and 12.

[34] *Hist.* 1. 46 f.

[35] Valerius Maximus 2. 6. 15.

[36] Cf. Minucius 24. 3; Tertullian, *Apol.* 15. 7; Lactantius, *Div. inst.*
1. 17. None of them, of course, mentions this specific temple but
all refer to the practice of temple prostitution. A. W. Newton, "The
Adversus Gentes of Arnobius: a Study in Christian Apologetics,"
Proc. Lit. and Philosoph. Soc. of Liverpool 52 (1897-8) 156, says
that Arnobius was disgusted with the Venus worship but he derives
this from the general criticism of the cult, not from any special
passage.

[37] Halm's 1865 edition of Valerius has at the passage cited not
Siccae but *Cirtae* and says in the apparatus that the former is to be
found in the 'deteriores' and that the epitome of Nepotianus reads
apud Cirtenses. I have submitted this problem to Dr. Dorothy M.
Schullian, an expert on the text of Valerius Maximus, who has
kindly furnished me convincing evidence to show that the weight
of the manuscript authority really is with *Siccae* and not with *Cirtae*.

[38] Cf. H. Dessau, "Sicca Veneria," *RE* 2 R., 2 (1923) 2187 f.;
S. Pétridès, *loc. cit.*; T. Mommsen, *CIL* 8, p. 197, inscriptions 1632-
1775. Siccan bishops were suffragan to Carthage and the names of
those who held the see in 256, 348, 411, 484, and 649 are known.
Cf. also Gabarrou (*Oeuvre* 5); P. J. Mesnage, *L'Afrique chrétienne,
évêchés et ruines antiques* (Paris 1912) 92.

[39] We know that the Romans did permit the continuance of temple
prostitution at the temple of Venus Erycina in a Sicilian town—see
W. W. Hyde, *Paganism to Christianity in the Roman Empire*
(Philadelphia 1946) 58—but it is probable that at the end of the
Third Punic War (149-146 B. C.) the cult was stamped out at
Sicca, not for reasons of a religious or moral nature but as the result
of the wholesale annihilation of the population.

[40] P. Godet, "Arnobe l'ancien," *DTC* 1. 2 (1931) 1985 f., accepts
the connection of Arnobius with Sicca without question. That
Arnobius was also a native of Sicca is assumed by the following: T.
Mommsen, *CIL* 8, p. 197; E. K. Rand, *CAH* 12 (1939) 609; H.

Leclercq, "Kef (El)," *DACL* 8. 1 (1928) 690, but Bryce-Campbell (xiii) rightly note the possibility that he was not a native. I am inclined, however, to believe that the weight of probability is that he was born there, since Sicca was by no means an important city, likely to attract a teacher from afar.

[41] J. K. Fotheringham, *Eusebii Pamphili Chronici Canones* (London 1923) 313.

[42] A. Puech, *Histoire de la littérature grecque chrétienne* 3 (Paris 1930) 177.

[43] See W. L. R. Cates, "Chronology," *Encycl. Brit.* 6 (11th ed., 1911) 305-18, esp. 312. Since the basic date of Abraham was 2016-5 B. C., the 2343rd year from Abraham could be either 326 or 327 A. D. So also in the case of the Olympiads and even the reign of Constantine which began on 25 July 306.

[44] F. H. Sandbach, "Lucreti poemata and the Poet's Death," *Class. Rev.* 54 (1940) 72-77, esp. 73. Cf. also J. W. Thompson—B. J. Holm, *A History of Historical Writing* 1 (New York 1942) 129.

[45] S. Colombo, "Arnobio Afro e i suoi sette libri Adversus Nationes," *Didaskaleion* 9 (1930) 3, admits the contradictions.

[46] Cf. 1. 26, 1. 65, 2. 5, 2. 77 f., 3. 36, 4. 36, 5. 29, 6. 27.

[47] A. Harnack, *Die Chronologie der altchristlichen Litteratur bis Eusebius* 2 (Leipzig 1904) 415, says 2. 5 and 4. 36 show the persecutions had not stopped.

[48] Optatus 1. 18; P. Monceaux, *Histoire littéraire de l'Afrique chrétienne* 3 (Paris 1905) 247.

[49] Bardenhewer 2. 521.

[50] Harnack 2. 414.

[51] Gabarrou (*Oeuvre* 6); U. Moricca, *Storia della letteratura latina cristiana* 1 (Turin 1923) 610; S. Brandt, "Über die dualistischen Zusätze und die Kaiseranreden bei Lactantius," *Sitzungsb. d. k. Akad. d. Wiss., philos.-hist. Cl.*, 120. 5 (Vienna 1890) 40.

[52] Bardenhewer 2. 518.

[53] This view is based solely on the master-pupil relationship of Arnobius and Lactantius which will be discussed later.

[54] Bryce-Campbell x.

[55] On Jerome's additions to the *Chronicon* of Eusebius see R. Helm, "Hieronymus' Zusätze in Eusebius' Chronik," *Philologus* Suppl. 21. 2 (1929) esp. 89 where Helm dates Arnobius in 303-310. See also S. v. Sychowski, *Hieronymus als Literarhistoriker* (*Kirchengesch. Stud.* 2. 2, Münster i. W. 1894).

[56] Cf. 1. 13: Trecenti sunt anni ferme, minus vel plus aliquid, ex quo coepimus esse Christiani et terrarum in orbe censeri.

[57] Modern scholars are fairly well agreed that the calculation upon which our present chronology is based was made by Dionysius Exiguus in the sixth century. He equated the Birth of Christ with the year we now call 1 B. C. and computed his own date therefrom. While there is no unanimity as to when the historic Birth took place, so far as our present investigation is concerned, it does not matter, for if an error was destined to be made by Dionysius, that fact was unknown to Arnobius.

[58] Cf. Tertullian, *Apol.* 7. 3: Census istius disciplinae, ut iam edidimus, a Tiberio est; Lactantius, *De mort. pers.* 2.

[59] Cf. Acts 11. 26. See J. A. Kleist, *ACW* 1 (1946) 127 n. 15a.

[60] Bryce-Campbell *ad loc.* translate clumsily as 1500 years but correct this in the errata and it is given properly in *ANF* 6, *ad loc.*

[61] See Cates, *loc. cit.* 313.

[62] L. Cincius Alimentus, fr. 4 in H. Peter, *Historicorum romanorum reliquiae* 1 (Leipzig 1914) 41, quoted from Dionysius of Halicarnassus, *Ant. rom.* 1. 74. 1: Ol. 12. 4 = 728 B. C.

[63] Dionysius (*ibid.*) quotes Fabius Pictor as giving the date as Ol. 8. 1= 747 (see Peter, 1. 19, fr. 6); also quoted by Syncellus, Eusebius, and Solinus.

[64] Quoted by Dion. Hal., *Ant. rom.* 1. 74. 3 = *Annales maximi*, fr. 1, Peter 1. 3. The same date is attributed to Q. Lutatius Catulus, fr. 12 from Solinus 1. 27 (Peter 1. 194) and to Nepos and Eratosthenes and Apollodorus: Ol. 7. 2 = 750 B. C.

[65] M. Porcius Cato, quoted by Dion. Hal., *Ant. rom.* 1. 74. 2, says Rome was founded 432 years after the fall of Troy = 752 B. C. See Peter 1. 61, fr. 17**.

[66] M. Terentius Varro, according to Censorinus (*De die nat.* 21), and before him T. Pomponius Atticus, fr. 1 of his *Annales* (Peter 2. 7), also attributed to Cicero, give Ol. 6. 3 = 753 B. C. The same date also appears in Plutarch (*Romulus* 12. 2), not mentioned by Peter. For a compilation and discussion of all these dates, see F. K. Ginzel, *Handbuch der mathematischen und technischen Chronologie* 2 (Leipzig 1911) 192-201. Ginzel cites evidence for still other dates, all earlier.

[67] *ANF* 6. 407.

[68] Varro is cited by name twelve times in all (see index) and three times is alluded to without being named (3. 1, 3. 34, 4. 13).

[69] Heraldus, cited by Orelli; Oehler xii; Bryce-Campbell xii; Crutt-

well 2. 631; Monceaux 3. 248; Bardenhewer 2. 521; Sihler 173; Colombo 4; Rapisarda (*Arnob.* 131).

⁷⁰ Eusebius, *Hist. eccl.* 8. 2. 14.

⁷¹ Cf. 4. 36: Nam nostra quidem scripta cur ignibus meruerunt dari? cur immaniter conventicula dirui?

⁷² LeNourry (*Diss. praev.* in *ML* 5. 392 f.) suggests that earlier persecutions may have provided this information. Freppel (34) thinks the tone too calm for the year 303. Colombo (5) emphasizes the disturbance among the Christians at the outbreak of the persecution. Cf. Lactantius, *De mort. pers.* 34; Eusebius, *Hist. eccl.* 8. 17. 6.

⁷³ In 1. 5 Arnobius alludes to the invasion of the Mediterranean basin by people from the lost Atlantis which he dates as "ten thousand years ago." The source is Plato, *Timaeus* 23e, where it is said that Solon was told by the Egyptian priests that the invasion took place nine thousand years before his time. Solon's dates are approximately 638-558 B. C., so Arnobius is therefore only roughly accurate at this point.

⁷⁴ Monceaux 3. 248.

⁷⁵ Moricca 1. 610, but on the same page he gives 284-311 as the outer limits.

⁷⁶ Dates of Arnobius by various writers are as follows: 296 A. D.: H. F. Clinton, *Fasti Romani* 1 (London 1845) 339, 381; 2 (*ibid.* 1850) 433; J. Tixeront, *Handbook of Patrology* (tr. by S. Raemers from 4th French ed., St. Louis 1939) 125. 297-298: LeNourry, *ML* 5. 393; N. Lardner, *Works* 2 (London 1815) 246; Freppel 33. 298: Elmenhorst, citing Meursius, quoted by Orelli 1. 292. *About* 300: Sihler 171, 173 (?); Gabarrou, *Oeuvre* 6; McGiffert 2. 39. 300-310 A. D.: Colombo 4. *Just before* 303: Newton 155. *As late as* 303: Cruttwell 2. 631. *During persecutions of* 303: Rand, *CAH* 12. 609. *Either* 297 *or* 303 (*preferably* 303): Schaff 2. 858. 303 A. D.: Rapisarda (*Arnob.* 241). 303-313: Moule 50 (but on 49 he says Arnobius was still teaching in 303). *After* 303: Krüger, *New Schaff-Herzog* 1. 300. 303-310 A. D.: Helm, *loc. cit.* 304-310: de Labriolle 1. 277 n. 2; C. Weyman 689; Micka 148 f. *Probably before* 305: Bryce-Campbell xii. *During persecution*: Altaner, *Patrol.* 109; Baynes, *CAH* 12. 652. 305 *during or soon after persecution*: Bardenhewer 2. 521. *About* 305: G. Brunner, *Jahrb. f. Liturgiew.* 13 (1935) 178; Jordan 229 f. 306 A. D.: Schoenemann, Orelli 1. xxi. The correct date is, however, neatly set down by G. Quispel (*Vigiliae Christianae* 2 [1948] 123) as " ± 300 A. D."

⁷⁷ Newton 155. B. Schmid, *Grundlinien der Patrologie* (2nd ed., Freiburg i. Br. 1886) 64, believes that he died after 325!

⁷⁸ Bryce-Campbell (xiv) and Coxe (*ANF* 6. 405) think martyrdom probable.

⁷⁹ Harnack, *Chron.* 2. 415.

⁸⁰ Brandt, *op. cit.* 40; Moricca, 1. 625.

⁸¹ Micka 146-7 n. 3, gives a long list of earlier scholars who accept the pupil-teacher story. On the relationship of Lactantius to Arnobius, see Micka 145-7. C. Bailey, in his edition of Lucretius 1 (Oxford 1947) 9, 11, says that Arnobius follows Lactantius in imputing the words *insanus, delirare, amens,* to Lucretius. Since Arnobius never applies these words to Lucretius, he can hardly be following Lactantius in this respect.

⁸² E. Ffoulkes, "Lactantius," Smith and Wace, *Dict. of Christ. Biogr.* 3 (London 1882) 613-7. B. Altaner, *Patrologie* (Freiburg i. Br. 1938) no longer states (cf. Rauschen-Altaner, *Patrologie* [Freiburg i. Br. 1931] 153) that Jerome's assertion was made "wohl zu Unrecht."

⁸³ Lactantius, *Div. inst.* 5. 1. 22 f.: Ex iis qui mihi noti sunt Minucius Felix non ignobilis inter causidicos loci fuit. . . . Septimius quoque Tertullianus fuit omni genere litterarum peritus, sed in eloquendo parum facilis et minus comptus et multum obscurus fuit. Ergo ne hic quidem satis celebritatis invenit. Unus igitur praecipuus et clarus exstitit Cyprianus. Note the criticism of the style of Tertullian, a point to which we shall revert a little later. Harnack (*Chron.* 2. 414) is singularly in error in saying that Lactantius had little reason to cite Arnobius.

⁸⁴ Micka 149.

⁸⁵ See above, pp. 2, 7.

⁸⁶ Micka (150) says Arnobius was no longer in contact with Lactantius who was called about 290 to Nicomedia and later to Gaul.

⁸⁷ The view that Lactantius does not mention Arnobius because he did not know of his work is accepted by the following: LeNourry (*ML* 5. 862); N. Dufresnoy, *Praef. in Lactantium* 7 (*ML* 6. 59); Brandt 19-21; Colombo 1 f. Bardenhewer 2. 531-3. McGiffert (2. 45) says that the two works were being composed about the same time.

⁸⁸ Freppel 92. Though the differences are many, a few may be cited by way of example: (1) Lactantius shows a much broader and much deeper knowledge of pagan literature; (2) Lactantius differs strongly on such doctrines as the immortality of the soul and the Divine Anger; and (3) Arnobius' attitude toward the Roman govern-

ment is one of opposition, whereas Lactantius boldly addresses Constantine. Cf. C. N. Cochrane, *Christianity and Classical Culture* (London-New York 1944) 191.

[89] Brandt 19 f.

[90] Micka 152 n. 15.

[91] Moricca 1. 649.

[92] G. Molignoni, "Lattanzio apologeta," *Didaskaleion* 5 fasc. 3 (1927) 151.

[93] Yet, as we have seen, some regard Arnobius as not a profound thinker and such a resemblance in any case is hardly significant.

[94] Brandt, *loc. cit.* and *CSEL* 19. 1, pp. cii, 89, 181, and the index of authors in *CSEL* 27. 2. 245.

[95] M. Pohlenz, *Vom Zorne Gottes* (*Forsch. z. Rel. u. Lit. d. alten u. neuen Test.* 12, Göttingen 1909) 49 n. 1. He objects to Brandt's views in regard to a comparison of Arnobius 2. 35 with Lactantius 2. 14. 4; Arnobius 5. 18 with Lactantius 1. 22. 9.

[96] Micka 152 n. 15 sees resemblances also between Arnobius 2. 51 and Lactantius; between Arnobius 3. 17 and *De op. dei* 17. 6, but on 152 f. he thinks Brandt's and Pohlenz' view of the dependence of Lactantius on Arnobius is not probable.

[97] Cf. Micka 147 f. and 152-4, 156.

[98] Micka 153. Cf. Monceaux 3. 290.

[99] Micka 157.

[100] Micka 151 n. 13.

[101] De Labriolle (1. 291) and Brandt (*CSEL* 19. xi) say it was Pico della Mirandola that first called Lactantius this.

[102] In 2. 7 there is a noncommittal reference to dreams as a subject for investigation.

[103] Oehler x.

[104] Bryce-Campbell x.

[105] *ANF* 6. 405.

[106] *CAH* 12. 609.

[107] Freppel 32.

[108] Moule 50.

[109] Gabarrou, *Oeuvre* 5 f., in reference to Arnobius 1. 45 and the argument against philosophy in Book Two.

[110] Cruttwell 2. 631.

[111] A. Neander, *General History of the Christian Religion and Church* 2 (tr. by J. Torrey, London 1851) 449. He quite naïvely speaks of the "free, independent manner in which he seems to have

come to Christianity, through the reading of the New Testament, especially the gospels."

[112] Cumont 220 n. 55.

[113] *Oeuvre* 5, derived from Monceaux 3. 245.

[114] De Labriolle 254.

[115] Monceaux 3. 245.

[116] Moricca 1. 609.

[117] Bryce-Campbell xi-xii.

[118] A. D. Nock, *Conversion: the Old and the New in Religion from Alexander the Great to Augustine of Hippo* (Oxford 1933) 258.

[119] Neander 2. 450; Schaff 2. 858.

[120] Bryce-Campbell x.

[121] Sihler 167.

[122] Rapisarda, *Arnob.* 7.

[123] LeNourry 5. 391.

[124] Freppel 32.

[125] *CAH* 12. 609.

[126] Geffcken 287.

[127] Salvatorelli 105.

[128] Cited by Rapisarda, *Arnob.* 7.

[129] Moule 50.

[130] *Sententiae episcoporum numero LXXXVII de haereticis baptizandis* 28 = *CSEL* 3 (Cyprian) 1. 447. 9-13 Hartel = *ANF* 7. 653. Cf. Mesnage 92 f.; H. Leclercq, "Kef (El)," *DACL* 8. 1 (1928) 690; *CIL* 8, p. 197; *RE* 2. R., 2 (1923) 2187 f.; Gabarrou, *Oeuvre* 5.

[131] Rapisarda, *Arnob.* 10.

[132] On the credibility of Jerome's account of Lucretius see C. Bailey's edition of the poet (Oxford 1947) 1. 1; 2. 1529, which is in general skeptical. For the opposite view see J. Masson, *Lucretius, Epicurean and Poet* (London 1907) 44: "It is one marked bias of the scholar to be skeptical as to any recorded event which is not conventional or commonplace, anything which transcends the experience of the persons among whom he moves."

[133] Lardner (245) regards the story as an interpolation, as, of course, it is, an interpolation by Jerome into Eusebius' *Chronicon*, but that does not mean that it is false. Gwatkin (1. 195) believes Arnobius' ignorance of Scripture shows that the Christians were afraid of him, but see below.

[134] Trithemus 53 (for the text, cf. below, n. 384). Moule (49) actually takes Trithemius to be a valid source on Arnobius.

[135] Cruttwell (2. 642) says he was not a *presbyter*; McGiffert (2. 43) that he was a layman.

[136] *ANF* 6. 405; M. Richard, " Enfer," *DTC* 6. 1 (1939) 61.

[137] Colombo 11-15.

[138] It is condemned by Micka 42 n. 47, who merely says that Arnobius shows a "marked tendency to cling to pagan ideas." Moricca (1. 613) says Arnobius was more a philosopher than a Christian. Monceaux (3. 242) thinks the references to the theater are autobiographical but no more is meant than that as a pagan he probably attended the theater.

[139] Gabarrou, *Oeuvre* 7.

[140] St. Jerome, *Epistula* 58 (*Ad Paulinum*) 10: Arnobius inaequalis et nimius est et absque operis sui partitione confusus.

[141] Freppel (35) comments on the regular plan of composition throughout and objects to Jerome's criticism but he thinks Book Two is moderately ("passablement") confused. Salvatorelli (107) says "Arnobio manca di sviluppo metodico delle idee," a statement hardly correct. Even Rapisarda, staunch defender of Arnobius as he is, says (*Arnob.* 1) that the *Adversus nationes* is "un opera nell' insieme poco ordinata."

[142] Cf. the remarks on the ridiculous nature of the pagan gods in 1. 28, a topic developed in detail in Books Three to Five.

[143] While it must be admitted that in later books Arnobius often appears to be answering hypothetical objections of hypothetical pagans in order to bring out his own contentions, it seems reasonably clear that in Book One he is answering only actual objections.

[144] Gwatkin (1. 194) calls this a most spirited answer though not so deep as that of Origen.

[145] Clement of Alexandria, *Protr.* 8. Cf. also Tertullian, *Apol.* 47 ff.; Ps.-Justin, *Cohort. ad Gent.* 35 f.

[146] See Book One, nn. 299 f. Cf. Rapisarda, *Arnob.* 108.

[147] Cf. 2. 1, 3. 2 and p. 11, above.

[148] Duchesne (2. 42) speaks of Arnobius' view of the immortality [sic] of the soul in such a way as to make it appear that he believes Arnobius espoused this doctrine but had an imperfect view of it.

[149] Cf. 2. 20 ff. De Labriolle (1. 281 f.) thinks this view of the soul shows Stoic influence.

[150] De Labriolle 1. 284.

[151] McGiffert 2. 39 f. In making the statement that only the first two books are of interest "for us," McGiffert may have meant the quoted words to apply only to persons interested, as he was in that

book, in the history of Christian thought, not in the broader aspects of Arnobius.

¹⁵² A highly illuminating example of the truth of this charge is to be found in the *Hippolytus* of Euripides though the example is not, in fact, used by Arnobius. Hippolytus is the unfortunate victim of a conflict between the desire of Aphrodite to cause all men to love and the contrary wish of Artemis to preserve Hippolytus' chastity. Artemis clearly points out (1325-34) that she would have been glad to interfere with Aphrodite's actions and save Hippolytus from death but that there is among the gods a law that no god will oppose the will of another but stand aside.

¹⁵³ Orelli 1. v.

¹⁵⁴ See above, p. 11.

¹⁵⁵ Kettner, *Introd.*

¹⁵⁶ Bryce-Campbell xii.

¹⁵⁷ The transposition at the beginning of Book Two is of another kind, palaeographic in character. See 2. 3 and n. 3.

¹⁵⁸ But Bardenhewer (2. 521) thinks the *Adversus nationes* is probably complete.

¹⁵⁹ I do not refer to passages in which there are *three* synonyms in a row, a rhetorical device characteristic of the period. Cf. E. S. Bouchier, *Life and Letters in Roman Africa* (Oxford 1913) 101-3.

¹⁶⁰ *Ibid.* 101.

¹⁶¹ Bryce-Campbell xiv; Cruttwell 2. 641, but far superior to Tertullian in clearness and neatness. Milton also thought the style of Arnobius bad: see K. E. Hartwell, *Lactantius and Milton* (Cambridge, Mass. 1929) 40.

¹⁶² A. Jülicher, *RE* 1 (1894) 1206 f.

¹⁶³ A. J. Festugière, *Mémorial Lagrange* (Paris 1940) 101 n. 3.

¹⁶⁴ Brandt 13.

¹⁶⁵ Freppel 92. The following sentence doubtless reflects the politics of the pre-Franco-Prussian War period: "Il faut en verité un aplomb tout germanique pour oser vanter la sobriété du style d'Arnobe." Orelli's dictum is found in *ML* 5. 1291c.

¹⁶⁶ Foakes-Jackson 169, but he is probably confusing Arnobius with Lactantius. See above, n. 1.

¹⁶⁷ Bryce-Campbell xiv-xv.

¹⁶⁸ Cf., e. g., 1. 31 and Micka 40-42.

¹⁶⁹ De Labriolle 1. 277.

¹⁷⁰ *Ibid.* 1. 288. He suggests particularly Voltaire's *Taureau blanc* and the *Lettres d'Amabed.* To Wright (140) the irony is inferior

but Rapisarda (*Arnob.* 196 f.) claims Arnobius made large contributions to the development of Christian literature. He sees (229) none of the pretended Semitic sources in the Latin but does see reflections of a knowledge of Greek (183).

[171] Rapisarda (*Arnob.* 256-8) thinks that if Arnobius modelled his style on any author, it was Cicero, not Sallust.

[172] The Arnobian *nimietas*, to use Jerome's trenchant criticism: *nimius est* (cf. above, n. 140).

[173] Sihler 168. On vocabulary paralleling that of Lucretius, Plautus, Cato, and Varro, see W. Tschiersch, *De Arnobii studiis latinis* (diss. Jena 1905). Tschiersch's belief that these archaistic reflections stem only from frequent use of a lexicon, rather than from reading of the authors, is preposterous.

[174] For the evidence, see below, n. 293.

[175] Freppel 90 f. No neologisms were noted by him but many archaisms.

[176] Compare the contention of H. L. Mencken, *The American Language* (4th ed. New York 1936) 127 f., that there are in " American " many such locutions which have become archaic in the English of the British Isles. I have deliberately refrained from discussing the much-vexed question of *africitas*.

[177] Oehler ix.

[178] Norden 2. 605 n. 1.

[179] On Arnobius' language, consult the following: LeNourry (ML 5.690-714); C. Stange, *De Arnobii oratione* (Progr. Saargemünd 1893); J. Scharnagl, *De Arnobii Maioris latinitate pars* 1 (Progr. Görz 1894, printed 1895); P. Spindler, *De Arnobii genere dicendi* (diss. Strassburg 1901); Tschiersch, *loc. cit.*; J. H. Schmalz, " Satzbau und Negationen bei Arnobius," *Glotta* 5 (1914) 202-8; F. Gabarrou, *Le latin d'Arnobe* (Paris 1921); K. J. Hidén, *De casuum syntaxi Arnobii*, in his *De Arnobii Adversus nationes libris VII commentationes* 3 (Helsingfors 1921); H. Koch, " Zum Ablativgebrauch bei Cyprian von Karthago und andern Schriftstellern," *Rhein. Mus.* 87 (1929) 427-432; Rapisarda, *Arnob.* 185-263.

[180] C. Stange, *De Arnobii oratione*: II. *De clausula Arnobiana* (Progr. Saargemünd 1893), while still approved by Rapisarda (*Arnobio* 260), is strongly criticized by E. Norden, *Die antike Kunstprosa* 2 (Leipzig-Berlin 1909) 946. Norden maintains that Arnobius observes the rule of the *clausulae* before all stronger stops, almost all of the weaker.

[181] T. Lorenz, *De clausulis arnobianis* (diss. Breslau 1910).

[182] E. Löfstedt, *Arnobiana, Lunds Univ. Arsskr.* (Lund 1917).

[183] H. Hagendahl, *La prose métrique d'Arnobe—contributions à la connaissance de la prose littéraire de l'empire,* in *Göteborgs Högskolas Årsskr.* 42 (1936) 1 (Göteborg 1937). See the reviews by B. Axelson, *Gnomon* 15 (1939) 89-99, and by H. D. Broadhead, *Class. Rev.* 52 (1938) 148, the latter unfavorable.

[184] Their formulations of the clausulae are as follows:

Lorenz:		Löfstedt	
I.	– ᴗ – – – ~	I.	᷑ ᴗ ᷑ ᷑ ~
II.	– ᴗ – – – ᴗ ~	II.	᷑ ᴗ ᷑ ᷑ ᴗ ~
III.	– ᴗ – – – ᴗ – ~	III.	᷑ ᴗ ᷑ ᷑ ᴗ ᷑ ᴗ.
IV.	– ᴗ – – – ᴗ – ᴗ ~		

Cf. G. Wiman, *Text Studier till Arnobius, Svenskt Arkiv f. hum. Avhandl.* 4 (Göteborg 1931) vi.

[185] L. W. Jones, *An Introduction to Divine and Human Readings by Cassiodorus Senator* (New York 1946) 39.

[186] St. Jerome, *Epistula* 62 (*Ad Tranquillinum*) 2: Origenem propter eruditionem sic interdum legendum arbitror, quo modo Tertullianum, et Novatum, Arnobium, et Apollinarium et nonnullos ecclesiasticos scriptores Graecos pariter et Latinos, ut bona eorum eligamus vitemusque contraria (*CSEL* 54. 583 Hilberg).

[187] Micka 158.

[188] Geffcken 287.

[189] On this point cf. Gwatkin 1. 195; Moule 50; Micka 75-6; de Labriolle 1. 278-80; Moricca 1. 611; Gabarrou, *Oeuvre* 64.

[190] Cf. 1. 17, 2. 58, 3. 10, 3. 12, 6. 2, 7. 5, 7. 8, 7. 36.

[191] Schaff (2. 858) says that Arnobius quotes from the New Testament once (1 Cor. 3. 19); Micka (74) that he knew the Scriptures, at least the New Testament (cf. 1. 74 f.), but read little of it or did not understand it well. Cf. Leckelt, *Uber des Arnobius Schrift: Adversus nationes* (Progr. Neisse 1884) 7.

[192] Newton 159.

[193] *Illud vulgatum.*

[194] Cf. Gwatkin 1. 145. Marchesi, *Questioni* 1026, says he had not read the Epistle.

[195] Reifferscheid 8, 289.

[196] Rapisarda (*Arnob.* 9-11, 102) will have none of this theory of Arnobius' ignorance of the Scriptures. Dr. Plumpe acutely remarks that the silence is doubtless caused by lack of a copy of the Bible; that numerous precious copies of the Bible were consumed by flames

during the persecution under Diocletian (cf. Eusebius, *Hist. eccl.*
8. 2. 14); and that Arnobius himself very probably alludes to this
(4. 26): nam nostra quidem scripta cur ignibus meruerunt dari?

[197] That knowledge of New Testament passages could have been
obtained orally from other Christians or in catechetical instruction is
the view of Leckelt (8); Monceaux (3. 266). F. P. Badham, " Arnobius and the ' Gospel of Peter,' " *Academy* 49 (1896) 177 f., compares
1. 46 with Matthew 15. 30 f. and thinks Arnobius was here indebted
to the apocryphal *Gospel of Peter.*

[198] De Labriolle (1. 285 f.) thinks that he had no thought of con-
verting the pagans, and, indeed, only a pagan already on the point
of conversion would have been likely to be greatly influenced by
Arnobius.

[199] I omit, as not quite in the same category, the inclusion in the
list of miracles in 1. 45, one not recorded in the Gospels, which is
probably a confusion of the speaking with tongues at the Day of
Pentecost. This is an error, not evidence of ignorance.

[200] Dr. Plumpe points out that something like this (Matt. 5. 44)
would be apt to stick in Arnobius' memory because it was based on
a principle diametrically opposed to the Jewish attitude, as indicated
by the Lord Himself in the preceding verse.

[201] Arnobius conveniently forgets that, according to pagan witnesses, various gods had actually appeared to human beings.

[202] So Marchesi, *Questioni* 1025, but for the opposite view, cf.
Rapisarda, *Arnob.* 11, 103, citing Nam quia proni . . . purgemus
(*Adv. nat.* 1. 27).

[203] In 7. 32 (see n. *ad loc.*) there is ignorance of Christmas and in
7. 26 the criticism of incense as used by the pagans implies that
either Arnobius did not know incense was used by Christians or that
it was not so used in his day. The latter alternative is certainly
correct.

[204] Cf. 1. 62.

[205] McGiffert 2. 43 f.

[206] The view that Christ is personally one with the Father and
indistinguishable from Him and the Sonship is only one of the
' modes ' or manifestations of God.

[207] The view that the Father and Son are completely separate
beings.

[208] Cruttwell 2. 633.

[209] Micka 53, citing J. Alzog, *Grundriss der Patrologie* (4th ed.,
Freiburg i. Br. 1888) 214.

[210] Brunner 174 f. Rapisarda (*Arnob.* 108) maintains on the contrary that the exposition of the Incarnation in 1. 53 and 1. 62 f. is not clear.

[211] Rapisarda (*Arnob.* 107, 124) thinks no occasion was offered for mentioning the dogma of the Trinity. He admits that the epithets of superiority frequently applied to God are intended to differentiate Him not from Christ but from the pagan pantheon. Cf. Book One, n. 101.

[212] Gabarrou, *Oeuvre* 13.

[213] Cf. 2. 49; Micka 61-65.

[214] Marchesi, *Questioni* 1025.

[215] Rapisarda, *Arnob.* 11, 110, but cf. 112 f. On the Resurrection, see *ibid.* 94.

[216] Cruttwell 2. 638.

[217] Marchesi, *Questioni* 1027. J. Hontheim, " Hell," *Cath. Encycl.* 7 (1910) 208, points out that Arnobius takes the view of the temporariness of the punishment in Hell (called by some writers ' annihilationism '), in which he is like some of the Gnostics (the Valentinians) but Hontheim does not make the point that he was consciously influenced by the Valentinians. B. B. Warfield, " Annihilationism," *New Schaff-Herzog Encycl.* 1 (1908) 184 f., calls Arnobius the earliest genuine annihilationist.

[218] McGiffert 2. 44.

[219] For example, one might conclude from 6. 19 that Arnobius had no conception of the all-pervading presence of God but for the fact that in 6. 4 there is a peculiarly beautiful formulation of that doctrine. Baynes (*CAH* 12. 652) says Arnobius denies Providence.

[220] Gabarrou, *Oeuvre* 65, citing 6. 3, 7. 1, 7. 26, 7. 28.

[221] Cf. 4. 36: *conventiculum*; see Book 4, nn. 263 f.

[222] Micka 60.

[223] For evidence on the Divine Anger in Scripture, see Micka 2-7. I cannot agree with Schaff (2. 859) who says that Arnobius' doctrine of God is scriptural.

[224] Micka 46.

[225] Micka 35-59, 65-74.

[226] For the evidence, see Micka 17-21.

[227] See Micka 25-30.

[228] See again Micka 21-34.

[229] For the pagan view, see Micka 7-17, 34.

[230] Micka (17) acutely remarks that the pagan position as exemplified by the philosophers must be distinguished from that of the

common people who not only believed in the gods' anger but sought to appease them. This point of view is expressed in the conversion passage (1. 39).

[231] Micka 76.

[232] Micka (2) says the Stoics and Epicureans were the chief Greek philosophers affecting Arnobius; elsewhere (8, 13) he makes them the only ones. On the Divine Anger among pagans, see Cicero, *De off.* 3. 28. 102: At hoc quidem commune est omnium philosophorum numquam nec irasci Deum, nec nocere. For the view that the gods dwell apart from humans, see Lucretius 2. 646-8; Cicero, *De nat. deor.* 1. 17. 45; 1. 18. 8; 1. 19. 51; 1. 20. 54; Plutarch, *De def. orac.* 19. 420 b; Seneca, *De ben.* 4. 19 f. On possible parallels with Stoicism, see Rapisarda, *Arnob.* 46 f.

[233] LeNourry (*ML* 5. 469). Cf. Micka 54 n. 57; J. Tixeront, *History of Dogmas* 1 (3rd English ed. tr. by H. L. B. from the 5th French ed., St. Louis 1930) 413 f.

[234] Micka (47, 59, 159) points out that Arnobius appears to have no fear of contradicting himself and that this inconsistency saves him from further errors. Cf. also de Labriolle 1. 290.

[235] See below, n. 293.

[236] E. Klussmann, "Arnobius und Lucrez oder ein durchgang durch den Epikuräismus zum Christenthum," *Philologus* 26 (1867) 362-6.

[237] C. Bailey in his edition of Lucretius (vol. 1, p. 8) says that Arnobius "attacks" Lucretius but I nowhere find any evidence to support this statement.

[238] Gabarrou (*Oeuvre* 27-36) thinks Francke exaggerates the Epicureanism in Arnobius.

[239] Cf. J. Jessen, "Über Lucrez und sein Verhältnis zu Catull und Späteren," *Jahresber. ü. d. Kieler Gelehrtenschule* 1872, 17-20: "Es scheint dass Arnobius, bei dem der rhetor bedeutend mehr als der philosoph hervortritt, den Lucrez mehr als stilmuster als wegen des epikuräischen inhalts studiert hat."

[240] F. Dal Pane, "Se Arnobio si è stato un epicureo: Lucrezio e gli apologeti cristiani Minucio Felice, Tertulliano, Cipriano, Lattanzio," *Riv. di stor. antica* 10 (1906) 403-35; 11 (1907) 222-36. I have been unable to find a copy of his work, *De Lucretii imitatione apud Arnobium* (Florence 1901) in which he studied merely the literary imitations. Cf. also Gabarrou, *Oeuvre* 27 ff.; Monceaux 3. 254, 262; G. Krüger, *Realencycl. f. prot. Theol. u. Kirche* 2 (3rd ed., Leipzig 1897) 116.

[241] A. Röhricht, *Die Seelenlehre des Arnobius nach ihren Quellen und ihrer Entstehung untersucht* (Hamburg 1893) 2-21: "Verhältnis des Arnobius zu Lucrez und dem Epikuräismus"; also his *De Clemente Alexandrino Arnobii in irridendo gentilium cultu auctore* (diss. Kiel: Hamburg 1892) 40.

[242] See the whole section (141-62). Elsewhere (174) he points out the importance of Epicurus' first Principal Doctrine for this view.

[243] Marchesi, *Questioni* 1024. Cf. H. Hagendahl, "De latinska apologeterna och Lucretius," *Eranos* 35 (1937) 41-67, esp. 49-67 on Arnobius.

[244] Atzberger 573 f.

[245] Geffcken 287. Cf. 2. 20 ff., 2. 54.

[246] Freppel 76.

[247] Micka 76 f.

[248] Rapisarda, *Arnob*. 25.

[249] Cruttwell 2. 641.

[250] *Ibid*.

[251] *Ibid*. 1. 182. In 2. 640 Cruttwell would have it that Arnobius hardly realized the exclusiveness of Christianity. G. Quispel, in his review of Rapisarda, *Vigiliae Christianae* 2 (1949) 123, alludes to affinities with Karl Barth.

[252] See Book Two.

[253] M. Leigh, "A Christian Skeptic of the Fourth Century: Some Parallels between Arnobius and Pascal," *Hibbert Jour.* 19 (1920-1) 319.

[254] Rapisarda, *Arnob*. 68; G. Quispel, *Vigiliae Christianae* 2 (1948) 123.

[255] W. R. Halliday, *The Pagan Background of Early Christianity* (Liverpool-London 1925) 170.

[256] Shahan 747; Schaff 2. 858; Altaner 10 (with some caution); Rand, *CAH* 12. 609; A. Ebert, *Allgemeine Geschichte der Litteratur des Mittelalters im Abendlande* 1 (Leipzig 1889) 71; Bardenhewer, 2. 522; Monceaux 3. 268; Moricca 1. 612; A. Stöckl, *Geschichte der christlichen Philosophie zur Zeit der Kirchenväter* (Mainz 1891) 186; Micka 43 n. 10 (he thinks 'primus' and 'princeps' imply the existence of other gods [2. 6, 2. 2], and cites the end of 3. 24 and 7. 23).

[257] LeNourry 2. 4 (ML 5. 399); Leckelt 9; Marchesi, *Questioni* 1009-18.

[258] Cruttwell 2. 640.

²⁵⁹ Leckelt 9 f. Micka (42 f.) says Leckelt's arguments are not cogent.

²⁶⁰ On the *daemones* cf. 1. 23, 1. 45, 1. 50, 1. 56, 2. 25, 2. 35. Micka (42 f.) thinks it surprising that Arnobius did not equate the *daemones* with the pagan gods and lists (43 n. 8) other Christian writers who did.

²⁶¹ In 2. 35 f.; cf. also 2. 62, 6. 3, 7. 35.

²⁶² Cf. 2. 62.

²⁶³ Cf. 6. 3. Geffcken (290) thinks the idea of lesser gods comes from Plotinus πρός τ. γνωστ. = *Enn.* 2. 9.

²⁶⁴ Even Micka (45 f.) says Arnobius' teaching is "quite perplexing" and that no conclusion can be reached; Salvatorelli (107), that on the existence of the gods Arnobius is vague.

²⁶⁵ Marchesi, *Questioni* 1016.

²⁶⁶ This is certainly wrong; cf. the evidence cited above.

²⁶⁷ I am unable to agree with Micka (72) who says that the words 'God' and 'gods' are used almost indiscriminately by Arnobius.

²⁶⁸ Micka (47) accuses LeNourry of trying to prove Arnobius orthodox and of reading into his text what is not there. Leckelt (15) and Dal Pane (228 f.) do not follow LeNourry, but Rapisarda (*Arnob.* 2, 52, 79, 125 and *passim*) is to date the strongest defender of Arnobius' orthodoxy.

²⁶⁹ E. v. Dobschütz, *Das Decretum Gelasianum de libris recipiendis et non recipiendis* (*Texte u. Unters.* 3. R., 8. 3, Leipzig 1912) esp. 315; ML 59. 163 and 178. See Colombo 26.

²⁷⁰ V. Dobschütz 12, line 320 of the text. In modern times a similar criticism was voiced against our author by French Jesuits. Cf. de Labriolle 1. 290.

²⁷¹ Bardenhewer 2. 521 f.

²⁷² Cf. 1. 59. It is the hypothetical pagan opponent who speaks here.

²⁷³ For the places in which all these writers are cited, consult the index. For a list of the authors cited, classified according to type of writing, see Gabarrou, *Oeuvre* 11.

²⁷⁴ Though this name is Roman, the work cited was in Greek.

²⁷⁵ Schaff (2. 858) says he quotes "freely" from Homer but there is only a single citation. There are, however, several allusions to the Trojan War and these may be what Schaff means. See following note.

²⁷⁶ Rapisarda (*Arnob.* 255) is sure Arnobius knew both the *Iliad* and *Odyssey*, Pindar, Hesiod, and Euripides.

²⁷⁷ If Flaccus is Granius Flaccus, then he is cited five times.

²⁷⁸ 'Valerianus' may be an error for 'Valerius Antias.'

²⁷⁹ In 1. 3, 2. 71, 7. 9, 7. 38, 7. 44 (bis), but I am not sure that Arnobius had actually read the annales.

²⁸⁰ Cf. 6. 11.

²⁸¹ Cf. 3. 11, 4. 14, 4. 15, 4. 18 (ter), 5. 5, 5. 8.

²⁸² Cf. 1. 3, 5. 1, 5. 15, 5. 18, 5. 32, 7. 28, 7. 44, 7. 46, 7. 49.

²⁸³ Cf. 2. 62.

²⁸⁴ Cf. 2. 73.

²⁸⁵ Rapisarda is convinced that Arnobius knew Horace (242), Vergil (248 f.), Ovid (253), Lucan (254) and Juvenal (254).

²⁸⁶ Sihler 168. Elsewhere (169) he maintains that Arnobius knew Plato, Epicurus, Epictetus, Lucretius, and Hermippus well. He is certainly right in regard to Plato and Lucretius, possibly right about Epicurus (for which author I am more cautious than Rapisarda), but we cannot be sure about the others.

²⁸⁷ See Book Four, n. 164.

²⁸⁸ Cicero, Tusc. 1. 4. 7; 1. 10. 22.

²⁸⁹ G. Bürner, Vergils Einfluss bei den Kirchenschriftstellern der vornikänischen Periode (diss. Erlangen 1902) 36-38 (merely a list, not always sound); P. Spindler, De Arnobii genere dicendi (diss. Strassburg 1901) 11-14; Rapisarda (Arnob. 165) gives a list also.

²⁹⁰ Röhricht, Seelenlehre 22. Cf. Sihler 169.

²⁹¹ Gabarrou, Oeuvre 17, 21-27. The same conclusion is affirmed by Rapisarda (78).

²⁹² For borrowings from Plato see the introductory note to Book Two and the notes on the following chapters: Book One: 5, 8, 52, 64; Book Two: 7, 9, 13, 16, 19, 21, 24, 25, 30, 36, 52, 62, 64, 69; Book Three: 30, 32, 35; Book Four: 16.

²⁹³ For imitations and borrowings from Lucretius and Epicurus, see the notes on the following chapters: Book One: 2, 3, 11, 17, 20, 25, 31, 33, 38, 39; Book Two: 2, 5-7, 9, 10, 14, 16, 20, 23, 26-30, 32, 33, 37, 43, 55, 57-59, 61, 66, 69; Book Three: 5, 9, 10, 13, 28, 32, 33, 41; Book Four: 2, 8, 21, 24, 35; Book Six: 8, 15, 20; Book Seven: 4, 17, 27, 32, 43, 49. See also Spindler 3-11; Wassenberg 32 f.; Röhricht, Seelenlehre 2-19; Gabarrou, Oeuvre 17, 28-37; Sihler 169; Dal Pane opp. citt.; H. Hagendahl, Eranos 35 (1937) 49-67. Bailey in his edition of Lucretius (vol. 1. 137) points out that in Lucretius there are many words which elsewhere appear only in Apuleius and Arnobius. On the resemblance of Arnobius to Apuleius, see Bouchier 101-3.

²⁹⁴ See above, n. 3. See 7. 16 for evidence that Arnobius was unacquainted with certain passages in Plutarch, Juvenal, and Ovid.

²⁹⁵ T. Zielinski, *Cicero im Wandel der Jahrhunderte* (3rd ed., Leipzig-Berlin 1912) 98, admits that Arnobius was indebted to Cicero. Cf. also LeNourry (*ML* 5. 397); Gabarrou, *Oeuvre* 17; de Labriolle 1. 287.

²⁹⁶ For dependence on Cicero's works, see the following chapters and the corresponding Notes: *De nat. deor.*: 3. 5, 3. 6, 3. 8-10, 3. 12-14, 3. 17, 3. 22, 3. 38, 4. 14, 4. 15, 4. 18, 6. 21; *Tusc. disp.*: 2. 9, n. 52; *De div.*: 1. 63, n. 304.

²⁹⁷ For pagan criticism of the pagan cults, see the following: P. Decharme, *La critique des traditions religieuses chez les Grecs des origines au temps de Plutarque* (Paris 1904); B. v. Borries, *Quid veteres philosophi de idolatria senserint* (diss. Göttingen 1918); de Labriolle 1. 286 f.

²⁹⁸ Cf. 4. 29.

²⁹⁹ Cf. 7. 1 f.

³⁰⁰ The reader will long have wondered whether a good deal of the learning displayed by Arnobius is not derived from secondhand reading of manuals available to him from earlier times. I think this is a possibility but not in every case. Cf. the review, by W. H. Stahl, of P. Courcelle: *Les lettres grecques en occident de Macrobe à Cassiodore* (Paris 1943), in *Class. Weekly* 41 (1947) 21: (The seemingly erudite compilers of the period) "often pretend to be drawing upon Plato and Aristotle, although it is evident that they are not familiar with the original works but are repeating clichés handed down through the centuries." The period described by Courcelle is somewhat later than that of Arnobius but the quotation is perhaps apt for him also.

³⁰¹ See M. Schanz—C. Hosius—G. Krüger, *Geschichte der römischen Litteratur* 3 (3rd ed., Munich 1922) 181. For the fragments see G. Kettner, *Cornelius Labeo, ein Beitrag zur Quellenkritik des Arnobius* (Prog. Pforta, Naumburg 1877), Part 3; Gabarrou, *Oeuvre* 46-53, cf. 17, 38-53; J. Mülleneisen, *De C. Labeonis fragmentis, studiis, adsectatoribus* (diss. Marburg: Leipzig 1889). Cf. also W. A. Baehrens, *Cornelius Labeo atque eius commentarius Vergilianus* (Leipzig 1918).

³⁰² This silence, while not necessarily a conclusive argument against the Labeonian theory, is very strong, and the Labeonians have not attempted seriously to meet it. Bardenhewer (2. 532) and Micka (154 nn. 19 f.) maintain that both Lactantius and Arnobius

do not ordinarily mention their sources, but I suspect that, so far as
Arnobius is concerned, they are basing their conclusion in large part
on the silence as to Labeo.

[303] W. Bousset, rev. of J. Kroll, *Die Lehren des Hermes Trismegistos* (diss. Münster i. W. 1913), in *Gött. Gelehrt. Anz.* 176. 12
(1914) 697-755; "Zur Dämonologie der späteren Antike," *Archiv f.
Religionsw.* 18 (1915) 134-75.

[304] B. Boehm, *De Cornelii Labeonis aetate* (diss. Königsberg 1913).

[305] F. Niggetiet, *De Cornelio Labeone* (Münster i. W. 1908).

[306] W. Kroll, "Die Zeit des Cornelius Labeo," *Rhein. Mus. n. F.*
71 (1916) 309-57. F. Tullius, *Die Quellen des Arnobius im 4., 5.
und 6. Buch seiner Schrift Adversus Nationes* (diss. Berlin: Bottrop
1934) 68 n. 157, expresses extreme doubt as to the date of Labeo. It
should be said for Kroll that while he believes that Arnobius used
Labeo in 2. 62, he thinks it very improbable that Labeo is all he
used; and that Porphyry and the *Oracula Chaldaica* were among the
other sources (66 ff.).

[307] Besides the other scholars already cited, see W. Kahl, "Cornelius Labeo, ein Beitrag zur spät-römischen Litteraturgeschichte,"
Philologus Suppl. 5, Heft 5 (1889) 717-807; Röhricht, *Seelenlehre*
30-42: "Verhältnis des Arnobius zu Cornelius Labeo"; F. Dal Pane,
"Sopra la fonte di un passo di Arnobio (V, 18)," *Stud. ital. di filol.
cl.* 9 (1901) 30; Geffcken 289; R. Agahd, "M. Terenti Varronis
rerum divinarum libri I. XIV. XV. XVI," *Jahrb. f. klass. Phil.* Suppl.
24 (1898) 123; de Labriolle 1. 287 n. 1; Cumont 278, nn. 49 f.;
Colombo 118-124; A. S. Ferguson, in W. Scott, *Hermetica* 4 (Oxford 1936) 474-83; Duchesne 2. 42; F. J. Dölger, IXΘΥΣ 2 (1922)
23 n. 1.

[308] St. Augustine, *De civ. Dei* 2. 11; 3. 25; cf. also 9. 1.

[309] The *gentilicium* is supplied from Macrobius, *Sat.* 1. 12. 21,
1. 16. 28, 1. 18. 21, 2. 4. 6.

[310] See above, n. 306.

[311] A. J. Festugière, 'La doctrine des "Uiri noui" sur l'origine et
sur le sort des âmes d'après Arnobe, II, 11-66,' *Mémorial Lagrange*
(Paris 1940) 97-132. G. Bardy, who prepared the 3rd edition of de
Labriolle's *Histoire*, remarks (287 n. 1) that the influence of Labeo
on Arnobius has probably been "beaucoup exagéré." Rapisarda, however, curiously enough, still holds (*Arnob.* 77) to the antiquated
conclusions of Kettner and Kahl.

[312] Tullius 73.

[313] Tullius 57 f.

[314] Tullius 8-10.

[315] Gabarrou, *Oeuvre* 21-3.

[316] Festugière, *table*, 128 f.

[317] Cf. Rapisarda, *Arnob.* 10.

[318] Cruttwell (2. 642), but he also thinks that Arnobius had hardly read Tertullian with whom he had little in common. Arnobius, he says, is unlike Minucius and not an imitator. He certainly is original.

[319] Colombo 28-30.

[320] Coxe, *ANF* 6. 405.

[321] Gabarrou, *Oeuvre* 17.

[322] *Ibid.* 73. He also thinks (68) that Francke is wrong in saying that Arnobius knew his predecessors well. I am glad to note that J. H. Waszink, the latest editor of *Quinti Septimi Florentis Tertulliani De anima* (Amsterdam 1947) 48*, believes that that work exerted no influence upon Arnobius whatever. See my review of Waszink in *Class. Jour.* 44 (1949) no. 5.

[323] De Labriolle 1. 287.

[324] His article in *Africa romana* (Milan 1935) 195 is cited by Rapisarda, *Arnob.* 10.

[325] Freppel 45.

[326] Geffcken 287 f.

[327] LeNourry (*ML* 5. 397).

[328] Bryce-Campbell xvii.

[329] Kettner 2.

[330] Coxe, *ANF* 6. 405.

[331] C. Brakman, *Miscella tertia* (Leyden 1917) 28.

[332] Colombo 118-124; Gabarrou, *Oeuvre* 17; de Labriolle 1. 287; Micka 71 n. 30; Moricca 1. 616; Geffcken 288 n. 1.

[333] Röhricht, *De Clemente*.

[334] Bouchier 102. This remark may hardly amount to opposition to Röhricht since he merely says Arnobius owes more to the pagans than to Clement.

[335] For example, he concludes (8-10) that in 6. 6 Arnobius and Clement had a common source, inferior to Clement in precision but copied blindly by Arnobius. This source must have been later than Sammonicus, the last author cited by Arnobius in the section dependent upon it, and, of course, earlier than Clement who used it.

[336] Hagendahl, *Prose métrique* 2. See the review of Tullius by B. Reynders, *Rech. théol. anc. méd.* 8 (1936) 109.

[337] E. Rapisarda, *Clemente fonte di Arnobio* (Turin 1939). Cf. also his *Arnobio* (Catania 1945) 1, 10, 49, 63.

[338] For the evidence, see the Notes on 3. 30, 3. 39, 4. 21, 4. 22, 4. 25, 4. 29, 5. 1, 6. 1, 6. 3, 6. 10, 6. 12, 7. 49.

[339] For the evidence, see 1. 39, n. 199; 3. 16, and 6. 21. The remaining parallel is to be derived from the *Octavius* 34. 10 where Minucius appears to favor the belief in the mortality of the soul, a cardinal doctrine with Arnobius. Coxe (*ANF* 4. 198, Elucid. III) denies, however, that this statement of Minucius is to be interpreted in such fashion. I dissent.

[340] Halm (*CSEL* 2. 30).

[341] R. Heinze, "Tertullians Apologeticum," *Ber. sächs. Ges. d. W.* 62. 10 (1910) 354 b. 2.

[342] W. Kroll, "Arnobiusstudien," *Rhein. Mus. n. F.* 72 (1917) 86.

[343] Tullius 17.

[344] This assumes that *Adversus nationes* is the right title and that *Adversus gentes* is wrong, but there is really little doubt on the point; see above, 5.

[345] Several good examples may be found in Tertullian, *Apol.* 9. In Arnobius the device is too frequent to require citation.

[346] Cf., for example, Tertullian, *Apol.* 13. 1: Sed nobis dei sunt, inquis.

[347] Tertullian, *Apol.* 21. 17—Arnobius 1. 50.

[348] Tertullian, *Apol.* 17. 5-6—Arnobius 2. 3.

[349] Tertullian, *Apol.* 3. 4; *Ad nat.* 1. 4—Arnobius 2. 5.

[350] Tertullian, *Ad nat.* 1. 10—Arnobius 2. 71.

[351] Tertullian, *Apol.* 10. 6—Arnobius 2. 71.

[352] Tertullian, *Apol.* 19—Arnobius 2. 71.

[353] Tertullian, *Apol.* 6. 8—Arnobius 2. 73.

[354] Tertullian, *Apol.* 15—Arnobius 3. 11.

[355] Tertullian, *Apol.* 20. 2, 40. 3 ff.; *Ad nat.* 1. 9—Arnobius 1. 3; 1. 5.

[356] Tertullian, *Apol.* 21. 3—Arnobius 1. 36.

[357] Tertullian, *Ad nat.* 1. 8—Arnobius 2. 20.

[358] Tertullian, *Ad nat.* 1. 11; *Apol.* 16. 1-4—Arnobius 3. 16.

[359] Tertullian, *Ad nat.* 2. 12—Arnobius 3. 29.

[360] Tertullian, *Apol.* 14. 3; *Ad nat.* 2. 11; Arnobius 4. 24.

[361] Tertullian, *Apol.* 14. 2 f.; *Ad nat.* 1. 10—Arnobius 4. 25.

[362] Tertullian, *Apol.* 14. 4—Arnobius 4. 25.

[363] Tertullian, *De spect.* 18—Arnobius 7. 1.

[364] Tertullian, *Apol.* 22. 10—Arnobius 3. 41.

[365] *Caccabulum* in *Adv. nat.* 6. 14; *silicernium* in 7. 24, both in Tertullian, *Apol.* 13. 4, 7.

[366] Tertullian, *Apol.* 10. 2—see above, pp. 30-3.

[367] Cf. n. 322.

[368] *Apol.* 10.

[369] Pindar, *Pyth.* 3. 54-58; Clement of Alexandria, *Protr.* 2. 30. 1 f.; Tertullian, *Ad nat.* 2. 14; *Apol.* 14. 5.

[370] Geffcken 288: " So hat er im allgemeinen nicht allzu viel Neues gebracht, so gute Quellen er gelegentlich benutzt; die meisten Argumente der anderen Apologeten kehren, ohne dass wir, wie es ja fast stets so geht, immer eine bestimmte Quelle anzugeben imstande wären, hier wieder."

[371] Ssee above, pp. 12-15.

[372] I omit from consideration passages in which there is some resemblance but not a significant one. As an example of an insignificant resemblance, cf. *Div. inst.* 5. 3. 9 where Lactantius alludes in passing to the possibility, which he, of course, denies, that the Miracles of Christ were performed by magic, with *Adversus nationes* 1. 43.

[373] Lactantius, *Div. inst.* 4. 27. 2: nam sicut ipse cum inter homines ageret, universos daemonas verbo fugabat hominumque mentes emotas et malis incursibus furiatas in sensus pristinos reponebat, ita nunc sectatores eius eosdem spiritus inquinatos de hominibus et nomine magistri sui et signo passionis excludunt. (The translation in the text is a revision of that of W. Fletcher [*ANF* 7. 129].) The words suggest that Lactantius may have himself been an eyewitness of the practice, whereas those of Arnobius do not.

[374] Note also some resemblance between Lactantius and a passage of Tertullian (*Apol.* 21. 17) already cited.

[375] *Div. inst.* 4. 15. 6-8: Virtutes eius fuerunt quas Apollo portentificas appellavit, quod quacumque iter faciebat, aegros ac debiles et omni morborum genere laborantes uno verbo unoque momento reddebat incolumes, adeo ut membris omnibus capti receptis repente viribus roborati ipsi lectulos suos reportarent, in quibus fuerant paulo ante delati. Claudis vero ac pedum vitio adflictis non modo gradiendi, sed etiam currendi dabat facultatem. Tum quorum caeca lumina in altissimis tenebris erant, eorum oculos in pristinum restituebat aspectum. Mutorum quoque linguas in eloquium sermonemque solvebat. Item surdorum patefactis auribus insinuabat auditum, pollutos et aspersos maculis repurgabat. Et haec omnia non manibus aut

aliqua medella, sed verbo ac iussione faciebat, sicut etiam Sibylla praedixerat:

πάντα λόγῳ πράσσων πᾶσάν τε νόσον θεραπεύων.

[376] This is probably an error, a confusion of Pentecost. See Book One, n. 227.

[377] *Adv. nat.* 5. 18—*Div. inst.* 1. 22. 1. See Book Five, n. *ad loc.* and cf. Brandt *ad loc.* (89).

[378] *Adv. nat.* 6. 21—*Div. inst.* 2. 4. 16-20. See Book Six, n. *ad loc.*

[379] Lactantius, *Div. inst.* 2. 14. 3 f.: sic eos diabolus ex angelis dei suos fecit satellites ac ministros. Qui autem sunt ex his procreati quia neque angeli neque homines fuerunt, sed mediam quandam naturam gerentes, non sunt ad inferos recepti sicut in caelum parentes eorum. Cf. Brandt *ad loc.* (163).

[380] See the text in Book Two, n. 293. Cf. Brandt *ad loc.* (181).

[381] *Div. inst.* 5. 9. 15-17.

[382] *Adv. nat.* 3. 8 (see n. 30)—*Div. inst.* 3. 11. 12.

[383] Rapisarda, *Arnob.* 161.

[384] Joannes Trithemius, *De scriptoribus ecclesiasticis* 53: Arnobius presbyter, philosophus et rhetor insignis, cum adhuc gentilis rhetoricam doceret, divina miseratione vocatus, Christianum se coepit profiteri, cumque ad episcopos accedens se baptizari expeteret, non credebant, veriti ne vir saecularis tumens eloquentia, sacramentis fidei conaretur illudere, et omnino sententiam differebant. Arnobius vero cernens sibi fidem minime adhiberi, in argumentum sinceritatis suae scripsit et obtulit episcopis insigne volumen:

Adversum Gentes	Lib. VIII.
In Psalterium quoque	Lib. I.
De Rhetorica institutione	Lib. I.

Alia quoque multa edidit, quae ad notitiam meam non venerunt. Docuit in Africa rhetoricam sub Diocletiano principe. Habuitque multos egregios et nobiles discipulos qui viri doctissimi evaserunt. Claruit ergo circa annos Domini nostri IESV Christi CCC. [This text is based on that printed in the preface to Sabaeus' 1542-3 edition of Arnobius.]

[385] K. Ziegler, *Iuli Firmici Materni V. C. De errore profanarum religionum* (Leipzig 1907). Consult his notes at the bottom of the page throughout.

[386] A new edition of this work with Latin text and German translation is expected at the moment of going to press.

[387] C. Brakman, *Miscella tertia* (Leyden 1917) 25-28.

[388] For possible borrowings by Firmicus Maternus, see the Notes on the following chapters: Book One: 29, 34, 53; Book Three: 29, 30, 33, 80; Book Four: 14, 25, 26, 28; Book Five: 6, 19, 21, 26, 28, 33; Book Six: 25; Book Seven: 3, 5, 12, 24, 28, 36. The quotation from the Tarentine poet in Firmicus 26. 1 is not, however, borrowed from *Adv. nat.* 5. 26, since it is given in Greek, and the formula in Firmicus 28. 1 is not derived from that in *Adv. nat.* 5. 26.

[389] Rapisarda, *Arnob.* 29-30. Cf. Eusebius' lost *Quaestiones evangelicae*; Ambrosiaster, *Quaestiones Veteris et Novi Testamenti*. Rapisarda also compares (78 f. and 94) Arnobius with Methodius of Olympus.

[390] Cod. Vat. 3852, membr. 4, fol. 130 (s. X).

[391] E. Bickel, " Ps.–Tertullian De execrandis gentium diis," *Rhein. Mus.* 67 (1927) 394-417.

[392] Colombo 23.

[393] In Rapisarda's view (9, 30, 34, 42 f., 147), however, Augustine had much in common with Arnobius though he never explicitly says that the Bishop of Hippo read the rhetor of Sicca. See the long list of passages (139) containing supposed parallels between the *Adversus nationes* and the *De civitate Dei*. Upon close examination, many of these do not appear to support Rapisarda's contention.

[394] For description of the MS, see the introductions in the editions of Reifferscheid and Marchesi discussed below in detail.

[395] The date of P has been universally determined on the basis of its minuscule script as the beginning of the ninth century and there is evidence to show that the scribe had before him another manuscript in the so-called ' cursive script' which was hard to read and was derived from a still earlier copy in the uncial script without separation of words. The probability is that P was prepared in a monastic *scriptorium* in either Switzerland or Germany. Corrections appear in a number of hands, of which Reifferscheid distinguished three and Marchesi only two, all of these in the ninth century, but in the sixteenth century an unknown scholar added others, utilizing for that purpose at least two and possibly three of the early printed editions, certainly Sabaeus (Rome 1542-3), Gelenius (Basel 1546), and, perhaps, Canterus (Antwerp 1582).

[396] Marchesi v.

[397] Oehler xx.

[398] J. Van den Gheyn, *Catalogue des manuscrits de la Bibliothèque Royale de Belgique* 2 (Brussels 1902) p. 20, no. 923.

[399] Reifferscheid viii. E. J. Goodspeed, *A History of Early Chris-*

tian Literature (Chicago 1942) 284, overlooks this MS when he says "only one manuscript has ever been found."

[400] This conclusion needs to be verified.

[401] Richardson (76) is probably wrong in listing an edition by Muralto (Zürich 1856) which I have not found. I have learned to be skeptical of his list, particularly when, as in this case, he marks an entry with a question. The following errors should be noted: (1) an edition by Stewechius (Antwerp 1586) which Oehler rightly calls a 'fabula'; (2) an edition by Heraldus (Geneva 1597) which is a misprint for 1599; (3) the edition he lists of Heraldus (Paris 1603) is an error for Elmenhorst's printed at Hannover in the same year; (4) the edition of Jo. Meursius (Lugd. 1598) which he lists is a real book: not, however, an edition but a work bearing the title "Criticus Arnobianus tributus in libros septem"; (5) the edition of Ernstius (Havre 1726 ??) should be H. Ernstius, *Notae brevissimae ad Arnobii libros disputationum adv. Gentes* (Copenhagen 1726, but the preface is dated 1651) and this too is not an edition. Oehler (xxvii) lists two other 'ghost' editions which never existed, as he says, one alleged to have been published at Paris in 1626 by the Benedictines of St. Maur, and another (London 1651) with notes by "Carthesius" (= Descartes ?), obviously a mistake for Salmasius' edition (Leyden 1651) which was printed without the editor's name on the title page.

[402] Cf. above, Bibliogr., p. 233.

[403] I do not understand why Guinagh implies (*Proc. Am. Phil. Assoc.* 67 [1936] xxxviii) that Reifferscheid did not examine the manuscript anew.

[404] The only important edition overlooked by Reifferscheid is that of Renatus Laurentius de la Barre (Paris 1580) which doubtless escaped his notice because it is included in an edition of Tertullian. The British Museum also contains a number of early editions having manuscript notes by important scholars as follows: (1) Ant. Carpentarius in the edition of Sabaeus; (2) I. Casaubon in the edition of Canterus (Antwerp 1582); (3) H. Estienne, same; (4) P. Scriverius, same; (5) T. J. Almeloveen, same, and (6) J. Walker, edition of Salmasius (Leyden 1651). The *Bibliothèque Nationale* in Paris contains similarly annotated editions: (1) Jacobus Dalechampius = Jacques Dalechamps, in Sabaeus' edition; (2) Jo. Passeratius = Jean Passerat, same; (3) Franciscus Pithoeus = François Pithou, same; (4) Nicholas Rigault, same; (5) L. Servin, Ursinus' edition (Rome 1583). Some of the latter series apparently were seen by Reiffer-

scheid. The University of Illinois Library possesses a copy of Oehler's edition with notes by Johannes Vahlen.

[405] See the bibliography.

[406] The entire publishers' stock of this edition was destroyed by bombing.

[407] The following reviews, generally favorable, have been noted: (1) Anonymous, *Supplément* to the *Bull. Budé* 1935 152; (2) S. Colombo, *Riv. fil. istr. cl.* 13 (1935) 390-2; (3) G. Costa, *Nuova riv. stor.* 20 (1936) 25; (5) K. Guinagh, *Class. Phil.* 31 (1936) 371 f. and (6) " Justifying the Newer Edition of Arnobius," *Proc. Am. Phil. Assoc.* 67 (1936) xxxvii-xxxviii; (7) W. Kroll, *Phil. Woch.* 55 (1935) 1082-4; (8) E. Malcovati, *Athenaeum* 14 (1936) 112; (9) A. Souter, *Class. Rev.* 49 (1935) 209; (10) O. Tescari, *Convivium* 7 (1935) 476 f.; (11) M. Valgimigli, *Leonardo* 6 (1935) 208.

[408] Hagendahl, *Prose métrique* 2; Wiman, *Eranos* 45 (1947) 129.

[409] At this point I should like to speak a good word for Orelli's commentary which Bryce-Campbell were inclined to criticize unduly. His material is not, as they say, well digested, but contains much information of great value.

[410] Oehler (xxix) has this to say of von Besnard: " Ea conversio tot vitiis verborumque stribiliginibus laborat, ut nisi textum latinum adhibueris vix verbum intellegas."

[411] C. F. Rössler, *Bibliothek der Kirchen-Väter in Uebersetzungen und Auszügen* 3 (Leipzig 1776) 308-44 contains, not a translation, as might be supposed from the title, but an extract based on Stewechius' edition (Antwerp 1604). My friend, Professor Keith C. Seele, has kindly examined this work in the Library of the University of Chicago.

[412] I am likewise indebted to the following friends who have patiently suffered many importunate requests for bibliographical assistance: Professor P. R. Coleman-Norton, Professor Lloyd W. Daly, Dr. Glanville Downey, Professor Gerald F. Else, Lt. Thomas F. Fawcett, Professor Revilo P. Oliver, Professor Keith C. Seele, and Professor Gertrude Smith. The willing assistance of the staffs of the Drake University Library and the Foreign Language Library of the State University of Iowa should be gratefully acknowledged. At the proper points in the Notes I have expressed my indebtedness to other scholars who have courteously given expert advice on special points.

BOOK ONE

The title, though missing in *codex Parisinus* 1661, appears in the *explicit* to Book Two (folio 64, see n. 484 of that Book). There is, however, no reason to believe that any part of the text has been lost. The introductory sentences also contain no dedicatory reference to any patron who suggested the writing of the work. This fact needs to be considered in the light of the testimony of St. Jerome that Arnobius composed the work as evidence of the sincerity of his Christian profession (see Introduction 2, 16 f.). Moreover, while the customary protestation of modesty is not lacking, it is far more restrained than one finds, for example, in such writers as Cyprian, *Ad Donatum* 1; Lactantius, *De opificio Dei* 1; *Divinae institutiones* 3. 1; Julianus Pomerius, *De vita contemplativa* 1. 1. f. (*ACW* 4. 14 f.).

Beginning with no reference to the Bishop of Sicca, Arnobius takes his point of departure from a charge which he says he had heard made by persons otherwise not specified (*nonnullos*) that the Christians were responsible for calamities then oppressing the world. So far as the simple statement of the text goes, we might believe that Arnobius had himself heard the charge made by opponents of Christianity; but the same criticism had been made as early as Tertullian's day (*Apol.* 30, repeated substantially in *Ad nat.* 1. 9; cf. *Ad Scap.* 3). Cyprian also wrote his *Ad Demetrianum* (252 A. D.) to refute the same charge, but he adopts a defense quite different from that of Arnobius: (a) the world was getting older and therefore running down; (b) the real cause was that the pagans did not worship the true God. (On this passage of Cyprian see the penetrating remarks of A. J. Toynbee, *A Study of History* 4 [London 1939] 7 f., in which the leading historian now living discusses the significance of both Cyprian and the poet Lucretius on the decline of civilizations.)

It is therefore at least a possibility that Arnobius had read Tertullian and Cyprian and from them derived his point of departure. This seems to be the view espoused by S. Colombo, "Arnobio Afro e i suoi sette libri Adversus Nationes," *Didaskaleion* 9 (1930) 28, who is sure that Arnobius had read Tertullian, *Apol.* 40, *Ad nat.* 1. 9, and Cyprian, *Ad Demetr.* 2 (see Introd. 41-51). The same charge against the Christians is also met with in writers subsequent to Arnobius, e. g. Lactantius, *Div. inst.* 5. 4. 3; Augustine, *De civ. Dei* 2. 3; 3. 31.

The whole of Book One is devoted in the main to the refutation of this and other similar charges. In general, it is a Book which appears to have benefitted by more thorough revision than some of the others—it presents almost no serious problems of interpretation. Repeated study leads me to remark that Book One seems characterized by the genius and personality of the author to a greater degree than most of the others in which the problem of source is more important.

[1] The verbs *insanire* and *bacchari*, the full force of which can hardly be rendered in English, suggest (a) that the critics of Christianity spoke in such a manner as to convey the impression that they believed themselves the mouthpieces of Apollo (cf. H. W. Parke, *A History of the Delphic Oracle* [Oxford 1939]) or of Dionysus (cf. Euripides' *Bacchae*); (b) that they resembled the typical priestess of these gods in that their words sounded either insane or drunken, and (c) that in Arnobius' opinion the critics were uttering statements worth no more than the babblings of the mad and intoxicated. Cf. Tertullian, *Ad ux.* 1. 6.

[2] Though Arnobius as a rhetorician might be expected to be competent in this sphere, this expression of modesty follows the convention. Cf. the passages cited in the Introductory Note to this Book.

[3] Cyprian, *Ad Demetr.* 2.

[4] Cf. Tertullian, *Apol.* 10. 2: Tunc et Christiani puniendi, si quos non colerent, quia putarent non esse, constaret illos deos esse.

[5] He soon forgets his intention to be dispassionate.

[6] The *numina* include not only the Olympian pantheon but all the other lesser divinities—see G. Wissowa, *Religion und Kultus der Römer* (2nd ed., Munich 1912). In the subsequent attack on the pagan deities, the only important omissions are the cult of the emperors and Mithraism, though in Book Two there are some passages which have been thought to show evidence of the latter religion (see n. 64 of that Book).

[7] A clear allusion to the *De rerum natura* of T. Lucretius Carus (first century B. C.). See the two most recent editions of Lucretius: (a) that of W. E. Leonard and S. B. Smith (Madison 1942) and (b) that of C. Bailey (Oxford 1947). All references have been checked against these two editions. See also below, 2. 70.

[8] Probably not an allusion to alchemism.

[9] *Machinae huius et molis.* Cf. Lucretius 5. 96: moles et machina mundi, and Bailey's note *ad loc.*

[10] Cf. Acts 17. 28.

[11] Cf. Lucretius 2. 147-9 and Bailey *ad loc.*; Vergil, *Aen.* 6. 640 f. Probably the source of the metaphor is Cicero's *Arati Phaen.* 294 (Müller.)

[12] Arnobius doubtless ignores the astronomical fact that unless periodic adjustments are made to the calendar, seasons will over a period of time change perceptibly in relation to the calendar.

[13] Again Arnobius is ignoring the reversed seasons of the Southern Hemisphere. Note the denial of the existence of the antipodes in Lactantius, *Div. inst.* 3. 24. 1.

[14] On this sentence see C. Weyman, " Textkritische Bemerkungen zu Arnobius adversus nationes," *Festschrift Sebastian Merkle* (Düsseldorf 1922) 386 f.

[15] *Prima incipiensque nativitas*, a good example of Arnobius' repetitive language.

[16] The MS reading (*inhabitabiles*) has caused difficulty to many editors for they take the prefix *in-* to be negative, a sense clearly inappropriate here. No dictionary consulted lists the adjective *inhabitabilis* = ' inhabitable ' except Forcellini (2. 841) where the only citations are to this passage and to 7. 47 (Orelli's numbering—in all other editions it is 7. 50) but the MS reading there, *inhabitabilia*, has been rightly emended to *ab Italia* by Oehler and editors subsequent to him. Dr. H. Haffter, of the *Thesaurus Linguae Latinae*, in a letter dated 27 July 1947, kindly informs me that he has been able to find no other example of *inhabitabilis* with a neutral prefix in the unpublished collections of the *TLL* at his disposal. Yet this interpretation of the prefix has been accepted by Orelli, Oehler, Hildebrand, and Marchesi, the last pointing out that *inhabitabilis* is derived from *inhabito* which as early as Seneca and Pliny sometimes = *habito*. A noncommittal position is taken by P. Thielmann, *Archiv f. lat. Lex.* 1 (1884) 80. J. Svennung, *Untersuchungen zu Palladius* (Uppsala 1935) 576 n. 3, cites an example of *ininhabitabilis* in which the first *in-* is negative, the second intensive. This seems strong confirmation, but B. Axelson, " Randbemerkungen zu Arnobius," *Eranos* 40 (1942) 182; " Textkritisches zu Florus, Minucius Felix und Arnobius," *K. Humanist. Vetenskapssamf. i Lund, Årsb.* 1944-5 No. 1, 40, takes *inhabitabiles* to = ' unbewohnt ' (' uninhabited ') and cites *illacrimabilis* which frequently has the sense of ' unwept ' and *habitabilis* = ' inhabited ' (Sil. Ital. 1. 541). This view is equally possible yet Rapisarda (*Arnob.* 15) translates ' inospitali.' Much less plausible is the earlier view of Klussmann that what

Arnobius wrote was *tres habitabiles oras* (i.e. Europe, Asia, Africa), and that a copyist reading in some MS ' III INHABITABILES ' confused ' III ' with ' IN.' Reifferscheid accepted this basic idea of Klussmann's but subtly changed to *duas habitabiles oras*, which does not improve much.

[17] Rulers, in Arnobius' view, would appear to be chosen by fate, not by divine right. Tertullian, on the other hand, seems to believe that the emperor ruled by divine sanction: Et merito dixerim, noster est magis Caesar, ut a nostro deo constitutus (*Apol.* 33. 1).

[18] *Leges*, enacted laws; *iura*, laws inherent in nature. For the view that Arnobius is precise in his use of juristic terminology in this and other passages, see C. Ferrini, "Die juristischen Kenntnisse des Arnobius und Lactantius," *Zeitschr. der Savigny-Stift. f. Rechtsgesch.* 15 (1894) 343-52, esp. 343-6.

[19] A reference to the Roman principle of *mos maiorum*. See J. C. Plumpe, *Wesen und Wirkung der* Auctoritas Maiorum *bei Cicero* (diss. Münster: Bochum-Langendreer 1935) Ch. 5: "Mos Maiorum."

[20] Gabarrou (*Oeuvre* 29) sees in this phrase an allusion to Lucretius 2. 306, 3. 151, and 4. 926, but the parallels are not very striking.

[21] *Sacramenta.* Cf. 2. 5 and Scharnagl 32.

[22] Cf. Cyprian, *Ad Demetr.* 8.

[23] *Vocamen.* Cf. 2. 35, 4. 3, 7. 46, and Lucretius 2. 657 and Bailey *ad loc.*

[24] See, for example, Livy 1. 31, 21. 62, 23. 21, 25. 7, 39. 27. These showers may have been either meteoric or volcanic—cf. H. Jordan, *Topographie der Stadt Rom im Alterthum* 1. 1 (Berlin 1878) 120.

[25] He can hardly mean the destruction of Pompeii, Herculaneum, and Stabiae, by Vesuvius in 79 A. D. since this occurred in the Christian area and that fact would vitiate the point. Tertullian (*Apol.* 40. 8) also mentions the Etruscan town of Volsinii (modern Orvieto) in the same connection (see *Ad nat.* 1. 9). Cf. Pliny, *Nat. hist.* 2. 52; Volsinii oppidum Tuscorum opulentissimum concrematum est fulmine.

[26] Scharnagl 35 makes *difficiles* = *rarae* but it seems as well to take it in the opposite sense.

[27] Cf. Livy 4. 30. 7 f. Twice (*Ad Scap.* 4; Apol. 5. 6) Tertullian tells the story that owing to prayers of Christians serving in the armies of Marcus Aurelius, rain was obtained during a drought.

[28] Cf. also 2. 71, 7. 9, 7. 38, 7. 39 and 7. 44.

[29] Marchesi's insertion of ⟨*terras*⟩ in this sentence seems un-

necessary. For description of the plague at Athens in 438 B. C., see Thucydides 2. 47-52; Lucretius 6. 1138-286 and Bailey *ad loc.*: Eusebius, *Hist. eccl.* 9. 8.

[30] See Livy 42. 10; Tacitus, *Ann.* 15. 5; Pliny, *Nat. hist.* 8. 29; 10. 65; 10. 85; Orosius 5. 11; Augustine, *De civ. Dei* 3. 31.

[31] The inhabitants of Gyara, an island in the Cyclades, were put to flight by mice, according to Pliny, *Nat. hist.* 8. 29. 104.

[32] Tertullian, *Apol.* 20. 2: Quod terrae vorant urbes, quod insulas maria fraudant; *ibid.* 40. 3: Legimus Hieran, Anaphen et Delon et Rhodon et Co insulas multis cum milibus hominum pessum abisse. Cf. also *Ad nat.* 1. 9 for the same story. Pagan writers (Pliny, *Nat. hist.* 2. 87. 202, and Ammianus Marcellinus 17. 7. 13) reported that the first four cities mentioned had come into existence through earthquakes. According to one explanation of the Lacus Curtius in the Forum Romanum (see Platner-Ashby 310 f.) there had been a yawning chasm even in Rome itself. Cyprian, *Epist.* 75. 10, reports earthquakes in Cappadocia and Pontus during the reign of Alexander Severus.

[33] In addition to the account in the Bible (Gen. 6-8) which Arnobius probably did not know, the Greeks had a similar tradition, Deucalion and Pyrrha corresponding to Noe and his family (cf. 5. 8; Apollodorus, *Bibl.* 1. 7. 2; Ovid, *Met.* 1. 244-415; Apollonius Rhodius 3. 1058-89; H. Usener, *Die Sintflutsagen* [Bonn 1899]).

[34] See Ovid, *Met.* 1. 750-2; Nonnus, *Dionys.* Bk 38, for the fullest accounts of Phaethon and the chariot of the sun which was said to have set the world on fire. Cf. also Hyginus, *Fab.* 154; Plato, *Tim.* 22.

[35] See Ovid, *Met.* 15. 262 ff. Tertullian, *Apol.* 40. 4, speaks of the sea tearing away a part of Lucania and thus forming the island of Sicily; and remarks: Haec utique non sine iniuria incolentium accidere potuerunt.

[36] Not fights in the arena but wars of extermination—see Aelian, *De nat. animal.* 17. 27.

[37] Pliny, *Nat. hist.* 8. 29, reports an attack of snakes upon the Spartan town of Amyclae. Rapisarda (*Arnob.* 254) thinks another source may be Lucan 9. 891 ff. but there is really little resemblance.

[38] Plato (*Tim.* 23e) states that the Egyptian priests told Solon (ca. 638-558 B. C.) that the events occurred 9,000 years before his time. If Arnobius was writing under Diocletian, this statement is roughly in harmony with Plato but not precise.

[39] Plato (*Tim.* 24e-25d). His *Critias* contains a history of the

commonwealth of Atlantis. Röhricht (*Seelenlehre* 22) lists the other passages in which Plato is mentioned (cf. 1. 8, 2. 7, 2. 13, 2. 24, 2. 36, 2. 52, 2. 64, 4. 16) and maintains that they are all genuinely Platonic and that the possibility in most of them of direct acquaintance with Plato " kaum zu umgehen ist." He raises the question of whether Arnobius could not have known only the *Timaeus* of Cicero but concludes (23 f.) that Arnobius is directly dependent on Plato or Cicero.

⁴⁰ Neither Plato nor Tertullian (*Apol.* 40. 4; *Ad nat.* 1. 9), who refers to the destruction of Atlantis, mentions Neptune in this connection, and it may be that in Arnobius' estimation the word has no more force than to say that Atlantis was out in the ocean.

⁴¹ This war of Assyria under Ninus with Bactria under a king called by some writers " Zoroaster," was described in a lost work of the historian Ctesias which Arnobius certainly knew, at least secondhand (cf. 1. 52), the history of the Assyrian Empire. E. Meyer, *Geschichte des Altertums* 1. 2 (Stuttgart-Berlin 1921) 347-9; " Bactria," *Encycl. Brit.* 3 (11th ed., 1911) 180, states that the whole history of Ctesias is a fantastic fiction and no such war ever took place. See F. Jacoby, " Ktesias," *RE* 11 (1922) 2032-73; Diodorus Siculus 2. 6; Orosius 1. 4; Augustine, *De civ. Dei* 21. 14.

⁴² Since Ctesias' work is lost, we cannot be sure that the confusion was not his. See 1. 52.

⁴³ Cf. 4. 13.

⁴⁴ Greek tradition attributed the abduction of Helen to the bribe of Paris (Alexander) by Aphrodite. Helen was harmful to later times through the destruction of Troy.

⁴⁵ Xerxes I, king of Persia, in his preparations for the second invasion of Greece (480 B. C.), caused a canal to be dug through the promontory of Mt. Athos (Herodotus 7. 22), and also built a bridge over the Hellespont (*ibid.* 7. 33).

⁴⁶ Alexander the Great.

⁴⁷ For other references to Christ, see the index.

⁴⁸ Tertullian (*Apol.* 40. 13) makes a similar point. In *Ad Scap.* 3 there is an allusion to an instance when there was a failure of crops owing to persecution of Christians.

⁴⁹ On this passage see Gabarrou, *Oeuvre* 63, who cites Matthew 5. 49 and Tertullian, *Apol.* 40. Cf. Rapisarda, *Arnob.* 22.

⁵⁰ Reifferscheid (index, p. 289) cites on this passage Matthew 5. 44; Romans 12. 17; 1 Thessalonians 5. 15; 1 Peter 3. 9, which undeniably contain the same sentiment, but as these central truths

of Christianity must have been well-known to all converts, as well as to many pagans, the present passage is no certain proof that Arnobius had read the New Testament.

[51] Cf. Isaias 2. 4 but the idea is commonplace.

[52] Reading with Marchesi the MS *facto*, rather than the corrector's *facio*, adopted by Reifferscheid.

[53] Tertullian, *Ad Scap.* 3, says that the calamities are signs of God's impending wrath.

[54] Earth, air, fire, water. Cf. Cicero, *De nat. deor.* 1. 18. 19: quem ad modum autem oboedire et parere voluntati architecti aër ignis aqua terra potuerunt? In *ibid.* 2. 23. 84 he lists earth, water, air, and ether, not fire. In *ibid.* 1. 18. 19 there is an allusion to the five solids: pyramid (fire), cube (earth), octohedron (air), dodecahedron (ether), eicosihedron (water), but they are not so specifically named.

[55] Astrological terms.

[56] In 1. 47, however, the miseries are really viewed as adverse to men, brought on by unalterable fate (*fatalibus inroganturque decretis*). This passage has been cited by Micka (58) against Colombo (109), who with reference to 7. 10 says that Arnobius does not maintain that all human events do not take place by inexorable fate but that Arnobius uses this idea for purposes of developing the theme of human misery.

[57] On *columen*, the topmost part of a building, see Vitruvius 4. 7. 100. Cicero often uses the word figuratively of persons (as does Arnobius here): cf. *Verr.* 3. 76. 176; *Flacc.* 17. 41; *Sest.* 8. 19; *Phil.* 12. 26. The word can also mean column or pillar: in Gal. 2. 9 St. Paul calls Peter and other Apostles pillars, στῦλοι (Vulg.: *columna*). Cf. also Clement of Rome 5. 2.

[58] *Timaeus* 22b-22e. Arnobius was very familiar with at least the introduction of this dialogue. See above, notes 38-40. Cf. Origen, *C. Cels.* 4. 20, where Plato is specifically quoted.

[59] Reading *etenim* (Reifferscheid) in place of *et*[*in*] (Marchesi) and *et in⟨sinuare⟩* (Brakman). Marchesi's suggestion (in the apparatus) of *et ait* is attractive but unproven.

[60] *Vectoribus* = carriers.

[61] As the following words make clear, the reason for drying the body is to make room for more drink. Tertullian (*Apol.* 40. 15) has a similar reference but with a different application: Nos vero ieiuniis aridi et omni continentia expressi, etc. Cf. also Minucius 2. 3: quod esset corpori meo siccandis umoribus de marinis lavacris

blanda et adposita curatio. Colombo (30) is right in maintaining that Arnobius had certainly read the chapter of Tertullian.

[62] To man but not to all animals. Cf. Lucretius 4. 640 f.; Pliny, *Nat. hist.* 10. 72. 197; 25. 5. 59; Hesychius *s. v. ἐλλέβορος.*

[63] A Vergilian echo: cf. *Aen.* 9. 59.

[64] Cicero, *De nat. deor.* 2. 53. 133; 2. 60. 152–61. 153, states that the gods have created the world for the sake of both gods and men.

[65] Cf. Tertullian, *Ad nat.* 1. 7, 1. 9. See Colombo 32.

[66] For the unreadable *erunt* of the MS Meiser suggests *serunt* (contrive); Sabaeus *adiierunt* (= ?); a corrector of the MS *ferunt* (bring); Klussmann *eruunt* (cast forth); Reifferscheid *ingerunt* (pile up); Brakman *creant* (create).

[67] Doubtless the computation is based on the Birth of Christ (see Colombo 4). See Introduction. Note that Tertullian (*Apol.* 7. 3) begins the Christian era in the reign of Tiberius: Census istius disciplinae (Christianae), ut iam edidimus, a Tiberio est. Cf. Lactantius, *De mort. pers.* 2.

[68] A. C. Coxe (*ANF* 6. 417) goes too far when he sees in this word proof that Arnobius was baptized when he wrote.

[69] *Feriae* = holidays.

[70] Note that here at least Arnobius is quite willing to consider himself a Roman citizen, but cf. 7. 51.

[71] Arnobius adopts the point of view of a consumer, not that of a producer. He was a rhetorician, not a farmer.

[72] Here is some awareness of the problems of economics. The reign of Diocletian was a difficult time (cf. his famous edict of 301 A. D. establishing prices in the eastern half of the Empire). See M. Rostovtzeff, *The Social & Economic History of the Roman Empire* (Oxford 1926) 453; H. Mattingly, *CAH* 12 (1939) 342. On the situation in Africa, see R. M. Hayward, in *An Economic Survey of Ancient Rome* 4 (Baltimore 1938) 1-121, pp. 115-9 on the period after 232 A. D. Though public works were built in this province under Diocletian (see C. E. Van Sickle, " The public works of Africa in the reign of Diocletian," *Class. Phil.* 25 [1930] 173-9), there is " no evidence of anything like an economic revival. . . . Unfortunately, evidence for price levels during this period is very rare." Cf. also Eusebius, *Hist. eccl.* 9. 8, for plague and famine in the reign of Maximinus (307-313 A. D.); also Monceaux 3. 247.

[73] That is, not successfully from the start of hostilities.

[74] A German tribe specified for the whole German nation. For

further data on the expansion of Christianity by Arnobius' time, see 2. 12.

[75] Cf. Minucius 12. 5: nonne sine vestro deo imperant, regnant, fruuntur orbe toto vestrique dominantur?

[76] The Roman provinces of Asia and Syria are meant.

[77] The MS here reads *cumaquitanos* which seems to point to Aquitania but this does not explain the *cum* and almost certainly another African name is required. Brakman and Marchesi prefer *Zeugitanos*, since Sicca, Arnobius' home, was near the region of Zeugitana. See T. H. Dyer, "Zeugitana regio," *DG* 2 (London 1870) 1338. Other suggestions: *tum aquitanos* (Sabaeus); *et Tingitanos* = Tangiers (Ursinus); *Garamantas* (Meiser); *Quinquegetanos* (Reifferscheid and Partsch).

[78] S. J. Case, *The Social Triumph of the Ancient Church* (New York-London 1933) 73, thinks that this is proof that Christian merchants had grown wealthy "by trading in foodstuffs during a period of high prices"; but all that our author says is that some Christians had grown rich or even wealthy.

[79] The change from plural to singular is probably only rhetorical.

[80] *Duelles* = 'warriors' but they must here be hostile.

[81] This use of the terminology of soothsayers is by no means an inconsistency in Arnobius who elsewhere criticizes that tribe strongly. He is here merely assuming their point of view for polemical purposes, a frequent procedure with him.

[82] This is the earliest reference in Arnobius to a doctrine repeated in 3. 25, 6. 2, 7. 5, and 7. 36, that God is never angry, and it is one of the most convincing proofs that Arnobius was ignorant of the Old Testament, a point emphasized by Gabarrou (*Oeuvre* 64) who correctly states that our author had no conception of the relationship of Judaism to Christianity (cf. also de Labriolle 2. 280), as well as an imperfect acquaintance with the New Testament. For evidence of the presence of the doctrine of Divine Anger in Holy Scripture, see the interesting and exhaustive dissertation of E. F. Micka, *The Problem of Divine Anger in Arnobius and Lactantius* (Stud. in Christ. Ant., 4 Washington 1943) 2-7. Micka rightly attributes to pagan philosophy Arnobius' contention that God cannot be angry and still be God, in particular to Stoicism and to an even greater extent to Epicureanism (cf. Cicero, *De off.* 3. 28. 102: At hoc quidem commune est omnium philosophorum . . . numquam nec irasci deum, nec nocere; *De nat. deor.* 1. 16. 42; 2. 28. 70; Micka 2, 8, 13, 76). This belief is a natural result of the peculiar view of

God's 'aloofness,' a fundamentally Epicurean concept, which is central to Arnobius' thinking, and to its corollary, the base condition of man, both of which establish the incompatibility of Divine Anger (Micka 65-74). Arnobius' doctrine of impassibility puts him into company with the pagans rather than with his Christian predecessors, of whom Micka distingiushes two groups: (a) writers who saw no particular difficulty in taking over the pagan belief of impassibility while aware of the many references to Divine Anger in the Bible, e. g. the apologists Aristides, Athenagoras, Justin Martyr in the first *Apology* (Micka, 17-21, cites the evidence), and (b) writers who adopted an orthodox view on this doctrine in their efforts to combat the heretical view of Marcion that the God of the Old Testament is to be distinguished from that of the New (Marcion eliminated all NT passages which conflicted with this view), e. g. Irenaeus, Tertullian, Novatian, Pseudo-Clement of Rome's *Recognitiones*, Clement of Alexandria, and Origen (see Micka 25-30). While pagan philosophers rather generally adopted the doctrine of the impassibility of God, the people, of course, believed heartily in the opposite view (see Micka 17 n. 82). Arnobius did not discuss the subject completely and systematically; his contemporary and pupil, Lactantius, did, however, devote a special work to the topic, the *De ira Dei* (*CSEL* 27. 1 Brandt). On Lactantius' divergent view, see Micka 81-145, 158-178; cf. also M. Pohlenz, *Vom Zorne Gottes* (Göttingen 1909).

[83] Reading *crucibus* with Zink and Reifferscheid rather than *cruces* (Heraldus, Orelli, Marchesi).

[84] *Alienatione* = the German 'Besinnungslosigkeit,' both here and in 5. 2. Cf. Scharnagl 31.

[85] Cf. Lucretius 3. 288 f.; Vergil, *Aen.* 12. 101 f.; Seneca, *De ira* 1. 1. 4; *Medea* 387-9. Cf. Rapisarda, *Arnob.* 164.

[86] Cf. Seneca, *De ira* 1. 1. 5; Vergil, *Aen.* 4. 499.

[87] Arnobius here follows the Stoics who distinguished between *adfectus, passio, perturbatio*. Cf. Seneca, *De ira* 2. 2. 5. Rapisarda (*Arnob.* 81, 176) points out the idea is not taken from Lucretius but possibly from Neo-Platonism.

[88] Since the Greeks regarded the gods as immortal, it followed that not only did the whole being of a god resist dissolution but also the parts. Thus, no food or drink was necessary to replace worn-out cells, but in order to supply the pleasures of the table, the gods ate *ambrosia* and drank *nectar*, instead of the life-giving food and drink.

See W. H. Roscher, "Ambrosia," *LM* 1. 280-3. Cf. also Cicero, *De nat. deor.* 2. 23. 59: nec his escis aut potionibus vescuntur.

[89] Plato (Rep. 377-8) banished poets from his ideal state because they represented the gods in similarly low moral character. Cf. Cicero, *De nat. deor.* 1. 16. 42.

[90] *Intestinis*, a Lucretian echo (2. 290 but see Bailey's note *ad loc.* which takes the word as = 'internal'). Cf. also Arnobius 1. 36, 6. 2, 6. 10, 7. 43.

[91] The same argument is found in Lactantius, *Div. inst.* 2. 4; 5. 21. 7, and there is a long passage on the impotence of the pagan gods in Clement of Alexandria, *Protr.* 4. 52-56.

[92] Something worse than ordinary "sour" wine.

[93] Cf. Tertullian, *Apol.* 41. 3: Aequalis est interim super omne hominum genus, et indulgens et increpans; communia voluit esse et commoda profanis et incommoda suis, ut pari consortio omnes et lenitatem eius et severitatem experiremur.

[94] The Greek word δαίμονες (= demons) is here used by Arnobius for the first time. In classical Greek it had no connotation of evil but was either equal to θεοί (= gods) or a more general sense connoting the divine power. Later, under the Christian influence, it came to be equated with evil spirits. That is the sense here. Bryce-Campbell translated "demigods" for what reason I do not know.

[95] The MS *errores* is now clearly seen to be mistaken and has been from both a palaeographical and theological point of view convincingly emended to *errones* which in classical times denoted runaway slaves who voluntarily returned to their masters. See Horace, *Serm.* 2. 7. 113; Tibullus 2. 6. 6; Ulpian, *Digest.* 21. 117, who, after defining the word, says: Quod bene arguteque congruit daemonibus quoque qui apud Christianos scriptores 'vagi' appellantur. Among the Christian writers, see Minucius 26. 7; Cyprian, *Quod idola dii non sint* 6; Commodian 1. 3. 22.

[96] In Cicero, *De nat. deor.* 3. 37–38. 90, the statement is made that the gods are not ignorant of what goes on but do not take note of everything.

[97] These worthies are, successively, the *haruspices* (diviners by inspection of entrails), *coniectores* (dream interpreters), *harioli* (same as *haruspices*), *vates* (prophets), and *fanatici* (guardians of *fana* or shrines). It is perhaps significant that Arnobius omits *augures* (experts on fortunetelling from the flight of birds). The great source on these subjects is Cicero's *De divinatione*, but since the second book contains a pagan criticism of divination, Arnobius

may possibly have refrained from citing the work. For other references to *haruspices*, see 1. 46, 4. 11, 4. 12, 7. 38, 7. 40; on *vates*, 1. 46, 2. 73, 7. 38, 7. 47. See also A. Bouché-Leclercq, "Haruspices," *DA* 3. 17-33; C. Thulin, "Haruspices," *RE* 7 (1912) 2431-68.

[98] Literally: "Sparse attendance is at its highest." Cf. Tertullian, *Apol.* 42. 8: Certe, inquitis, templorum vectigalia cottidie decoquunt; stipes quotusquisque iam iactat?

[99] It seems better to include this sentence in the soothsayer's words but this is not certain.

[100] An Epicurean concept. Cf. the Epicurean virtue of ἀταραξία (calm). Cf. Cicero, *De nat. deor.* 1. 19. 51: Nihil enim agit (deus), nullis occupationibus est implicatus, nulla opera molitur.

[101] *Deum principem. Princeps* in this sense (= 'first,' 'chief,' etc., not 'prince,' a later development) is frequently applied by Arnobius to God in various ways: cf. *deus princeps* in 2. 48, 2. 53, 2. 55, 2. 60, 2. 61, 2. 65; *principe deo* 1. 53; *deo principe* 2. 16; *deo principi* 2. 2; *deus rex et princeps* 2. 55; *deo, regi ac principi* 2. 74; *summi regis ac principis* 1. 27, 3. 6; *dei regis ac principis* 2. 36; *rerum princeps* 2. 48; *principali ab rege* 2. 6; *principali e capite* 2. 3; and *principalis* 2. 22. Cf. Introd., n. 211.

[102] *Fessis rebus*, a phrase used again in 1. 28, 3. 24; Vergil, *Aen.* 3. 145; Tacitus, *Ann.* 15. 50.

[103] I cannot agree with Coxe (*ANF* 6. 419) when he maintains that Arnobius was no longer among the *catechumens* when he wrote these words. The passage is not evidence for so precise a conclusion.

[104] If this is a reference to the persecution of Diocletian in 303 A. D., as some appear to think (see Introd. 10), one does not get the impression that Arnobius momentarily expected the arrival of the imperial police at his door.

[105] Orelli prints a long note by Heraldus which maintains that *exurit* refers not to "vivicomburium (cf. Tertullian, *De an.* 1. 6 and Waszink's note, p. 95) sed ad cruces et tormenta," but this view is based on the false assumption that here is a series of gradual steps leading up to execution, rather than a list of divers methods, two or more of which, to be sure, may have been combined.

[106] The MS reading *profan-us* (with either *e* or *i* erased) was emended to *profanos* by Ursinus, in which case the translation should be "Does the Dodonian or the . . . Jupiter call us profane," etc. Pithoeus, however, emended *profan-us* to *Trophonius* and is followed by Marchesi. On this epithet of Zeus, see Cicero, *De div.* 1. 34. 74; *De nat. deor.* 3. 19. 49; Livy 45. 27. 8; Pliny, *Nat. hist.* 34. 8. 19;

31. 2. 11. The shrine of Zeus Trophonius was at Lebadia in Boeotia. Cf. A. B. Cook, *Zeus* 2 (Cambridge 1925) 1073-6 (appendix k).

[107] Dodona in Epirus was a famous shrine of Zeus with an oracle which used oak leaves. Cf. Cook, *op. cit.* 1. 851; 2. 1333, for index to references to this cult.

[108] According to the myths, Apollo was born by Leto on Delos. On this passage, see Clement of Alexandria, *Protr.* 2. 11. 2 which lists the following oracles: the Clarian, the Pythian, Didymaean, that of Amphiaraus, the (Trophonian ?), and that of Amphilochus; but the two lists seem independent of one another. At Claros near Colophon in Ionia there was a spring used in inspiring oracular responses from the god Apollo. Another existed at Didyma near Miletus. According to O. Höfer, "Philesios," *LM* 3. 2304, "Philesian" was a cognomen of Apollo at the shrine in Didyma. Cf. L. Preller-C. Robert, *Griechische Mythologie, I: Theogonie und Götter* (Berlin 1894) 283 n. 5. Apollo was also called "Pythian" from the Pythia, the mouthpiece of Apollo at Delphi. Finally, the MS *ethis* is unintelligible. One solution is to find another epithet of Apollo and I have adopted Reifferscheid's suggestion of *Smintheus* (see his apparatus). Other scholars give other suggestions.

[109] The word is *imperator* = 'general' (in republican Latin) or 'emperor' (in imperial).

[110] Cf. Prudentius, *Apoth.* 402 f.: torquetur Apollo nomine percussus Christi; Lactantius, *Div. inst.* 5. 22.

[111] *Summi regis ac principis.* See note 101.

[112] *Magister* = 'teacher.'

[113] On the Lares Grunduli (or Grundules), see Wissowa 174. This epithet of the traditional Roman household gods is thought by Wissowa to bear some connection with graves of children. The Lares Grunduli and the following divinities were doubtless chosen as examples of trivial worship. On the Lares proper, see also 3. 41-43.

[114] An altar to Aius Locutius (the speaking voice) stood on the Palatine in Rome as a memorial of an unheeded voice which had warned the Romans of danger. See Livy 3. 5. 32; 5. 50. 5; Cicero, *De div.* 1. 101; 2. 69; A. Gellius 16. 17; R. Peter in *LM* 2. 191; Wissowa 55; A. Aust, *RE* 1 (1894) 1130; K. Ziegler, "Palatium," *RE* 18 (1948) offprint p. 14.

[115] The *limentinus* was the god of the threshold. See Tertullian, *De idol.* 15; *De cor.* 13; Augustine, *De civ. Dei* 4. 8, 6. 7; W. Schur, *RE* 13 (1927) 571 f. Cf. also 4. 8.

[116] On the worship of the shepherd god Faunus see Wissowa

208-19; W. Otto, *RE* 6 (1909) 2054-73; Fowler 256-65. On Fatua, variant for Fauna, wife of Faunus, cf. Vergil, *Aen.* 5. 28; Lactantius, *Epit.* 22; Wissowa 211; Fowler 103. The *genius* was to a city what the *lar* was to a household (Wissowa 175-81). On Pavor, the god of terror, see Wissowa 149. There were two goddesses named Bellona: one a native goddess of war (Wissowa 151 f.), the other an importation from Cappadocia (*ibid.* 348-50). See A. Aust, *RE* 3 (1899) 254-57; Fowler 95, 100 (Bona Dea = Maia), 123.

[117] Elmenhorst (quoted by Salmasius *ad loc.* and Orelli 1. 308 = *ML* 5. 751), doubtless on the testimony of Lactantius, *Div. inst.* 1. 20. 1-7, which he cites among other authorities, suggests three examples of the condemned practice: the Greek Leaena, the Roman Laurentia and Flora, but the source of Arnobius is more probably Minucius 25. 8. Only the first of the examples is even possibly historical and all three are capable of interpretation as aetiological. On divine honors actually paid to historical *hetaerae*, see W. S. Ferguson, *Hellenistic Athens* (London 1911) 119; K. J. Beloch, *Griechische Geschichte* 4. 1 (2nd ed., Berlin-Leipzig 1925) 434; W. W. Tarn, *CAH* 6 (1927) 501; K. Schneider, "Hetairai," *RE* 8 (1913) 1331-72.

[118] Cf. Vergil, *Aen.* 8. 40.

[119] The ancient Egyptian religion is meant. Clement of Alexandria, *Protr.* 2. 39.25, lists various animals worshipped in Egypt. Cf. Cicero, *De nat. deor.* 1. 36. 101; 1. 16. 43; 1. 29. 81 f.; 3. 19. 47; Theophilus, *Ad Autol.* 1. 10; Origen, *C. Cels.* 1. 20; Cyprian, *Ad Demetr.* 12; Lactantius, *Div. inst.* 5. 20. 12.

[120] Cf. Pliny, *Nat. hist.* 30. 11. 99; Juvenal 15. 2; Lactantius, *Div. inst.* 2. 5. 36; Martianus Capella 2. 170.

[121] Micka (44) thinks this proviso (cf. 1. 19, 6. 1, 7. 2, 7. 35; W. Kroll, *Rhein. Mus.* 72 [1917-8] 63 ff.) indicates that Arnobius was attempting to steer a middle course, but it is probably nothing more than a statement of a hypothesis: "if the pagans are right in thinking the gods exist, their actions are inconsistent and reprehensible."

[122] Cf. Cicero, *De nat. deor.* 1. 32. 91; Vergil, *Aen.* 6. 724-34.

[123] Perhaps imitated by Firmicus Maternus, *De errore prof. rel.* 8. 1 (cf. C. Brakman, *Miscella tertia* [Leyden 1917] 25).

[124] Cf. 2. 16; 7. 28.

[125] Reading *foturos* with G. Wiman, *Eranos* 45 (1947) 129, in preference to *feturas* (Axelson) or *futuros* (P).

[126] For other references to these gods, see Index.

[127] This *testimonium* is no. 290 f. in E. J. and L. Edelstein,

Asclepius: a Collection and Interpretation of the Testimonies (Pubs. Inst. Hist. of Med., Johns Hopkins Univ. 2. ser., Texts and Doc. 2, Baltimore 1945) vol. 1.

[128] Colombo 11-15 points out that some elements of this beautiful prayer (as Micka 42 calls it) might well have been taken from pagan sources and that therefore it is a possibility that Arnobius was never a Christian. This, Micka rightly says, is hardly sound.

[129] The lacuna has been supplied by Marchesi to make sense. Meiser (11) thinks that this chapter (and also 3. 19, 6. 2, 7. 15) are in part echoes of Lucretius 2. 646-51.

[130] This phrase, repeated in 2. 58, is clearly a reflection of Lucretius 1. 472: nec locus ac spatium. See also Bryce-Campbell *ad loc.* who call attention to the fact that the Peripatetics referred to God as the τόπος πάντων.

[131] The punctuation here follows Axelson (42).

[132] The atheists meant may be Diagoras of Melos (fl. 420 B. C.) and Theodorus of Cyrene (fl. 310 B. C.), both mentioned by Cicero (*De nat. deor.* 1. 1. 2; 1. 33. 63; 1. 42. 117; 3. 37. 89), or Euhemerus of Acragas (fl. 300 B. C.), Hippo of Melos (fifth cent.), Nicanor of Cyprus, who, in addition, are mentioned by Clement of Alexandria, *Protr.* 2. 24. 2. Minucius (8. 2) mentions Theodorus, Diagoras; Lactantius (*Div. inst.* 1. 2), Diagoras. The skeptic is of course Protagoras of Abdera (see n. 133) who is mentioned by Cicero, Clement, Minucius, and Lactantius. See A. B. Drachmann, *Atheism in Antiquity* (London 1922) and cf. Justin Martyr, *Apol.* 1. 6, who calls attention to the fact that the Christians were themselves termed ἄθεοι.

[133] Protagoras of Abdera (*ca.* 480-*ca.* 410 B. C.), a sophist, was charged with impiety at Athens for having written a book which began with the words: "As for the gods, I am unable to say whether they exist or whether they do not exist."

[134] The atomists: Leucippus, of whom little is known except that he probably flourished in the fifth century B. C.; Democritus of Abdera (fifth cent. B. C); Epicurus of Samos (342-270 B. C.), and the Roman poet, T. Lucretius Carus (*ca.* 98-55 B. C.), whose influence on Arnobius is great. On Lucretius' view of the atom, see J. Masson, *Lucretius, Epicurean and Poet* (London 1907) 76-141. On Leucippus, see Stenzel, *RE* 12 (1925) 2266-77 (no. 13).

[135] The text here reads *diversitatis impetu* (by propulsion of diversity). One thinks, of course, of atoms but Arnobius does not

use the word *atomus,* common though it is in Latin. Bryce-Campbell translate " atoms of different shapes." Perhaps so.

[136] *Averruncetur amentia,* a proverbial phrase which goes back to one preserved from the poet Pacuvius by Varro (*De ling. lat.* 7. 102). The phrase is also known to St. Ambrose (*De fide* 1. 9. 60, 1. 11. 73). Cf. A. Otto, *Die Sprichwörter und sprichwörtlichen Redensarten der Römer* (Leipzig 1890) 18.

[137] In Arnobius' psychology the infant apparently is born with a potential, if not an actual, awareness of where he came from and this is what he means here. Cf. the reference to Epicurus' doctrine of *prolepsis* in Cicero, *De nat. deor.* 1. 43.

[138] The chief temple of Jupiter Optimus Maximus, the most important god of the Capitoline triad and indeed of the Roman pantheon, was on the Capitoline Hill. See Platner-Ashby 297-302; C. Thulin, " Iuppiter " no. 15, *RE* 10 (1919) 1135-9; Cicero, *De nat. deor.* 2. 25. 64.

[139] Zeus, the Greek counterpart of the Roman Jupiter, was the son of Cronus and Rhea, his sister, and therefore was grandson of Uranus and Gaea in both lines, having, as Arnobius overlooks, but one pair of grandparents instead of the usual two. Hades and Poseidon were his brothers. See E. Fehrle, *LM* 6. 578 ff.

[140] This phrase is added here by Marchesi in place of *dicitur,* inserted by Reifferscheid, following Klussmann, in the next clause. Both seem redundant.

[141] Here *et,* added by Sabaeus, is retained by Reifferscheid and Marchesi; but it is unnecessary and disturbs the chiasmus.

[142] Cf. 3. 41.

[143] Cf. Tertullian, *Apol.* 21. 3: Sed et vulgus iam scit Christum ut hominem aliquem, qualem Iudaei iudicaverunt: quo facilius quis nos hominis cultores existimaverit.

[144] Here the word *crux* is used but Arnobius employs it interchangeably with *patibulum.* The former denoted an instrument of punishment as early as Plautus (*Asin.* 548; *Miles gl.* 372; *Mostell.* 359—see *TLL* 4. 1255).

[145] The same point is made by Lactantius, *Div. inst.* 4. 16. 1.

[146] Cf. 3. 6, 3. 29, 3. 44, 6. 25. On Janus, the two-headed god of doors and gates, founder of the Janiculum, see Wissowa, 103-112; W. H. Roscher, *LM* 2. 15-55.

[147] In 3. 29 Arnobius wrongly calls the Janiculum a town. For a possible explanation, see above, p. 44.

¹⁴⁸ On Saturn, god of corn and father of Jupiter, see Wissowa 204-8; Thulin, *RE* 2. R., 2 (1923) 218-23. Cf. Cicero, *De nat. deor.* 3. 24. 63, and Arnobius 3. 29.

¹⁴⁹ See above, n. 116.

¹⁵⁰ Faunus is also mentioned in 2. 72, 5. 1, 5. 2 (*bis*).

¹⁵¹ On this syncretism of later Roman times, see Wissowa 216.

¹⁵² According to Wissowa (18 ff.) the *indigitamenta* were the original gods of the Roman religion, as distinguished from *novensiles* or newer additions taken over from other cults. See R. Peter, *LM* 2. 129-233; F. Richter, *RE* 9 (1916) 1334-67; Fowler 191 f., 341; G. Wissowa, *Hastings Encycl.* 7 (1915) 217 f.

¹⁵³ The allusion is to a passage of the *Aeneid* 12. 794 f. and Servius' commentary *ad loc.* Cf. Livy 1. 2; Ovid, *Met.* 14. 581-618; *Fasti* 3. 647 and Frazer's note *ad loc.*; Tibullus 2. 5. 43 f.

¹⁵⁴ The Greek god of healing, son of Apollo and the nymph Coronis, slain by Zeus lest he make all men immortal. His most important shrine was at Epidaurus in the eastern Peloponnesus. See E. Thrämer, *LM* 1. 615-40; *RE* 2 (1896) 1642-97 (no. 2); Edelstein and Edelstein, *testim.* 29c; Cicero, *De nat. deor.* 3. 22; Apollodorus, *Bibl.* 3. 10. 7; Hyginus, *Fab.* 202.

¹⁵⁵ The Roman god Liber was equated with the Greek Dionysus (Bacchus), god of wine, and son of Zeus and Semele, daughter of Cadmus, the legendary founder of Thebes which was the center of the cult of Dionysus. At Semele's request, Zeus appeared to her (as the god of lightning, however) before the birth of her child and as a result she was killed but Dionysus was saved by Zeus (or Hermes). See G. Wissowa, *LM* 2. 2021-9; W. Schur, *RE* 13 (1927) 68-76. Except for two references (4. 15, 6. 21) to this god as Dionysus and two allusions to the Bacchanalia (5. 19 *bis*), Arnobius always uses the Roman name Liber.

¹⁵⁶ Cf. 7. 44.

¹⁵⁷ The Roman god Mercury, whose province was the protection of commerce, was later equated with the Greek god Hermes, son of Zeus and Maia, eldest of the Pleiades, the seven daughters of Atlas and the Oceanid, Pleione. On the epithet *candida*, cf. Vergil, *Aen.* 8. 138; Macrobius, *Sat.* 1. 12. 19 f.; Apollodorus, *Bibl.* 3. 10. 1 f. See H. Steuding, *LM* 2. 2802-31; F. M. Heichelheim, *RE* 15 (1932) 975-1016.

¹⁵⁸ Cf. 2. 70, 4. 15, 4. 22, 6. 12.

¹⁵⁹ Diana (= Greek Artemis) and Apollo were the children of Zeus and Latona (Greek Leto). After they had been conceived, their

mother wandered about for a long time until she reached the island of Delos where she gave them birth. Delos had previously been a floating isle of rock but was now fixed to the bottom of the sea. They are called archers (*arquitenentes*) because they slew with arrows the giant Tityus for having insulted their mother. See T. Birt, *LM* 1. 1002-11; G. Wissowa, *RE* 5 (1905) 326-38.

¹⁶⁰ Venus (= Aphrodite), the goddess of love, perhaps taken over from oriental cults, was by the Greeks regarded as daughter of Zeus and Dione. She bore to the Trojan Anchises, king of Dardanus on Mt. Ida, the hero Aeneas whose wanderings form the subject of Vergil's *Aeneid*. She is called *intestini decoris publicatrix* to indicate that like *meretrices* she made her body public property. Cf. Cicero, *De nat. deor.* 3. 24. 62; 2. 27. 69.

¹⁶¹ Ceres (= Demeter), daughter of Cronus and Rhea and therefore sister to Zeus, nevertheless bore to Zeus, Proserpina (= Persephone) who, gathering flowers on the Nysian plain, was carried off by Pluto (= Hades, god of the lower world). (For another version, cf. 5. 24-27.) This story gave rise to the beautiful explanation of the recurrence of the seasons; Ceres shared her daughter with Hades for six months of each year. While Proserpina was with her mother, vegetation flourished; while she was with Hades, it died. For a different view, see W. C. Greene, " The Return of Proserpina," *Class. Phil.* 41 (1946) 105-7. See also T. Birt, *LM* 1. 859-66.

¹⁶² Cf. 3. 33, 4. 15, 4. 27, 5. 21, 5. 24, 5. 32, 5. 37, 5. 40, 7. 21.

¹⁶³ Hercules (= Heracles), the great national hero of the Greeks, was the son of Zeus and Alcmene, wife of Amphitryon, king of Tiryns. His boyhood was spent in Thebes where his mother and her husband passed an exile as the guest of King Creon. His life was a succession of heroic exploits of which the celebrated Twelve Labors were but a few. His wife Deianeira sent him as a gift a shirt daubed on the inside with the blood of the centaur Nessus whom Hercules had slain. Burned by the magic inherent in Nessus' blood, Hercules in agony mounted on a funeral pyre on Mt. Oeta and died. On the Tyrian Hercules, see Cicero, *De nat. deor.* 3. 42; Arrian 2. 16; Pomponius Mela 3. 6; Pausanias 5. 25; cf. A. Furtwängler, " Herakles," *LM* 1. 2135-52 and R. Peter, " Hercules," *ibid.* 2253-98; F. Haug, *RE* 8 (1913) 550-612.

¹⁶⁴ Castor and Pollux, here referred to as frequently by the joint name of " Castors," were, with Helen and Clytaemnestra, the children of Leda. Concerning their father, there are variant traditions: (a) Zeus, in the form of a swan, was father of all four; (b)

Zeus was father of only Pollux and Helen, Tyndareus, king of Sparta, being father of the others; (c) Zeus was the father only of Helen; and (d) Tyndareus was father of all four. Arnobius attributes both Castors to Tyndareus but elsewhere they are frequently referred to as the Dioscuri (sons of Zeus). Castor was a horse-tamer, Pollux a boxer, and when the mortal Castor was slain in battle, his immortal brother shared life with him thereafter on alternate days. See also 2. 70, 4. 15, 4. 25, and (as Dioscuri) 4. 22. See A. Furtwängler, LM 1. 1154-77.

[165] Marchesi reads *Titanes*, Reifferscheid *Tisianes*. W. Kroll, a keen student of the text of Arnobius, inserted into RE 2. R., 12 (1937) 1478 a note on "Tisianes et Bucures," calling them, solely on the basis of this passage, Moorish gods. Cf. also Oehler's note *ad. loc.*

[166] Undoubtedly a reference to the Dea Syria (Atargatis), identified by the Greeks with Aphrodite who, according to one legend, was hatched from an egg found by some fish in the Euphrates. The fish pushed the egg onto the river bank where it was cared for by a dove. See Ovid, *Fasti* 2. 459-74; *Met.* 5. 331; Cicero, *De nat. deor.* 3. 15. 39; E. Meyer, LM 1. 645-55; F. Cumont, RE 4 (1901) 2236-43; Cumont, *Religions orientales* 95-99; F. J. Dölger, ΙΧΘΥΣ 2 (1922) 292; W. W. Hyde, *Paganism to Christianity in the Roman Empire* (Philadelphia 1946) 55-59.

[167] I have translated *proditus* as 'betrayed' rather than 'born' which the other translations have, because there would be no stigma attached to mere birth in the Peloponnesus. This sentence is in harmony with, though almost certainly not derived from, a statement in Apollodorus, *Bibl.* 2. 1. 1 (on which see Frazer's note *ad loc.*). In his account of the descendants of Inacchus, Apollodorus tells of the children of Phoroneus and the nymph Teledice who were Apis and Niobe. Apis became a tyrannical ruler and was betrayed by Thelxion and Telchis and died childless. In Egypt he was equated with Serapis. See also 6. 6. Cf. Eusebius, *Chron.* p. 41 Fotheringham; Augustine, *De civ. Dei* 18. 5; Theophilus, *Ad Autol.* 1. 9.

[168] Cf. 2. 73, 4. 29, 6. 23.

[169] Isis, the Egyptian goddess, wept for her brother-husband, Osiris, slain by Seth, and for her son Horus. See Plutarch, *De Is. et Osir.*; Lactantius, *Div. inst.* 1. 21. 21. On Egyptian deities in Roman religion, see Cumont 69-94; Hyde 49-55.

[170] Ops was the wife of Saturn. Cf. also 2. 70, 2. 71, 3. 30, 4. 20. Orelli cites a conjecture of Oudendorp (on Apuleius) which would,

he thinks, justify changing *regias* (royal) to *egregias* (out of the ordinary) in an ironic sense, but this is unnecessary.

[171] On wounding ears, cf. Vergil, *Aen.* 8. 582; Lactantius, *Div. inst.* 7. 1. 14.

[172] Note that there is no reason given for the Incarnation. Cf. Monceaux 3. 268; Micka 53.

[173] Pagans realized this and Euhemerus of Sicily (fl. 300 B. C.) advanced the view that has since been known as euhemerism, i. e. that the polytheistic deities came into being through the apotheosis of heroes. Cf. Cicero, *De nat. deor.* 1. 42. 119. Cf. 4. 29; Jacoby, " Euemerus " no. 3, *RE* 6 (1909) 952-72.

[174] Arnobius means such writings as those of Euhemerus and the others he mentions in 4. 29.

[175] *Manum . . . dantes,* cf. Lucretius 2. 1043, where Leonard-Smith and Bailey point out the military origin of the metaphor.

[176] That is, a human being, not a god. E. Klussmann, " Arnobius und Lucrez oder ein durchgang durch den Epicuräismus zum Christenthum," *Philologus* 26 (1867) 362-6, points out the very striking parallelism between the praise of Christ in this chapter and a similar eulogy of Epicurus in Lucretius (5. 1-54). In both mythological references and in diction, the passages are similar. So also C. Brakman, *Miscella altera* (Leyden 1913). Only on the basis of a belief in imitation of Lucretius by Arnobius can the remarkable statements of the second half of the chapter be explained. There Arnobius attributes to Christ many teachings having no counterpart in the extant Gospels. Indeed, Christ is regarded as a kind of Greek philosopher with a system which He taught to His disciples. Arnobius was apparently so recent a convert to Christianity that he was unaware that the Man of Galilee had not given lectures on physics and metaphysics. A more accurate picture of Christ's teaching appears in other Christian writers, e. g. Clement of Alexandria, *Protr.* 10. 110. Whether the Epicureanism of this and other passages is to be explained on the basis of Arnobius' own former adherence to that school is a point we have discussed in the Introduction (see pp. 23 f., 29). I find it difficult, however, to follow Marchesi (*Questioni* 1024) when he says that Arnobius was a " sdegnoso avversario " of Epicureanism, maintaining (1022) that 2. 60 f. is a contradiction and retraction of 1. 38 which in part it is.

[177] Cf. Lucretius 5. 8: deus ille fuit, deus. Cf. Cicero, *De nat. deor.* 1. 16. 43: venerari Epicurum et in eorum ipsorum numero de

quibus haec quaestio est habere debeat. Bailey ignores this passage of Cicero in the note to Lucretius 5. 8.

[178] So always in Arnobius. See Cumont 197.

[179] Edelstein-Edelstein, *testim.* 367, vol. 2,141.

[180] Athena (= Minerva) in her contest with Poseidon for possession of Attica struck the earth of the Acropolis with her spear and an olive-tree sprang forth. Cf. Vergil, *Georg.* 1. 19. See A. Furtwängler, "Athene," *LM* 1. 675-704 and G. Wissowa, "Minerva," *ibid.* 2. 2982-99; F. Dümmler, *RE* 2 (1896) 1941-2020.

[181] Triptolemus, the first priest of Demeter, was the inventor of agriculture. His name was explained as τρὶς πολεῖν (three ploughings) but a better etymology would derive it from τρὶς πτολεμεῖν (three fights). Cf. also 3. 6, 5. 25; F. Schwenn, *RE* 2. R., 13 (1939) 213-30.

[182] Cf. 1. 36, 2. 3, 2. 13, 2. 65, 2. 70, 2. 74, 3. 24, 3. 32, 4. 14, 4. 17, 4. 22, 4. 24, 6. 12, 7. 21, 7. 22.

[183] To Colombo (20) the rest of this chapter has almost the flavor of a litany; to Rapisarda (*Arnob.* 137) the chapter resounds with Isiac mysticism.

[184] Marchesi (*Questioni* 1022) points out the inconsistency between the apparent interest in scientific investigations shown here and what is said in 2. 60 f.

[185] The MS reads *animalibus*; the editors *an aliis*, but Hagendahl recently has declared himself in favor of *animalium* or *animalibus*, i. e. whether the moon alternates her light for the benefit of living creatures. Cf. Cicero, *De nat. deor.* 2. 16; Macrobius, *Sat.* 1. 14.

[186] Meiser calls attention to Plato, *Apol.* 40c of which the present passage may be an echo.

[187] Usually *nuper* implies recent events but two passages in Horace (*Carm.* 3. 26. 1; *Ars poet.* 227) use it in the sense of 'formerly,' 'once.' Klussmann (*Philologus* 26 [1867] 366) sees a parallel to Lucretius 5. 1194 ff. For another reference to the recency of the conversion, see 3. 24. On this chapter, cf. Colombo 18.

[188] That is, statues made of ivory, as were the flesh parts of the great statue of Athena by Pheidias on the Acropolis.

[189] On the worship of trees, stones, and springs, see Wissowa 100, and the literature cited in his note 7. Cf. Servius on Vergil's *Aen.* 1. 374; Plutarch, *Timol.* 29. 3; Lucan 1. 135-43.

[190] Meiser wishes to add here " or with a wreath," citing a number of passages in which these two elements of worship are joined. On

this passage, see Clement of Alexandria, *Strom.* 7. 4; Gen. 28. 18; 31. 13; 35. 14; Theophrastus, *Char.* 16.

191 C. Pascal, *Riv. Filol. Istr. Cl.* 32 (1904) 1, emends to *digna de divis* (worthy feelings about the gods).

192 Moule (50) points out that this may be a doubtful allusion to the Second Coming of Christ, but it is possible that the reference is to rewards for righteous living to be received after death.

193 *Patibulum*, a forked stick on which lowest classes of criminals were tied to be beaten or executed.

194 Modern opinion seems to be agreed that Pythagoras was probably born in Samos about 582 B. C. and died in Metapontum (southern Italy) late in the century, perhaps about 510 B. C. It is certain that the school bearing his name encountered opposition when it began to engage in political activity so that it was stamped out in the middle of the fifth century, the meeting houses of the Pythagoreans being everywhere sacked and burned. Of the various accounts of Pythagoras' death, that in Diogenes Laertius (8. 39) seems to be in harmony with Arnobius who mentions Pythagoras also in 2. 9, 2. 10, 2. 13. Cf. Plutarch, *De Stoic. repugn.* 2. 1051; Iamblichus 1. 35; Suidas *s. v.* Πυθαγόρας.

195 Socrates the Athenian (469-399 B. C.), known to us best through the Dialogues of Plato, left no writings of his own.

196 The three have nothing in common except the violence of their deaths. Aquilius = M.' Aquilius, consul in 101 B. C., put to death by having molten lead poured down his throat (Appian, *Mithr.* 21— see E. Klebs, "Aquilius" no. 11, *RE* 2 [1896] 324). Trebonius = C. Trebonius, prominent in the age of Caesar, slaughtered in bed by orders of Dolabella (Appian, *Civ.* 3. 26—see F. Münzer, "Trebonius" no. 6, *RE* 2. R., 6 [1937] 2274-82). Regulus = M. Atilius Regulus, consul in 267 and 256 B. C., captured by the Carthaginians and supposedly put to death by torture. To the Romans he was a great hero (Livy, *Epit.* of Bk. 18; A. Gellius 7. 4) but the stories of his life are suspected of being fictionalized (see E. Klebs, "Atilius" no. 51, *RE* 2 [1896] 2086-92; cf. Minucius 37).

197 According to the tradition, the boy Dionysus, not the Theban god but the son of Zeus and Persephone, was set upon while at play by Titans sent by Hera. They tore him to pieces, cooked and ate the limbs, and Hera gave the heart to Zeus to eat. This variant of the myth was doubtless suggested by the epithet Zagreus ('torn to pieces'). Cf. Clement of Alexandria, *Protr.* 12. 18. See O. Kern, *RE* 5 (1905) 1010-46.

[198] Edelstein-Edelstein, *testim.* 368, vol. 2. 141.

[199] See note 153.

[200] Words bracketed by Reifferscheid (praef. xv) and Marchesi as probably repeated in error.

[201] See note 163.

[202] These Galli (no inhabitants of Gaul, as Bryce-Campbell translate) were castrated priests of the Phrygian god Attis whose worship was connected with that of Magna Mater (see 5. 5-7). Cf. F. Cumont, " Gallus " no. 5, *RE* 7 (1912) 674-82.

[203] Cf. 2. 68, 3. 16, 3. 39, 4. 3, 7. 26.

[204] The story is told by Livy 1. 16; Ovid, *Fasti* 2. 494; Cicero, *De rep.* 1. 41. See Wissowa 153-6.

[205] Cf. 4. 3.

[206] On what is known of the large temple of Quirinus in Rome, which stood on the Quirinal Hill and had 76 Doric columns, dipteral-octostyle, see Platner-Ashby 438 f.

[207] Reading *faciatis*, with Axelson, for the MS *faciamus*.

[208] *Praesidem*, sometimes translated 'president.' It is used frequently in Book Three to denote the relationship of divinities to their respective spheres of influence—cf. 3. 23, 3. 38.

[209] The phrase *interiorum potentiarum* is not clear. Orelli (ad. loc.) surmises that the angels may be referred to; or the hidden powers of nature.

[210] *Virtutes* is the regular Scriptural word for 'miracles' and is used in that sense here and in 1. 65, 2. 11. In 2. 58 the word is used of the power that moves the earth in its orbit. Cf. the English phrase " by virtue of."

[211] Names of angels were part of the paraphernalia of magicians; for some excellent examples, see J. Barbel, *Christos Angelos* (Theoph. 3, Bonn 1941) 219 f. For mention of angels by Arnobius, cf. 2. 35. See Origen, *C. Cels.* 1. 22; Justin Martyr, *Apol.* 1. 30; Geffcken 289.

[212] Arnobius uses the word *daemones* also in 1. 23, 1. 45, 1. 50, 1. 56, 2. 25, 2. 35.

[213] Cf. 1. 46, 2. 62, 4. 12, 7. 24.

[214] On affecting the results of horse racing by the use of magic, see Jerome, *Vita Hilar.* 20; F. J. Dölger, *Ant. u. Christ.* 1 (1929) 219.

[215] Aposiopesis.

[216] Matt. 8. 28-33; Mark 5. 1-16; Luke 4. 41; 8. 2; 8. 26-39; 13. 32. The references to the miracles in this chapter are hardly proof that Arnobius had read the Gospels; if he had, he was citing the miracles from memory.

[217] Matt. 8. 28-34; Mark 5. 6-17; Luke 8. 26-33.

[218] Matt. 8. 2-3; 10. 8; 11. 5; 26. 6; Mark 1. 40-42; 14. 3; Luke 5. 12-13; 7. 22; 17. 12. *Vitiligines* = skin diseases marked by blotches, including leprosy. My friend, Frederick L. Santee, M. D., tells me that the term "is still used by dermatologists to mean a disease not well understood in which there are depigmented areas of the skin, a leukoderma."

[219] Reifferscheid's text has *cutibus* (skins) but in his preface (xv) he restores the *visceribus* of the MS on the ground that Arnobius uses this word as equal to *corpus or corpora*. Rather it is used in the sense of flesh, as in Lucretius 1. 837.

[220] Cf. Matt. 9. 20; Mark 5. 25; Luke 8. 43 f.

[221] Dr. Santee writes: "*Intercutes* is, I believe, an adjective agreeing with *undae*. Taken literally (between skin) it can only mean blisters or wheals. However, I suspect the fluid is really subcutaneous."

[222] Matt. 11. 5; 15. 31; 21. 14; Luke 7. 22; 14. 13; 13. 21. F. P. Badham, "Arnobius and the 'Gospel of Peter,'" *Academy* 49 (1896) 177, whose interest in the problem of the apocryphal Gospel according to St. Peter led him to untenable beliefs, maintains that a comparison of Arnobius with the *Acta Pilati* and with Lactantius' *Divinae institutiones* makes it clear that all three were following that Gospel. Cf. *Div. inst.* 4. 15.

[223] Reading with Wiman: *et iam operis res erat ⟨parvi⟩*, in place of Marchesi's *et iam operis res erat*; Reifferscheid's *et iam † operis res erat*; C. Weyman, "Textkritische Bemerkungen zu Arnobius adversus nationes," *Festschrift Sebastian Merkle* (Düsseldorf 1922) 387 f.: *et iam profecti operis res erat*; Meiser: *iam pes incedere poterat*.

[224] Matt. 12. 10; Mark 3. 1-3; Luke 6. 6-8; John 5. 3. Badham is inclined to see in the sentence a reference to the hunchback of the *Acta Pilati*.

[225] Matt. 9. 6; Mark 2. 9-11; John 5. 11-12.

[226] Matt. 9. 27; 11. 5; 12. 22; 20. 30; Mark 8. 23; 9. 46; Luke 7. 21-22; 4. 18; John 5. 3, 9. 1.

[227] The particular occasion is not clear since none of the Gospels specifies the exact number of healings except where single cases are recorded. Badham suggests Matt. 15. 30 f. and calls attention to Lactantius, *Div. inst.* 4. 15. 5-8, which he likewise thinks was derived from Pseudo-Peter. On the number and kinds of Christ's miracles, see A. Wikenhauser, "Wunder," *LTK* 10 (1938) 984 f.

[228] Matt. 8. 24-27; Mark 4. 37-41; Luke 8. 23-25.

²²⁹ Matt. 14. 25-28. The detail that His feet were not made wet is not in the Gospel.

²³⁰ Matt. 14. 17; Mark 6. 38; Luke 4. 13; John 6. 9.

²³¹ Reading *corpora*, Sabaeus' correction of the MS *corpore*, now approved by Wiman.

²³² A syncretism of the raising of the daughter of Jairus (Mark 5; Luke 8) with the raising of Lazarus (John 11-12) and details from the Resurrection story.

²³³ Probably a reference to the conversation at Sichar (John 4). Cf. also John 2. 25.

²³⁴ No such miracle is recorded in the Gospels. Oehler's suggestion that Arnobius is thinking of Pentecost has evident merit, particularly since a search through apocryphal literature has had negative results.

²³⁵ If this is not a veiled reference to the Transfiguration, or the Sermon on the Mount, then no specific event is meant but the whole of the ministry.

²³⁶ Events on the road to Emmaus, at the tomb, etc.

²³⁷ As Christ had Himself foretold (Mark 16. 17): *In my name shall they cast out devils.*

²³⁸ See n. 98.

²³⁹ Marchesi wrongly marks this sentence a question, a conclusion which I had reached independently of the excellent discussion by G. Wiman, *Eranos* 45 (1947) 130 f.

²⁴⁰ The three classes of unfortunates, not fitting the form of the sentence, are bracketed by Reifferscheid as interpolated, though Marchesi does not follow him. Badham (see 1. 45) cited for the remainder of this chapter Lactantius, *Div. inst.* 4. 26; *Acta Pilati* 1.

²⁴¹ Colombo (109) says this passage and 7. 10 do not indicate Arnobius' belief in fate but Micka (58) rightly objects.

²⁴² Note the fatalism of this and other passages.

²⁴³ Aesculapius is meant.

²⁴⁴ Cf. F. J. Dölger, *Ant. u. Christ.* 2 (1930) 158; Edelstein-Edelstein, *testim.* 576a, 584, vol. 2, pp. 134, 185. Cf. also Lucretius 5. 1200; Rapisarda, *Arnob.* 175.

²⁴⁵ On the theology underlying this chapter see Marchesi, *Questioni* 1024-1032: "La responsibilità del peccato" in which he maintains, I think wrongly, that Arnobius does not know the doctrines of original sin and redemption (1025); that Arnobius had not read the Pauline Epistles (1026), a point on which he is probably right; and that there is no relationship between Arnobius and Gnosticism

(1027). Note that there is a redundant *qui* in this sentence in the MS.

[246] A denial of free will and choice. Cf. Micka 64; LeNourry, *ML* 5. 463 f.

[247] The MS reads *sed* which is attacked by Micka 64 n. 9. Reifferscheid reads *seu* which Micka prefers, but Marchesi changes to *et*, citing an example in 1. 42 of *sed* for *et*. Cf. also on this passage LeNourry, *ML* 5. 464; Colombo 40 f.

[248] The same point is made by Origen, *C. Cels.* 1. 46; Lactantius, *Div. inst.* 4. 27. 2. See also Ps.-Barnabas 5. 9 and J. A. Kleist's remarks: ACW 6 (1948) 172 n. 51. Cf. Mark 9. 38; Luke 9. 19; Acts 3. 1-10; 14. 8-10.

[249] Tertullian, *Apol.* 21. 17, in describing the scene on the Cross, uses the phrase *cum verbo* of the way in which Christ died: *spiritum cum verbo sponte dimisit.* The point is different in the two writers and the parallelism is doubtless illusory.

[250] So the MS: *per admirationem.*

[251] So called because his most important temple was on the Capitoline.

[252] A priest of a *curia* or division of the city population. Cf. B. Kübler, *RE* 4 (1901) 1836-8; Fowler 304; there was a *curio maximus* (Fowler 303 f.).

[253] The chief religious magistrate of Rome. The name, of course, appears to mean 'bridge builder,' whether or not that was its original significance. It was later adopted as a designation of the Bishop of Rome at least as early as the third decade of the third century (cf. Tertullian, *De pud.* 1. 6—217-222 A. D. ?).

[254] The *flamen Dialis* was a special priest of Jupiter. He is also mentioned in 4. 35, 7. 43. See E. Samter, "flamines," *RE* 6 (1909) 2484-92; Fowler 86-8, 204, 221, 313.

[255] Reifferscheid and Marchesi both retain the MS *quod eius est* which has given much trouble to all editors. The reading adopted is that of G. Wiman, *Eranos* 45 (1947) 131: *quod ⟨pecus⟩ eius est* (cf. 7. 43; Catullus 63. 13). Less preferable are Hagendahl (*Prose métr.* 244): *qui Diovis est,* and Axelson (cf. n. 16): *qui d⟨omesticus⟩ eius est.*

[256] According to A. J. Festugière, *Mémorial Lagrange* (Paris 1940) 98 n. 1, Arnobius is here indebted for the comments on the myth of Er (in Plato's *Rep.* 10) to Numenius and Cronius whom he mentions in 2. 11. Cf. H. C. Puech, " Numénius d'Apamée et les

théologies orientales au second siècle," *Mélanges Bidez* 2 (Brussels 1934) 747 n. 2.

²⁵⁷ Doubtless a reference to the legend that Zoroaster had appeared from a hill blazing with fire.

²⁵⁸ Arnobius is here doubtless thinking of the founder of Zoroastrianism. Despite the passage of time, the very full notes on this chapter in Orelli's edition (1. 342-6 = *ML* 5. 787-90) are still worth reading.

²⁵⁹ Hermippus of Berytus (Beirut)—see S. Heibges, *RE* 8 (1913) 853 f.— wrote five books on dream interpretation. He flourished in the reign of Hadrian.

²⁶⁰ Here Arnobius is confusing the founder of Zoroastrianism with the Bactrian king (see nn. 41-42). W. Kroll, *Oracula Chaldaica* (Breslau 1898) 28, demonstrates that this *Zoroaster Armenius* and *familiaris Pamphylus Cyri* is Er, the confusion going back to an apocryphal work cited by Clement of Alexandria, *Strom.* 5. 14. 103. 3.

²⁶¹ On Armenius, cf. E. Riess, "Armenius" no. 1, *RE* 2 (1896) 1188. See Plato, *Rep.* 614b.

²⁶² Apollonius of Tyana, first century A. D. whose life by Philostratus is extant. See J. Miller, "Apollonius" no. 98, *RE* 2 (1896) 146-8.

²⁶³ Damigeron the Magus (*RE* 4 [1901] 2055 f.) wrote (in the 2nd cent. A. D.) a book on the power of stones. Cf. Apuleius, *Apol.* 90. 20; Tertullian, *De an.* 57. 1 (who mentions Osthanes, Typhon, Dardanus, Damigeron, Nectabis, Berenice, and somewhat later, Simon Magus).

²⁶⁴ On Dardanus, see Pliny, *Nat. hist.* 30. 1. 9.

²⁶⁵ Belus is a proper name (cf. Baal) but nothing, apparently, is known of this person.

²⁶⁶ This Julianus is either no. 8 or no. 9 of the list given in *RE* 10 (1919) 15 f. He was a "Chaldaean" of the age of Marcus Aurelius —see A. J. Festugière, *Mém. Lagrange* (Paris 1940) 126.

²⁶⁷ On this Baebulus, see E. Riess, *RE* 2 (1896) 2734, where he is briefly identified as an "Erzzauberer." Ochsner, cited by Orelli, says that there is no reference to Baebulus in ancient literature.

²⁶⁸ The same point is made by Origen, *C. Cels.* 1. 6; Lactantius, *Div. inst.* 5. 3. 9.

²⁶⁹ *Principe deo.* See n. 101.

²⁷⁰ *Elementa turbata*, possibly imitated by Firmicus Maternus, *De err. prof. rel.* 24. 2.

²⁷¹ Note the dramatization of the Gospel narrative of the phe-

nomena accompanying Christ's death (Matt. 27. 51-54, Mark 15. 38, Luke 23. 44 f.), though the most remarkable detail—the rising of the dead (Matt. 27. 52)—is not mentioned. Cf. Tertullian, *Apol.* 21. 19-21: Eodem momento dies medium orbem signante sole subducta est. . . . Sed ecce die tertia concussa repente terra, etc.

²⁷² Cf. the same two words (*vanus, mendax*) in Vergil, *Aen.* 2. 79 f.

²⁷³ That is, different regions under different parts of the heavens.

²⁷⁴ At least after the first persecution.

²⁷⁵ *Praeconibus = apostolis.*

²⁷⁶ The MS reads *animis hominibusque* (to souls and men) but in Arnobius the word *homo = corpus* in several places (1. 62, 1. 65, 2. 28). Wiman's *summis humilibusque* is unnecessary. See also Tertullian, *De an.* 35. 6 and Waszink's note *ad loc.*

²⁷⁷ That is, no one outside these nations knew them and they themselves could not make known their existence. Scharnagl (35) is wrong in stating that the passive is here used for the active.

²⁷⁸ An exceedingly obscure sentence aside from possible corruptions of the text. The MS and Marchesi read *sed numquam fuerit* which is certainly not clear. Kroll suggested a lacuna and Bryce-Campbell translated: "But it will never avail them that it be gathered from written testimony ⟨only⟩." Wiman ingeniously attempts to fill the lacuna as follows: *sed numquam fier⟨ri non pot⟩erit.*

²⁷⁹ *Res*, a word defying adequate translation.

²⁸⁰ This may be a reference to the κοινή Greek. Cf. Origen, *C. Cels.* 2. 26. Clement of Alexandria (*Protr.* 8. 77. 1) says that the Scriptures are "bare of embellishment, of outward beauty of language, of idle talk and flattery." The charge that the Christian writings, notably the Bible versions, reeked with barbarisms of language and style were common, and defense against the assertion, commonplace: cf. Origen, *In Iesu Nave hom.* 8. 1; *In Gen. hom.* 15. 1; *De princ.* 4. 26; Lactantius, *Div. inst.* 3. 1; Jerome, *Epist.* 53. 10; Isidore of Pelusium, *Epist.* 4. 28, etc. Cf. Geffcken 289; A. v. Harnack, *Die Mission und Ausbreitung des Christentums in den ersten drei Jahrhunderten* 1 (4th ed., Leipzig 1924) 388 f.; Bardenhewer 1. 68-72. For other passages in which the fact that among the evidences for Christianity was the testimony of quite uneducated persons, see the note of J. H. Waszink to Tertullian's *De an.* 6. 7 (Amsterdam 1947) 141 f.

²⁸¹ Collectiones = συλλογισμοί (cf. Scharnagl 31-43).

²⁸² One wonders whether at his conversion Arnobius renounced his devotion to rhetoric.

[283] See the unsigned note by L. Havet, *Rev. de Phil.* n. s. 2 (1878) 84, calling attention to the fact that this passage demonstrates that the two accents were pronounced differently.

[284] Reading *sapientiae* with the corrector of the MS rather than ⟨*in*⟩ *sapientia* (Hildebrand, Reifferscheid). The allusion is probably to Epicurus: cf. Dion. Hal., *De comp. verb.* 24 fin. (= fr. 230 Usener); Quintilian 2. 17. 15; 12. 2. 24; Diog. Laert. 10. 6 (= fr. 33, p. 129 Bailey); 10. 13; Cicero, *De fin.* 1. 5. 14; *De nat. deor.* 1. 21. 59; R. Philippson, "Philodems Buch über den Zorn," *Rhein. Mus.* 71 (1916) 424-60, a study of Philodemus *On Rhetoric.* But cf. J. S. Reid in J. Masson, *Lucretius, Epicurean and Poet*, complementary volume (London 1909) 191 f. Cf. also C. Bailey, *Epicurus, the Extant Remains* (Oxford 1926) 149, from the *Vita Epicuri* 14: "He uses current diction to expound his theory, but Aristophanes the grammarian censures it as being too peculiar. But he was clear in expression."

[285] On this passage see G. E. McCracken, "Arnobius Adversus Genera," *Class. Jour.* 42 (1947) 474-6; E. Schwentner, "Arnobius über das grammatische Geschlecht," *Wörter und Sachen*, n. F. 20 (1939) 92 f. Schwentner merely quotes the passage without comment. It should be noted that in expressing grammatical gender by using the appropriate form of the demonstrative, Arnobius is following a practice which began at least as early as the first century B. C. Cf. G. Funaioli, *Grammaticae Romanae fragmenta* (Leipzig 1907), who cites *hoc pollen* (from Caesar, p. 153, fr. 17); *hic naevus* (from Varro, p. 196, fr. 25); *hos pugillares* (from Asinius Pollio, p. 499, fr. 5); *hos lodices* (from Asinius, p. 500, fr. 8); and *allecem hanc* (from Verrius Flaccus, p. 517, fr. 14). The practice lasted long: cf. D. T. Starnes—G. E. Noyes, *The English Dictionary from Cawdrey to Johnson, 1604-1755* (Chapel Hill 1946) 200, and E. Coyle's review of it, *Class. Weekly* 41 (1947) 26.

[286] *Hic* (this) and *paries* (wall) are both masculine; *haec* (this) and *sella* (chair) both feminine.

[287] Coxe (*ANF* 6. 430 n. 3) appears to believe that these examples of doubt as to gender are taken from the New Testament, for he refers to testimony as to Biblical texts.

[288] *Haec utria* = ' these wineskins.' The gender here is neuter and was used by the dramatist Livius Andronicus in place of the more usual masculine (*hos utres*). For references to passages in which the anomalous forms cited in this chapter occur, see *TLL* (so far as this

has appeared), and *Harper's Latin Dictionary*, edited by Lewis and Short.

²⁸⁹ *Caelus*, a masculine form for the more usual neuter, *caelum* (heaven), is found in Lucretius, Vitruvius, and Petronius, as well as in the grammarians Charisius and Diomedes. On the god Caelus (= Uranus) see 2. 71, 3. 29, 3. 37, 4. 14, 4. 24. See *TLL* 3. 79.

²⁹⁰ *Pileus* = *pilleus*, the masculine form being more usually found than the neuter *pileum* = *pilleum* (felt cap) which was, however, used by Plautus.

²⁹¹ This word means saffron. The masculine is found in Vergil, Ovid, Propertius, and Juvenal; the neuter in Sallust, Celsus, Pliny, Isidore of Seville, Servius, Diomedes, Charisius, while the word is cited for the feminine form in Apuleius, *Met.* 10. 34. See *TLL* 4. 1215.

²⁹² Usually *fretum* (strait) is neuter but it was treated as masculine by Lucilius, Naevius, Lucretius, Livy, Varro, and Jordanes. See *TLL* 6. 1311.

²⁹³ *Hic panis* (this bread) is the more normal but the neuter form is cited as having been used by Plautus: *Curc.* 367. Cf. F. J. Dölger, *Ant. u. Christ.* 1 (1929) 18.

²⁹⁴ *Hic sanguis* (this blood) is usual but *hoc sanguen* (neuter) was used by Ennius, Cicero, Cato, Varro, Lucretius, and Petronius.

²⁹⁵ Apparently only Arnobius speaks of the masculine form here used but there is evidence also for a variant *candelabrus* of which he may have been thinking. *Iugulus* is used by Juvenal; *iugulum* by Cicero and Tacitus. Note the chiasmus.

²⁹⁶ All were grammarians: (a) Cornelius Epicadus, freedman of Sulla, mentioned by Charisius, Keil's *Grammatici Latini* 1. 110; (b) L. Caesellius Vindex, age of Hadrian (see G. Goetz, *RE* 3 [1889] 1305); (c) Verrius Flaccus who lived under Augustus (see Schanz-Hosius, *Geschichte der römischen Literatur* 2 [4th ed., Munich 1935] 361-7); (d) Q. Terentius Scaurus, first half of second century A. D. (see P. Wessner, *RE* 2. R., 5 [1934] 672-6); (e) Nisus, briefly mentioned by a number of grammarians in Keil's *Grammatici Latini* 1. 26; 2. 503; 7. 76; 7. 155. It is tempting to believe that one of these lost grammarians was Arnobius' source, and, indeed, A. Gellius (6. 2) presents evidence to show that Caesellius, at least, did discuss the question of variable genders of nouns.

²⁹⁷ All these names are expressed in the plural, a favorite form of intensification with Arnobius.

²⁹⁸ Axelson may be right in wanting this to be 'knew' instead of

'willed'; the MS reads *noluit* which editors usually change to *voluit* but the deletion of the letter *l* (= *novit*) is quite as simple a change.

[299] *Adsumpsit.* Cf. G. Brunner, *Jahrb. f. Liturgiew.* 13 (1935) 177: "Das *adsumpsit* des Arnobius ist der in der Theologie üblich gewordene terminus technicus für die Annahme der menschlichen Natur durch den Logos an Stelle des *accepit* der Vulgata. Mit *tegmen* gibt Arnobius das paulinische σχῆμα, was die Vulgata mit *habitus* übersetzt. *Tegmen, forma, similitudo* stehen bei Arnobius, wie bei Paulus, im Unterschied zur *primigenia natura* bzw. forma Dei, die Christus besass, bevor er in der Fülle der Zeiten Mensch wurde, oder, um es mit einem Worte des Arnobius auszudrücken, als er noch in *incognitis regnis* weilte, von wo aus ihn der höchste Gott in die Welt gesandt hat."

[300] *Sine homine simulato* has a Docetic ring (cf. McGiffert 2. 43), but Brunner emphasizes the fact that this word is found in a quotation and therefore does not represent Arnobius' own views. Cf. W. Kroll, *Rhein. Mus.* 71 (1916) 333; Rapisarda, *Arnob.* 108.

[301] Plato (*Rep.* 611b) makes the same point: nothing synthesized is immortal (see 2. 14). Cf. Tertullian, *De an.* 10.

[302] Rapisarda (*Arnob.* 110) notes the striking parallel with Lactantius (*Div. inst.* 4. 10): homini . . . quem induerat gerebat. Micka (54) says of this passage that Arnobius "seems . . . to be teaching Docetism," but that his views are more akin to those of the later Nestorius. He rightly objects to the view of Brunner (173) that on the Incarnation Arnobius is correct. Colombo (18 ff.) says, however, that Arnobius is merely describing Christ in terms of a pagan deity, a view which has much that is attractive in it. Badham (see n. 222) maintains that these statements show Arnobius to have been a Docetic and is inclined to think that the source was the apocryphal Pseudo-Peter. E. S. Bouchier, *Life and Letters in Roman Africa* (Oxford 1913) 102, thinks the chapter contains Gnostic errors.

[303] The Pythian Sibyl—so Brunner (178).

[304] Bacis was a Boeotian prophet—see Cicero, *De div.* 1. 18. 34; Helenus, son of Priam, a Trojan prophet (*ibid.* 1. 40. 89); Marcius, a Roman prophet (*ibid.* 1. 50. 115). This suggests strongly that Arnobius was acquainted with the *De divinatione* although he never cites it. He might have made the point stronger by alluding to Helenus' sister Cassandra, also possessed of prophetic powers, since she, according to the legend followed in Aeschylus' *Agamemnon*,

was slain by Clytaemnestra and Aegisthus while vainly attempting to warn Agamemnon. On Bacis, see O. Kern, *RE* 2 (1896) 2801 f.

[305] Reading, with Wiman, *succubuisset vis tanta, ⟨tanta⟩ si non agenda res esset.*

[306] This word *fati* is Gelenius' correction of the MS *satis* which Axelson would retain. If he is right, then the translation should be "the inscrutable plan did not have to be revealed in completely hidden mysteries."

[307] *Latrones* = robbers, but, as Scharnagl (32 f.) says, in early Latin, which Arnobius is fond of imitating (but see Introduction, p. 24), the word = *milites* (cf. Plautus, *Trinummus* 599; Varro, *De ling. lat.* 7. 52). Cf. Forcellini 3. 40. Dr. Plumpe remarks that there may be a confusion of the *milites* who crucified with the *latrones* (Matt. 27. 38) who were crucified with Christ.

[308] An exceedingly corrupt passage, the MS reading: *Cum enim de animarum periculis multa, mala de illarum contra insinuator,* etc. There appears to be a lacuna in which stood at the very least a feminine noun in the ablative and some verb form which can govern *multa.* Marchesi attempts to purify the sentence by changing *mala* to *multa, insinuator* to *insinuaret,* and inserting *⟨salute⟩* after *contra.* This does not satisfy either me or Wiman whose alternative is *Cum enim de animarum periculis multa, mala de illarum contra ⟨indole vitiorum sollicite cogitans multa⟩ insinuator,* etc. This is better since it keeps closer to the text as given in the MS, preserves the word *insinuator* which certainly is right, but is open to the objection that the expansion of the lacuna is very lengthy. I have, however, followed it in the translation.

[309] For examples of ἱεροσυλίαι (temple robbing) see 6. 21; Cicero, the Fourth Verrine Oration: *De signis; De nat. deor.* 1. 29. 82; 1. 31. 86; 3. 34. 83; Suetonius, *Iulius* 54; *Caligula* 57; Clement of Alexandria, *Protr.* 4. 52.

[310] A famous example was that of Antony and Octavian in which both Marcus Cicero and his brother Quintus were among the victims in 43 B. C.

[311] The presence of *indigetes* immediately following suggests that Arnobius was thinking of Roman examples, in which case we might cite the rape of Rhea Silvia, daughter of King Numitor of Alba Longa and herself a Vestal Virgin, by the god Mars.

[312] Prior to the time of Diocletian, under whom Arnobius was writing, the title of *divus* or *diva* had been officially conferred after death upon Julius Caesar, thirty-four emperors, and twenty-seven

other members of the imperial family—see R. Cagnat, *Cours d'épigraphie latine* (4th ed., Paris 1914). If this is really a veiled reference to emperor worship, it is the only one in Arnobius.

[313] A difficult sentence to interpret. The following are mentioned: (a) critics of immorality and luxury (e. g. Juvenal?); (b) proponents of communistic marriage (e. g. Plato?); (c) pederasts; (d) misanthropes. One would have expected Arnobius to view the first with approval, but if the second and third be taken as examples of the vices, then there are only two classes, both hostile to the pagans and yet treated with respect by them.

[314] A clear case of hendiadys: the MS reads *luxurias et vitas vestras*, which Reifferscheid did not improve by changing to *vitia vestra*.

[315] Plato (*Rep.* 457d) argued that the female guardians should provide themselves as wives in communistic fashion for the male guardians. He did not advocate communistic marriage for the population.

[316] Doubtless a reference to Socrates and Plato but see C. Murley, "The Didactic Significance of Erotic Figures in Plato," *Class. Essays Pres. to James A. Kleist, S. J.* (St. Louis 1946) 61-73, who brings together evidence tending to prove that the references to pederasty in Plato may usually, if not always, be taken in a non-physical sense.

[317] An early pagan criticism of the Christians was that they were haters of the human race (Tacitus, *Ann.* 15. 44).

[318] Stertinius Avitus, a contemporary of Martial, wished to put a bust of the poet in his library (cf. the introductory epigram to Martial, Bk. 9).

[319] Brakman wishes to read *duratum* (hardened); Lorenz, *pravatum* (depraved).

[320] *Praeconium salutare. Salus* first meant health and then acquired the religious sense of salvation. Here there is a play on both senses.

[321] Sihler (173) thinks that the persecution of 303 A. D. had not yet started when Arnobius wrote this chapter and 2. 78.

[322] Cf. Cicero, *De nat. deor.* 1. 26. 71; in *De div.* 2. 24. 52 the statement is attributed to Cato the Elder: "I wonder that a soothsayer doesn't laugh when he sees another soothsayer."

[323] *Virtutum omnium dominus* = 'Lord of every virtue' but the reference is probably also to miraculous power as well as to virtue. See n. 210.

[324] See 2 Tim. 1. 10: *Our Savior Jesus Christ who hath destroyed death.*

BOOK TWO

With Book Two, the longest and in many ways the most important and the most original, Arnobius reaches the height of his philosophic and literary powers. This Book was regarded by its author as a sort of digression from his main theme (cf. 2. 1 and 3. 2) and may be briefly summarized as an attack on the method and results of the philosophers, in particular the idealism of Plato and the Neo-Platonists, and also the doctrine of the *novi viri* which was a combination of hermetism (cf. Rapisarda, *Arnob.* 136), Neo-Platonism, the *Oracula Chaldaica*, and other writings of the period (see chapters 11-66). Rapisarda (*ibid.* 76 f.) makes the interesting point that in the attack against Neo-Platonism, Arnobius really limits himself to a criticism of the theories of Plato himself, but elsewhere (41) emphasizes the importance of the work as showing that contemporary African Christianity realized the danger of Neo-Platonism. The extremely original controlled experiment designed to refute Plato's doctrine of recollection (see chapters 20 ff.) is worthy of considerable attention, but the cardinal teaching of this Book is the important belief, surprising as it is, that the human soul is not intrinsically immortal.

Attention is invited to the following special bibliography on Book Two:

L. Atzberger, *Geschichte der christlichen Eschatologie innerhalb der vornicänischen Zeit* (Freiburg i. Br. 1896) 573-82.

J. Carcopino, " Le tombeau de Lambiridi et l'hermétisme africain," *Rev. Arch.* 15 (1922) 283-90.

———. *Aspects mythiques de la Rome païenne* (Paris 1941) 293-300. (Cf. de Labriolle 1. 277.)

S. Colombo, " Arnobio e i suoi sette libri Adversus Nationes," *Didaskaleion* 9 (1930) esp. 45-74.

A. J. Festugière, 'La doctrine des " Uiri noui " sur l'origine et sur le sort des âmes d'après Arnobe, II, 11-16,' *Mémorial Lagrange* (Paris 1940) 97-132. [This is a most penetrating study of these chapters.]

K. B. Francke, *Die Psychologie und Erkenntnisslehre des Arnobius* (diss. Leipzig 1878).

H. W. Fulford, " Conditional Immortality," *Hastings Encycl.* 3 (1913) 822-5.

O. Grillnberger, " Studien zur Philosophie der patristischen Zeit,

II: Die Unsterblichkeitslehre des Arnobius," *Jahrb. f. Philos. u. spek. Theol.* 5 (1891) 1-14.

G. J. Joyce, "Annihilation," *Hastings Encycl.* 1 (1913) 544-9.

C. Marchesi, "Il pessimismo di un apologeta cristiano," *Pègaso* 2 (1930) 536-50.

A. Röhricht, *Die Seelenlehre des Arnobius nach ihren Quellen und ihrer Entstehung untersucht. Ein Beitrag zum Verständnis der späteren Apologetik der alten Kirche* (Hamburg 1893) esp. 43-64.

A. D. Nock–A. J. Festugière, *Corpus Hermeticum* (2 vols., Paris 1946).

E. F. Schulze, *Das Übel in der Welt nach der Lehre des Arnobius. Ein Beitrag zur Geschichte der patristischen Philosophie* (diss. Jena 1896).

[1] Zeus and Alcmene are clearly meant. Cf. 2. 70, 4. 22, 4. 26, 5. 22, 7. 33.

[2] The verbs *praetendit* and *amovit* follow Reifferscheid and Wiman, rather than the *praetenderit* and *amoverit* of Marchesi's text.

[3] At this point there is a transposition in the text, doubtless caused by a loose leaf wrongly replaced, a dislocation which took place prior to the compilation of P. The translation follows the rearrangement of the pages found in both Reifferscheid and Marchesi. Wiman, however, would begin chapter 2 with: *et non omnium virtutum vi cinctus et lumen praetendit vitae et periculum ignorationis amovit?*

[4] *Salutaria* = wholesome things.

[5] So the MS (*optaret*) which was changed by Meursius to *aptaret* and by Heraldus, followed by Reifferscheid, to *apertaret* (opened), but the MS is really intelligible.

[6] *Officiosior.*

[7] *Motu . . . vitali.* Cf. 2. 16: *motum . . . vitalem,* and Lucretius 2. 717: vitalis motus.

[8] *Imperator.* See Book One, n. 109. The word is used again in 2. 36.

[9] Cf. 3. 26, 4. 25, 4. 27, 5. 41, 5. 45, 6. 3, 6. 11, 6. 12.

[10] Following Heraldus, Orelli, and Meiser, I have adopted *Da puerum iudicem* for *Da verum iudicium,* since otherwise *dubitabit* lacks a subject. What Arnobius says is "Let even a child decide."

[11] Arnobius may here be imitating, with unwonted restraint, a passage in Tertullian, *Apol.* 17. 5 f., which lists no fewer than six colloquial expressions used by pagans in similar fashion: *deus magnus, deus bonus, quod deus dederit, deus videt, deo commendo,* and *deus*

mihi reddet, or Minucius 18. 11: Quid? quod omnium de isto habeo consensum? Audio vulgus: cum ad caelum manus tendunt, nihil aliud quam ' deum ' (note the single word, as in Arnobius) dicunt et ' deus magnus est ' et ' deus verus est ' et ' si deus dederit.'

[12] Rapisarda (*Arnob.* 53) thinks this refers to angels, not to aeons.

[13] The Greek word τῦφος means vanity, as well as affectation, humbug, delusion, and also serves as the name of four kinds of fever. Arnobius is fond of it but uses it again only in this Book: Chapters 12, 16, 19, and 63, which suggests that he may have found it in a source used in Book Two only. J. Gibb-W. Montgomery, *The Confessions of Augustine* (Cambr. Patr. Texts, Cambridge 1908) 57, cite this example as the earliest they have found of a usage common in Augustine. They call this rightly a conscious use as a loan word. Neither Reifferscheid nor Marchesi print the word in Greek characters, though the fact that five of the six occurrences are corrupt suggests that a scribe, perhaps he who produced P, had difficulty in reading the Greek word which he saw before him. In 3. 29 both editors rightly print Greek characters because in the MS the word χρόνος appears with only one letter (the *n*) clearly in Roman script. In 3. 41 they both print λαύρας though P reads quite clearly in Roman script *laude*. I therefore believe that the MS originally had Greek characters at this point, though the fact does not become patent in a translation. See *Vigiliae Christianae* 3 (1949) 40.

[14] *Latronibus* which in 1. 63 (see n. 307) has the sense of ' soldiers.'

[15] Cf. Origen, *C. Cels.* 2. 10.

[16] [C. E.] Freppel, *Commodien, Arnobe, Lactance, et autres fragments inédits* (Paris 1893) 52, points out that this idea appears in Pascal's *Pensées*, art. 10. 1 (148-53 Havet). Resemblances between Arnobius and Pascal have also been noted by M. Leigh (see below, n. 44).

[17] Bryce-Campbell wrongly take *redarguat* to mean ' to show to be true ' because they went astray on the meaning of *quod* (because).

[18] H. M. Gwatkin, *Early Church History to A. D. 313*, 1 (London 1912) 201, refers this passage to the argument of Gamaliel (Acts 5. 38).

[19] *Sacramenta*—an early Christian loan word taken from the Roman military sphere, where it = soldiers' oaths of allegiance. Like *mysterium*, with which it is frequently identical in meaning, it has a very wide range of significance in early Christian literature (cf. below, *militiae sacramenta*). Cf. the very illuminating notes of J. P.

Christopher (*ACW* 2. 108 f.) and J. H. Waszink (Tertullian's *De anima* [Amsterdam 1947] 90 f.) and the voluminous bibliography cited by both scholars. On the parallel with Mithraism, see Cumont 207 n. 5.

[20] Note how the rhetorician gives first place to those professions connected with his own experience.

[21] This sentence closely parallels one of Tertullian, *Apol.* 3. 4: Uxorem iam pudicam maritus iam non zelotypus eiecit, filium iam subiectum pater retro patiens abdicavit, servum iam fidelem dominus olim mitis ab oculis relegavit: ut quisque hoc nomine emendatur, offendit. Cf. also *Ad nat.* 1. 4. If in this passage Arnobius is imitating Tertullian, then it is quite possible that he was writing before the persecution of Diocletian, yet Colombo (4) maintains that this sentence does refer to that persecution, perhaps rightly.

[22] *Salutaris militiae sacramenta deponere.* When a Roman recruit was inducted, a token of identification, *signaculum*, attached to a chain or cord, was suspended from his neck. The *signaculum* bore the name (or portrait?) of the emperor, and on this the military oath was administered to the soldier. The entire ceremony constituted a religious rite and was known as *sacramenta militiae*. Cf. F. J. Dölger, "sacramentum militiae," *Ant. u. Christ.* 2 (1930) 268-80. To a Christian *militiae sacramenta deponere* meant to abandon the allegiance sworn to Christ in baptism. The ancient Christian concept of life as a war, struggle—*militia*—to obtain salvation, is the theme of a famous study by A. Harnack, *Militia Christi: die christliche Religion und der Soldatenstand in den ersten drei Jahrhunderten* (Leipzig 1905).

[23] *Inaniter* = as an atom in the void, by chance alone.

[24] An allusion to the Epicurean theory of atomic collisions.

[25] This word *credulitas* has, when used by the pagan critics of Christianity in a sarcastic tone, precisely the same meaning as its English cognate. When used by Christians it has the sublime sense of belief in Christ.

[26] *Conditi*, so the MS, approved by Löfstedt, Stangl, and Marchesi; *contincti* = 'sprinkled' (Wensky); *aliti* = 'nourished' (Reifferscheid); *candidi* = 'bright' (Kistner); *praediti* = 'endowed' (Meiser). Weyman rightly maintains that *conditi* is derived from *condire*, not from *condere*.

[27] G. Bortolucci, "Arnobio, Adversus Nationes II, 6 ed una ipotesi di Pietro Giordani," in *Mélanges de Droit Romain dediés à Georges Cornil* 1 (Gand-Paris 1926) 129-36, wrongly deduces from this

passage the conclusion that the pagans imputed to the Christians " una estrema ignoranza e della grammatica e della letteratura e della logica e del diritto, opponendo che se i Cristiani cotali cose ignoravano che tutti sanno, altre e migliori a più importanti ne conoscono e più atte alla disciplina dello spirito e del viver civile." All that may rightly be derived is that Arnobius rebukes the pagans for foolishly thinking that their command of knowledge in the fields specified entitled them to special consideration.

[28] *Declinare.* Note the several examples of chiasmus in the passage. Cf. 1. 59.

[29] *Obsignatum memoria tenetis,* perhaps a Lucretian echo (cf. 2. 581: *obsignatum . . . habere,* and Bailey *ad loc.*).

[30] The point is that they were thoroughly learned in literature, knowing even minor works. This is the only extant allusion to the third satire of the 29th book of Lucilius (*ca.* 180-103 B. C.) who is also mentioned in 5. 18. Cf. F. Marx's edition of the fragments (Leipzig 1904), fr. 1177, text in 1. 80, commentary in 2. 372 f. See also E. H. Warmington, *Remains of Old Latin* 3 (London-Cambridge, Mass. 1938) 294 f. The latter translates *Fornix* as 'Brothel' —the word really means 'arch' and its evil connotation (cf. 'fornicate') was derived from the practice of vice near arches. See H. Degering, " Fornix," *RE* 7 (1912) 8-12; I. Hilberg, " Der Fornix des Lucilius und der Marsya des Pomponius," *Wien. Stud.* 25 (1903) 156-8.

[31] The juxtaposition of the allusion to the satirist Lucilius makes it highly probable that this is a reference to an otherwise unknown work of the master of the so-called Atellan farce, Pomponius of Bononia (fl. 80 B. C.), on whom see M. Schanz-C. Hosius, *Geschichte der römischen Litteratur* 1 (4th ed., Munich 1927) 245-53; J. W. Duff, *A Literary History of Rome* (London 1909) 220-2. Bortolucci (*loc. cit.*), however, gives considerable attention to a theory of Pietro Giordani (b. 1774) that this Pomponius was the jurisconsult Sextus Pomponius who lived, according to Giordani, either under Hadrian or under Alexander Severus. Giordani believed that the clauses immediately following the name of Pomponius give the contents of the work called *Marsyas* which took its name, he thought, from the statue of the Phrygian satyr standing in the Forum (see Platner-Ashby 499). But, as Bortolucci points out, the presence of *quia* (because) directly following the name sets off the sentence from what follows.

[32] A clear reference to 1 Cor. 3. 19: *For the wisdom of this world*

is foolishness with God. Note that Arnobius uses *hominis* in place of *mundi* which is found in the Vulgate (agreeing with the Greek manuscripts) and adds his own touch (*primum*) to make sure that the Christian God will be clearly understood. Some earlier editions eliminated the problem of this word by placing it in the next sentence. On the epithet, see Micka 43 n. 10. It should be noted that the words *illud vulgatum* suggest that Arnobius knew the phrase in common speech, rather than that he had read the Epistle. He might have met it also in Clement of Alexandria, *Strom.* 5. 1; Origen, *C. Cels.* 1. 13; Cyprian, *Test.* 3. 69. On Arnobius' knowledge of Scripture in general, see Introd. pp. 25-7.

[33] A difficult passage: *invidia* may as well be taken as nominative in which case there is a case of chiasmus.

[34] In the first *Alcibiades* (129e), a dialogue which is sometimes suspected of being spurious (cf. P. Shorey, *What Plato Said* [Chicago 1933] 415), Alcibiades is represented as not being able to explain what man is; but Socrates at once brings him to the necessary conclusion (see Bryce-Campbell *ad loc.*). LeNourry (cited by them) thinks the reference is to *Phaedrus* 230a where Socrates says he investigates himself, not mythological questions. Röhricht (*Seelenlehre* 25 f.) concludes from a study of these passages that Arnobius used Plato directly.

[35] The ancient theory of abiogenesis or spontaneous generation. Cf. Lucretius 2. 871 and the notes of Leonard-Smith and Bailey *ad loc.*

[36] *Theaetetus* 158cd, but since Socrates is here developing Protagoras' theory from his point of view, it can hardly be said of Plato that he is in doubt. See Bryce-Campbell's n. 3. Röhricht (*Seelenlehre* 27) says that this passage is derived from direct acquaintance with Plato.

[37] Cf. A. Gellius 5. 16. 2: Stoici causas esse videndi dicunt radiorum ex oculis in ea quae videri queunt emissionem aerisque simul intentionem.

[38] An African would probably overlook blond hair.

[39] Here the word is *animus*, but in the discussion which makes up the rest of Book Two, Arnobius regularly uses *animae* (feminine plural). On Lucretius' use of these terms (*animus* = 'mind,' 'spirit,' 'understanding'; *anima* = 'soul' and 'life'), see J. Masson, *Lucretius, Epicurean and Poet* (London 1907) 205, and the notes on the two words in J. H. Waszink's edition of Tertullian's *De an.* (Amsterdam 1947) 201, 254.

[40] *Deus = divinus* (see nn. 232, 237, 375). Cf. Cicero, *Tusc.*
1. 26. 65; *Somn. Scip.* 8 = *De re publ.* 6. 24. 26; also Dionysius Cato
(290 A. D.):

> Si deus est animus, nobis ut carmina dicunt,
> Hic tibi praecipue sit pura mente colendus.

E. Baehrens, *Poetae latinae minores* 3. 216 = *Oxford Book of Latin
Verse* (Oxford 1944) p. 368, no. 211.

[41] Reading *defessus deliret futura et insana* (Marchesi) but perhaps Reifferscheid (*defessus, delira ecfuttiat et insana*), following
Oehler, is right, and the translation should be: " prattles about crazy
and mad things." On this passage, see Lucretius 3. 444-71.

[42] This passage, as Klussmann pointed out, reflects the well-known
lines of Lucretius 3. 445-69 which are used to demonstrate, in the
estimation of the poet, that the soul is mortal.

[43] Reading *quod* (Reifferscheid) instead of *ut* (Marchesi).

[44] M. Leigh, " A Christian Skeptic of the Fourth Century: Some
Parallels between Arnobius and Pascal," *Hibbert Jour.* 19 (1920-21)
319-25, sees parallels between Pascal's Art. 23. 10 and this chapter,
as well as many other points of similarity between the two writers.
See above, n. 16.

[45] The word *meraco* implies that the draught is not watered down
but is pure wine (*merum*). Though I find it difficult to believe that
a rhetor like Arnobius could be unacquainted with Horace, I cannot
agree with Rapisarda (*Arnob.* 242) that this is surely a conscious
imitation of *Ep.* 2. 2. 137.

[46] A reference to the taking up of a newborn child from the ground
as a sign of recognition of its legitimacy.

[47] This act of faith is also mentioned by Origen, *C. Cels.* 1. 11;
Theophilus, *Ad Autol.* 1. 8.

[48] Clement of Alexandria (*Protr.* 5. 64. 1 f.) has a passage somewhat like this. He mentions Thales, Anaximenes of Miletus, Diogenes of Apollonia, Parmenides of Elea, Hippasus of Metapontum,
Heraclitus of Ephesus, and Empedocles of Acragas. The passages
are similar but quite obviously independent of each other. Cf.
Cicero, *De nat. deor.* 1. 10. 25; which mentions Thales but apart
from this allusion lacks clear evidence of Arnobius' indebtedness to
Cicero. The same is true of a reference to Heraclitus on fire (*ibid.*
3. 14. 35).

[49] Thales of Miletus (*ca.* 624-*ca.* 550 B. C.) believed that all things
came from water (see W. T. Stace, *A Critical History of Greek*

Philosophy [London 1920] 21; T. Gomperz, *Greek Thinkers, a History of Ancient Philosophy* 1 [trans. by L. Magnus, New York 1901] 48); Heraclitus of Ephesus (*ca.* 535-*ca.* 475 B. C.) taught that the fundamental reality was fire (Stace 78, Gomperz 1. 63). Heraclitus is also mentioned in 5. 29. On Thales, see W. Nestle, *RE*, 2. R. 5 (1934) 1210-12.

[50] Pythagoras of Samos (fl. 6th century B. C.) whom Arnobius thrice mentions (1. 40, 2. 10, 2. 13) was a famous mathmatician who believed that number was the basic reality (Stace 34, Gomperz 1. 99-122; R. Scoon, *Greek Philosophy before Plato* [Princeton 1928] 35-50). Archytas of Taras, a contemporary of Plato, developed mechanics on mechanical lines and was a geometer of considerable ability (Scoon 273).

[51] An allusion to the celebrated "Theory of Ideas."

[52] This reference to the fifth element shows that Arnobius is indebted to the following passage in Cicero, *Tusc.* 1. 10. 22: Aristoteles longe omnibus—Platonem semper excipio—praestans et ingenio et diligentia, cum quattuor nota illa genera principiorum esset complexus, e quibus omnia orerentur, quintam quandam naturam censet esse, e qua sit mens; cogitare enim et providere et discere et docere et invenire aliquid et meminisse, et tam multa alia, amare odisse, cupere timere, angi laetari; haec et similia eorum in horum quattuor generum inesse nullo putat: quintum genus adhibet vacans nomine et sic ipsum animum ἐνδελέχειαν appellat novo nomine quasi quandam continuatam motionem et perennem. On the Greek word see the very illuminating note in J. E. King's translation of Cicero, *Tusc.*, Loeb Classical Library (London-New York 1927) 28, and cf. also the following passages in Aristotle: *Metaphys.* 4. 2 (1013a); *Phys.* 2. 3 (194b); see W. D. Ross, *Aristotle's Physics* (Oxford 1936), analysis, pp. 361 f.; and Bryce-Campbell's note 2 (72).

[53] The followers of Aristotle were called Peripatetics (from περιπατεῖν, 'to walk about'), either from his habit of walking about as he lectured or from the περίπατος (a covered walk) of the Lyceum. The chief Peripatetics were Theophrastus, Eudemus of Rhodes, Strato of Lampsacus, Andronicus of Rhodes, and Alexander of Aphrodisias.

[54] Reading with Wiman *arsuram* for Marchesi's *arsurum.*

[55] Chrysippus of Soli (*ca.* 280-206 B. C.) was a teacher of Zeno of Tarsus. He was renowned as a dialectician and prodigious worker (reputedly wrote 705 works!). Panaetius of Rhodes (second century B. C.) came to Rome and taught philosophy there. Arnobius, or his

source, appears to be in error in including Zeno in this category, since he is said not to have accepted the Stoic view of a final conflagration.

[56] Three representative atomists. On Metrodorus, cf. Cicero, *De nat. deor.* 1. 31. 86; 1. 33. 93; 1. 40. 113.

[57] On Arcesilas of Pitane (316-241 B. C.), founder of the so-called 'Middle Academy,' see H. v. Arnim, "Arcesilas" no. 19, *RE* 2 (1896) 1164-8. On Carneades (214-129 B. C.), a leader of the Academics, see v. Arnim, *ibid.* 10 (1919) 1964-85.

[58] On the Academics, see Cicero, *De nat. deor.* 2. 1. 1-2; *Academica*, *passim*. The chief difference between the older and later Academic school was that the latter softened the pure skepticism of the former by stating what was "probably" true.

[59] Cf. Lucretius 1. 635-704; Lactantius, *Div. inst.* 1. 5. 15-18.

[60] *Comprehendere* = both 'comprehend' and 'include,' a play on words.

[61] *Fides*, i. e. a willingness to believe (in a good sense), contrasted with *credulitas*, which has the same meaning in a bad sense.

[62] Reading *nostra cum credulitate* with Ursinus, Stewechius, and, more recently, Lorenz, in place of the MS *nostra in credulitate* (Marchesi).

[63] This suggests the second principle of Gorgias of Leontini that if anything exists, it cannot be recognized or known.

[64] On the philosophical sources used by Arnobius in 2. 11-66, see A. J. Festugière, *Mémorial Lagrange* (Paris 1940) 97-132. From his résumé the doctrine may be summarized as follows: (1) The soul is the child of the First God, even a portion of his substance. (2) In the hierarchy of primary divinities, the soul holds fourth place, after the First God and the Two Intellects [see below n. 163]. (3) Born the child of God, the soul is divine, immortal, incorporeal, naturally omniscient and all-wise; endowed with an indestructible perfection which causes it to practice all the moral virtues and renders it incapable of sin; not subject to the laws of fate. (4) Sprung from the same source, all the souls possess in common the same spirit, the same conduct, the same judgment. (5) The soul descends to earth, that is, enters human bodies, by virtue, apparently, of a spontaneous choice. (6) During the descent, when the soul passes through the circles of the spheres, it acquires 'active principles' (*causae*) which render it the slave of all the passions and vices. (7) Man is therefore composed of three elements: a) from his divine part he is endowed with reason, is superior to the animals, and, of himself, immortal,

omniscient, incapable of sin, not subject to fate; b) from the qualities which he receives from the stars man becomes completely bad, but the sins he commits should be charged against the astral causes, not against the divine part of man, the real man, which remains incapable of sin and necessarily immortal; and c) from his terrestrial body, man is subject to death. (8) After the visible death, the soul flies back to God its Father. (9) To obtain or facilitate the return, three methods or 'ways' are offered to the soul: a) the way of the half-wise (*scioli*): to detach the divine part as much as possible from the material; b) the way of the Magi: to learn prayers thanks to which the soul will remove the evil powers which oppose its return, and c) the way of the Etruscans: to provide, by the sacrifice of some animal to some divinity, that the soul will become divine and not die. In an elaborate table (128 f.) Festugière lists passages in the *Corpus Hermeticum*, Numenius, Porphyry, Iamblichus, the *Oracula Chaldaica* [cf. Cumont 115], the Gnostics in Plotinus, *Enn.* 2. 9, Zoroaster, Osthanes, and others, and magical papyri (Mithraic liturgies) which he believes correspond to the various elements of the doctrine of the 'viri novi' here summarized.

It need not be pointed out that Arnobius accepts none of this doctrine but opposes it whole-heartedly with Christian fervor, though the result is not always orthodox. That hermetism inspired Arnobius is also maintained by Cumont (238 n. 50), citing J. Carcopino, " Le tombeau de Lambiridi et l'hermétisme africain, *Rev. Arch.* 15 (1922) 283-90.

[65] So the MS: *Platoni*, but Ursinus reads *Plotino* which Heraldus and Bryce-Campbell preferred.

[66] The MS reads *Crotonio*, i. e. either a man named Crotonius of whom nothing is known or the 'man of Croton,' perhaps an allusion to Pythagoras. But it is much more probable that Ursinus was right in correcting to *Cronio*, an allusion to an eminent Pythagorean, also mentioned by Eusebius, *Hist. eccl.* 6. 19. 8; Porphyry, *De ant. nymph.* 21; *Vita Plotini* 14; Longinus in Porphyry, *Vita Plotini* 20; Iamblichus in Stobaeus 1, pp. 375, 380, where, as Festugière points out, Cronius' name is coupled with that of Numenius as here. Because Theodoret (*Graec. aff. cur. serm.* 2: *De princ.* 33 [MG 83. 852B]) mentions in the same connection Plato, Plotinus, and Numenius, Gelenius wanted to change *Crotonio* in the text to *Plotino*. Orelli offers some other less probable suggestions. See Festugière 98 n. 1. For the fragments of Numenius, see E. A. Leemans, *Studie over den wijsgeer Numenius van Apamea met*

uitgave der fragmenten (Brussels 1937) 113-46; the fragments of Cronius, 153-7. On Numenius, cf. Origen, *C. Cels.* 4. 53; 5. 57; Rapisarda, *Arnob.* 46.

⁶⁷ *Fideliter* = with faith or belief in their authenticity rather than devotion to them.

⁶⁸ Cf. 1. 48 for similar questions asked about the pagan gods.

⁶⁹ *Scabies* = either an itch or a scab. The point of *callus* (in place of *cutis*) is probably to indicate that a sliver may be more easily removed from hard than from soft skin.

⁷⁰ *Luculentissimis*, a word applied by St. Jerome (*Chron. ann. Abr.* 2343 = 326-7 A. D.) to Arnobius' own books. See Introd. n. 19.

⁷¹ *Levigatis* has the possibility of an ironic sense, i. e. slippery, too smooth, which is doubtless not wanted here.

⁷² Kistner suggests *acumina* (subtleties) which is tempting (cf. Cicero, *Orat.* 31. 110: *argutiis et acumine*) but is rejected by Marchesi and Löfstedt.

⁷³ The antecedent is *vis* (power).

⁷⁴ All editors have resisted the temptation to insert a negative in this sentence. What Arnobius means is that the deeds are so well-known that, if he wished, he could specify them, not that their very fewness would permit them to be counted. On the expansion of Christianity at this period, see also Lactantius, *Div. inst.* 5. 13. 1, which, however, shows no dependence on Arnobius.

⁷⁵ Orelli thinks this " India " = Ethiopia and he may be right, but there is literary evidence in addition to support Arnobius' statement. Cf. the third-century *Acts of Thomas* (see M. R. James, *The Apocryphal New Testament* [Oxford 1924] 364-438), confirmed by the apocryphal work on the Assumption (*ibid.* 203 f., 218) and the Apostolic History of Abdias (see McGiffert and Wace in Schaff-Wace, *Nicene and Post-Nicene Fathers* 1 [New York 1890] 225 n. 6, which tends to show that this " India " is not India proper), where it is stated that Pantaenus went to " India " and found there a Hebrew version of the first Gospel brought there by Bartholomew; and Jerome, *De vir. ill.* 36 and *Ep.* 70 (*Ad Magnum*), which shows that Jerome was thinking of India proper (cf. the reference to Brahmins). A. Harnack, *Mission and Expansion of Christianity* 2 (2nd ed., London 1908) 152, appears to accept the evidence of the *Acts of Thomas* at its face value. Not so H. W. Gwatkin, *Early Church History to A. D. 313*, 2 (London 1912) 163, and K. S. Latourette, *History of the Expansion of Christianity* 1 (New York 1937) 337, both of whom favor an Arabian site. C. R. Beazley, " Christian

Missions," *Hastings Encycl.* 8 (1916) 705, takes a neutral position. E. J. Rapson, *Cambridge History of India* 1 (New York 1922) 579 f., points out the chronological possibility of the data in the *Acts of Thomas*, but appears to be hesitant about accepting the tradition they preserve. On this point I have applied for information concerning possible archaeological evidence, tending to substantiate the existence of Christianity in the Indian subcontinent prior to 300 A. D., to Father P. DeLetter, S. J., St. Mary's Theological College, Kurseong, India. In a letter dated 10 May 1947, Father DeLetter quotes the following statement of his colleague, Father J. Bayart, Professor of Indian Religions: ". . . the viewpoint of Western scholars has always been this (and not fully rightly): the 'India' or 'Indi' of early Christian writers (or of classical authors) is *not* the real India, unless this can be proved; whereas the historical evidence about trade relations between India and the West at the beginning of the Christian era would rather justify the contrary: 'India' means India unless the opposite be clearly proved."

[76] The Seres were an ancient oriental people usually identified with the Chinese, but Lucan 10. 29 makes them neighbors of the Ethiopians, dwellers near the sources of the Nile. They are mentioned again in 6. 5. See Herrmann, " Seres," *RE* 2. Reihe, 2 (1923) 1678-83.

[77] Cf. Eusebius, *Hist. eccl.* 6. 19. 15 f.

[78] Note the curious absence in this list of Africa (except Egypt), and of Spain, Gaul, Britain, and northern Europe in general.

[79] Tertullian (*Adv. Iud.* 7) states that Christianity had spread to such an extent that it was now possessed *ab omnibus gentibus supra enumeratis*, which include: Parthians, Medes, Elamites; inhabitants of Mesopotamia, Armenia, Phrygia, Cappadocia; dwellers in Pontus, Asia, Pamphylia, Egypt, trans-Cyrenaic Africa; the Jews in Jerusalem; the Gaetuli, Mauri, Spaniards, Gauls, Britons, Sarmatians, Dacians, Germans and Scythians. Note the absence of " India " in this list. Cf. also the celebrated passage in Tertullian, *Apol.* 37. 4: Hesterni sumus, et vestra omnia implevimus, urbes, insulas, castella, municipia, conciliabula, castra ipsa, tribus, decurias, palatium, senatum, forum. Sola vobis reliquimus templa. Cf. Irenaeus, *Adv. haer.* 1. 2 (Harvey).

[80] According to Livy 1. 19, Numa gave the Romans their religious customs. The allusion is perhaps a veiled attack on augury which Arnobius, curiously enough, never mentions elsewhere. See Book One, n. 97.

[81] *Res.* This may possibly refer, on the other hand, not to the

religious traditions but to actual property rights which would have
to be abandoned at conversion. Cf. Clement of Alexandria, *Protr.* 10.

[82] Cf. Minucius 31. 7: et quod in dies nostri numerus augentur.

[83] The context makes it seem certain that "they" are the people
of Rome and that Arnobius is viewing the contest as having taken
place there.

[84] According to G. N. L. Hall, "Simon Magus," *Hastings Encycl.*
11 (1921) 514-25, Arnobius is the earliest writer to give a version
of the story in which Simon lived after his attempted flight. For
other writers who mention Simon, cf. H. Lietzmann, "Simon
Magus," *RE*, 2. Reihe, 5 (1927) 180-4; E. Amann, "Simon le
Magicien," *DTC* 14. 2 (1941) 2130-40; and see Rapisarda, *Arnob.*
51 f. Incidentally, by his offer of money for the power to give the
Holy Spirit (Acts 8. 17 ff.), Simon fathered the term 'simony.'

[85] Cf. N. H. Baynes, *CAH* 12 (1939) 664, citing Eusebius, *Hist.
eccl.* 7. 10. 4.

[86] Brunda = Brundisium (modern Brindisi). See C. Hülsen,
"Brundisium," *RE* 3 (1899) 902, where the *Schol. Bern.* to Lucan
2.609 is cited for the form 'Brunda.'

[87] *Pudore.* A. Souter (*Class. Rev.* 49 [1935] 209), suggests *paedore*
('stench') which gives a more vivid sense in connection with *cru-
ciatibus.* No doubt there was both *pudor* and *paedor.*

[88] *Secta* has a basic meaning of the trodden path and there is a
play, doubtless, in the juxtaposition of it with *deverticula.*

[89] Mercurius = Hermes Trismegistus on whom see J. Kroll, *Die
Lehren des Hermes Trismegistos* (2nd ed., Münster i. W. 1928).
According to Festugière (99 n. 1), Arnobius here distinguishes three
groups: (a) hermetism; (b) the Platonici-Pythagorici, and (c) the
'novi viri,' whom he mentions in 2. 15: "et qui se croient issus du
même premier Dieu Noûs, ce que les rend nécessairement ὁμονοοῦντες."
On the necessity of going back as far as Pythagoras, Festugière cites
fr. 9 of Numenius (Leemans).

[90] On the association of the three in this order, see Iamblichus,
De myst. 1. 2.

[91] Festugière's 'first way' (102 f.) of facilitating the return of the
soul to God after death (see above, n. 64). The thought is repeated
in 2. 62 and 2. 66. Röhricht (*Seelenlehre* 27) thinks Plato was here
directly used.

[92] *Theaetetus* 173e where Plato merely says that the outer form
of the philosopher is in the city—his mind is "flying all abroad"
as Pindar said, "measuring earth and heaven and the things which

are under and on the earth and above the heaven, interrogating the whole nature of each and all in their entirety, but not condescending to anything which is within reach." Cf. Cicero, *Somn. Scip.* 3 = *De re publ.* 6. 15.

⁹³ Cf. Minucius 34; Origen, *C. Cels.* 1. 7; and Rapisarda, *Arnob.* 94.

⁹⁴ Röhricht (*Seelenlehre* 27) thinks Arnobius used Plato directly.

⁹⁵ *Politicus* 270de. Cf. Gabarrou, *Oeuvre* 21-3.

⁹⁶ Wiman understands *vos* to refer to *Platonici* and this makes the sentence logical.

⁹⁷ Wiman transposes this word (*quod*) from where it appears between *non* and *vitiis* and places it before *metus*. He cites other examples of such transpositions in 3. 43 (*cogat*), 5. 6 (*formas*), 5. 35 (*in*) and 7. 15 (*primum*), to which I may add two other examples of transposed *non* (2. 49 and 4. 32). But Professor A. D. Nock, in a letter of 28 March 1948, dissents from Wiman's transposition and believes *quod* means 'as for the fact that.' This I have followed in the translation.

⁹⁸ Festugière's 'second way' (120 f.), repeated in 2. 62 but not in 2. 66, as he maintains. He also appears to be mistaken in attributing to this chapter a reference to the 'third way,' sacrifice of animals. I find no allusion to animal sacrifice here. He points out (99 n. 2) that here Arnobius distinguishes between " éloignement des passions (matière) et prières théurgiques " as also in 2. 62, 2. 65. Cumont (265 f., n. 91) expresses doubt as to Arnobius' dependence on Labeo at this point.

⁹⁹ Gabarrou (*Oeuvre* 31) sees in chapters 14, 26 f., much influence of Lucretius. Cf. Lucretius 3. 459 f., 470, 668. Gabarrou also maintains (73) that the doctrine of the mortality of the soul, expounded by Arnobius in Book Two, shows that he had read the *De anima* of Tertullian. Apart from the fact that a careful comparison shows no great similarity of treatment in the two works, Tertullian explicitly states (16) that both God and Christ were angry. It seems difficult to believe that anyone who knew that on occasion Christ had exhibited anger could maintain, as Arnobius does in 1. 17 and elsewhere, the belief that God is incapable of anger. Cf. Introd. n. 322.

¹⁰⁰ Arnobius uses here both *hostes* (national enemies) and *inimici* (personal foes). The idea of this sentence seems Gnostic.

¹⁰¹ *Phaedo* 112a-114a. It may be recorded here that in the assertion of the mortality of the human soul which makes up the bulk of Book Two, Arnobius is not followed by his brilliant pupil, Lactantius, *Div. inst.* 3. 13; 8. 8 f., *Epit.* 65, and *De ira Dei, passim.* Röhricht (*De*

Clemente 40) maintains that Arnobius is not attacking Plato here but contemporary Neo-Platonists.

[102] Festugière (99 n. 3) points out that Plato speaks neither of demons nor pain of fire.

[103] Reading with the MS *pravae* in place of the emendation *parvae* (small) adopted by Canterus and Reifferscheid. In either case the word is complimentary to Plato as elsewhere (cf. 1. 8).

[104] See 1. 62, n. 301; Cicero, De *nat. deor.* 3. 14. 34: Etenim aut simplex est natura animantis, ut vel terrena sit vel ignis vel animalis vel umida, quod quale sit ne intellegi quidem potest; aut concreta ex pluribus naturis, . . . nullum igitur animal est sempiternum; *De off.* 1. 30; Gregory Thaumaturgus, *De an.* 5.

[105] Cf. Lactantius, *Epit.* 38; Theophilus, *Ad Autol.* 3. 6.

[106] Neither mortal nor immortal; they have a choice. Tatian (13) maintains that the soul is mortal, and this seems to be a proper conclusion from Minucius 34. 10: sicut de nihilo nasci licuit, ita de nihilo licere reparari? Cf. Justin Martyr, *Apol.* 1. 18, where proofs of the immortality of the soul are given; but in *Dial. c. Tryph.* 5 Justin admits that some souls are mortal. Note the sentence in the celebrated chapter of the *Ep. ad Diogn.* 6 in which the Christian relationship to the world is compared to the relationship of soul and body (trans. by J. A. Kleist, *ACW* 6 [1948] 140: "Immortal, the soul is lodged in a mortal tenement; so, too, Christians, though residing as strangers among corruptible things, look forward to the incorruptibility that awaits them in heaven." Regarding the view of the early Fathers on the human soul, see J. Bainvel, "Ame, III: doctrines des trois premiers siècles," *DTC* 1. 1 (1930) 977-1001 (Arnobius: 999).

[107] *Minas* of the MS; *misericordias* (Reifferscheid) and *venias* (Kistner and Wensky). Festugière (100 n. 1) approves *minas* and condemns *misericordias* as unnecessary. Doubtless, the difficulty which has perplexed some scholars is that *minas* ('threats') is thought too harsh to be used of Christ.

[108] On this point see *Corpus Hermeticum, Asclepius* 27-29, vol. 2, pp. 331-6 Nock-Festugière = W. Scott, *Hermetica* 1 (Oxford 1924) 364-370; A. J. Festugière, "Une source hermétique de Porphyre: l'Egyptien du De abstinentia II, 47," *Rev. des ét. gr.* 49 (1936) 586-95, esp. 590 ff.

[109] Here Bryce-Campbell maintain that Arnobius shows himself ignorant of Jewish teaching on this point—see I. Broydè, "Demonology," *The Jewish Encycl.* 4. 514-21, and L. Blau, "Gehenna," *ibid.*

5. 582-4, but according to Festugière (100 n. 3) the meaning is not that the demons did not exist before Christ but that their true nature was unknown.

[110] Festugière (100 n. 4): "sciens = ὁ ἐν γνώσει, ὁ γνωστικός, essentiellement 'celui qui connait Dieu,' etc."

[111] Festugière (100 f., plan of the thesis of the 'novi viri' 101-5) emphasizes the importance which Arnobius attaches to the view of the 'novi viri' the basis of which consists of 2. 15 and the first sentence of the next chapter.

[112] *Novis viris*: the Ms has *nobis*, emended to *novis* by Gelenius, but cf. Orelli's *bonis* in an ironic sense which is in keeping with the rest of the chapter. *Novis* is, of course, certainly right.

[113] The MS has *deum* which Zink, Reifferscheid, and Marchesi change to *idem*, but cf. Festugière 105 n. 2. Cf. also *Corpus Hermeticum* 18. 14.

[114] An allusion to the well-known proverb: *quot homines, tot sententiae* (first met with in Terence, *Phorm.* 454); cf. A. Otto, *Die Sprichwörter und sprichwörtlichen Redensarten der Römer* (Leipzig 1890) 166 f.

[115] Cf. Plato, *Phaedo* 81ce; Cumont 302 n. 28.

[116] Festugière (105 n. 3) points out the juridical vocabulary and remarks that the passage recalls a mode of condemnation often used in regard to Christian virgins.

[117] See n. 13. I cannot follow Wiman in eliminating this genuinely Arnobian word *typhus* for *institorium superciliumque* even if the translation of Irenaeus carries such an expression.

[118] Festugière (106 n. 1) points out that such triads (other examples in 2. 43, 2. 45, 2. 48, 2. 54, 2. 64, and almost *passim*) are a malady of the times found also in Minucius, Lactantius, and *Asclepius*.

[119] *Favore*, which Pascal emends to *furore* ('madness').

[120] *Differitas*, poetic for *differentia*, used by Lucretius 4. 636 for metrical reasons (see Bailey *ad loc.*). Cf. Munro's note on Lucretius 1. 653 which lists other such forms used only by Lucretius "or his constant imitator Arnobius" (Munro's 4th ed., Cambridge 1886). The word also occurs in 5. 36, 7. 23, 7. 27.

[121] *Animantium numero*, but the following sentence makes clear that animals are meant.

[122] Cf. Lucretius 2. 934-6, 5. 222-7, 5. 925-30; Rapisarda, *Arnob.* 71-3.

[123] *Conciliis*, a Lucretian echo. Cf. Lucretius 1. 183, 484, 517, 772,

1082; 2. 110, 120, 563, 564, 920, 935; 3. 805, and the Leonard-Smith note on 1. 183, which states that the noun is the Latin rendering of σύγκρισις (Epicurus 1. 40) and is technically used by Lucretius of the union of atoms. Here it has a more general sense. Cf. also Bailey's notes on 1. 183, 2. 120.

[124] The theory of metempsychosis or transmigration of souls. Cf. Micka 62.

[125] *Semotae* (Souter) in preference to *exutae* = 'doffed' (Reiffer-scheid); *seiunctae* = 'disjoined' (Klussmann, Marchesi).

[126] Cf. *Corpus Hermeticum, Asclepius* 37; Festugière 106 n. 4.

[127] Rapisarda (*Arnob.* 71, 247) thinks this passage is influenced by Lucretius 5. 228-34; Vergil, *Georg.* 1. 145.

[128] *Suspicio*, in Arnobius, frequently means not 'suspicion' but some idea conceived by a human being through conjecture and not proved by knowledge.

[129] *Suppara* were linen garments worn, usually, by women (but cf. Varro in Nonius 540. 15) and were shirts worn over undershirts. See E. Saglio, "Supparum," *DA* 4. 1564.

[130] Except for grammar which here occupies the place of arith-metic, we have the four liberal arts of the medieval *quadrivium* which, with the *trivium* (grammar, rhetoric, and logic) made up the seven liberal arts.

[131] Cf. the Gnostics attacked by Plotinus, *Enn.* 2. 9. 8; 18, and Festugière 107 n. 1.

[132] *Continentias* = περιοχή (cf. Scharnagl 31).

[133] This probably reflects rather accurately the state of affairs in the age of Diocletian.

[134] Plato, *Phaedo* 72e-74d; Tertullian, *De an.* 23. 6 (Waszink 302) and Arnobius 2. 28. Waszink marks the word *reminiscentia* as occurring only in Tertullian and Arnobius.

[135] In this and the following chapters Arnobius anticipates by many centuries the modern scientific 'controlled experiment.' Its defect lies in his inability to contrive a method for achieving *perfect* isolation of the subject from every outside contact. A somewhat similar experi-ment, of an inferior character, is attributed by Herodotus (2. 2, cf. also Tertullian, *Ad nat.* 1. 8, which Arnobius may have known) to Psammetichus, king of Egypt, who, wishing to know which nation was oldest, placed two new-born infants to be reared in isolation from other human contact, particularly that of speech, by a shep-herd. When the boys were examined at a later period, they stretched forth their hands and said βηκός. Upon inquiry it was found that

this was the Phrygian word for 'bread.' *Ergo*, the Phrygians were the oldest nation. But it is probable that the word spoken was merely the boys' way of pronouncing the only utterance which they had ever heard, that of the sheep. The whole purpose of Arnobius is to show that the mind of the child is a *tabula rasa*, affected only by its experiences, and that therefore the soul does not come from God.

[136] *Nothum* = spurious, bastard (King Darius II Nothus), artificial (cf. 5. 36 and Lucretius 5. 575: lunaque, sive notho fertur loca lumine lustrans; Catullus 34. 15 f.: tu potens Trivia et nothos [notho es] dicta lumine Luna). For references to other thinkers who noted that the moon had no light of its own, see Leonard-Smith's note on Lucretius 5. 575.

[137] Reading *modo* (Zink) for *non* of the MS. There must be at least one door. Kistner's *sane* has the right sense but is less satisfactory palaeographically. See *Vigiliae Christianae* 3 (1949) 41.

[138] Reifferscheid correctly suspected a lacuna at this point but it is clear that it ought to be placed before *natum* and that the lost word had the sense of 'newly.' I suggest that *modo* be inserted before *natum*. It is true that *mox* means 'presently,' 'directly,' but I think that should be taken with *deinceps*. See *Vig. Christ., loc. cit.*

[139] Cf. Plato, *Apol.* 25a.

[140] Plato, *Apol.* 21a.

[141] Hagendahl would change *alicuius* to *eloquium*, i. e. 'for speech' instead of 'to say anything.'

[142] Cf. Lucretius 5. 1416.

[143] The MS reads *a deō*. Vahlen's conjecture gives the right sense: *atque*, but is palaeographically impossible. Wiman is certainly right: *et ideo* (cf. 2. 15).

[144] Reading *portionem particulamque* (Meiser).

[145] Reading with Wiman *tam lautae* for *iam laetae*. *Laetus* is also sound for *lautus* in 7. 41.

[146] *Milvus*: perhaps we should read 'mule,' following Stewechius' conjecture of *mulus*.

[147] A cake made of meal mixed with must, the unfermented juice of the grape, was served at weddings. *Carduus* is here translated 'artichoke' because if a thistle is meant, it must be an edible variety. This word is sometimes masculine and sometimes neuter—it might well have been used in 1. 59.

[148] *Stragula*, used alone, is a pall or a horse-cloth; with *vestis*, as here, the word appears to mean 'bedspread,' etc.

[149] *Strophium*: a band of some kind, either a chaplet or breast band.

[150] *Fascia*: either a band for use as girdle or a religious ornament, or a bandage, or swaddling clothes.

[151] *Calautica*: a veil which covered both head and shoulders of a woman.

[152] *Mastruca*: a garment made from skins of wild sheep from Sardinia.

[153] Reading *seliquastrum*, first suggested by Meursius (cf. Festus 460 Lindsay) in place of *siliquastrum* = pepperwort, a kind of plant, which seems out of place in this list.

[154] An ancient book shaped like a modern book in distinction from a *liber* = roll of parchment or papyrus.

[155] *Formatura*: cf. Lucretius 4. 552.

[156] Deaf-mutes cannot articulate through being unable first to hear—a situation exactly paralleling that of the subject of this experiment.

[157] By questioning an uneducated slave, Socrates (*Meno* 81-84) brings out the principle of the Pythagorean theorem which proves, he says, that the slave has 'recollected' this knowledge from a previous existence. Cf. Cicero, *Tusc.* 1. 24. 57 f. Röhricht (*Seelenlehre* 26) and Gabarrou (*Oeuvre* 26) rightly maintain that Arnobius possessed direct knowledge of the *Meno*. For a similar confutation of Plato's doctrine of recollection, see Tertullian, *De an.* 24 and the excellent discussion in the notes in J. H. Waszink's edition (Amsterdam 1947) 303-7: "Still more important is the fact that he (= Tertullian) misinterprets the essence . . . (of the doctrine) . . . by making it appear that this 'renewed recollection' should lead to an immediate and complete knowledge of the 'Forms'; he does not in the least take into account the fact that . . . Plato understands a faded remembrance of a former existence, which only gradually may develop into real knowledge." Though Waszink does not say so, precisely the same criticism may be brought against the confutation by Arnobius.

[158] Reading, with Wiman, *rationis muneri admoto*, in place of Marchesi's *rationibus numeri admota* which is certainly not clear.

[159] The slave in the *Meno*.

[160] Both Reifferscheid and Marchesi read *sesqueoactavus aut sesquetertius † ultimus*, but Wiman is certainly right in brilliantly suggesting *sesquetertius ⟨s⟩altim*. The scribe who produced P found, according to Wiman's theory, *sesquetertiusaltim*, the letters *ss* having been reduced to one by haplography. He therefore took

the remainder, *altim*, in which an *a* might easily be mistaken for *u*, to be an abbreviation of *ultimus*.

[161] Cf. Vergil, *Aen.* 6. 471. Marpesian (= Parian) rock or granite chosen merely as a stock example. Cf. Rapisarda, *Arnob.* 249.

[162] Meursius marked this an interpolation but it is characteristic of Arnobius to repeat in this fashion.

[163] The MS here reads *post mentes geminas* ('after the twin intellects') and this reading is preserved by Orelli and defended in his commentary. Klussmann's suggestion of *daemonas et genios*, adopted by Reifferscheid, is rightly rejected by Marchesi who with little more reason conjectures *potentias geminas* on the basis of other references to *potentiae* in 2. 20, 7. 34. But the MS reading is really correct, as was long ago pointed out by W. Kroll, *De oraculis chaldaicis* (Breslau 1894) 28 n. 2, and reiterated in his review of Marchesi's edition (*Phil. Woch.* 55 [1935] 1084). It has been more recently approved, with convincing argument and independently, by two scholars, Festugière (108 n. 3) who prefers to translate as 'intellects' rather than as 'esprits,' and Wiman, citing Plotinus, *Enn.* 2. 3. 7; 2. 9; 5. 1. 2. But cf. Plato, *Phaedrus* 246e-247a, where Plato places Zeus first, followed in turn by an army of θεοί and δαίμονες, after which man occupies fourth place. See *Vigiliae Christianae* 3 (1949) 41 f.

[164] *Ex crateribus vivis*. A *cratera* is normally used in mixing wine and water. The reference is to Plato, *Timaeus* 41d, where the Creator mixes the vital essences of the soul. Cf. Arnobius 2. 22: ex fontibus vitae derivatum; J. H. Waszink on Tertullian, *De an.* 20. 6, p. 290.

[165] *Mundus minor*. M. Pohlenz, *Vom Zorne Gottes* (Göttingen 1909) 47 n. 2 (cf. Micka 62) makes the claim that so far as he knows, Arnobius is the only writer of the early Church who calls into doubt the description of man as a microcosm.

[166] Reading *similitudinemque mundi* with Reifferscheid.

[167] *Nesciat* implies ignorance of their very existence, but how about the nurse?

[168] The translation here follows Wiman: . . . *saxo? Qui nesciat homines et in mutis semper solitudinibus degat demoret⟨ur, is numquam ulli rei verum vocabulum⟩ iners valeat indere, quamvis,* etc. This involves only changing the MS *inaere* to *indere* and then supplying an object for the infinitive. It is distinctly better than Marchesi's *valeat inaniter* ('grows strong to no purpose'), and far

superior to any of the many other attempts to correct the unreadable MS.

[169] Arnobius appears to be ignorant of the fact that the homing of the dove is instinctive, rather than the result of training.

[170] Rigaltius' conjecture of *circulis* for *saeculis* has recently been approved by W. Kroll, *Phil. Woch.* 55 (1935) 1084, and it has considerable merit. If correct, the text should read " about the higher circles"; but Festugière (109 n. 2) would equate *saeculis* with αἰώνων.

[171] *Ex docta, ut dicitur, elementariam fieri*: A. Otto, *Die Sprich-wörter der Römer* (Leipzig 1890) 123 f., suggests, "aus einem Professor ein Abcschütze werden."

[172] Except for 2. 28, where the word is repeated, *repetentia* is found elsewhere only in Lucretius 3. 851. *Retinentia*, the suggestion of Avancius and Lachmann (editors of Lucretius), is rejected by all subsequent editors I have been able to consult. Bailey makes the point that the use of the word twice by Arnobius is good evidence that Lucretius used it. He means, of course, that it confirms the evidence of the manuscripts of Lucretius.

[173] Micka (49) maintains that the idea of the corporality of the soul (cf. 2. 30, 7. 5; K. B. Francke, *Die Psychologie und Erkenntnis-lehre des Arnobius* [Leipzig 1878] 16) was the only alternative to the pre-existence of the soul. Leckelt, *Über des Arnobius Schrift: Adversus Nationes* (Progr. Neisse 1884) 16, explains the error by saying that Arnobius may have confused the natural and the super-natural life of the soul. Cf. M. Baumgartner in F. Ueberweg's *Grundriss der Geschichte der Philosophie, II: Die mittlere oder die patristische und scholastische Zeit* (10th ed., Berlin 1915) 112 f.; O. Grillnberger, "Studien zur Philosophie der patristischen Zeit, II: Die Unsterblichkeitslehre des Arnobius," *Jahrb. f. Philos. u. spek. Theol.* 5 (1891) 1-14; LeNourry (*ML* 5. 484 f.).

[174] Cf. Lucretius 3. 161-7, 175 f.

[175] The MS reading *suaderi* is suspect. Ursinus changed to *videri*; Oehler and Reifferscheid to *sua de vi*, which, as Marchesi says, is possibly right, but *sua de re*, suggested by Wiman, is even better and has been adopted.

[176] The MS reads *in corporibus*, changed by the editors to *sine corporibus*. Kroll and Festugière reject this, the latter saying (109 n. 4) that it destroys the argument. But does it?

[177] The argument is Platonic. Arnobius means, I think, that the

number is a Platonic 'idea' incarnated in a thousand bodies, yet loses nothing of its identity, as indeed it does not.

[178] *Pati*: the literal meaning of this word, here adopted because there is no perfect English equivalent, means more nearly 'to experience,' with no connotation of good or evil, though sometimes the latter sense is present and in this example and others in the next few chapters the word bears something of the idea of 'subject to dissolution and death through union with the body.' Cf. the excellent note by R. B. Tollinton, *Clement of Alexandria* 2 (London 1914) 15 f., on the meaning of the Greek cognate πάθος which likewise is not perfectly translatable into English.

[179] There is a play between *passivum* in the preceding sentence and *passioni* here. Both have the same sense, i. e., anything which is passive is subject to corruption.

[180] Cf. Lucretius 1. 1112: ianua Leti; 2. 960: Leti iam limine; 3. 67: Leti portas; 5. 373: Leti . . . ianua; 6. 762: Ianua . . . Orci. Munro (note to 1. 1112, vol. 2, p. 117 of his 4th ed. [Cambridge 1886]) says the same figure was adopted by Vergil, Ovid, Statius, and Valerius Flaccus. "In this the poets have idealized the solid stone doors of their tombs." Cf. also Bailey, *ad loc.*

[181] Literally, 'they have life for use.'

[182] A clear echo of Lucretius 3. 971: vitaque mancipio nulli datur, omnibus usu. See the very illuminating note in the Leonard-Smith edition *ad loc.* on the difference between *usus* and *mancipium*; also Bailey *ad loc.*

[183] At this point the MS reads *abeamus ne videamus* ('depart lest we see') which is manifestly impossible. The words *ne videamus* have been omitted in the translation, following Castiglioni's unpublished suggestion to Marchesi who brackets them as spurious. Assuming that they are a corruption of a genuine reading, other scholars have endeavored to emend: 'lest we be mocked' (Meursius and Reifferscheid); 'lest we seem' (Sabaeus and Hildebrand); 'let us hear' (Gelenius, combining the word with what follows); 'we are eager to hear' (Ursinus); 'we are eager to know' (Salmasius); 'let us inquire' (Kistner). Klussmann's suggestion (*videamus ne audiamus*) seems to me impossible and I have no confidence that any other is right.

[184] *Ante hominem*: here and at the end of the sentence *homo* means 'body' and not 'man,' a frequent use in Arnobius. Cf. 1. 55: *animis hominibusque*; 1. 65: *hominem suum* (cf. 2. 57); 2. 62: *post hominis functionem.* See Reifferscheid's index (324 f.).

[185] *Magis est*: cf. E. Löfstedt, " Arnobiana. Textkritische und sprachliche Studien zu Arnobius," *Lunds Univ. Årsskr.* n. f. avd. 1, bd. 12, no. 5 (Lund 1917) 70; T. Stangl, " Bobiensia," *Rhein. Mus.* 65 (1910) 93.

[186] Cf. Plotinus, *Enn.* 2. 9.

[187] Cf. 2. 16, 2. 26, and n. 173.

[188] *Momen*, also used in 2. 35, 2. 50, 6. 20 (Marchesi: *momine*; Reifferscheid: *nomine*), and Lucretius 3. 144, 188 f.; Paulus-Festus 123 Lindsay. Leonard-Smith (n. to Lucretius 3. 144) and Bailey (n. to 3. 189) think that the image may come from the balance.

[189] *Proletarii*: men whose wealth was assessed at 1500 *asses librales* (A. Gellius 16. 10. 10) were tax-exempt and, except in critical situations, not subject to military service. Their designation suggests that their only contribution to society was children, *proles* (cf. the Marxian use of the term 'proletariat'). This class was the second-lowest (cf. n. 191). See also the masterly note on the word in A. J. Toynbee, *A Study of History* 1 (2nd ed., London 1935) 41. It is quite impossible to reproduce in English translation the irony-laden language borrowed in this section from the Roman fiscal terminology.

[190] *Classicus* was originally an adjective applicable to any class of Roman citizens in the census but came to be applied only to the first or highest class of taxpayers (cf. A. Gellius 6. 13) and sometimes metaphorically to literary excellence (Gell. 19. 8. 15)—hence our word 'classic.' Cf. B. Kübler, *RE* 3 (1889) 2628 f.

[191] *Capite . . . censeatur*: 'counted by the head,' since they possessed even less than the *proletarii*. Their rating was 375 *asses librales* (A. Gellius 16. 10. 11-4). Marius was the first Roman general to enroll the *capite censi* in the army.

[192] The Roman household god of the hearth. A poor man had a poor *lar*.

[193] A reference to the patrician-plebeian controversy in early Roman history. Cf. 2. 48: *patricii generis*.

[194] Reading *veros* with Löfstedt and Wiman.

[195] Klussmann, followed by both Reifferscheid and Marchesi, interpolated ⟨*non*⟩ at this point, to which both Kroll and Wiman strongly and rightly object. The latter, with Axelson, changes *censetis* to *cessatis* and reads *accidere* with a long *i*; but see his later doubts in *Eranos* 45 (1947) 136.

[196] If the soul is immortal, why lead a virtuous life to protect it from punishment by death? The argument overlooks the possibility of painful punishment in an afterlife.

[197] Festugière (111 n. 1) equates this (*inpotens*) with Plato's ἀκρατής (*Laws* 734b, 886a).

[198] Arnobius is here thinking of the Epicurean theology and ethics, which he mentions in the following chapter. Assuming that the soul is immortal and the gods live apart and care little for men, why should not men indulge their appetites?

[199] An elliptical question—the last three words must be supplied. Arnobius' answer to this objection seems very weak—the punishments of the lower world were reputed to be very painful, either physically or mentally, and it was a cardinal point of the Epicurean ethics to avoid pain and disturbance (ἀταραξία).

[200] Here *torrentium* has both its original and derived senses: the water is hot and in addition a torrent.

[201] The MS here reads *non* (out of normal position, however), and it has rightly been deleted from the text.

[202] Festugière (111 n. 3) says this is philosophical suffering: "état de ce qui pâtit sous l'action d'une cause extérieure."

[203] Cf. Lucretius 3. 417-829 where the seventeen proofs that the soul is mortal are discussed. The passage in Diogenes Laertius 10. 63-8= p. 41, Bailey's edition of the fragments of Epicurus, seems to be the one referred to.

[204] Cf. Plato, *Phaedo* 64c-65c, where the soul is represented as thinking best when it is in least contact with the body.

[205] Soul and body perish together.

[206] In addition to the passage of Lucretius cited in n. 203, cf. Lactantius, *Div. inst.* 7. 12.

[207] Cf. Plotinus, *Enn.* 2. 9. 15, who reproaches the Gnostics for always saying: βλέπε πρὸς θεόν without ever practicing virtue or curbing their passions.

[208] The wicked man in the preceding chapter.

[209] Bryce-Campbell pretend to see in this reference an allusion to the Stoic doctrine that the soul must be material because, unless soul and body were of the same substance, there could be no common feeling (see Cleanthes in Nemesianus, *De nat. hom.* 2, p. 33) or to another Stoic doctrine that only the souls of the wise remained after death, and these only to the final conflagration (for this view Bryce-Campbell cite Stobaeus, *Ecl. phys.* 1. 101 Meineke) which awaits the world and ends the Stoic great year. Other Stoics maintained that the souls of the wise became demons and demi-gods (Diog. Laert. 7. 151 and 157). But there is no need to go so far afield to find examples. All that is needed is a reference to Plato's belief that

the soul is immortal as discussed in the *Phaedo* confronted with the opposite view that it is mortal, as discussed in the third book of Lucretius already cited.

[210] Here and in the next sentence ' they ' = the souls.

[211] This looks suspiciously like high praise for Epicurus, since, as we have seen, the proof that the soul is mortal is derived from him indirectly through Lucretius, but the word *summus* is used just below of God and it may be that Arnobius thinks the normal mortality of the soul is an essentially Christian doctrine. Cf. 1. 38 where there is a similar confusion of Christ with Epicurus.

[212] Perhaps, as Orelli thought, a reference to John 17. 3: Haec est autem vita aeterna, ut congoscant te solum Deum verum et quem misisti Iesum Christum. Festugière (112 n. 2) points out that immortality, conditioned by the γνῶσις θεοῦ, is exactly what hermetism teaches. Cf. *Corpus Hermeticum* 2. 24-26; *Harvard Theol. Rev.* 31 (1938) 1 n. 4.

[213] LeNourry and Bryce-Campbell following him rightly reject Heraldus' attempt to see in these straightforward words a veiled allusion to the sacraments of baptism and the Eucharist.

[214] Amulets. See L. Deubner, " Greek Amulets," *Hastings Encycl.* 3 (1913) 433-9; R. Wünsch, " Roman Amulets," *ibid.* 461-5.

[215] The Psylli were an African people living southwest of the Syrtis Major, celebrated as snake charmers. See E. B. James, " Psylli," *DG* 2 (1870) 676 f. The Marsi, a people of Latium, were famous for this accomplishment as well as for wizardry. Cf. Horace, *Epod.* 17. 29; Pliny, *Nat. hist.* 7. 2; 21. 13; 25. 2; 28. 3; Aelian, *De nat. animal.* 1. 57; Lucilius, fr. 605 f. in E. H. Warmington, *Remains of Early Latin* 3 (London—Cambridge, Mass. 1938) 190 f. See also H. Philipp, " Marsi," *RE* 14. 2 (1930) 1977-9.

[216] According to Plotinus, *Enn.* 2. 9, the Gnostics believed that the soul upon creation, that is, upon coming into contact with matter, lost its wings.

[217] Cf. 2. 62: *ab legibus mortalitatis*; Lucretius 3. 687: *Leti lege*.

[218] Chorus, a dancing group. Cf. Dionysius Hal., *De comp. verb.* 24. 5 where the Greek word χορός is used in a derogatory sense of the Epicureans.

[219] Here the MS has: *atque ad in finem adducere*. Most editors refuse to believe that Arnobius could use two prepositions of practically the same sense before a single noun (with asyndeton) but the reading, though bizarre, is correct. Cf. M. Leumann-J. B. Hofmann's edition of Stolz-Schmalz, *Lateinische Grammatik* (Munich

1928) 541, who call the double preposition *adin* " erst mittelalterlich."
See *Vigiliae Christianae* 3 (1949) 42 f.

[220] The usual word for miracles (*virtutibus*). Cf. Book One,
n. 210.

[221] Cf. Horace, *Carm.* 1. 2. 37: nil mortalibus ardui est.

[222] A. S. Ferguson in W. Scott, *Hermetica* 4 (Oxford 1936) 480
n. 7, maintains that this distinction " is known to have been made by
Labeo," but Festugière (113 n. 1) objects that the passage cited (cf.
Augustine, *De civ. Dei* 9. 19) says rather that Labeo named ' good
demons ' those whom others call ' angels.' Festugière further objects
that the notion of angels as good demons or as superior demons could
have come to Arnobius from other sources (cf. F. Cumont, " Les
anges du paganisme," *Rev. de l'hist. des Rel.* 36 [1915] 159-82; F.
Andres, " Angelos," *RE* Suppl. 3 [1918] 101-4) and that the distinction of gods, angels, demons, appears in a fragment of the *De regr. an.*
of Porphyry (Augustine, *De civ. Dei* 10. 9).

[223] Cf. Augustine, *De civ. Dei* 8. 23: ille autem Aegyptius
(= Hermes Trismegistus) alios deos esse dicit a summo Deo factos,
alios ab hominibus; Lactantius, *Div. inst.* 1. 6; Rapisarda, *Arnob.* 139.

[224] The position of *solum* is as translated but perhaps it modifies
immortalem also.

[225] The position of *mortalium* (*hi omnes quos opinatio credidit
deos esse mortalium*) seems to preclude the possibility of taking it,
as do Bryce-Campbell, with *opinatio*, but the word seems redundant
if it is to be taken with *deos*.

[226] Arnobius has of course been much criticized for this statement.
See Introd. pp. 30-3.

[227] On this chapter, cf. Lactantius, *Div. inst.* 2. 14. 3 f. (*CSEL*
19. 162 Brandt-Laubmann): Sic eos diabolus ex angelis dei suos
fecit satellites ac ministros. Qui autem sunt ex his procreati quia
neque angeli neque homines fuerunt, sed mediam quandam naturam
gerentes, non sunt ad inferos recepti sicut in caelum parentes eorum.
Cf. Pohlenz 49 n. 1; Micka 152 n. 15.

[228] Plato is mentioned by name, or by the specific citation of one
of his works, fifteen times in Arnobius. Usually this is without
special praise: cf. 1. 5, 2. 7, 2. 9, 2. 11, 2. 13 (*bis*), 2. 24, 2. 34, 2. 52,
2. 64, and 4. 16, but in addition to the present instance Plato is given
high praise in 1. 8 and 2. 52.

[229] Röhricht at first (*De Clem.* 40) expressed doubt as to whether
this passage was borrowed from Plato directly or from Cicero's
version of the *Timaeus*, but in *Seelenlehre* (22 f.) he concludes

that there is evidence of the direct use of Plato. The passages are Plato's *Timaeus* 41 and Cicero's *Timaeus* 11 which are also compared with this chapter by Gabarrou (*Oeuvre* 23-27) who reaches the same conclusion as Röhricht in his *Seelenlehre*.

[230] Plato (*Timaeus* 41) represents the Creator as telling the gods whom he has created that "that which is bound may be dissolved, but only an evil being would dissolve that which is harmonious and happy. And although you are not immortal you shall not die, for I will hold you together" (Jowett). Cf. Cicero, *De nat. deor.* 1. 8. 8.

[231] The MS *salutari iussione donari*, here translated, has been much emended. Reifferscheid thought a lacuna should be indicated before *donari* in which something like *dono immortalitatis* is missing. Gelenius and Lorenz prefer *missione*; Salmasius and Bastgen, *vinctione*; Meiser, *mansione*; Hildebrand, *nexione*; while Brakman would insert *perpetuitatis* before *salutari*. "Alii alia," says Marchesi, retaining the MS reading, perhaps on the basis of Pascal's opinion in *Riv. fil. istr. cl.* 32 (1904) 3.

[232] *Filias*: the feminine is doubtless used because *anima* is feminine. See other similar locutions in nn. 40, 247, 375. Rapisarda (*Arnob.* 43. 53) says Arnobius denies that God is the Creator of the souls because he believes in *filiation*, rather than *creation*.

[233] P has *sententia* but Ursinus, Reifferscheid, and Marchesi adopt *essentia*.

[234] Micka (48 f.) points out the inconsistency between this statement, categorical though vague, and supported by the references to the secondary beings (2. 53), and the emphatic profession of ignorance earlier in 2. 47. On the Second Creator God, see W. Bousset, rev. of J. Kroll, *Die Lehren des Hermes Trismegistos*, *Gött. Gel. Anz.* 176 (1914) 711-6.

[235] E. S. Bouchier, *Life and Letters in Roman Africa* (Oxford 1913) 102, calls attention to the Gnostic errors in this chapter, as does Cruttwell (2. 639) who also states that Arnobius is both unorthodox and historically inaccurate. The same comment is made by Festugière (114 n. 1) who also points out that the vocabulary is taken from the language of the Imperial Court at the end of the third century. Cf. *CAH* 12 (1939) 361-3 (*ordo salutationis*).

[236] *Potestatis principalis*. As Gabarrou (*Oeuvre* 37) remarks, this passage probably owes something to the discussion, in Lucretius 5. 158-234, of the indifference of the gods to human affairs.

[237] *Virtute*: here the word appears to have the more usual sense

in place of that usually found in Arnobius (cf. Book One, n. 210).
Perhaps " the highest perfection " is the meaning here.

[238] *Pituitas* which gives us 'pituitary.' There is an echo here of
the ancient physiological theory of four (the first two are mentioned
by Arnobius) humors or fluids determining a person's health and
temperament: phlegm, blood, yellow bile, and black bile.

[239] Cf. Lucretius 4. 1026; 5. 174-6; Rapisarda, *Arnob.* 71 f.

[240] Lucretius 5. 165-9; Lactantius, *Div. inst.* 7. 5. 6.

[241] Oehler is right in regarding this sentence as a statement by the
opponent, whereas the editors wrongly mark it a question.

[242] So Reifferscheid and Marchesi (*picarios*) but Sabaeus suggested
'drivers of two-horse teams' and K. E. Georges, *Philologus* 33
(1874) 334, 'dealers in paints.'

[243] Cf. Plautus, *Aul.* 508: stat fullo, phrygio, aurufex, lanarius.

[244] Bastgen would makes this 'artisans.'

[245] On the thought of this chapter, cf. 4. 21.

[246] *Rex mundi*: so Marchesi; but Reifferscheid's reading, suggested
by Vahlen, is *rerum dominus* ('Lord of things ').

[247] *Deae*: cf. n. 232.

[248] Reading *temporariae*, with Kroll, *Phil. Woch.* 55 (1935) 1084,
in place of *terrariae* (Reifferscheid and Marchesi).

[249] Cf. Lucretius 5. 229 f.:

> Nec crepitacillis opus est, nec cuiquam adhibendast
> Almae nutricis blanda atque infracta loquela.

[250] H. Hagendahl, " En Ovidiusreminiscens hos Arnobius," *Eranos*
35 (1937) 36-40, sees in the repeated passages beginning with these
words reminiscences of Ovid, *Met.* 1. 131; 1. 138-40.

[251] *In hominibus.*

[252] Orelli thinks Arnobius was imitating Sallust, *De con. Cat.* 5:
simulator ac dissimulator.

[253] Cf. Sallust, *Cat.* 10. 5: aliud clausum in pectore, aliud in
lingua promptum habere (similarly, Augustine, *Enchir.* 6. 18).

[254] Cf. Cicero's famous work, *De finibus bonorum et malorum.*

[255] Essentially, if not strictly, true—some species of animals do
build houses, e. g. the beaver, the bee, etc., and cf. what Arnobius
himself says, somewhat inconsistently, in 2. 17.

[256] Here Arnobius seems to have a clear consciousness of the
travails of the farmers, as in 1. 14 he appeared to appreciate the
point of view of the consumer.

[257] Reading *insomniam* (Hildebrand and Marchesi) but *in somnia*
of the MS may be right.

[258] Cf. Horace's greedy capitalist: *Carm.* 2. 18. 23 ff.; also Julianus Pomerius, *De vita contempl.* 1. 13. 2. See C. Lécrivain, " Latifundia," *DA* 3. 956-71.

[259] This clause appears in the MS at a point three clauses earlier but it was restored to its proper place here by Heraldus.

[260] *Fuligine.*

[261] *Vibrare* = ' to curl '; Cf. Vergil, *Aen.* 12. 100: *crines vibratos*; Pliny, *Nat. hist.* 2. 78. 80.

[262] Cf. Firmicus Maternus, *Math.* 8. 7; Clem. Alex., *De paed.* 3. 3; Tertullian, *De app. fem.* 2. 5-8.

[263] Cf. Lactantius, *Div. inst.* 5. 9. 16: *testamenta supponant.*

[264] This means to win away the loyalties of a slave as well as of a wife.

[265] Orelli says that *botuli* = German *Blutwürste*; cf. Tertullian mentioning (*Apol.* 9. 14) *botulos cruore distentos.*

[266] *Castellamenta.* Cf. *TLL* 3. 524: *cuppedii carnei ut videtur genus fortasse castelli specie factum* (cites only Arnobius 2. 42); Du Cange 2. 208 derives the word from *catillare* and concludes: " *Proprie vero ita vocasse videntur farcimina aut botulos minutis carnibus inculcatos, quod avide a Cartillonibus expererentur.* "

[267] Cf. Cicero *In Pisonem* 10. 22: *cum illum suum saltatorium versaret orbem.*

[268] The ancient *sambuca* was a triangular stringed instrument. The notes were shrill and unpleasant, the players reputed to be of bad character.

[269] The translation follows Marchesi's emendation of a corrupt passage chiefly because no other suggestions seem better.

[270] The MS reads *habitare atque habitare*. The text follows Löfstedt's suggestion of *abire*, accepted by *Marchesi*, in place of the first *habitare*. Other suggestions: *visitare* (Meiser); *aditare* (Oehler); *abitare* (Brakman).

[271] Cf. Lucretius 2. 177-81; 5. 195-9.

[272] Reading Wiman's ⟨*errorum*⟩ in place of Marchesi's ⟨*malorum*⟩. Cf. *evagandi* immediately below.

[273] Reading *pri⟨m⟩us*, with Wiman, instead of *prius* which Marchesi allows to stand at the end of the sentence. *Prius* was deleted by W. Kroll; Axelson prefers *peius*.

[274] Yet cf. 1. 3, where God is said to be the highest procreator. Cf. Micka 46 f. LeNourry (*ML* 5. 483) says, however, that Arnobius did not mean God had no part in the creation of the souls but was carried away by zeal at this point. Micka explains by recurrence

to the idea that the 'aloofness' of God was fundamental to Arnobius' thinking. There is, of course, the possibility that the MS of the *Adversus nationes* never underwent a thorough final revision to eliminate inconsistencies of this kind.

[275] On the figure, cf. Tertullian, *De an.* 53. 5 and the literature cited by Waszink (545).

[276] Perhaps an allusion to cannibalism?

[277] *Columen*: a word used abundantly with names of people—see *TLL* 3. 1736-7.

[278] Cf. Micka 52; U. Moricca, *Storia della letteratura latina cristiana* 1 (Turin 1923) 612, 615; R. Pichon, *Lactance, étude sur le mouvement philosophique et religieux sous le règne de Constantin* (Paris 1901) 52 f.

[279] A corollary of the excellence of God.

[280] A. C. McGiffert, *A History of Christian Thought*, 2 (New York 1933) 39 f., compares this view with a similar position taken by Celsus in the second century.

[281] Note the dualism—cf. Micka 58, 61; P. Monceaux, *Histoire littéraire de l'Afrique chrétienne*, 3 (Paris 1905) 270. Cf. also Minucius 26. 11, who attributes a similar view to Osthanes.

[282] Inconsistent, as Micka (48 f.) says, with 2. 46 and 2. 53. On this chapter Rapisarda (*Arnob.* 139) would cite Augustine, *De civ. Dei* 12. 25 (and 11. 15 which appears to be a misprint).

[283] *In suae [et] integritatis perfectione finitum.* Kistner would add *naturae* after *suae* and keep *et.*

[284] *Ex mediocribus familiis* where the adjective not only suggests that their families are not highborn but also even insignificant ('mediocre'). There is a suggestion also of the 'neutral character' of the souls mentioned in previous chapters.

[285] *Generositas principalis.*

[286] *Caput rerum*, a term used by Ovid (*Met.* 15. 736) to denote Rome.

[287] *Viri*, not *homines*. This passage is doubtless an answer to the view mentioned by Cicero (*De nat. deor.* 3. 5. 12) that the souls (*animos*) of very famous men are divine and immortal.

[288] Reading *et admiratione ⟨quarum non nisi laboriosa⟩ congregatione conquiritur*, with Wiman, in place of *adcuratiore congregatione* (Reifferscheid and Marchesi).

[289] The word *non* here is clearly misplaced in the MS, hence it is inserted before *modo* and bracketed before *parvi.*

[290] *Philosophi* = 'lovers of wisdom.'

[291] The MS reads *animorum*, corrected by Meursius to *animarum* to conform to Arnobius' general usage, but doubtless our author may be permitted some inconsistency.

[292] The MS reads *inperfectum inprobabilem* and the first word is marked as a gloss. Some editors delete *inprobabilem* (e. g. Sabaeus) while others change to *probabilem* (Salmasius) but the sense is not 'needing no correction' but as given in the translation.

[293] Micka (152 n. 15) and Brandt (*CSEL* 19. 1. 181) profess to see resemblance between this chapter and Lactantius, *Div. inst.* 3. 2. 9: Non ergo sapientiae student qui philosophantur, sed ipsi studere se putant, quia illut quo quaerunt ubi aut quale sit nesciunt. Sive igitur sapientiae student sive non student, sapientes non sunt.

[294] Cf. Cicero's statement (*De nat. deor.* 1. 1. 1) that the Academics prudenter . . . a rebus incertis adsensionem cohibuisse.

[295] Cf. A. J. Festugière, " Εἰς ἄνθρωπον ὑποφέρεσθαι," *Rev. de sc. phil. et théol.* 20 (1931) 476-82, a study of the passage in Clement of Alexandria, *Protr.* 9. 82. 2: ὑμεῖς δὲ εἰς θάνατον (Festugière restores ἄνθρωπον ὑποφέρεσθε). Cf. likewise Festugière, "Tomber dans l'homme," *ibid.* 26 (1937) 41 f.

[296] An exceedingly dubious passage: *et ⟨in⟩ nihil expositum iaculatio mentis illata?* (Marchesi); *et † nihil ex positu iaculatio mentis in latentia?* (Reifferscheid); *et nihil ⟨habens in luce⟩ positum iaculatio mentis intuta* (Meiser); *nihil exposta* (Hidén).

[297] Cf. Plato, *Timaeus* 41 f. It is the Creator who does the mixing but since the passage is contained in a speech by Timaeus, Arnobius attributes the act to the one who tells the story. Gabarrou (*Oeuvre* 23-37) compares this passage with Plato's *Timaeus* 41 and Cicero's *Timaeus* 12, and comes to the conclusion that Arnobius knew both Plato and Cicero firsthand. The same conclusion was reached earlier by Röhricht (*Seelenlehre* 23).

[298] This is the reading of Thörnell (*Patristica* 2): *vivere. Quid enim, ⟨si⟩,* approved by Wiman, in place of Marchesi: *vivere, qui⟨a ea⟩dem.*

[299] Cf. 2. 9 f., and Festugière 118 n. 2.

[300] Plato, *Timaeus* 41.

[301] Micka (51) believes that Arnobius realized the difficulty caused by the conflict of his view that the soul is mortal and the Christian belief in a life after death and to get out of the dilemma, invented the concept of the neutral character.

[302] *Ab rebus non principalibus*: cf. Tertullian, *De an.* 23.

[303] In this sentence 'you' (*vos*) is plural while the vocatives (*ineptissime, fatue*) are singular. 'You' therefore equals the pagan party of which a single member is being addressed. Bryce-Campbell translate these vocatives as adverbs: "What [is that] to you? [In so believing, we act] most absurdly, sillily." For another example of the use of the singular and plural second person in a single sentence, cf. 4. 31. C. Weyman, "Textkritische Bemerkungen zu Arnobius adversus nationes," *Festschrift S. Merkle* (Düsseldorf 1922) 290, wishes to regard *ineptissime* as an adverb and *fatue* as a vocative, and cites examples in 2. 14 and 2. 52.

[304] *Ab Orci faucibus*: cf. Vergil, *Aen.* 6. 273; Apuleius, Met. 7. 7.

[305] With this digression on the problem of evil (2. 54-60) compare an earlier one (1. 7-12). Geffcken (287) says that in the present chapter Arnobius uses the Stoic argument, and Rapisarda (*Arnob.* 139) sees parallels with Augustine, *De civ. Dei* 20. 1.

[306] Here the MS reads *nesciente, ignaro ac nescio*. Marchesi bracketed *nesciente* on the advice of Castiglioni but it is almost certain that Arnobius wrote three words. Cf. *quaerere pervestigare rimari* (2. 16); *turpitudinum criminum malitiarum* (2. 43); *ut exercerent, ut gererent, ut percelebrarent* (2. 43); *sator et conditor, procreator* (2. 45); *agi fieri statui* (2. 48); *aspernaris, contemnis et despicis* (2. 64). Since *nesciente . . . nescio* is harsh, I am inclined to think that either Orelli or Ursinus (with Reifferscheid) is right in changing, respectively, to *insciente* or *inscio*. Cf. Festugière 106 n. 1.

[307] Röhricht (*Seelenlehre* 7) thinks 2. 55-61 clearly stems from Lucretius 2. 398-443, 631 ff.; 5. 574 f.

[308] P has been thought to read *nominaliter*, but Löfstedt emphatically maintains that the reading is not *nominaliter* but *noninaliter*. For this reason Marchesi accepts *non inaniter*, the reading in the *Codex Bruxellensis*, and so does Weyman (390) independently of Marchesi, citing an impressive list of parallels. W. A. Baehrens, *Berl. phil. Woch.* 37 (1917) 1293 suggests *unanimiter*.

[309] Reading *ducetis* with the MS and Marchesi, in place of *ducentes* (Sabaeus, favored also by Wiman, while *ducentis* is preferred by Axelson).

[310] The MS reads *quinimmo potius magis*. Reifferscheid attempted to correct *potius* by suggesting *optimum* but this is bad palaeographically. The solution to the problem is furnished by Wiman who transposes *potius* to an earlier position and reads *tutius* which he derives from a sentence in 4. 16: *nonne potius ibit domum seseque*

abstinens ab negotiis talibus tutius esse arbitrabitur nihil horum contingere, etc.

[311] Bryce-Campbell here mistranslate *Quid ergo nos? unde?* as "What, then, do we say? whence?" and the German translators (von Besnard and Alleker) similarly go astray. The questions under discussion are (1) *Quid sumus?* (2) *unde sumus?*

[312] The conclusion is reached (cf. Micka 55 f.) as the result of the aloofness of God and its corollary, the impassibility of God.

[313] Bryce-Campbell profess to find these sentences exceedingly obscure but the meaning seems to be that the question of the origin of the soul has no pertinence in regard to the much more important question, its salvation.

[314] This evidently refers to the principle of the conservation of matter as discussed by Lucretius 1. 146-58; 2. 294-307 (where see Bailey's notes *ad loc.*) and the ancient sources cited by Orelli.

[315] Doubtless the allusion is to Plato's *Timaeus* 41. Cf. 2. 52.

[316] The Stoics. Cf. Diog. Laert. 7. 134 and 141; Seneca, *Consol. ad Polyb.* 2.

[317] Acceptance of *subripiant* (corrector of the MS and Marchesi) involves the view that the philosophers pilfer each other's arguments not to use them but to prevent their use by their opponents. How this could be done is not clear. I have therefore accepted Ursinus' suggestion of *subruant* which seems better than Sabaeus' *subrumpant.*

[318] Cf. Plato, *Timaeus* 32; Cicero, *De nat. deor.* 1. 8. 19: earth, air, fire, water. See also Bailey's edition of Lucretius, vol. 2, p. 1032.

[319] This is very likely an echo of Lucretius 1. 712 f.:

> Adde etiam qui conduplicant primordia rerum
> Aera iugentes igni terramque liquori.

This is overlooked by Bryce-Campbell who attribute to Orelli more than he says which is that the twin elements are earth and water. They allude to Diog. Laert. 7. 134, where the elements (ἀρχάς) of the world are given as two—the active and passive, but in searching for the source of allusions in Arnobius, the best rule is to look first in Lucretius.

[320] *Ex singulis:* the reference seems to be to the Eleatic monists, especially Xenophanes (*ca.* 580) and Parmenides (*ca.* 540). Plato admired the latter greatly and named one of his dialogues after him.

[321] *Individua corpora:* the founder of Atomism was Leucippus (Miletus?—*ca.* 475). The greatest exponent was Democritus of Abdera (*ca.* 460-370), who was also a mathematician, physician, and globe-trotter.

322 The atheists, see 1.31.

323 E. g., Protagoras. See 1.31, n. 133.

324 The Epicureans.

325 *Terrenas administrare rationes.* Cf. Cicero, *De nat. deor.* 1.1, 12, 19, 23, etc.

326 Plato will serve as an example.

327 The Epicureans again.

328 *Aliquid eis ad vitam dari.* This is the Stoic view. Cf. Cicero, *Tusc.* 1.31: Stoici . . . diu mansuros aiunt; semper negant.

329 This chapter shows almost certainly that Arnobius was ignorant of the opening chapters of Genesis.

330 *Virtutis*, a clear example of the use of this word in the sense of power. Cf. Book One, n. 210.

331 A Lucretian echo; cf. 1.31, and Lucretius 1.472.

332 Perhaps a reminiscence of Lucretius 2.934: huic satis illud erit planum facere atque probare. On the thought, cf. F. A. Norwood, "Attitude of the Ante-Nicene Fathers toward Greek Artistic Achievement," *Jour. of the Hist. of Ideas* 8 (1947) 436.

333 *Primus dies* may possibly refer to the initial day rather than the beginning of every day.

334 A clear allusion to Epicurean physics in which the stars were regarded as being actually the same size as they appear to be. See the very illuminating note by J. S. Reid in J. Masson, *Lucretius, Epicurean and Poet*, Suppl. Vol. (London 1909) 189, with reference to Masson's own pp. 158 f.

335 This passage has been much subjected to the tender mercies of emendation (see Marchesi's apparatus). The best suggestion seems to me Wiman's which I have translated: [*quod*] *imbresve ⟨quod nivem in plumeas subaperiat crustulas⟩.*

336 Arnobius, of course, had no idea of the variety of seasons at different points on the globe. It should be pointed out that he had a lively interest in scientific matters, despite the agnosticism which he here expresses concerning natural phenomena. We should not forget that while modern science has many "answers" for these problems which he presents, the ultimate answer has no more been achieved in our time than in his.

337 *Integritas.*

338 Klussmann, followed by Reifferscheid and Marchesi, added these words to balance *vel frigidae*, but it is by no means certain that Arnobius wrote them.

339 *Viscera* = 'flesh' in Servius, *Aen.* 1.211: viscera non tantum

intestina dicimus, sed quicquid sub corio est, ut in Albano Latinis visceratio dabatur, id est caro; 6. 263: viscera sunt quicquid inter ossa et cutem est.

[340] Orelli thinks the *alites* were birds used in augury, the *volucres* other birds, but this is unnecessary.

[341] *Avena* means oats in general but must here be a wild variety. Cf. Vergil, *Georg.* 1. 153.

[342] Reading *mel oleum vinum* with Wiman which is decidedly better than Marchesi's *melo cuminum* (P has *meloneum vinum*), since cumin is hardly an *ordinary* article of food (cf. *mediis in generibus*, immediately below). The passage may perhaps be an imitation of Vergil, *Georg.* 1. 152-4 (Rapisarda, Arnob. 249).

[343] These words were first bracketed by Heraldus. They are clearly a gloss and one which contributes nothing. On the thought, cf. Lucretius 3. 267: est odor et quidam calor et sapor, where Bailey reads *color* instead of *calor*—see Arnobius, a little below.

[344] ⟨*Alicuius*⟩ (Marchesi) is palaeographically better than ⟨*vel*⟩ (all other editors since Gelenius).

[345] Marchesi (*Quest.* 1022) says that this view of a lack of interest in such investigations is a contradiction and retraction of what has already been said in 1. 38.

[346] This statement (cf. also 1. 42) contradicts the claim of Gabarrou (*Oeuvre* 61) that Arnobius nowhere states positively the divinity of Christ. Cf. Micka 52 f.

[347] *Auras nescio quas eius sibi contemplationis adfingere*: on this use of *auras*, cf. Lactantius, *Div. inst.* 2. 17. 11. The force of *sibi* escapes me, except it be used inadvertently for *nobis*.

[348] No such words are attributed to Christ by the Evangelists, but doubtless they are a paraphrase of many passages in which claims of supremacy are made.

[349] Marchesi's text reads: *in dei rerum capitis [et] cognitione defixus*. The MS has a line over *dei* which is emended to *deo* (Sabaeus), *domino* (Zink), *domini* (Pascal), *dei domini* (Kirschwing). Pascal would change *capitis* (MS *capite*) to *captu* making this correlative with *cognitione* and keep *et* as genuine. If this be right, then the translation should read: " intent upon the comprehension and understanding of the God of the universe."

[350] The antecedent of the subject of *inquit* is clearly Christ, and therefore Arnobius is here again placing his own words in the mouth of the Divine Savior. Where the " quotation " was meant to end is doubtful. The opening words of this chapter have been much

emended, some suggestions eliminating the verb *inquit* entirely, e. e.
Pascal's *quid est enim quid vobis*, or changing it to first person, e. g.
Brakman's *quid ⟨opus⟩ est, inquam*.

³⁵¹ Cf. J. Masson, *Lucretius, Epicurean and Poet* (London 1907)
158 f., and J. S. Reid in the Supplementary Volume to the same
(London 1909) 189.

³⁵² Cf. Lucretius 5. 575 f.; 705-750, and Bailey's long note on the
latter passage.

³⁵³ *Supernatum* probably means ' superior to the necessity of being
born ' and indeed Ursinus changed to *super natum* in this sense.

³⁵⁴ Marchesi reads *in utilitate* which gives the opposite sense from
what is needed. Reifferscheid: *inutiliter* adopts Sabaeus's rendering.

³⁵⁵ Festugière's (120 f.) ' first way,' also mentioned in 2. 13 and
2. 66.

³⁵⁶ Cf. Plato, *Rep*. 2. 364, where Adeimantus (not Glaucon, as
Bryce-Campbell say) speaks of mendicant magi who go about making
claims for themselves and the powers which they say they possess.

³⁵⁷ Festugière's (120 f.) ' second way,' repeated from 2. 13.

³⁵⁸ Other references to *disciplina Etrusca* in 3. 40 (*bis*), 5. 18.

³⁵⁹ These books were said (cf. Servius, *Aen*. 8. 399) to have been
composed by Tages (mentioned by Arnobius in 2. 69), and appear
to have contained directions for expiatory sacrifices. W. Kahl, " Cornelius Labeo, ein Beitrag zur spätrömischen Litteraturgeschichte,"
Philologus Suppl. 5 (1889) 717-807, has a section on Arnobius' use
of Labeo (720-5) in which he maintains that this passage owes something to Labeo. An earlier writer, G. Kettner, *Cornelius Labeo, ein
Beitrag zur Quellenkritik des Arnobius* (Progr. Pforta: Naumburg
1877), cites many passages of Arnobius thought to have been derived from Labeo but he overlooks this one. F. Niggetiet, *De
Cornelio Labeone* (Münster 1908) maintains that Arnobius 2. 13-62
goes back to Labeo, thinking that the latter had himself borrowed
the idea of the good and bad angels from Porphyry, *De abstin*.
2. 36-43. Niggetiet would date Labeo quite late, but B. A. Bohem,
De Cornelii Labeonis aetate (diss. Königsberg 1913) demonstrates
that the *terminus ante quem* for *Labeo* must be 125 A. D. and denies
that 2. 13-62 could be derived from Labeo, the general spirit of
Labeo's fragments being in harmony with the later Stoicism. Next,
W. Bousset, rev. of J. Kroll, *Die Lehren des Hermes Trismegistos*,
Gött. gelehrt. Anz. 176 (1914) 753-5; " Zur Dämonologie der späteren
Antike," *Archiv f. Religionsw*. 18 (1915) 134-75, attempts to re-
concile these divergent views by accepting both the earlier date for

Labeo and Arnobius' indebtedness to him for 2. 13-62 but maintains that the ultimate source was not, as had been thought, Neo-Platonism (Porphyry) but hermetism and the *Oracula Chaldaica*, which would put the date back to the second half of the first century A. D. His views appear to have found favor with A. S. Ferguson, in W. Scott, *Hermetica* 4 (Oxford 1936) 474-83, but, meanwhile, an article by W. Kroll, "Die Zeit des Cornelius Labeo," *Rhein. Mus.* n. F. 71 (1916) 309-57, maintains that Arnobius used Labeo for the present passage but that it is very improbable that Labeo is all he used; that he certainly used Porphyry and through him without doubt the *Oracula Chaldaica*; that if Labeo is to be dated in the first century, then 'novi viri' becomes absurd. A further attack on the "myth" of Labeo has recently been published by Festugière (122-4). His principal objection concerns the date but he also points out that, according to the Bousset-Ferguson theory, Arnobius borrows from Labeo and he in turn from hermetism, a passage in which animal sacrifice is suggested, yet this practice was wholly foreign to hermetism. Moreover, he sees difficulty in believing that a Roman of about 100 A. D. would couple the Magi and the *haruspices* together. He therefore concluded that about all that one can attribute to Labeo is the reference to the Etruscan method of divination. Whence, then, did Arnobius derive the other two methods, asceticism and prayers of appeasement? Festugière (125-32) answers that Arnobius found them in hermetism and Zoroastrianism, and cites a text of the alchemist Zosimus of about the end of the third century (see his article, "Alchymica," *L'ant. class.* 8 [1939] 71-95). For the text see R. Reitzenstein, *Poimandres* 103, and the other scholars listed by Festugière. He sees in this passage a number of parallels to Arnobius and concludes that Arnobius used this source. His final thesis is that the 'novi viri' is not a designation of a single sect but of a great number of different sources listed in the table (128 f.).

[360] Festugière's (120 f.) 'third way.' Cf. n. 64.

[361] Cf. 2. 33.

[362] Added by Wiman: *omni⟨no ni⟩ si* in place of *eni siqui* of the MS.

[363] Strong evidence to support the view that Arnobius believed the pagan gods existed, but see the Introd. pp. 30-3.

[364] Bryce-Campbell mistake this word (*alii*) for a nominative plural and are forced to explain in a note who the mythical "others" might be.

[365] Weak reasoning, for he overlooks the possibility of delegated

authority which he himself strongly maintains in 1. 50 where the point is emphasized that the supernatural power of Christ to perform miracles was passed on to His followers.

[366] So the MS and the texts of both editors. Reifferscheid, however, suggests in his apparatus that for *ratio* we should read *oratio* (prayer) and makes this an allusion to the petition in the Lord's Prayer (Matt. 6. 13). He would at the same time insert *Christi*, written Χρι between *per* and *mandatum*. The idea is very tempting, since what plausibility does a demand of *reason* have in this connection and what is the meaning of the commandment?

[367] Others, e. g. Justin Martyr (cf. *Apol.* 1. 46), had taken up this problem before.

[368] Retaining *ut* with Marchesi, although Gelenius and Reifferscheid deleted it, perhaps rightly, as Marchesi says.

[369] Bryce-Campbell are right in maintaining that if there is no precise reference to a specific place in the New Testament, the " quotation " is in harmony with the whole of Christ's teaching. Cf. John 6. 37: " Him that cometh to me, I will not cast out." They are, however, with their usual virulence, unnecessarily hard on Orelli who saw a parallel to the bread of life (John 6. 35). On the fountain of life, *fons vitae*, see Apoc. 21. 6. The metaphor is quite popular in the didactic books of the Old Testament. Cf. Ps. 35. 10; Prov. 13. 14, 14. 27, 16. 22; Eccli. 21. 16.

[370] The idea of refusing permission to drink occurs in the *Odyssey* 11. 49 f. where in the lower world Odysseus uses his sword to prevent the shades from drinking of the blood of the sacrifices until he has obtained the necessary information from Teiresias.

[371] *Quid invitans expectat*, the reading of the MS, in preference to *expectat⟨ur⟩*, suggested by Reifferscheid and adopted by Marchesi.

[372] Röhricht (*Seelenlehre* 25) compares with this passage Cicero, *De nat. deor.* 3. 22. 56 and Plato, *Phaedrus* 274c (cf. *Philebus* 18b), and Arnobius 2. 7 with *Phaedrus* 230a, *Alcibiades* 129e, and concludes (26) that there is evidence of direct use of Plato.

[373] Plato (*Rep.* 2. 379) makes Socrates say that God is not the author of all things but of a few only. Cf. *Rep.* 10. 617 where the statement is made that the souls will choose their own genius, for virtue is free. On man's freedom of choice cf. Justin, *Dial.* 102; Irenaeus, *Adv. haer.* 4. 59 (Harvey); Tertullian, *De exhort. cast.* 2, etc.

[374] An obscure passage.

[375] *Deos = divinos.* Cf. 2. 7: *deus* (= *divinus*); 2. 36: *filias* (souls); 2. 39: *deas,* in the same sense.

[376] Marchesi: ⟨*vani*⟩ *animi contentio*—hardly a satisfactory restoration of a corrupt passage which has been much emended, usually in the sense, if not the words, of Marchesi's text. Kroll, *Phil. Woch.* 55 (1935) 1083, complains that this one is not rhythmical. Cf. Wiman, *Textkritiska Studier till Arnobius* 28 f.

[377] Note the anacoluthon in this sentence. *Iniunctum* and *traditum* ought to be made to agree with *partes* (so Reifferchesid), but Kroll and Marchesi prefer to keep the anacoluthon as possible evidence of Arnobius' haste.

[378] *Pontificium,* originally the power and right of a Roman *pontifex* or priest, came as early as the time of A. Gellius (1. 13. 3: *cuius id negotium pontificiumque*) to be used on occasions in a more general sense. Under the early Church, of course, it was used more specifically as the right and power of a bishop over his diocese. The fact that Arnobius uses the word here of Christ is no indication that he was familiar with the *Epistle to the Hebrews* 2. 17 where Christ is also called a high-priest (Vulgate: *pontifex*). Cf. J. C. Plumpe, " Pomeriana," *Vigiliae Christianae* 1 (1947) 227-33, esp. 227 f.; E. Löfstedt, " Some Changes of Sense in Late Medieval Latin," *Eranos Rudbergianus* = *Eranos* 44 (1946) 340-54, esp. 343-6.

[379] Cf. 1. 36, 1. 38, 1. 41, 2. 70, 2. 74, 3. 33, 3. 39, 3. 44, 4. 17, 4. 22, 4. 29, 5. 6, 5. 11, 5. 19, 5. 28, 5. 29, 5. 39, 5. 43, 5. 45, 6. 12, 6. 23, 6. 25, 7. 21. See Book One, nn. 155, 197.

[380] Edelstein-Edelstein, *Testim.* 290d.

[381] On Juno, see Index.

[382] On Fortuna, cf. 3. 40, 3. 43, 6. 25.

[383] See Index.

[384] Bryce-Campbell suggest that this qualifying phrase shows unfamiliarity with the Scriptural passage. They are strongly criticized by Coxe (*ANF* 6. 540, Elucid. 1) who rightly maintains, I think, that the phrase qualifies the figure and not the passage.

[385] Gabarrou (*Oeuvre* 64) professes to see here an allusion to John 10. 7-10; 14. 6.

[386] *Per hanc* (Meursius, Reifferscheid, Marchesi) but *per hunc* is in the MS, i. e. through Christ.   •

[387] Cf. John 10. 9, 14. 6, which, if not clearly in the mind of Arnobius as he wrote, certainly afford complete justification for his statement.

[388] Cf. 1. 13, 1. 58.

[389] In this phrase Arnobius overlooks the fact that the Roman religion was in reality a syncretism of the " religion of Numa " with the anthropomorphic polytheism of the Greeks and many foreign and barbarous rites from the orient. In 2. 73, however, he alludes to the syncretism but there is defending the Christians from the charge of introducing something new rather than something barbarous and foreign. Had Christianity, or Judaism, not been intransigently monotheistic, doubtless the pagans would have been quite willing to take over or tolerate these religions as well. But such acceptance or incorporation postulated a recognition of the Roman state gods and religion, including emperor worship, a condition which clashed with the very essence of the Christian credo and with which no compromise whatever was possible. Christianity could only reject the Roman state religion and this was ultimately interpreted as serious treason against the state, and the persecutions arose as a result. Cf. A. Bigelmair, " Christenverfolgungen," *LTK* 2 (1931) 912-17; W. R. Halliday, *The Pagan Background of Early Christianity* (Liverpool-London 1925) 23 f.

[390] *Fruges*, that is, cultivated plants, as opposed to those items of diet growing wild.

[391] What is here meant is not the superior fruit of the wild strawberry which is the usual translation of *arbuta* (neut. pl., cf. *TLL* 2. 431) but a berry or fruit consumed by primitive men before they had learned to obtain better foods (cf. Pliny, *Nat. hist.* 15. 24. 28, 23. 8. 79; Varro, *De re rust.* 2. 1. 4; Vergil, *Georg.* 1. 148, 2. 520; Lucretius 5. 939-42; Servius, *Georg.* 1. 148: arbuta . . . sunt rubra poma silvarum, quae Plinius unedones vocat, quod asperitate sui plura edi non possunt).

[392] Cf. Lucretius 5. 953-7.

[393] Reading, for the MS *aversionem a religionem*, the suggestion of Wiman, *aversionem et relictionem*, approved by Kroll and now reiterated in *Eranos* 45 (1947) 140, against Reifferscheid's and Marchesi's *aversionem a religione*.

[394] Cf. Tertullian, *Apol.* 6. 9: Laudatis semper antiquitatem et nove de die vivitis; Prudentius, *C. Symmach.* 2. 203-13.

[395] An allusion to the five classes of citizens divided according to wealth for military purposes, an institution ascribed (by Livy 1. 43; cf. also Dion. Hal., *Ant. Rom.* 4. 18) to King Servius Tullius. See nn. 189-91.

[396] Since no *comitia militaria, urbana,* or *communia* are otherwise known, it is probable that Arnobius is here referring to the *comitia*

centuriata, curiata, and *tributa,* respectively. On the *comitia,* see W. Liebenam *RE* 4 (1901) 679-715; G. W. Botsford, *The Roman Assemblies from their Origin to the End of the Republic* (New York 1909) esp. 138.

[397] For the neglect of such omens, see Cicero, *De div.* 2. 36. 76 f.; *De nat. deor.* 2. 3.

[398] Cf. Vergil, *Aen.* 8. 1: Ut belli signum Laurenti Turnus ab arce extulit.

[399] The *fetiales* (hence *ius fetiale*) were an ancient Roman institution—a college of twenty priests, appointed for life, whose office was the expediting of international law and relations; for example, the conclusion of treaties and alliances, declarations of war, armistices, extradition of criminals, etc. Cf. Wissowa 550-4; E. Samter, *RE* 6 (1909) 2259-65. For the fetial ritual, see Livy 1. 24; Polybius 3. 25 f.

[400] The final act of the fetial was to cast a spear into the enemy territory. The phrase *discrimen Martium* may be an imitation of Lucan (3. 336: *discrimina Martis*) as Rapisarda (*Arnob.* 254) suggests.

[401] A reference to the *leges annales* which prescribed the age of eligibility (*aetas legitima*) and the order in which the various magistracies (*certus ordo magistratuum*) had to be held. Cf. Livy 40. 44, regarding the *Lex Villia annalis* (*annaria*) of the year 180 B. C.: quot annos nati quemque magistratum peterent caperentque. See A. H. J. Greenidge, *Roman Public Life* (London 1930) 186. Under Vespasian the *princeps* was exempted from these laws (*ibid.* 350). On the word, see *TLL* 2. 109 which cites examples only from Festus (25 Lindsay): Annaria lex dicebatur ab antiquis ea, qua finiuntur anni magistratus capiendi; also Lampridius, *Vita Commod.* 2. 4.

[402] On the *Lex Cincia,* cf. R. Leonhard, "Donatio," *RE* 5 (1905) 1535 f. C. Ferrini, "Die juristischen Kenntnisse des Arnobius und des Lactantius," *Zeitschr. d. Sav.-Stift. f. Rechtsg.* 15 (1894) 343-6, cites this as an example of Arnobius' precise knowledge of legal terms. Cf. Tertullian, *Apol.* 6. 1 f.: Nunc religiosissimi legum et paternorum institutorum protectores et ultores respondeant velim de sua fide et honore et obsequio erga maiorum consulta, si a nullo desciverunt, si in nullo exorbitaverunt, si non necessaria et aptissima quaeque disciplinae oblitteraverunt. Quoniam illae leges abierunt sumptum et ambitionem comprimentes. He then goes on to give specific examples of luxury.

[403] Numerous laws passed by the censors to curb luxury—known as *leges sumptuariae*. Cf. A. Gellius 2. 24.

[404] Reading with Wiman: *in penetralibus ut olim ignis perpetuos fovetis focis?*

[405] The table as well as the hearth was sacred to the household gods. The salt-cellar (*salinum*) which was never missing on the table, was sacred to them. See Horace, *Carm.* 2. 16. 14; Livy 26. 36. 6. Cf. F. J. Dölger, *Ant. u. Christ.* 2 (1930) 216.

[406] *Maritorum genios* may probably mean "genii of husbands" as Bryce-Campbell translate it (cf. also Wissowa 176), but apparently the significance of this remark is not well understood by the experts on private antiquities. Cf. C. Lécrivain, "Matrimonium (Roman)," *DA* 3. 1654-62, esp. 1655, where this passage is cited among examples of obscurities.

[407] The *hasta caelibaris* was not properly a spear but a small dart or needle with which the bride's hair was divided into six plaits, the sign of chastity. See Ovid, *Fasti* 2. 560; Plutarch, *Romulus* 15; *Aetia* 87; Festus 55 (Lindsay); Pliny, *Nat. hist.* 28. 3. 7; Lécrivain, *loc. cit.* 1655; Klingmüller, "Hasta," *RE* 7 (1912) 2503.

[408] C. Lécrivain (*loc. cit.*) says that on the eve of the wedding the future bride consecrated her *toga praetexta* to some divinity, probably to the lares of the family (Propertius 1. 1133; Nonius 538. 14), but that according to Arnobius in this passage it was to Fortuna Virginalis (cf. Wissowa, 257; J. G. Frazer, note on Ovid, *Fasti* 6. 569, vol. 4, p. 295).

[409] The womanly virtue of industry in the household tasks was highly prized by both the Greeks (e. g. Penelope in the *Odyssey*) and the Romans (e. g. Lucretia: see the account given by Livy 1. 57. 9).

[410] Cf. Tertullian, *Apol.* 6. 4-6: cum mulieres usque adeo vino abstinerentur, ut matronam ob resignatos cellae vinariae loculos sui inedia necarint. He then gives examples of primitive severity and continues: At nunc in feminis . . . prae vino nullum liberum est osculum; repudium vero iam et votum est, quasi matrimonii fructus.

[411] Cf. A. Gellius 10. 23; Tertullian, *Apol.* 6. 5.

[412] The highest peak (943 m. above sea level) of the Alban volcano, lying about seventeen miles southeast of Rome between the Via Latina and the Via Appia. From the summit may be obtained a magnificent view of the sea and the whole of the Campagna, and on clear days St. Peter's is visible. Here were celebrated the Feriae Latinae at the temple of Jupiter Latiaris (cf. Fowler, 95-7, 227 f.,

who, however, says nothing of the reddish bulls but speaks only of a white heifer). Cf. Wissowa 40, 124 f.

[413] Doubtless the same magnificent breed of cattle still used in the neighborhood for agricultural purposes.

[414] Pompilius = Numa Pompilius, traditionally the second king of Rome.

[415] *Madida* = 'boiled' but Kroll wants *arida* ('dry'). Cf. Wiman, *Textkritiska Studier till Arnobius* 31 f.

[416] The MS reads *Tullio* = Servius Tullius, sixth king of Rome, but both Reifferscheid and Marchesi correct to *Tullo* = Tullus Hostilius, third king, on the basis of the previous references to the first two.

[417] *Leviter animata*: perhaps corrupt. Alleker's "fast lebend" ('almost alive') may suggest the right sense or perhaps *animata* refers to blowing upon the coals.

[418] Dis is mentioned also in 4. 26, 5. 28, 5. 32, 5. 35, 5. 40, 5. 43, 6. 3.

[419] Cf. 5. 1 and Dion. Hal., *Ant. Rom.* 1. 30; Minucius 30; Lactantius, *Div. inst.* 1. 21; Macrobius, *Sat.* 1. 7. 31.

[420] On κοιναὶ ἔννοιαι, cf. Tertullian, *De an.* 2. 1 and Waszink's note *ad loc.* (100).

[421] An Etruscan demon or divinity who taught the *disciplina Etrusca*. Cf. 2. 62; Cicero, *De div.* 2. 23. 50; Censorinus, *De die natal.* 4; Ovid, *Met.* 15. 553-9.

[422] That is, after he emerged as a boy from the furrow that was being ploughed; cf. Cicero, *loc. cit.*

[423] According to Plato (*Phaedrus* 274c) Theuth was an Egyptian god who invented numbers and arithmetic, geometry, astronomy, draughts, dice, and letters. Gabarrou (*Oeuvre* 23-37), who compares this passage in Plato with another reference to Theuth in Cicero, *De nat. deor.* 3. 22. 56, concludes, rightly, I think, that it is the Greek source which is followed by Arnobius.

[424] Röhricht (*Seelenlehre* 25) thinks this allusion to Atlas stems from tradition. Cf. Cicero, *Tusc.* 5. 3. 8; Vergil, *Aen.* 1. 741; Ovid, *Met.* 4. 631 ff.

[425] Cf. 1. 28.

[426] Pluto. Cf. Vergil, *Aen.* 4. 638, where Pluto is called the Stygian Jupiter.

[427] Neptune.

[428] On the Muses, cf. 3. 21, 3. 37, 3. 38, 3. 44, 4. 15, 4. 24.

[429] Cf. 1. 36, 4. 15, 4. 25.

[430] Cf. 3. 37. Mnemosyne, mother of the Muses, is meant. See P. Weizsäcker, *LM* 2. 3076-80; S. Eitrem, *RE* 15 (1932) 2265-9; A. B. Cook, *Zeus* 2 (Cambridge 1925) 1157. Cf. Hippolytus, *Ref.* 1. 23; Origen, *C. Cels.* 1. 23.

[431] The MS: *Alchmena*, changed to *Alcmena*, by all editors, but Castiglioni suggested *Alcumena* in order to explain the error. Alcmene, wife of Amphitryon, bore Heracles to Zeus. Cf. also 4. 22, 4. 26, 5. 22, where she is again mentioned and 2. 1 and 7. 33 where there are veiled allusions to her.

[432] Mother of Mercury (Hermes).

[433] Mother of Mars.

[434] Mother of Apollo and Diana. On Latona, cf. 4. 22, 5. 22.

[435] Mother of Castor, Pollux, Clytaemnestra, and Helen, but see Book One, n. 164 and cf. H. W. Stoll, O. Höfer and L. Bloch, " Leda," *LM* 2. 1922-32. She is mentioned again in 4. 22, 5. 22, 7. 33.

[436] Mother, according to variant traditions, of Aphrodite (*Iliad* 5. 370), of Dionysus (Euripides, fr. 177), of Pelops and Niobe (Hyginus, *Fab.* 9. 82).

[437] Mother, according to another tradition, of Dionysus. On Semele, see 3. 44, 4. 22, 5. 28, 5. 44.

[438] Jupiter. The MS reads *dies patri* but the *a* of *patri* has been corrected from *a* to *e* and then to *i*. This form of the name also appears again in the same chapter and in 4. 20, 5. 3, 5. 20. Rapisarda (*Arnob.* 242) lists this use of the name as an imitation of Horace, *Carm.* 1. 34. 5. This is possible but not proven.

[439] Brakman inserts *queunt* and changes *fuere* to *fuisse*, since *fuere* is a poetic form. If he is right, the translation should read " can they have been."

[440] The MS has *quadringentos* which is surely right, though many editors follow Ursinus in changing to *trecentos*. If in 1. 13 Arnobius indicates that three hundred years more or less have passed since the origin of Christianity, then it could possibly have existed three hundred years previously. It has escaped notice that this sentence is taken from the remark of the adversary who must be presumed to be ignorant of so fine a point as exactly how many years have elapsed since Christianity began. Arnobius is careful to compose these remarks of his adversary on the basis of the presumed knowledge of such a person. How any one could accept *trecentos* here and still date the *Adversus nationes* in the fourth century, as many do, passes understanding. Cf. Freppel 33. See also Zeno of Verona, *Tract.* 1. 5. 4: Quum ante annos ferme quadringentos vel eo amplius, etc.,

and M. F. Stepanich, *The Christology of Zeno of Verona* (diss. *Cath. Univ.*: Washington 1948) 10. See *Vigiliae Christianae* 3 (1949) 43 f.

[441] Cf. Otto, *Sprichwörter* 211.

[442] Tertullian (*Apol.* 10. 6) likewise begins with Saturn: Ante Saturnum deus penes vos nemo est; ab illo census totius vel potioris et notioris divinitatis.

[443] Uranus. Note that the dialogue is here Platonic in flavor. Uranus is also mentioned in 3. 29 (*bis*), 3. 37, 4. 14 (*bis*), 4. 24.

[444] On Caelus and Hecate, as parents of Janus, cf. 3. 29.

[445] Cf. 5. 1 and 5. 2. Picus is also the father of Faunus in Tertullian, *Ad nat.* 2. 10.

[446] This implies ignorance of the age of various ancients mentioned in Genesis 5.

[447] Cf. 3. 39.

[448] Bryce-Campbell (*ANCL* 19. 141) clumsily translate *quinquaginta et mille* as 'fifteen hundred' but correct the error in the errata (so also in *ANF ad loc.*). In spite of this they say that it is "important to note that Arnobius is inconsistent." Not so—he is merely inexact, a far different thing. Assuming the year 753 as the date of the founding of Rome (see Introd., nn. 60-66), 1050 less 753 gives 297 A. D. which is certainly one of the possible dates for the composition of the *Adversus nationes* (see Introd. pp. 7-12).

[449] Lactantius' reckoning for Saturn (*Div. inst.* 1. 23. 5, based on Theophilus of Antioch—cf. the notes in Waszink's edition of Tertullian's *De an.*, 254 f.) is not more than 1800 years; for Jupiter (*ibid.* 2. 5. 2), 1700 years.

[450] *Periculo corruptionis*: the latter word is not clear, but it seems possible that it refers to putrefaction of unburnt parts of the sacrificed animal. Cf. 7. 15 *in sedem fabricata faetorum* and 7. 16. It must be remembered, however, that pagan priests at least at times sold unburnt portions on the market (see Acts 15. 29 and 1 Cor. 8. 7).

[451] Cf. Tertullian, *Apol.* 19. 2: et (puto adhuc minus dicimus) ipsos, inquam, deos vestros, ipsa templa et oracula et sacra unius interim prophetae scrinium saeculis vincit, in quo videtur thesaurus collocatus totius Iudaici sacramenti, et inde iam et nostri.

[452] Cf. Ennius in Cicero, *De off.* 1. 51 (= fr. 398 Vahlen); *Pro Balbo* 36:

> Homo, qui erranti comiter monstrat viam,
> Quasi lumen de suo lumine accendat, facit.
> Nihilo minus ipsi lucet, cum illi accenderit.

453 For the same thought, though not, in the Vulgate, the same words, see Isa. 9. 2, quoted in Matt. 4. 16; cf. also Luke 1. 74; Rom. 2. 19.

454 Cf. Tertullian, *Apol.* 6. 8: Serapidem et Isidem et Arpocratem cum suo Cynocephalo (= Anubis, cf. *Ad nat.* 1. 10 where Varro is cited), Capitolio prohibitos inferri, id est curia deorum pulsos, Piso et Gabinius consules, non utique Christiani, eversis etiam aris eorum abdicaverunt, etc. Piso and Gabinius were consuls in 58 B. C. The reference to Varro as the source makes it possible that Arnobius is following him either directly or through the *Apologeticus.*

455 See G. Lafaye, *DA* 4. 1248-51.

456 Cf. E. Meyer and W. Drexler, *LM* 2. 360-548; W. Ruge, *RE* 9 (1916) 2048-132; J. Burel, *Isis et Isiaques sous l'empire romain* (Paris 1911).

457 Reading *in[e]violabili* for *memorabili,* with Axelson.

458 Cybele, the chief divinity of the Phrygians. Cf. A. Rapp, "Kybele," *LM* 2. 1638-72; F. Schwenn, "Kybele," *RE* 11 (1922) 2250-98; H. Graillot, *Le culte de Cybèle* (Paris 1912).

459 Cf. 5. 7, 5. 18.

460 In the Second Punic War (218-202 B. C.). The cult of Cybele was introduced to Rome in the year 204 B. C., when her "sacred black stone" was brought there from Pessinus. Cf. Wissowa 300 f., and Livy 29. 10. 4-11. 8; 15. 5 ff. Note that Arnobius, good Roman as he frequently is, applies to Hannibal, his fellow-African, the word 'Punic' (*Poenus* = Phoenician) which to the Romans must have suggested poena = 'punishment' quite as much.

461 Cf. 1. 36 and note *ad loc.* The reference seems to be to the *sacrum anniversarium Cereris,* introduced shortly before the Hanni-balic War and celebrated in August; its origin and character were entirely Greek. J. G. Frazer (note on Ovid, *Fasti* 3. 308) seems to be wrong in citing this passage as evidence that the *Cerealia* were introduced not long *after* Cannae.

462 It is suspected that this refers to M. Terentius Varro; but Gabarrou (*Oeuvre* 39) would have it be Cornelius Labeo (cf. Macrobius, *Sat.* 1. 12. 21).

463 Numa Pompilius, second king of Rome.

464 *Sospitator,* not *salvator,* is repeated in the present chapter and in 2. 75.

465 Probably not a dislocation of the calendar, but a difference in the weather.

466 Edelstein-Edelstein, *Testim.* 128.

[467] *Moderator.*

[468] *Generibus virtutum tantis et [potestatibus] potestatum.* Most editors have bracketed *potestatibus*, but so good a scholar as Castiglioni thought the MS correct. It is clear that here as elsewhere in Arnobius *virtutes* refers more to the miraculous power used than to the beneficent result. See Book One, n. 210.

[469] The moment of the Incarnation.

[470] Sabaeus took this word (*centenarios*) as modifying *vagitus* (his form of the MS *vagitum*) and found it therefore necessary to change to *stentoreos*, i. e. their cries were like the voice of Stentor, but it really modifies *infantes*, as will be clear from the next note.

[471] Herodotus (1. 68, quoted by A. Gellius 3. 10) speaks of the bones of Orestes as having been found when a well was dug and proved to be seven cubits = 12.25 Roman feet (so Gellius) in length. For the idea that human stature had declined, see Juvenal 15. 70.

[472] *Rex summus.* The present passage sounds very much like a limitation upon the power of God.

[473] Cf. ·Minucius 12. 4; Clement of Alexandria, *Strom.* 4. 11; Eusebius, *Hist. eccl.* 5. 1. 60.

[474] *Pignorum*: I have kept the literal meaning because of the legal flavor of the following phrase but it must be admitted that in many writers from Ovid and Pliny onward *pignus* = 'pledge of love' or children, and then, by transference, other dear ones. The presence of *sterilitatem* immediately before *amissionem* strongly suggests the latter alternative: the first misfortune is never to have children, the second to lose those one has. Each reader must choose for himself.

[475] Moule (50) emphasizes the unorthodoxy of this point.

[476] On *in carunculae huius folliculo*, see Orelli's useful note.

[477] Reading *voluntatem* for *voluptatem* (P and Marchesi). On this idiom, cf. Cicero, *Phil.* 2. 32. 79: tu eius perfidiae voluntatem tuam adscripsisti, and Wiman, *Eranos* 45 (1947) 141. It is dangerous, however, to argue as he does, that because Christians have never been taught to take pleasure in misfortune, Arnobius cannot have said that.

[478] According to Reifferscheid's apparatus, the MS reads *in egressum* which Marchesi prints, although his apparatus indicates the MS reads, rather, *inegressum*. Ursinus attempts to solve the difficulty by omitting the word. Reifferscheid suggests *in ingressu*, Klussmann *lumine cassum*, Meiser *in perpessu*, Kistner *ingravissimam*, Wiman *vi fessum*, and Castiglioni *in aggressu*. None of these seems to me satisfactory and they are deficient in proportion as they abandon what appears to me the necessary root, that of the verb *egredior*.

For any prisoner, egress from his prison is the most important thought. I therefore suggest that we read *in carcerem datum* ⟨*s*⟩*in*⟨*e*⟩ *egressu*[*m*]. The *e* of *egressu* was omitted by haplography after omission by oversight of the *s* of *sine*. Having overlooked the presence of *sine*, the influence of a supposed *in*, together with the idea of entrance in *datum*, suggested the accusative. While not certain, this gives a better sense than any other suggestion. Dr. Plumpe, who would make *sine egressu* mean 'without an outlet,' 'without an opening,' comments: "In the following the escape of the prisoner as the result of the berserk actions of the jailer is no consideration; but the admission of light to dispel the gloom of the prison cell is important for the analogy drawn." See *Vigiliae Christianae* 3 (1949) 44.

⁴⁷⁹ *Pelliculis . . . et cutibus.*

⁴⁸⁰ This may be a more specific reference to the impending persecution than that in the preceding chapter or in 1. 26. Sihler (173) thinks, however, that the persecution has not yet begun.

⁴⁸¹ *Ad salutarem deum.*

⁴⁸² The historian, Flavius Arrianus, a Bithynian born *ca.* 95 A. D., was a pupil and friend of the Stoic philosopher Epictetus (*ca.* 60-140 A. D.), whose lectures he copied down and later published. The present passage is printed as fr. 181 in the Schweighauser edition of Epictetus, as fr. Xa in the edition by Schenkl.

⁴⁸³ *Volumus* (Reifferscheid) is better than *molimur* (Meiser, Marchesi); *ponimus* (Kroll); *novimus* (Wiman).

⁴⁸⁴ The *explicit* of Book Two and the *incipit* of Book Three are as follows: A̅r̅n̅o̅u̅i̅i̅ A̅d̅u̅e̅r̅s̅ Nationes L̅i̅b̅. II Ex̅p̅. Incipit L̅i̅b̅. III. This is the only place in the manuscript where the title of the work appears.

BOOK THREE

In the estimation of its author (cf. 2. 1 and 3. 2) Book Three marks a resumption of his main theme after the digression on the mortality of the soul which consumes most of Book Two, and is principally devoted to a vigorous attack on the anthropomorphic conception of the pagan gods.

Here and there are passages which suggest some dependence upon Cicero and there are scholars who believe that Cornelius Labeo is one of Arnobius' sources in this Book (see the remarks on that shadowy figure in the Introduction, 38-40). While Friedrich Tullius generally confines his attention in his dissertation, *Die Quellen des Arnobius im 4., 5. und 6. Buch seiner Schrift Adversus Nationes* (diss. Berlin: Bottrop i. W. 1934), to later Books, he concludes (73) that the real source in Books Three and Four was not Labeo but a theological manual in existence as early as 100 A. D., not written by M. Terentius Varro.

¹ Rapisarda (*Clemente* 1) thinks this an allusion to Minucius Felix, Tertullian, and Cyprian, and he is probably right.

² Probably a reference to 2. 1 although *paulo ante* might seem to imply something still more recent.

³ Reading nostris (*n̄ris*) for vestris (*ūris*) with Axelson.

⁴ *Alia numinum capita* (Rigaltius) for *alienum capita* (P). The statement in the previous sentence holds good only if such gods as are mentioned really do exist. On this question, see Introd. 30-33. The discussion there should be kept clearly in mind throughout the reading of this Book.

⁵ *Etsi* (Klussmann and Reifferscheid) for *et* (P, Marchesi); Wassenberg would delete *et*.

⁶ Micka (43) cites this passage as referring to demons and says that Arnobius found it difficult to come to a decision concerning them.

⁷ *Plebs.* This passage seems to Micka (43 n. 10) to imply the existence of other deities (cf. 7. 23). He also believes that the phrases *deus princeps* (2. 2) and *deus primus* (2. 6) imply the existence of other gods. Perhaps so in the latter instance but in the former *princeps* need mean nothing more than that God is the Beginning.

⁸ The day of purification (*dies lustricus*) for Roman males was the ninth, for females the eighth, after birth. On this day they also received their name. Cf. Macrobius, *Sat.* 1. 16. 36; Festus, 107 f. (Lindsay). For Greeks it was the tenth. Cf. also F. J. Dölger, *Ant. u. Christ.* 1 (1929) 188.

⁹ *Videbatis* (P and Marchesi); *videratis* (Meursius, Reifferscheid).

¹⁰ *Popularis vulgaritas.*

¹¹ Here the MS has *popularem* which, as it is meaningless as it stands, has been omitted, following bracketing by Ursinus, Castiglioni, and Marchesi. Zink thinks something omitted; Reifferscheid indicates a crux. Other suggestions: *populares* (Sabaeus), *populatim* (Rigaltius), *propriatim* (Wensky), *eorum* (for *eos*) *populum* (Pascal), *populari censura . . . dicit* (Meiser), *personaliter* (Wassenberg).

¹² An exceedingly corrupt passage which Marchesi prints as follows: *unde tamen vobis* † *quae nominibus huius censum complent* † *an sint aliqui vobis incogniti neque in usum aliquando notitiamque perlati?* Wiman improves a great deal by changing as follows: *quae⟨so, est scire, ordinis hine, qui noti sunt⟩ nominibus, huius censum comple⟨a⟩nt an sint,* etc. *Compleant* is due to Salmasius; Meursius first suggested *quaeso.*

¹³ *Usus* is here taken by Orelli and accepted by Marchesi as equivalent to *cultus,* but Meursius and Reifferscheid read *visum* (sight).

¹⁴ *Numero* for *numeri* (Bastgen).

¹⁵ *In rerum natura,* a Lucretian echo.

¹⁶ Cf. Cicero, *De nat. deor.* 1. 30. 84: numerus . . . deorum autem innumerabilis.

¹⁷ *Alii [et] ceteri,* a characteristic of the overdone synonym, repeated in *alia cetera* (6. 11).

¹⁸ On the question of the existence of the pagan gods, see Introd. pp. 30-3.

¹⁹ *Illam* appears to be the MS reading and *illa* in Marchesi a misprint.

²⁰ Cf. Cicero, *De nat. deor.* 1. 34. 95: nam quod et maris deos et feminas esse dicitis; Lactantius, *Div. inst.* 1. 16.

²¹ *Homines pectoris vivi.*

²² M. Tullius Cicero (106-43 B. C.) was first called *disertissimus* in a poetic note by Catullus 49. 1-3:

> Disertissime Romuli nepotum,
> Quot sunt quotque fuere, Marce Tulli,
> Quotque post aliis erunt in annis.

Arnobius mentions him again in 3. 7 and 5. 38. Cf. Tertullian, *Apol.* 11. 16: eloquentior Tullio.

²³ *Secundas ut dicitur actiones.* Cf. Horace, *Epist.* 1. 18. 14.

²⁴ *Aucupia verborum,* a phrase which means literally, " setting snares for, catching at words as if they were birds," is used by Cicero himself (*Pro Caec.* 23. 65; *Orat.* 25. 84; 58. 197, in these last: *delectationis aucupium*).

²⁵ *De hoc* is taken by Orelli to be the equivalent of *propter hoc* (a meaning of *de* which is well-attested), but this would imply that Cicero's writings were criticized for their verbal brilliance, a point that seems very unlikely. The alternative is to render the phrase, as do Bryce-Campbell, as " on this subject," the antecedent being

vaguely the skeptical position taken by Cicero in the *De natura deorum,* mentioned in the preceding chapter, rather than *aucupia verborum splendoremque sermonis.*

[26] Livy (40. 29) records that in 181 B. C. a chest containing certain books of religious and philosophic character was discovered in a field below the Janiculum. These books were forged on the name of Numa Pompilius, second king of Rome (cf. Livy 1. 19 f.). Because of their Pythagorizing tendency, thought subversive of the Roman religion, they were burnt *in conspectu populi* by decree of the Senate. Cf. Plutarch, *Numa* 22; Val. Max. 1. 1. 12; Pliny, *Nat. hist.* 13. 13. 84-7; Wissowa 68.

[27] Arnobius returns to this subject of sex among the gods in 7. 19. Cf. Lactantius, *Epit.* 6.

[28] Lactantius, *Div. inst.* 1. 8, takes the view that God has no body and needs no sex; in 1. 16 that beings who have sex cannot be gods.

[29] Cf. A. Gellius 2. 28. 3: Eas ferias si quis polluisset piaculoque ob hanc rem opus esset, hostiam " si deo, si deae " immolabant, idque ita ex decreto pontificum observatum esse M. Varro dicit, quoniam et qua vi et per quem deorum dearumve terra tremeret incertum esset.

[30] Cf. Cicero, *De nat. deor.* 2. 23. 59 f., where it is stated categorically that the gods do not have bodies. Earlier the Epicurean spokesman (*ibid.* 1. 33. 92) has stated that the gods have no need of limbs or organs, and there is a considerable passage (1. 35. 93) on the question of the parts of the bodies of gods. Moreover, Zeno the Stoic is cited as having stated the belief that the gods have only semblance of body (1. 25. 71). In 1. 27. 77 it is admitted that the gods are *represented* in human form.

[31] *In significata et generum disiunctione* (Marchesi); *insignificatam esse generum disiunctionem* (Reifferscheid), neither of which is very clear.

[32] Cicero, *De nat. deor.* 2. 50. 127) makes the same point more succinctly. In this chapter Arnobius is thinking of sex; in 1. 59 of grammatical gender.

[33] *Sufficere prolem.* Cf. Vergil, *Georg.* 3. 65; Lucretius 3. 704.

[34] Reading *supter* (Castiglioni and Marchesi) for the MS *super* (above). Other noteworthy suggestions: *superi et inferi,* gods above and below (Pascal); *superbas leges,* proud laws (Wiman).

[35] Cf. Cicero, *De nat. deor.* 1. 33. 92: Habebit igitur linguam deus et non loquetur, dentes palatum fauces nullum ad usum; quaeque procreationis causa natura corpori adfinxit ea frustra habebit deus.

[36] Reading *improbum in illis lusum ludere,* Haupt's correction,

accepted by Reifferscheid. Kroll rightly criticizes Marchesi's version (*improvidam in illis suam ludere*) as impossible. If *improbum* . . . *lusum* is wrong, then *inprovidentiam* (the MS has *improvida* . . . *suam*) is much better than *improvidam*. Of the other suggestions none seems quite satisfactory.

[37] Orelli takes this actively, " to cause an abortion," perhaps rightly.

[38] *Chalcidicis*. Cf. 4. 33. According to Platner-Ashby 111, 603, the Chalcidicum in Rome was an annex to the Curia Julia built by Augustus and a sort of *porticus*, perhaps a repository for records. Here the reference is by no means so specific: a part of the heavenly *curia* is used for the whole. Cf. A. Mau, " Chalcidicum," *RE* 3 (1899) 2039-42.

[39] Despite his great indebtedness to Lucretius, this is the sole reference in Arnobius to the Epicurean poet by name. Cf. Lucretius 4. 1168: at tumida et mammosa ' Ceres ' est ' ipsa ab Iaccho.'

[40] A Hellenistic deity, son of Aphrodite and Dionysus, whose cult originated at Lampsacus on the Hellespont. He was a god of fruitfulness with whom art and literature (*Priapea*) often associated lewdness in its crudest form. He was also used by the Romans as a sort of scarecrow: cf. Horace, *Serm.* 1. 8, and Lactantius, *Div. inst.* 2. 4. 1-4. See F. Cumont, *DA* 4. 645-7; O. Jessen, *LM* 3. 2967-90.

[41] On Juno Lucina, the goddess of childbirth, see W. H. Roscher, " Iuno," *LM* 2. 581-5.

[42] Cf. Tertullian, *Apol.* 15. 7: . . . nescio, ne plus de vobis dei vestri quam de Christianis querantur.

[43] Cf. 1. 3, 15-20.

[44] The word (*theologi*) is also used of pagan writers in 4. 14, 15, 18 (*ter*), 5. 5, 8. See Cicero, *De nat. deor.* 3. 21. 53 f.

[45] Gabarrou (*Oeuvre* 65) cites on this chapter P. de Labriolle, " Le cas d'Arnobe," *Revue de Fribourg* 40 (1909) 744 f., an article not available to me unless it be identical with a section bearing the same title in his *Histoire de la littérature latine chrétienne* 1 (3rd ed., Paris 1947) 276 f.

[46] On forms of gods, cf. Cicero, *De nat. deor.* 1. 1. 2; 1. 12. 41: Xenophon [*Mem.* 4. 3. 13] . . . facit Socratem disputantem formam dei quaeri non oportere; 1. 29. 80: Si una omnium facies est, florere in caelo Academiam necesse est; si enim nihil inter deum et deum differt, nulla est apud deos cognitio, nulla perceptio; 1. 29. 81; where much is said about specific appearances. See also Minucius 19. 13; Lactantius, *De ira Dei* 11. 13.

[47] Micka (75 f.) maintains that Arnobius had a poor opinion of

the Old Testament, citing de Labriolle 256 f. (= 3rd ed.: 1. 279 f.), Moricca 1. 611. LeNourry (*ML* 5. 453) appears to divide Jewish writings into two classes, those of the Sadducees, not pertaining to Christianity, and the Old Testament, but Micka is rightly unimpressed.

[48] Bryce-Campbell are right in saying that Arnobius evidently confuses the skeptical Pharisees with their opponents, the Sadducees and Talmudists. Cf. E. G. Hirsch, "God," *The Jewish Encycl.* 6. 3-12. The most recent works on the Pharisees are L. Finkelstein, *The Pharisees* (Philadelphia 1938) and R. T. Herford, *The Pharisees* (New York 1924). Cf. H. L. Strack—P. Billerbeck, *Kommentar zum Neuen Testament aus Talmud und Midrasch* 4 (Munich 1928) 334-52: 'Die Pharisäer und Sadduzäer in der altjüdischen Literatur.'

[49] Reading *tribuamus et nos* (with the editors) for the MS *tribuant et nos*. Salmasius corrected *nos* to *os* ('they attribute shape and countenance'); Wiman and Kroll prefer *annos* ('shape and years').

[50] For *auctoritate* of the MS Brakman prefers *antiquitate* and Löfstedt *ut* (?) *vetera*, both having allusion to the authority of more ancient testimony. Wiman's suggestion: *et revelat⟨ionis⟩ certa antiqua auctoritate* does not seem very good.

[51] *Filum*—cf. Lucretius 2. 341 (and Bailey, *ad loc.*), 4. 88, 5. 571, 5. 589; TLL 6. 763, citing Plautus, *Merc.* 755; Lucilius, fr. 816; Nonius 313; Varro, *De ling. lat.* 10. 4, and others.

[52] Cf. Lucretius 3. 220 f. (and Bailey, *ad loc.*); 4. 647.

[53] *Collectum*. Marchesi declines to attempt a correction. Meiser suggests *confectum* ('made'); Kistner thinks the place desperate. Reifferscheid has *colli erectum* ('upright on the neck').

[54] Orelli quaintly remarks: "Eleganter comparat Arnobius nares cum imbrice, id est tegula cava, quae tectis applicatur, ut per eam defluat aqua, *Dachrinne, Dachtraufe.*" Cf. also Cicero, *De nat. deor.* 2. 57. 143; Aristotle, *Hist. animal.* 1. 11; Lactantius, *De op. Dei* 10.

[55] The three kinds: (1) τομεῖς, *primores* (Pliny, *Nat. hist.* 7. 16) or *praecisores* (Isidore, *Etym.* 11. 1. 52)—modern incisors; (2) κυνόδοντες, *canini* (Isidore, *loc. cit.*)—canines or cuspids; (3) γομφίοι or μύλοι, *molares* (Isidore), *mollientes* (Pliny), *genuini* (Cicero, *De nat. deor.* 2. 54. 134)—molars.

[56] Arnobius' physiology is Ciceronian. Cf. *De nat. deor.* 2. 55. 138: et sanguis per venas in omne corpus diffunditur et spiritus per arterias; utraeque autem crebrae multaeque toto corpore intextae vim quandam incredibilem artificiosi operis divinique testantur; A. Gellius 18. 10.

[57] Eating, instead, ambrosia and drinking nectar. Cf. Book One, n. 88.

[58] Cf. Cicero, *De nat. deor.* 1. 29. 80.

[59] Here Arnobius imitates Cicero (*ibid.*): Ecquos si non tam strabones et paetulos esse arbitramur, ecquos naevum habere, ecquos silos flaccos frontones capitones, quae sunt in nobis, but as usual sows with the sack. Note how many of these descriptive adjectives and phrases were used by the Romans for *nomina* and *cognomina*: Capito, Cilo (cf. *cilunculus*), Fronto, Labeo, Mento, Naevius, Nasica, Macer (cf. *macilentus*), Crassus, Crispus (cf. *crispulus*), Calvus (cf. *calvities*), Glabrio (cf. *glabritas*), Aquila (from *Aquilus* or *aquila*), Caesius, Ravilla (cf. *ravus*). For a contrast drawn between the bald realism of Roman nomenclature and the idealism and beauty found in Greek personal names, see J. C. Plumpe, "What's in a Greek or Roman Personal Name," *Class. Bulletin* 13 (1937) 57 f.

[60] At this point P reads *in his* (translated earlier in the sentence as "among them") but Reifferscheid changes to *simos* ('having snubbed noses'), without palaeographic probability; though, if he is right, Roman comedy has a proper name, Simo, to match.

[61] Here the text is defective, reading *sacrivoces* which, besides being unattested, would have no sense ('holy-voiced'). The translation follows Salmasius' conjecture of *saccibucces*. *Acrivoces*, the conjecture of Reifferscheid, seems hardly better than *sacrivoces*.

[62] Rightly bracketed by Marchesi, omitted by Reifferscheid, as a MS reduplication not fitting the sense.

[63] By curious coincidence there has been preserved to our day at Pompeii an instance of divine beings represented in art as fullers. These are the cupids painted on the wall of a room in the house of Cn. Poppaeus Habitus, believed to have been the proprietor of the neighboring fuller's shop. From these cupids the house formerly was named the "Casa degli Amorini Dorati." Arnobius, of course, could have known nothing of these frescoes since they were buried by the eruption of Vesuvius in 79 A. D. Cf. T. Warscher, *Pompeji, ein Führer durch die Ruinen* (Berlin-Leipzig 1925) 103-8, and her English *Pompeii* (Rome 1930) 89-101; A. Mau, *Pompeii, its Life and Art* (New York 1902) 333; A. Mau-W. Barthel, *Führer durch Pompeii* (5th ed., Leipzig 1910) 77-9.

[64] *Rudes*, a term used by St. Augustine in his *De catechizandis rudibus* (see ACW 2. 4) for prospective converts.

[65] *Aenigmata.* Cf. Clement of Alexandria, *Strom.* 5. 7. 41. 2 ff.

Scharnagl (31) lists this word among those which have unusual senses in Arnobius.

[66] *Causae = res* (cf. Scharnagl). See also 5. 26 (*rebus atque causis*); 7. 3 (*causis et rebus*).

[67] *Accipiant*, cf. 7. 22: *accipienda*.

[68] *Animalis*, the point being that there is little difference between worshipping a dumb animal and a human being.

[69] *Nisi forte*, etc., a favorite introduction, conveying irony or sarcasm, to objections attributed to the opponents, occurs fourteen times: 2. 6, 2. 39, 3. 16, 3. 23, 4. 4, 4. 19, 5. 4, 5. 10, 5. 36, 5. 42, 6. 22, 6. 23, 7. 3, 7. 48.

[70] Cf. Xenophanes of Colophon in Clement of Alexandria, *Strom.* 5. 14. 109. 3 [= fr. 15 Diels]: 'Now if oxen ⟨and horses⟩ or lions had hands so as to limn with these hands and make the works of art that men make, then would they limn their gods—horses like unto horses and oxen unto oxen—and sculpt them in the manner of the frame they themselves bear.' Cf. Eusebius, *Praep. ev.* 13. 13 (*MG* 21. 1121B); Theodoret, *Graec. aff. cur.* 3. 49 (*MG* 83. 885AB).

[71] Curiously enough, Tertullian (*Apol.* 16. 1-4; *Ad nat.* 1. 11) reports the slander against the Christians that they did worship an ass's head. Cf. also Minucius 9. 3, 28. 7. Whether Arnobius chose to make this supposition because he had read these predecessors, we cannot, of course, be certain, but they are strongly supported by the discovery in 1856 on the Palatine Hill in Rome, in a building along the western side known as the *domus Gelotiana* or the *Paedagogium*, i. e. a school for pages in the imperial household, of a *graffito* representing a caricature of the Crucifixion. It is a figure with an ass's head hanging on the cross and adored by a youth standing on the left. Underneath are the words: ΑΛΕΞΑΜΕΝΟΣ ΣΕΒΕΤΕ ΤΟΝ ΘΕΟΝ ("Alexamenos worships his god"). See G. Lugli, *The Classical Monuments of Rome and its Vicinity* 1 (trans. by G. Bagnani, Rome 1929) 294-6, with a photograph; the same, *Roma Antica: il centro monumentale* (Rome 1946) 521-3. For ready reference, see also M. M. Hassett, "Ass," *Cath. Encycl.* 1 (1907) 793; H. Leclercq, "Croix et crucifix," *DACL* 3. 2 (1914) 3050-56. The figure on the cross has been thought by some to represent not Christ but the Egyptian god Seth.

[72] Numa Pompilius, second king of Rome.

[73] More probably M. Porcius Cato of Tusculum (234-149 B. C.) than his great-grandson who died a suicide at Utica in 46 B. C.

[74] The allusion is undoubtedly to Ennius, quoted by Cicero, *De*

nat. deor. 1. 35. 97 [= *Sat.* 23 Warmington]: atque, ut Ennius, 'simia quam similis turpissima bestia nobis.' Ennius is also mentioned and by name in 4. 29. Cf. W. C. McDermott, *The Ape in Antiquity* (Johns Hopkins Univ. Stud. in Archaeology 27, Baltimore 1938) 141.

[75] Micka (158 n. 15) professes to see correspondence between this chapter and Lactantius, *De op. Dei* 17. 6.

[76] Cf. Cicero, *De nat. deor.* 1. 31. 88.

[77] The adversary is doubtless thinking in polytheistic terms, but Arnobius answers him in monotheistic, as in the preceding chapter, where the fact is a little more certain.

[78] Lactantius, *Div. inst.* 1. 18. 21, carries this *reductio ad absurdum* still further by suggesting that the pagans should worship gods who are potters and shoemakers. Cf. also *Epit.* 2. 7.

[79] E. g. Vulcan.

[80] E. g. Aesculapius.

[81] E. g. the fates who spin the thread of life.

[82] Meursius found difficulty in *nautas*, since Neptune, though having dominion over the sea, is not strictly a sailor. He therefore suggested *naccas* = *fullones*, but no modern editor follows him. Cf. the Castors and Portunus, sea divinities.

[83] Apollo.

[84] Pan.

[85] Diana.

[86] Pan or Faunus.

[87] Ceres, Pales. Marchesi makes this sentence interrogatory.

[88] Apollo, Zeus, Themis.

[89] The MS and Marchesi read *ceteri enim dii non sunt* to which both Löfstedt (*Arnobiana* 79) and Wiman (*Eranos* 45 [1947] 142), perhaps rightly, object. Both maintain that a word in the sense of *musici* (Reifferscheid) is needed and the former inserts it after *sunt*, while the latter suggests *ceteri enim melici* [or *melii*] *non sunt*. Though I do not feel absolutely certain that the sentence must be balanced, I tentatively suggest that *dii* may be at fault and should have been *di⟨vin⟩i*. Confirmation may perhaps be supplied by the fact that in Book Two (cf. n. 375) Arnobius has three examples of the use of *deus* = *divinus*, *deae* = *divinae*. The present use of *dii* may be really a case in point, and represent no more than *dii* = *divini*, even when *divinus* means not 'divine' but 'diviner.' See *Vigiliae Christianae* 3 (1949) 44 f.

[90] Lactantius, *Div. inst.* 1. 11. 9 f., makes the same point, referring

to the fact that Jupiter refrained from a union with Thetis because an oracle had foretold that her son would be greater than his father. He also mentions Themis as foretelling to Jupiter events which he would otherwise not have known. In *ibid.* 1. 13. 4 he asks, apropos of Saturn's attempt to prevent his son from becoming greater than himself as a result of a similar oracle: cur enim responsum ab alio potius accepit?

[91] Mercury. Cf. 3. 21.

[92] Bryce-Campbell and von Besnard make the remaining sentences of this chapter interrogatory. The nine subordinate clauses beginning with 'that' (*ut*) prove them wrong, since these clauses answer the initial question.

[93] Arnobius is in harmony with the prevailing tradition that the number of the Muses was nine, the second and third sets listed by Cicero, *De nat. deor.* 3. 21. 54, which were, respectively, the children either of Jupiter and Mnemosyne or of Pierus and Antiope (cf. Pierides, Pieriae). The first set were four in number: Thelxinoe, Aoede, Arche, and Melete, and were children of Cicero's "second Jupiter." Cf. O. Bie, *LM* 2. 3238-95.

[94] *Scitulae* but Oehler and Reifferscheid read *scitule* ('gracefully') with great probability.

[95] *In sidereis motibus*: an obscure phrase which Sabaeus attempts to change to *montibus*, Meursius to *montes*. The context suggests that, whether the passage is corrupt or not, it denotes a place where Diana, the moon goddess (cf. *CIL* 6. 124, Wissowa 251) may conduct her hunts. Hence, the meaning must approximate "the moon among the stars."

[96] Apollo, son of Latona.

[97] Apollo was inspired by Zeus, who in turn owed certain knowledge of the future to Themis; cf. Lactantius, *Div. inst.* 1. 11. 10.

[98] Diomedes wounded Aphrodite (*Iliad* 5. 334-42). Cf. also 4. 21, 4. 25.

[99] Aesculapius, whose chief seat of worship was at Epidaurus. His cult was introduced in Rome in 292 B. C.

[100] In the *Iliad* 18 Hephaestus (= Vulcan) appears as the forger of the new shield of Achilles designed to replace the one stolen by Hector from Patroclus.

[101] Minerva, so called after several rivers (in Arcadia, Boeotia, Crete) named Triton with which the myth of her birth was connected. Cf. Vergil, *Aen.* 5. 704; Ovid, *Met.* 2. 783; 5. 250; 5. 270; 6. 1; *Fasti* 6. 655. See also H. Kruse, "Tritogeneia," *RE* 2 R. 7. 1. (1937) 244 f., for the older version of her origin from the sea.

[102] Mercury, grandson of Atlas through his mother Maia. Cf. Horace, *Carm.* 1. 10. 1; Rapisarda, *Arnob.* 242.

[103] An obvious truth often lost sight of by modern educators.

[104] Cf. Cicero, *De nat. deor.* 1. 32. 90: di enim semper fuerunt, nati numquam sunt, siquidem aeterni sunt futuri.

[105] Note the caution of this sentence which prevents the point from being disproven if the pagan gods are not really immortal.

[106] It is maintained by W. Kahl, "Cornelius Labeo, ein Beitrag zur spätrömischen Litteraturgeschichte," *Philol.* Suppl. 5 (1889) 720-5, that Arnobius uses Cornelius Labeo as his source in this and the following chapter.

[107] In the text as preserved by the MS no name of a divinity appears: *per maria tutissimas praestat commeantibus navigationes,* but a corrector of the MS reads *permarini* for *per maria* which Oehler suggested, perhaps independently, as equal to "sea gods," thus providing a subject for the verb. Sabaeus, however, inserted *Portunus* (Matuta's son) after *praestat*. Reifferscheid inserted *Mater Matuta* after *maria* and this is accepted by both Brakman and Marchesi, though they omit *Mater*. Both of them cite Cicero, *Tusc.* 1. 12. 28, where, however, nothing is said of Matuta as a sea-goddess. Nor does Marchesi's reference to Lucretius 5. 654 (really 656) help out. But his final reference, in which he alludes to Ovid, *Fasti* 6.543-7 (cf. Frazer's note *ad loc.*, vol. 4. 287-90), provides what is needed:

Numen eris pelagi, natum quoque pontus habebit.
   In vestris aliud sumite nomen aquis:
Leucothea Grais, Matuta vocabere nostris;
   In portus nato ius erit omne tuo,
Quem nos Portunum, sua lingua Palaemona dicet.

It must be remembered, however, that palaeographically *Matuta* has no support whatever.

[108] Beginning at this chapter and continuing well into Book Four, Arnobius appears to be following some source unknown to us, which he exploits in an unsystematic fashion, since some of the gods reappear in Book Four. According to Kroll (66 ff.), this consisted of (a) a source of unknown character; (b) an antiquarian source; and (c) Cornelius Labeo, in whom Kroll recognizes Varronian elements. Tullius (68) is inclined to think only one source involved, one which R. Agahd, "M. Terenti Varronis rerum divinarum libri I. XIV. XV. XVI," *Jahrb. f. klass. Philol.*, Suppl. 24 (1898) 123, thinks is Labeo. But Tullius (68 f.) is very skeptical of the theory

that Labeo was the source, chiefly because the principal connection between Labeo and Arnobius is the distinction between *numina bona et mala* which can be found in other possible sources. Analysis of all the passages leads Tullius (73 f.) to the conclusion that the real source was a systematic treatment of pagan theology by an unknown author belonging at the latest to the first century A. D., since all the authorities cited by Arnobius in the section involved belong to the end of the Republic or first half of the first century A. D. The author was, according to him, neither Varro nor Labeo.

[109] P has *sed*, an excellent reading which Gelenius, followed by the editors, changed to *et* on the basis of an assumed parallelism with the later phrases.

[110] Consus was an ancient agrarian divinty, god of crops and their safe transfer into bin and granary. His proper sphere of patronage was early forgotten and misinterpreted: because on his feast day, the *Consualia*, races with horses and mules took place, he came to be regarded as a god of horses; and because his name (derived from *condere*) was given a wrong etymology (*Consus = deus consilii*), he came to be regarded—so here by Arnobius—as a god of counsel, secret planning, etc. See Wissowa 201-3; A. Aust, "Consus," no. 2, *RE* 4 (1901) 1147 f.

[111] On Pales see G. Wissowa, *LM* 3. 1276-80; on Inuus, H. Steuding, *LM* 2. 262 f.

[112] The MS here reads *genetrix* but Ursinus changed to *meretrix*, probably on the basis of Lactantius, *Div. inst.* 1. 20. 6; Minucius 25. 8, where Flora is clearly so called. Cf. H. Steuding, *LM* 1. 1483-7. Flora is mentioned again in 7. 33.

[113] There is no special subject for *adurit* in P and Wassenberg supplies *ardor* but Orelli cites abundant evidence (e. g. Vergil, *Georg.* 1. 93; Ovid, *Fasti* 1. 680; Silius 4. 68; Tacitus, *Ann.* 13. 35) to show that this verb can be used of cold and heat as well.

[114] Apollo.

[115] Edelstein-Edelstein, *Testim.* 343, vol. 2, p. 140.

[116] Originally *ceroma* meant the oil used to anoint the body of the wrestlers, then was extended to the place and even to the combat itself. Cf. *TLL* 3. 877; Rapisarda, *Arnob.* 211.

[117] An unfair objection on Arnobius' part. No solution of this fundamental dualism in competition was achieved until the last century when Alice in Wonderland said, "All have won and all shall have prizes." For another aspect of the same problem, see 4. 4.

[118] *Praesidatus.*

[119] An allusion to Arnobius' recent conversion. Cf. 1. 39.

[120] *Rex poli.*

[121] Added here by Löfstedt, following Ursinus who also balances *servis* with *ingenuis*, which Reifferscheid accepts, though Löfstedt and Marchesi do not. Cf. also Weyman 390-2.

[122] *Fessis rebus*: cf. also. 1. 25, 1. 28, and the notes.

[123] Unxia and Cinxia were epithets given to Juno as the protectress of the bride in marriage. As the bride entered the house of her husband, she consecrated herself to Juno Unxia by fastening wool around the doorposts and anointing them with oil and fat. As Cinxia the goddess presided over the untieing of the *cingulum*, the girdle: she was to guard the bride's fidelity to her husband. See Martianus Capella 2. 149. For Unxia, cf. H. Steuding, "Indigitamenta," *LM* 2. 227; for Cinxia, Steuding, *ibid.* 2. 195; for both, W. H. Roscher, "Iuno," *ibid.* 2. 589; L. v. Preller, *Römische Mythologie* 2 (3rd ed. by H. Jordan, Berlin 1883) 217. See also below, 7. 21.

[124] On Victua, see R. Peter, "Indigitamenta," *LM* 2. 231.

[125] On Potua, see Peter, *ibid.* 2. 217. Doubtless these four *di indigetes* were for illustration as examples of the ridiculous lengths to which the old Roman religion went.

[126] Kroll takes this passage to be from his "antiquarian source," while Agahd thinks it comes from Labeo.

[127] Cf. the Epicurean position in Cicero, *De nat. deor.* 1. 16. 42: ... et quae poetarum vocibus fusa ipsa suavitate nocuerunt, qui et ira inflammatos et libidine furentes induxerunt deos feceruntque ut eorum bella proelia pugnas vulnera videremus, odia praeterea discidia discordias, ortus interitus, querellas lamentationes, effusas in omni intemperantia libidines, adulteria vincula cum humano genere concubitus mortalisque ex inmortali procreatos. Cf. also 2. 28. 70: deorum cupiditates aegritudines iracundias.

[128] Cf. 4. 24. See G. Wissowa, "Laverna," *LM* 2. 1917 f.

[129] On Bellona, see A. Procksch, *LM* 1. 774-7. Cf. 1. 28.

[130] *Discordia* is the Latin translation of the Greek Eris—see W. H. Roscher, *LM* 1. 1179, and on Eris, W. Deecke, *ibid.* 1337-9. It is also the Latin designation of an Etruscan goddess in the third region of the heavenly temple of Martianus Capella (1. 45 ff.). See Deecke, *ibid.* 1. 1139.

[131] See A. Rapp, "Furiae," *LM* 1. 1159-64.

[132] *Laeva numina*: according to Kettner (8), Boehm (45), Mülleneisen (35), and Röhricht (*Seelenlehre* 31 f.), the source of this

chapter is Cornelius Labeo, since we know from Augustine (*De civ. Dei* 2. 11, 3. 25) that Labeo made the distinction between *numina bona* and *numina mala*. But Tullius (68 f.) cited evidence that other sources also made the same distinction and he therefore is skeptical of Labeo as the source here. On gods of the left (*laeva numina*), see also 4. 5, 7. 23, and Introd. pp. 38-40.

[133] Most editors since Meursius have made this future (and in 5. 19 also), but Marchesi, following Brakman, preserves the present of the MS in both places.

[134] *Cupidines*. Cf. 4. 15.

[135] Cf. Cicero, *De nat. deor.* 2. 28. 70.

[136] *Concitor* (Hildebrand, Kroll, Marchesi) for the MS *conditor* (Reifferscheid). Cf. F. M. Heichelheim, "Mars," RE 14 (1930) 1919-64.

[137] E. g., Eteocles and Polyneices in Aeschylus, *Septem c. Thebas.*

[138] The figure is taken from the ripping open of the seam of a garment.

[139] If Arnobius is thinking in this clause and the following of any well-known example, the allusion may be to the Oedipus legend.

[140] *Viri*. Heraldus remarks that Arnobius is here speaking like a Stoic.

[141] E. g., Phaedra in Euripides, *Hippolytus* 777. It is quite possible that here Arnobius means no specific example, known to history or literature, but the general prevalence of suicide among adherents of a faith that offered no hope of immortality as the reward for righteous living.

[142] Dido would doubtless be present in the mind of any African as a famous example of this rather unusual method of suicide.

[143] Cf. Ovid, *Her.* 15. 164 ff.

[144] *Constantiam* (P, Marchesi), *substantiam* (Reifferscheid) but Marchesi points out that *constantia* = *essentia*. Cf. also Scharnagl (31); Lucretius 1. 581: constant = sunt; M. Zink, *Fleckeisen's Jahrb.* 111 (1875) 869.

[145] Epicurean theology.

[146] According to Kahl (725) chapters 29-42 owe much to Cornelius Labeo. So also Röhricht (*Seelenlehre* 35), but he admits the proof is lacking.

[147] *Interioris*: the figure may be taken from the wine cellar where the older, and therefore the better, wine is in the jars farthest from the front. Cf. Horace, *Carm.* 2. 3. 8: interiore nota Falerni.

[148] See 1. 36.

¹⁴⁹ Cf. Ovid, *Fasti* 1. 117 ff.; Macrobius, *Sat.* 1. 9; Joannes Lydus, *De mens.* 1. f.

¹⁵⁰ The beginning of the day was sacred to him, hence he was called Janus Matutinus; the beginning of the year was dedicated to him, hence the name January. Cf. Martial 8. 2. 1; Lucan 5. 6. As people begin the year with January, so Arnobius begins with Janus.

¹⁵¹ A contemporary of Cicero, the scholar P. Nigidius Figulus, thought that Janus was originally a sun-god; see Macrobius, *Sat.* 1. 9. 5 ff.; Wissowa 108.

¹⁵² On Caelus, see H. Steuding, *LM* 1. 844 f; on Hecate, see W. H. Roscher, *ibid.* 1. 1885-1910. Cf. Cicero, *De nat. deor.* 2. 24. 63; 3. 17. 44.

¹⁵³ Historically, the Janiculum was not a town, though its name parallels those of some towns (e. g. Tusculum, Otriculum) but a hill, the largest and most important of those opposite the site of primitive Rome. In Vergil, *Aen.* 8. 358, and Ovid, *Fasti* 1. 245, it is called an *arx* which is what we should expect here. Cf. R. Gall, " Ianiculum," *RE* 9 (1916) 691 f. It seems hardly possible that Arnobius could have had personal acquaintance with the Eternal City and still make this mistake. He may have derived the error from a careless reading of Minucius 21. 6: Itaque latebram suam, quod tuto latuisset, vocari maluit Latium, et urbem Saturniam idem de suo nomine et Ianiculum Ianus ad memoriam uterque posteritatis reliquerunt. If he thought that the word *urbem* applied equally to Saturn and Janus, then Janiculum might become an *oppidum*. But note that in 4. 24 he tells this same story about Saturn's giving his name to Latium (derived from *latere*) and there does not include the derivation of *Saturnia* from Saturn. Cf. Tertullian, *Apol.* 10. 8; Lactantius, *Div. inst.* 1. 13. 9; 5. 5. 9.

¹⁵⁴ On this god of springs, see H. Steuding, "Fons," *LM* 1. 1496-8. The form in Arnobius (*Fonti*) is taken by Steuding to be a genitive and this gives rise to a nominative *Fontus*, but the god was elsewhere called *Fons*, though there is epigraphic evidence for the nominative as *Fontanus* (*CIL* 2. 150; 10. 6071). Cf. also Cicero, *De leg.* 2. 22. 56; *De nat. deor.* 3. 20. 52.

¹⁵⁵ See G. Wissowa, "Volturnus," *LM* 6. 370; G. Lafaye, *DA* 5. 965.

¹⁵⁶ On Juturna, goddess of springs, see G. Wissowa, *LM* 2. 762-4.

¹⁵⁷ Cf. Ovid, *Fasti* 1. 171-4:

> Mox ego: 'Cur, quamvis aliorum numina placem,
> Iane, tibi primum tura merumque fero? '

' Ut possis aditum per me, qui limina servo,
      Ad quoscumque voles' inquit ' habere deos.'
Cf. also Frazer's note *ad loc.*, vol. 2. 111; Macrobius, *Sat.* 1. 9.

[158] *Mensum* may be taken either as the participle of *metior* or the genitive plural of *mensis*, but *mensum = mensium* is well-attested in early Latin which Arnobius is fond of imitating.

[159] The Greek word χρόνος means ' time,' whereas the word Κρόνος, the name of the Greek father of Zeus (= Jupiter, son of Saturn) is identical with it save for the aspiration of the initial letter. Cf. Cicero, *De nat. deor.* 2. 24. 63; Plutarch, *De Is. et Osir.* 32. 363d; Macrobius, *Sat.* 1. 22. 8; Athenagoras, *Apol.* 22; Tertullian, *Ad nat.* 2. 12; Lactantius, *Div. inst.* 1. 12. 9.

[160] The phrase may be imitated by Firmicus Maternus, *De errore prof. rel.* 16. 2 and 27. 2: perpetua continuatione. Brakman (*Miscella tertia* 26) is quite sure Maternus is following Arnobius. See Introd. p. 52.

[161] Accius in Macrobius, *Sat.* 6. 5. 11; Vergil, *Aen.* 7. 179.

[162] In 6. 12 Saturn is also called the *cum obunca falce custos ruris.* Cf. Cyprian, *Quod idola dii non sint* 2.

[163] Kroll (68), Boehm (32), and Wahl (770) conjecture Labeo as the source for the identification of Jupiter = Sol but their view is attacked by Tullius (69).

[164] Cf. Macrobius, *Sat.* 1. 23. 1; A. B. Cook, *Zeus* 1 (Cambridge 1914) 400, 429.

[165] Plato (*Phaedrus* 246e-247a) represents Zeus as driving a winged chariot, arranging all things and caring for all things, followed by an army of gods in eleven squadrons.

[166] Cicero, *De nat. deor.* 1. 15. 40; 2. 28. 66; Servius, *Aen.* 1. 47; Varro, *De ling lat.* 5. 70; Minucius 19. 10; Augustine, *De civ. Dei* 4. 11.

[167] See G. Wissowa, " Ops," *LM* 3. 931-7.

[168] Cf. also 4. 25. See Lucretius 2. 624 ff.; Origen, *C. Cels.* 3. 141; Athenagoras, *Apol.* 30; Eusebius, *Praep. ev.* 3. 11. 37.

[169] The name Ἥρα contains the same letters as the word ἀήρ. See Cicero, *De nat. deor.* 2. 26. 66; Plutarch, *De Is. et Osir.* 32. 363d; Minucius 19. 10; Firmicus Maternus, *De errore prof. rel.* 4. 1; Athenagoras, *Apol.* 22; Servius, *Aen.* 7. 311; Augustine, *De civ. Dei* 4. 10; Macrobius, *Sat.* 3. 3.

[170] Cf. Vergil, *Aen.* 1. 46 f.: Iovisque et soror et coniunx; Firmicus Maternus, *De errore prof. rel.* 4. 1. Regarding the cult-names mentioned for Juno in the following: Fluvionia (or Fluonia) proba-

bly designates Juno as goddess of menstruation (hence also Dea Mena: cf. Augustine, *De civ. Dei* 7. 2). See Martianus Capella 2. 149; W. H. Roscher, " Iuno," *LM* 2. 580 and R. Peter, " Indigitamenta," *ibid.*, 198 f.; G. Wissowa, " Fluonia," *RE* 6 (1909) 2773 f. —Pomana appears to be a corruption of some cognomen whose meaning is unknown. See O. Höfer, " Pomana," *LM* 3. 2747, and G. Wissowa, " Pomona," *ibid.* 3. 2749.—Ossipagina is the reading here, but in 4. 7 and 4. 8 Ossipago is Canterus' correction of the reading of P in both instances. Other emendations suggested: Ossilago, Opigena. The word apparently reflects *ossa* and *pangere*, i. e. the goddess who puts strength into the bones of children.— Februtis, probably from Februlis (Februa): Juno as goddess of fruitfulness; see Wissowa 185.—Populonia, venerated especially by the Oscans and Sabellians; see Wissowa, *ibid.* 187 f.—Cinxia: see 3. 25 and n. 123.—Caprotina, Juno as the protectress of woman's sex life: see Varro, *De ling. lat.* 6. 18; Macrobius, *Sat.* 3. 2. 14; see W. H. Roscher, *LM* 2. 588; Wissowa 184 f.

[171] At first sight the reference to Granius suggests that Aristotle's works were not directly known to Arnobius and that he gained his opinion of the Stagirite entirely through Granius. But Aristotle is mentioned in 2. 9, and when we compare the following sentence of Cicero, (*Tusc.* 1. 4. 7): Sed ut Aristoteles, vir summo ingenio, scientia, copia, and another (*ibid.* 1. 10. 22): Aristoteles longe omnibus—Platonem semper excipio—praestans et ingenio et diligentia, with what Arnobius says, we see that the ultimate source is Cicero. Cf. Lactantius, *Div. inst.* 1. 5. 22.

[172] This Granius was either Granius Flaccus or Granius Licinianus if, indeed, these were not one and the same man. See G. Funaioli, " Granius " nos. 12 f., *RE* 7 (1912) 1819-22. That this sort of equating of gods began long before the time of Labeo, whenever that was, is shown by the reference to Aristotle. Cf. Tullius (69); Wissowa (91 ff.) See other references to Granius in 3. 38 f., 6. 7 and (as Flaccus?) 5. 18. Gabarrou (*Oeuvre* 40) identifies this Granius with the first-century historian Licinianus and is sure that Arnobius read Labeo, his proof being the reference to Apollo in 3. 33.

[173] Cf. Macrobius, *Sat.* 1. 17. 70.

[174] *Aetherium verticem.* Cf. Macrobius, *Sat.* 3. 4. 8; 1. 17. 70; Augustine, *De civ. Dei* 7. 16.

[175] G. Wissowa, " Minerva," *LM* 2. 2982 f., cites this and other attempts to establish etymologies for the name Minerva (older spelling: Menerva) and declares himself satisfied that the root is

related to the Sanskrit *man* and the Greek μένος, Latin *mens, memini, moneo,* etc. as did Orelli long ago. See Festus 109 Lindsay; Macrobius, *Sat.* 1. 17; Cicero, *De nat. deor.* 2. 26. 67; 3. 4. 62.

[176] Metis (Μῆτις), one of the daughters of Oceanus and Tethys, according to Hesiod (*Theog.* 886), the first wife of Zeus and mother of Athene. See P. Weizsäcker, *LM* 2. 2938-41. Both Sabaeus and a corrector read *Mentis,* and their view is supported by the reference to Mens in 3. 37 and by a fragment of Afranius in A. Gellius 13. 8.

[177] The MS reads *Victoriae* ('of Victory') which Marchesi corrects to *Victoria est* on the ground that *Victoria* (= Νίκη) is a cognomen of Athene. Reifferscheid suspects a lacuna and suggests something like *socia* or *genetrix.* Brakman suggests *Victoria era.* Cf. also 4. 1.

[178] Reading, with Axelson, *nulla Iovis enata de cerebro, inventrix oleae nulla, ⟨nulla⟩,* etc. Cf. L. W. Daly, *Am. Jour. Phil.* 69 (1948) 119.

[179] Here Arnobius refers to existing etymologies of the name: e. g. Cicero, *De nat. deor.* 2. 26. 66 (= Firmicus Maternus, *De errore prof. rel.* 17. 2): Neptunus a nando, "Neptune is derived from 'to swim'" (!); cf. also Varro, *De ling. lat.* 5. 72.

[180] In 2. 70 also Pluto is mentioned by this periphrasis.

[181] Poseidon Σεισίχθων or Ἐνοσίγαιος. Orelli thinks Arnobius is here quoting some tragic or comic poet.

[182] *Medicurrius* (*medius + currere*) = 'one who runs back and forth.' Arnobius is the earliest of three Christian writers who give this derivation: Augustine, *De civ. Dei* 7. 14: nam ideo Mercurius quasi *medius currens* dicitur appellatus, quod sermo currat inter homines medius, etc., repeated in Isidore, *Etym.* 8. 11. 45, who also reports another derivation (from *merx*) which is given by Festus (111 Lindsay). Apparently no other author uses the word *medicurrius.*

[183] Because Mercury = Hermes is the god of eloquence.

[184] Cyllene, Hermes' birthplace, was a lofty mountain in northeastern Arcadia.

[185] The *caduceus,* a herald's staff, was the symbol of Mercury. See H. Steuding, "Mercurius," *LM* 2. 2805 f., illustration on 2825; E. Samter, "Caduceus," *RE* 3 (1899) 1170 f. Cf. 4. 22, 5. 25, 6. 25, and notes *ad locc.*

[186] Cf. Lucretius 2. 993 f. and Bailey *ad loc.* That this identification, Magna Mater (the Asiatic Cybele) = *terra* = Ceres = Vesta, goes back to Labeo is denied by Tullius (69).

[187] The derivation of the name of Ceres from the root *gerere* = 'to

bear' (see Varro, *De ling. lat.* 5. 64; Cicero, *De nat. deor.* 2. 26. 67, 3. 20. 52, 3. 24. 62) is rejected by T. Birt (*LM* 1. 860) who declares for the root found in *crescere* and *creare*, confirming Orelli's derivation of *cereo = creo*.

[188] Cf. Plato, *Phaedrus* 247a (Hestia alone remains at home); Dion. Hal., *Ant. rom.* 2. 50, 64-8; Ovid, *Fasti* 6. 267 and Frazer's note *ad loc.* vol. 4, p. 202; 6. 288 and Frazer's note p. 220; Isidore, *Etym.* 8. 11. 67 f.

[189] Arnobius shares the pre-Copernican view of the fixity of the earth.

[190] P. Nigidius Figulus (cf. 3. 40 f.), friend and associate of Cicero in suppressing the Catilinarian conspiracy, and after Varro, the most learned of the Romans, was a Pythagorean. See W. Kroll, "Nigidius" no. 2, *RE* 17 (1936) 200-212; Cumont 152.

[191] Cf. Augustine, *De civ. Dei* 7. 16; Isidore, *Etym.* 8. 11. 40-42.

[192] *Venus* is derived, according to this etymology, from *venire* ('to come'). Cf. Cicero, *De nat. deor.* 2. 27. 69; Quae autem dea ad res omnes veniret, Venerem nostri nominaverunt. Cf. also *ibid.* 3. 24. 62; Varro, *De ling. lat.* 5. 62; Isidore, *Etym.* 8. 11. 76-9.

[193] This attempt to derive the name *Proserpina* from *proserpinare* ('to steal forth') is rightly rejected by J. B. Carter, *LM* 3. 3141-9, following H. Usener, "Proserpina," *Rhein. Mus.* 22 (1867) 435 f., who derives it from the Greek Περσεφόνη (cf. Cicero, *De nat. deor.* 2. 26. 66; Isidore, *Etym.* 8. 11; Varro, *De ling. lat.* 5. 68).

[194] Cf. also 4. 14, 4. 17, 4. 22, 6. 12; Macrobius, *Sat.* 1. 17 f.; Augustine, *De civ. Dei* 7. 16; Varro, *De ling. lat.* 5. 68.

[195] An allusion to Lucretius' poem? Cf. 1. 2, 2. 70, 3. 35.

[196] Liber, son of Semele.

[197] Apollo.

[198] On this epithet of Apollo, see Lactantius, *Div. inst.* 1. 7. 9; Macrobius, *Sat.* 1. 17; Ammianus 22. 11; K. Wernicke, "Apollo Smintheus," *RE* 2 (1896) 68 f.

[199] For the MS *tribiali* Marchesi suggests *triviali* ('commonplace'). Orelli points out that this is probably an allusion to the *cognomen* of Diana Trivia. Tullius (69) again denies that Labeo can be the source.

[200] Actaeon, son of Aristaeus and Autonoë, a famous Theban hunter and hero trained by the Centaur Chiron, accidentally, rather than purposely, as Arnobius implies, saw Artemis on Mount Cithaeron in the circumstances mentioned and was changed by her into a stag which was pursued and killed by his own fifty hounds. Cf.

Ovid, *Met.* 3. 155 ff; Apollodorus, *Bibl.* 3. 4; Hyginus, *Fab.* 180; Fulgentius, *Mythol.* 3. 3; G. Wentzel, "Actaeon," *RE* 1 (1894) 1209-12.

201 Cf. Cicero, *De nat. deor.* 1. 11. 27, who says that Alcmaeon of Croton attributed divinity to the sun, moon, and other heavenly bodies and to the soul. Lactantius, *Div. inst.* 2. 5 f., is devoted to the refutation of the view that the stars and planets are gods.

202 *Animans,* Salmasius' conjecture for the MS *animas.*

203 Cf. Plato, *Timaeus* 30; Augustine, *De civ. Dei* 4. 12, 7. 6; Lactantius, *Div. inst.* 2. 6.

204 A reference to the relative recency in which the pagan gods began to be worshipped. Cf. 2. 71.

205 That is, men deified parts of the universe (e. g. Sol. Luna, etc.) without change of name.

206 *In unius sensus simplicitatemque conflari,* but Kistner suggests ⟨*animi*⟩ *sensum,* Brakman *sensus* ⟨*finem*⟩.

207 Cf. Cicero, *De nat. deor.* 2. 27. 68; 3. 21. 54; Lactantius, *Div. inst.* 2. 5; Firmicus Maternus, *De errore prof. rel.* 17. 1.

208 *In rerum natura:* see above, n. 195.

209 *Vos* (Sabaeus), *nos* (P).

210 The following passage is attributed to Labeo by Kahl (791 ff.) and Röhricht (*Seelenlehre* 13), but this is denied by Tullius (70) who prefers as a source some encyclopedic work.

211 Cf. 7. 22, 7. 32.

212 Not Mnaseas of Berytus but Mnaseas of Patara in Lycia, pupil of Eratosthenes, who flourished in the 3rd and 2nd centuries B. C. His fragments are found in C. Müller, *Fragm. gr. hist.* 3. 149 f., where this is fr. 25a and 25b. See R. Laqueur, "Mnaseas Πατρεύς," *RE* 15 (1932) 2250-2.

213 Cf. 2. 70.

214 R. Peter, "Mens," *LM* 2. 2798-2800, thinks that the reference in this passage is only a translation of Μῆτις. Mens was an ancient goddess to whom the Romans prayed especially in times of distress, e. g. after the defeat at Lake Trasimenus. Cf. Tertullian, *Ad nat.* 2. 11; Lactantius, *Div. inst.* 1. 20. 13; Cicero, *De nat. deor.* 2. 31. 79; A. Marbach, "Mens," *RE* 15 (1932) 936 f.

215 This is fragm. 162 of Ephorus' *De inventis* in C. Müller, *Fragm. gr. hist.* See E. Schwartz, "Ephoros" no. 1, *RE* 6 (1909) 1-16. Pausanias (9. 29. 2) gives the three names as Μελέτη, 'Αοιδή, Μνήμη. Cf. also Hesiod, *Op.* 6; Cicero, *De nat. deor.* 3. 21. 54: Iam Musae primae quattuor Iove altero natae, Thelxinoë Aoede Arche

Melete, secundae Iove tertio et Mnemosyne procreatae novem, tertiae Piero natae et Antiopa, quas Pieridas et Pierias solent poetae appellare, isdem nominibus et eodem numero quo proxime superiores.

[216] Myrtilus (again mentioned in 4. 24) is probably no. 7 (discussed by R. Hanslik) in the list in *RE* 16 (1935) 1166. The seven muses, according to Epicharmus, were Neilous, Tritone, Asopous, Heptapolis, Acheloïs, Tipoplous, Rhodia.

[217] Orelli thinks this was Crates of Mallos (see W. Kroll, " Crates " no. 16, *RE* 11 [1922] 1634-1641) but it seems equally possible that it was Crates of Athens (*ibid.* 1633, no. 12) or even Crates of Thebes (*ibid.* 1625-31, no. 6 Stenzel).

[218] Cf. Hesiod, *Theog.* 75-9: Clio, Euterpe, Thalia, Melpomene, Terpsichore, Erato, Polyhymnia, Urania, Calliope, and cf. also the names of the books of Herodotus. See Rapisarda, *Arnob.* 255.

[219] Weak reasoning, since when there is a difference of opinion, one may be right. Cf. Cicero, *De nat. deor.* 1. 2. 5: Res enim nulla est de qua tantopere non solum indocti sed etiam docti dissentiant; quorum opiniones cum tam variae sint tamque inter se dissidentes, alterum fieri profecto potest ut earum nulla, alterum certe non potest ut plus una vera sit.

[220] *Integrare.* Cf. 2. 15.

[221] Cf. Cicero, *De nat. deor.* 2. 28. 71: Cultus autem deorum est optimus idemque castissimus atque sanctissimus plenissimusque pietatis et eos semper pura integra incorrupta et mente et voce veneremur.

[222] Ephorus.

[223] Hesiod.

[224] L. Calpurnius Piso Censorius Frugi, consul in 233 B. C., enacted the *Lex Calpurnia de repetundis* and was a writer of annals. Cf. C. Cichorius, " Calpurnius " no. 96, *RE* 3 (1899) 1392-5. This is fragm. 45 in H. Peter, *Hist. rom. fragm.* (Leipzig 1883) p. 86 = *Hist. rom. rel.* 1 (Leipzig 1914) 138 (on Piso, see *ibid.* clxxxi-cxcii). On Novensiles, cf. also 3. 39, 3. 42-4; S. Weinstock, " Novensides di," *RE* 17 (1936) 1185-9.

[225] Here Arnobius is doubtless referring to the Umbrian town of Trebia (modern Trevi), rather than the place of the same name in Latium, but locates it erroneously, either from ignorance or from confusion with Trebula Mutuesca (modern Monteleone) which was *in Sabinis.*

[226] Cf. 3. 31 and n. 172.

[227] L. Aelius Stilo Praeconinus, also mentioned in 3. 39, was a

Stoic teacher and speechwriter (153-73 B. C.) who taught both Cicero (for his tribute see *Brut.* 56. 205-7) and Varro, and is mentioned by Varro and Gellius many times. See G. Goetz, "Aelius" no. 144, *RE* 1 (1894) 532 f.

[228] M. Terentius Varro, the celebrated antiquarian. See H. Dahlmann, "M. Terentius Varro," *RE* Suppl. 6 (1935) 1172-1277.

[229] Cf. Censorinus, *De die nat.* 14.

[230] Cornificius Longus, a grammarian, is also mentioned in 3. 39. His date is determined approximately by the fact that he cites Cicero and and is cited by Verrius Flaccus. Cf. G. Wissowa, "Cornificius" no. 11, *RE* 4 (1901) 1630 f.

[231] T. Manilius, who was senator in 97 B. C. and lived in the age of Sulla, of whom Pliny, *Nat. hist.* 10. 2. 4, says: maximis nobilis doctrinis doctore nullo. See F. Münzer, "Manilius" no. 4, *RE* 14 (1930) 1115.

[232] Cf. Pliny, *Nat. hist.* 2. 53. 138; Seneca, *Quaest. nat.* 2. 41.

[233] L. Cincius Alimentus, also mentioned in 3. 39, was praetor in 210 B. C. and a well-known Roman historian. See F. Münzer—C. Cichorius, "Cincius" no. 5, *RE* 3 (1899) 2556 f.

[234] See Wissowa 18-20, 43-7.

[235] Servius, *Aen.* 8. 187: Sane quidem veteres deos Novensiles dicunt, quibus merita virtutis dederint numinis dignitatem. Cf. Cicero, *De nat. deor.* 2. 24. 62 (listing Hercules, Castor and Pollux, Aesculapius, Liber, Romulus-Quirinus). Minucius 21. 8-10 lists Romulus and Juba. Cf. Cyprian, *Quod idola dii non sint* 1.

[236] If Marchesi is right in rejecting with hesitation (see his apparatus) Reifferscheid's insertion of *Novensiles* at this point, then some similar word must be inserted into the translation.

[237] Macrobius, *Sat.* 3. 4. 6: Nigidius enim de dis libro nono decimo requirit num di Penates sint Troianorum Apollo et Neptunus, qui muros eis fecisse dicuntur, et num eos in Italiam Aeneas advexerit. Cf. Servius, *Aen.* 3. 12. The partisans of the Cornelius Labeo theory base their view that he is the source for this chapter on Macrobius, *Sat.* 3. 4. 6 and Servius, *Aen.* 1. 378, 2. 296, 2. 325, 3. 119, 3. 148. As Tullius (70) points out, in these passages Labeo is mentioned only twice and each time in connection with other writers on the Penates. He therefore concludes that Varro, who is mentioned more often than Labeo, is more likely as a source, particularly since Arnobius mentions Varro and not Labeo. On the *di Penates*, also mentioned in 3. 42 f., see Cicero, *De nat. deor.* 2. 27. 68;

Cyprian, *Quod idola dii non sint* 4; W. W. Hyde, *Paganism to Christianity in the Roman Empire* (Philadelphia 1946) 15; G. Wissowa, "Penates," *LM* 3. 1879-98; S. Weinstock, "Penates," *RE* 19 (1937) 417-57.

[238] *Immortalibus*: Reifferscheid's correction of the MS *immortalium*, in place of *immortali* (Marchesi), criticized by W. Kroll, *Phil. Woch.* 55 (1935) 1084: "die conditio ist doch nicht unsterblich."

[239] Cf. C. Thulin, "Etrusca disciplina," *RE* 6 (1909) 725-30.

[240] Who this Caesius was is not clear but he may have been Caesius Bassus, a lyric poet of the age of Nero who is said to have written a commentary on Aratus' *Phaenomena* (see Orelli's note).

[241] On the Genius Iovialis, see Wissowa 180, 280 f. Concerning Pales and the unsolved problem whether or not there were two divinities of this name, one male, one female, see Wissowa 199-201.

[242] Cf. 2. 62 and 5. 18.

[243] A group of twelve gods, six of them male and six female, supposedly acting as a council to Jupiter. See G. Wissowa, "Consentes," *LM* 1. 922 f.; *Religion und Kultus* 61; for a description of the *Porticus Deorum Consentium* at Rome, Platner-Ashby 421 f.

[244] This term is understood by W. H. Roscher, *LM* 1. 913 f., to be synonymous with *Consentes*, though he speaks of the "etwas unklare Notiz bei Arnobius." So also G. Wissowa, "Complices dii," *RE* 4 (1901) 795.

[245] *Quod una oriantur et occidant una*: an extremely obscure passage. The translation follows Orelli's suggestion that the verbs may point forward to the activity of these divinities as Jupiter's counsellors, as is set forth in a later clause.

[246] *Miserationis*, so the MS. But cf. *memorationis* (Ursinus), *viscerationis* (Scaliger), *venerationis* (Hildebrand), *mire notionis parcissimae* (Wiman), *nationis barbarissimae* (Gelenius).

[247] *Participes* (Scaliger and Reifferscheid) is inferior to the MS *principes*.

[248] Cf. Macrobius, *Sat.* 3. 4. 8; Servius, *Aen.* 3. 12.

[249] *Veritati suae proxima suspicione coniciens*, a most obscure passage for which Meiser suggests *veritatis vi promiscua suspiciones continens*.

[250] Here also the source is believed to be Labeo by Kahl (791) and Mülleneisen (39 f.) but Tullius (70) says this is without ground. Cf. Hyde 15.

[251] On these divinities, normally of the household, see G. Wissowa,

"Lares," *LM* 2. 1868-98, esp. 1887 where he lists occurrences of the *lares viales*: Plautus, *Merc.* 865; Servius, *Aen.* 3. 302; *CIL* 2. 2417, 2518, 2572, 2987, suppl. 5634, 5734; 3. 1422; 8. 9755; 11. 3079; 12. 4320.

[252] *Vicus* means either 'street,' 'row of houses,' or 'village,' 'hamlet,' 'villa.'

[253] Here *iter* has lost its original sense of 'journey' and become a synonym for the highway on which the journey is made. Cf. also the word *itinerare* (hence our 'itinerary') which in the late Empire stood for a sort of guide listing the posting stations on the highways. See Vegetius, *De re mil.* 3. 6, and cf. Varro, *De ling. lat.* 5. 22.

[254] Liddell and Scott, *Greek-English Lexicon*, rev. by H. S. Jones and R. McKenzie (Oxford 1925-40), cites (1032) examples from the *Odyssey* 22. 128, 137; Pindar, *Pyth.* 8. 86; Herodotus 1. 180; Hermesianax 7. 65; *P. Oxy.* 1449. 6 (3rd cent. A. D.), for the word in the sense of 'alley,' 'lane,' 'passage,' and Theocritus, *Ep.* 4. 1 for 'avenue'; in Plutarch, *Crassus* 4, 'path,' and in *P. Oxy.* 242 (1st cent. A. D.), a block of houses.

[255] On the Curetes who lived in Crete and had a part in the worship of Jupiter, see the notes on Lucretius 2. 629 in Leonard-Smith and Bailey. Lucretius appears to be confusing the Curetes with the Corybantes, a fault not found in Arnobius or his source. See also 3. 43, 4. 24. Cf. Ovid, *Fasti* 4. 207 and Frazer's note *ad loc.*, vol. 3, pp. 208-13; Lactantius, *Div. inst.* 1. 21. 38; Hyginus, *Fab.* 139.

[256] Cf. Lucretius 2. 629-39 esp. the following lines:

633 Dictaeos referunt Curetas, qui Iovis illum
634 Vagitum in Creta quondam occultasse feruntur,

* * *

637 Armatei in numerum pulsarent aeribus aera.

[257] The term *Digiti Samothracii* is equivalent in sense to *Idaei Dactyli*, divinities associated with the Idaean Mother who were smiths and sorcerers. They are called Samothracian because they went to Samothrace as Orpheus' teacher (Diodorus 5. 64). Cf. Cicero, *De nat. deor.* 3. 16. 42: Tertius est ex Idaeis Digitis, cui inferias adferunt. See L. von Sybel, "Daktyloi," *LM* 1. 940 f.; O. Kern, "Daktyloi," *RE* 4 (1901) 2018 f.

[258] On the Manes, the departed spirits of the dead, often referred to in the inscriptions by the phrase *Dis Manibus*, see H. Steuding, *LM* 2. 2316-2323; A. Marbach, *RE* 14 (1930) 1050-1060. On the

supposed old Roman goddess Mania, see G. Wissowa, *LM* 2. 2323 f.; A. Marbach, " Mania " no. 8, *RE* 14 (1930) 1110 f.

²⁵⁹ Perhaps Tertullian (*Apol.* 22. 10) had something like this in mind: Habent de incolatu aeris et de vicinia siderum et de commercio nubium caelestes sapere paraturas.

²⁶⁰ These Larvae were not divinities but forms of the old Italic superstition which in the lower world plagued the souls of the dead. They have nothing to do with the Lares. See G. Wissowa, *LM* 2. 1901 f.; P. Kock, *RE* 12 (1925) 878-80.

²⁶¹ *Consolationem* (P), *consultationem* (Sabaeus).

²⁶² *Refertis* (P), *referatis* (Sabaeus) but as Brakman points out, the indicative is often used by Arnobius, perhaps in conscious imitation of early Latin, when the Ciceronian norm would require the subjunctive.

²⁶³ I. e. one of the gods of the underworld—*di inferi*: see *Schol. Hor. Carm.* 3. 8; Servius, *Aen.* 6. 244; H. Steuding, " Inferi," *LM* 2. 234-61; Wissowa 239 f.

²⁶⁴ One of the gods above—*di superi*.

²⁶⁵ Saturn and Hercules. Cf. Vergil, *Aen.* 3. 405 and Servius *ad loc.*; Festus 462 Lindsay; Macrobius, *Sat.* 3. 6. 11.

²⁶⁶ Apollo. Cf. Cicero, *De div.* 1. 46. 104.

²⁶⁷ The MS reads *cogat offendat et necessario piaculum contrahi*. Oehler and Reifferscheid read *offendi*; Castiglioni and Marchesi transpose *cogat* to follow *contrahi*. This is approved by Wiman, *Eranos* 45 (1947) 133.

²⁶⁸ *Averruncate*, a word of great antiquity (cf. 1. 32, 7. 13), peculiar to the language of prayers. There was a divinity Averruncus or Auruncus (cf. *TLL* 2. 1316-7; Varro, *De ling. lat.* 7. 102; A. Gellius 5. 12. 14).

²⁶⁹ P has *terreor* which is better than *torreor* (Gifanius, accepted by Reifferscheid).

²⁷⁰ See 3. 40 and n. 241.

²⁷¹ *Proloquium*, cf. 5. 3, 5. 37; Stilo in Varro, *De ling. lat.* 24; A. Gellius 16. 8. 2.

²⁷² Summanus was the god of light by night. See S. Weinstock, *RE* 2 R. 4 (1932) 897 f.; R. Peter, *LM* 4. 1600-1601. See also 5. 37 and 6. 3.